After Spanish Rule

a book in the series

LATIN AMERICA OTHERWISE:

LANGUAGES, EMPIRES, NATIONS

series editors

WALTER D. MIGNOLO, DUKE UNIVERSITY

IRENE SILVERBLATT, DUKE UNIVERSITY

SONIA SALDÍVAR-HULL, UNIVERSITY OF

CALIFORNIA, LOS ANGELES

After Spanish Rule

Postcolonial Predicaments

of the Americas

EDITED BY

MARK THURNER AND

ANDRÉS GUERRERO

DUKE UNIVERSITY PRESS DURHAM & LONDON 2003

BOWLING GREEN STATE
UNIVERSITY LIBRARIES

© 2003 Duke University Press

All rights reserved

Printed in the United States of America

on acid-free paper ∞

Designed by C. H. Westmoreland

Typeset in Quadraat by Keystone Typesetting, Inc.

Library of Congress Cataloging-in-Publication Data

appear on the last printed page of this book.

This work has been subsidized by the Center

for Latin American Studies at the

University of Florida.

ABOUT THE SERIES

Latin America Otherwise: Languages, Empires, Nations is a critical series. It aims to explore the emergence and consequences of concepts used to define "Latin America" while at the same time exploring the broad interplay of political, economic, and cultural practices that have shaped Latin American worlds. Latin America, at the crossroads of competing imperial designs and local responses, has been construed as a geocultural and geopolitical entity since the nineteenth century. This series provides a starting point for redefining Latin America as a configuration of political, linguistic, cultural, and economic intersections that demands a continuous reappraisal of the role of the Americas in history, and of the ongoing process of globalization and the relocation of people and cultures that have characterized Latin America's experience. *Latin America Otherwise: Languages, Empires, Nations* is a forum that confronts established geocultural constructions, that rethinks area studies and disciplinary boundaries, that assesses convictions of the academy and of public policy, and that, correspondingly, demands that the practices through which we produce knowledge and understanding about and from Latin America be subject to rigorous and critical scrutiny.

After Spanish Rule: Postcolonial Predicaments of the Americas is a significant addition and makes a signal contribution to *Latin America Otherwise*. First, the volume is centered on a South-South dialogue and, therefore, it provides a re-centering that is at the same time a de-centering. Contributions by scholars from the North embrace the change of perspectives and by so doing they offer a telling example of the possibilities that the postcolonial paradigm, in sensu largo, offers to the still hegemonic and Euro-centered postmodern paradigm. Secondly, the volume makes a decisive contribution to the process of redoing the history of the Americas and, therefore, it enters into dialogue with American Studies at the same time that it indirectly questions many of the assumptions under which Latin American Studies has been operating since its foundation in 1964. After Spanish rule, "The Americas" became a place of different, contending national projects, which resulted in the marginalization of the non-Latin and non-Anglo population, that is, of indigenous people and people of African descent. This volume opens the door to explorations that have been absent in "Latin" American Studies.

Contents

Acknowledgments

This project springs from a moveable feast of wide-ranging conversations in places as varied as they are connected: Ecuador and Florida, Spain and Mexico. The idea for a workshop (which would become the groundwork for this volume) emerged during long conversations on a Mexican bus traversing the country, and then on a crumbling balcony of a cheap hotel on the beach near Puerto Vallarta. Having just come from a panel on the postcolonial question at the Latin American Studies Association Congress in Guadalajara, it became clear as the seaside horizon that a wider and deeper conversation was necessary.

The workshop, which took place in Gainesville, Florida in October 1999, brought together more than a dozen scholars and Valeria Millholland, our editor from Duke, thanks to the generous support of the Wenner-Gren Foundation for Anthropological Research, Inc., and the Center for Latin American Studies at the University of Florida. Alejandra Osorio and Juan Carlos Callirgos played critical facilitating roles at the workshop, for which we are most grateful.

We wish to thank all the participants at both meetings. Last but not least we particularly want to thank Shahid Amin for his brave travels in the New World.

This volume is very much a postworkshop creation in that it includes significantly revised papers as well as some new contributions from authors not present at the workshop. It has also been reshaped as a result of our extended transatlantic conversations.

Our labor on this book is for the love of Alejandra and Marie, both of whom made countless critical and amorous contributions to this project.

SHAHID AMIN

Foreword

I have been given the honor of writing the foreword to this volume. I have, of course, no special expertise in matters after Spanish rule, or in post-coloniality for that matter. There are others in the Subaltern Studies collective who would have a better purchase on the theoretical traffic that has marked the recent intellectual exchange between South Asia and South America. The volume editors' invitation to me, a historian from north India, to write the foreword to a group of essays on the new Latin American history I take as a reflection of a larger South-South dialogue. In fact, it is the outcome of two such meetings initiated by SEPHIS, the Dutch South-South Exchange Programme in the History of Development: one a conference in New Delhi in spring 1996 where I met Andrés Guerrero and Silvia Rivera Cusicanqui, and the other an invitation by Silvia to the Andes where I encountered Mark Thurner's searching probes about the "poetics of history" that I was then retailing breathlessly in Lima, Cuzco, and La Paz. My offerings in this foreword are quite literally the afterthoughts of an actual attempt to travel with my kind of history across anglophone certitudes, colonized affinities, and postcolonial hiatuses; in short, across "area studies," as these came to be demarcated in the U.S. academy after World War II. Indeed, it is these cartographic enclosures that have more often framed than freed historical understanding of the differing colonialisms with whose aftermaths we live variously in the South.

One must, I think, begin with the basic fact that we in the South are relatively ignorant of each other's histories. All of us in our separate ways know "our" Europe better than I know Bolivia, for example, or some academic in Cochabamba knows Nigeria. It might be only a slight exaggeration to say that an average historian of India would "know all about" the tin miners of Cornwall or the colliers of Newcastle, and precious little about the silver miners of Potosí. Dipesh Chakrabarty has argued provocatively that it is neither us nor our respective countries but rather Europe that is the subject of all our histories. Insofar as the academic discourse of history is concerned, "Europe" remains the sovereign, theoretical subject of all histories, including the ones we call "Indian," "Chinese," "Kenyan," and so on. There is a peculiar way in which all of these other histories tend to become variations on a master narrative that could be called "the history of Europe."

We in India have a fragmentary and contingent acquaintance with the histories of other areas of the South even in this variant mode described by Chakrabarty. Histories of the South have so far reached us in India through three major routes: the history of capitalism; national or regional histories; and what after World War II has come to be called area studies. While histories of capitalism have largely been histories of the "universalizing mission of capital" on a world scale, national and regional histories have tended to ghettoize the production and reception of histories of the South. It is not a simple question of limited funds and academic specialization: area studies, although based on expertise and authority, are productive of a certain ghettoization. So we get "Indian histories" or "Bolivian histories," which can be of interest only to Indians or Bolivians, or, at a pinch, to "Indianists" and "Latin Americanists."

The present political conjuncture (marked by the relative absence of the liberation movements of the 1960s and 1970s and the emergence of newer political concerns) of gender and of difference; the growth of majoritarian and sectarian identities the world over; the need to write anew the history of colonialism, nationalism, and the nation-state; the presence of "Third World" intellectuals in the West—all of this has begun to have an effect on the production of what within the profession is called "minority histories." It is in this context that some scholars have voiced the need for "a non-hierarchical cross-regional dialogue, [which] is not the application of a concept, part and parcel, without contextualization, to another area."[1]

What characterizes the essays brought together in this volume is this desire to write a new postcolonial history in South America while also critically engaging with what Subaltern Studies, for example, has to offer beyond the India-grounded analysis of the "colonial encounter." In his introductory essay Mark Thurner sums up the points of departure of this collection when he writes: "The array of historical trajectories and lived critical predicaments suggest that colonialism and its after are not everywhere and at all times the same; that no 'postcolonial theory' adequately accounts for colonial and postcolonial American histories; and that colonialism, although never identical with an essential image of itself, is not finished in the Americas."

Postcolonial theorizing, suggests Thurner and other volume contributors, suffers from the same universalizing impulse that it ascribes to the West. Several of the authors in this volume write with an express desire to insert the Latin American experience in any account of colonialism, as they underline the specificity of the Creole phenomenon that places the intellectual, political, racial, and ethnic aspects of the Latin American experience at variance with the life histories of settler or bureaucratically administered colonies. Thus, what emerges in Jorge Cañizares-Esguerra's analysis of the Creole cleric's critique of European travel accounts of the natural history of the new continent are both the intimations of the later national and postnational questioning of the limits of a parochial European reason as well as a revision of the view that saw these Creole clerics as outsiders in their own racially differentiated homelands. Cañizares-Esguerra hopes that this book will "open the gates to a more catholic, generous understanding of the postcolonial," and it is his intent "to call attention to [postcolonialism's] 'prehistory'—one located in Mexico and Peru, not India."

Similarly, Javier Morillo-Alicea in his ingenious short life history of the Spanish Overseas Archive, circa 1863–1898, after the empire was reduced to two far-flung outposts in Cuba and the Philippines, asks new questions about the official recording of distant subjected populations while at the same time seeking to redress the analytical indifference to the Spanish materiel in recent theorizing on colonial discourse. Much of the South Asian work in this overcrowded field has been insufficiently attentive to the internal economies of "rule by record" and "rule by report" in the constitution of colonial subjects as the site for colonial power and knowledge. The historical ethnography of the truncated late-nineteenth-century Spanish colonial archive that Morillo-Alicea presents is not simply a "welcome addition," to use that well-worn phrase of prefactory prose, it is a call for an "archive-centered approach to understanding [the] colonial knowledge" of the various historically constituted "Indians" that people its hallowed cellars, both offshore and within the nation.

To seek the "prehistory" of a recently emergent critical stance across several centuries and continents is, then, surely to reach beyond the sturdy conventions of comparative colonial history. An insistence on inserting South American histories into all understandings of the postcolonial is not only to give that term a longer duration and provenance, it is also to open the door to newer interpretative differences between the pasts of, say, the Cauca and the Gangetic valleys, as it is to make accounts of commodity production in two disparate areas of the South travel as histories across nonidentical social forms of the reproduction of labor in two different southern countrysides. To fashion all future dialogues across our two distant continents only or necessarily through theoretical interlocution is to say in effect that unlike our theorists and novelists our historians are by the nature of their craft doomed to produce particularistic narratives. This would have the paradoxical effect of keeping historical narratives in the South from ever traveling as tellable tales outside the provenance of a southern nation or an identifiable "area." And this would indeed be a sad ghettoization, for it would amount to a hobbling of historical accounts, precisely at the very moment when epistemic and fictional "truths" from beyond the West are laying claim to an insistent nonparticularity.

All of the essays in this volume no doubt tell important stories, whether that of a sense of "disappointment at the failure of the new rules of politics after independence" (Guardino); the modalities behind the necessary exclusion of "populations" that are administered both by the state and the "natural citizen" as these constitute themselves in postcolonial times (Guerrero); or the "inappropriate others" that such nonnatural citizen-intellectuals become in a postcolonial nation-state, at the same time as their project of difference contributes to the life of the nation-state form (Rappaport). Still, I may be excused for reverting to and ending with my earlier concern about telling our differing pasts as histories across the boundaries of area studies.

I wish to begin this penultimate part of my argument by asking whether in today's context of the blurring of genres and the hybridity of being we need to talk across cultures and histories only through theory. I emphasize the latter because that is how dialogue normally takes place across specializations in the academy, as well as outside it. I recall an interlocutor in La Paz asking me to justify theoretically what I had to say in that day's talk. The implication that if it is not "postcolonial theory" it is of no epistemic value to kindred spirits in the Andes or on the Mekong Delta has to be mulled over for one to realize how differently the sluice gates of theory function today from the flood of ideas that assailed the 1960s readers of Edgar Snow's *Red Star Over China* or even Frantz Fanon's *The Wretched of the Earth*.

It might be useful to phrase this predicament rather sharply as follows: fenced and patrolled as our different histories are by claims on national pasts and to the production of knowledge about specialized areas, how do the writers of alternative histories transmit their stories across borders with a minimum of baggage and duty-free allowances? I have put the point about newer ways of writing "southern" histories thus for two good reasons. First, because theory travels faster (and lighter) than histories—alternative, subaltern, or any other. Second, histories, particular as these invariably are (and will be), are unable to land in distant locations on their own, and for what they are as histories. And that is because there are, so to speak, no historical precedents for reading particularistic histories from the "Third World" as histories, without the area-specific tag of South Asian or South American attached to them for necessary identification, handling, and recovery.

How to tell unfamiliar stories without letting the detailed reconstruction choke the narrative drive is a problem that the writing of the newer histories will have to address sooner or later. If such histories can compel "thoughtful contemplation rather than distracted enjoyment or theory-seeking speed reading" among nonnationals and nonexperts, they will have helped to break through the chalk circles that circumscribe the retelling of our separate national pasts.[2]

NOTES

1 Florencia Mallon, "The Promise and Dilemma of Subaltern Studies: Perspectives from Latin American History," *American Historical Review* 99:5 (December 1994), 1493.

2 I am grateful to Mary Margaret Steedly for letting me borrow her words quoted in the sentence above.

1. ESCRITURA

On Imagining/Writing Postcolonial Histories

ANDRÉS GUERRERO

Point and Counterpoint

Translated by Mark Thurner

✳ In his foreword to this volume Shahid Amin makes a suggestive reading of the problem of the lack of communication
among the localities of "the South."[1] I cannot help but hear in his
prose a note of nostalgia that conjures up an orphan's mourning—
even if the reverberations ring only in my ears and not in his words.
Studies in the derivative perspective of the periphery, the great debates of old on the variations from the model of Europe (to which
one would have to add the United States the omitted *alter*, shadow of
the constitutive dialogue of modern Europe since well before Alexis
de Toqueville), now float without a home and no longer make sense.

What occurs to us now is perhaps not unlike what Hegel proposed
in the dialectic of master and slave. When the master (*patrón* in
Spanish, which has the double meaning of owner and model) dies,
the dependent consciousness, the slave, who longed for her master's
death so as to be free, celebrates her autonomy. But the fiesta lasts
but one night, then the day dawns and it is time to take stock. The
now autonomous consciousness discovers that with her master gone
she must now face, on her own, the implacable Lord of the Absolute,
the chaos of finitude without order, of death without sense. Is this
what afflicts us when we from the South get together to tell our histories in these new times without masters, without *patrones*? Is it the
discovery of that weighty and ill-stowed notion that the enjoyment of
autonomy does not in itself guarantee the creation of signification?

The order of things in the world is not what it once was. That old
order of nearly natural facts given by and for their very existence,
once and for all time, is past. Now the order of things is an always
questionable creation, a task forever in need of restarting: ephemeral
equilibria, nothing more. For, as Shahid Amin reminds us, the grand

furrows of history that only yesterday we ploughed so enthusiastically (those channels that seemed so secure, with the lines of signification always clearly traced and perennial, like those of Nazca) lent meaning to the labor of narrating the history of each in his or her South. It was the history of her variant of capitalist development, of his specific constitution of the nation and its productions, of her subalterns and his national projects. Similarly, in the universities it was the history that embraced one's original area studies interest, demarcated and bounded by competing academies, each with their patent and indispensable revisions and critiques.

Those well-worn perspectives of a discursive construction within which we naively and inexhaustibly conjured up historical narratives are revealed to us today as merry journeys among the universal images of counterpoised mirrors, as illusive representations that copy one another time and again, where reality becomes an abyss at the point of escape from the reflections. Yet we also cannot escape that watery canal that flows from the wheel (*noria*) of reality by grasping for the tree of theory, for an Esperanto in which only academics and intellectuals may be initiated, so as to dialogue among ourselves in a Tower of Babel of particular histories of the South. In grasping for the theory, Shahid Amin warns (with emphasis on the singular, perhaps, so as not to preclude all those lighter-traveling theories that circulate these days), we run the risk of closing the sluice gate that retains the seas of imagination and the torrents of ideas.

I WISH TO BEGIN . . .

Shahid Amin's foreword to this volume, it seems to me, advances three proposals, of which I would like to expand on a little. The first proposal is that perhaps the postcolonial, as the instituted fiction of a historical unity, may build bridges across the dispersed archipelagos of the histories of the South. Not in the sense of offering "the new theory" that would allow us to finally understand one another (a new conceptual universalism albeit from the periphery, in the style of what dependency theory was in the 1960s), but rather as a proposal for a new style or profile of sensibility. No doubt this would be a risky and ambitious invention, an imposition on the chaos that may not be entirely justified. It would appear to consist in refocusing historical reflection from the vantage point of a new temporal and processual watchtower. After the colonial, the postcolonial would demarcate something like a Bahktinian contact zone where historical discourses about the Ganges or Cauca valleys would engage in conflicts of hybridization (stylization, representation, dialogue). The postcolonial, as it were, as a flyover of the imagination above those themes and areas of study that connect otherwise dispersed histories. This effort would require working on the assumption, with the parameter of the postcolonial instituted in the center, and with the scope of visibility it extends, that clusters or conjunctions of unity (*conjuntos de unión*), in the mathematical sense, would appear in the particular histories around those themes selected for a common characteristic.

These common themes would not appear in all postcolonial histories of the South but rather only in those associated by bonds of kinship, preference, or affinity. These would be the units of signification that, after Wittgenstein, carry the sense and pragmatic use of notions with an extension or domain unenclosed by a limit. For example, the meaning of the word *play* (*juego*) is understood by another only when an indication such as "that play" or "that's how you play" is given, or because there is a definition by consensus that fixes a precise limit, contingent and temporal, in reference to the context of the moment. The importance of such open units is manifest in that they allow one to imagine (and thus visualize) communities of problems and concepts among historical phenomena that otherwise remain dispersed and fragmented, when not hidden in the shadows.

The second proposal would be that which is now being developed by certain authors who, ignoring academic boundaries, investigate transverse themes and compose narratives of individuals or social groups that link histories across imperial, national, or regional boundaries. This is no doubt a method rich in promise that could be expanded by the ongoing process of lending as well as unconscious cross-fertilization that is now occurring among the histories of the South. But because Mark Thurner develops this proposal in the essay following I will pass on to Amin's next suggestion.

Amin's third and final proposal is double-faced: it demands an effort in reading and another in writing. Even if the first two proposals are implemented there is still a residue which, like all things superficial, remains indispensable for the necessary task of communication. The heap of histories of the South whose object is immediate readings and performative writings are each entangled in the world called the local—that world signified by the political field and the cultural creativity of everyday life. Are these histories readable to third parties? Or, rather, from what moorings might "aliens" read them? The problem is complicated. In principle, a particular history torn from the local context, from the conjuncture and purpose (implicit and explicit, individual and social) that guide the author, would appear to fall into the nonsensical when it arrives from the South, for someone who, besieged by more pressing urgencies, reads it immersed in her or his other world of the South. We should remember that *before* we used to read—although I suspect that we continue to read, after the midnight hour—the local histories of the center as the place of history. All the questions about the significance of reading the particular of the center elicited an obvious answer: these were not stories, nor were they local, and even less particular; these were universal tendencies that pushed world processes and fixed the style of narration.

It is well known that reading requires a labor of elaboration, the creation of refracted significance in the discourses that populate the world of the reader. Perhaps it would be possible to propose a pedagogy in the world of common sense. It might consist of inventing a tradition among southerners—until it became customary practice— around diverse manners of reading that could be carried out with a sensibility open to the search for *familial airs (aires de familia)* (linkages, associations, suggestions) between the *particular world* of the author and the *local world* of the reader. Such an invented tradition would not fail to cultivate the search for models (concepts and epistemologies) that would also be reinterpreted from a connective sensibility that, unaccepting of binary copy, always insists on a minimally triangular recreation; that is, the invention of something else, of something that exists in a position of disparity vis-à-vis the model. Is it an almost Nietzschean *thoughtful contemplation* that Amin proposes? A reading driven by a curiosity that revels in a state of admiration, without the search for functionality? An appropriation without replication? An inspiration? Amin brings this theme to the writing of histories so that they may be read from that open sensibility that would become customary. The problem does not reside in finding one form of writing but rather in cultivating as many styles of writing as there are of reading.

Histories exist that are written to be read within the atmospheres in which they flowered. This is the idyllic situation where an author and a reader coincide in the same here and now, real and imaginary—as when we read Frantz Fanon in the 1960s, or so Amin recalls in a moment of nostalgia. Are there any histories written to be read in other local worlds? This would suppose that an author could have addressed himself not only to unknown readers but to unimaginable ones as well. I find this question intriguing. Perhaps it was this kind of differentiated writing and reading that the Subaltern Studies group brought from the South: an almost involuntary proposal to re-create writing and reading. This group (I say group but I suspect that its existence was more than anywhere else in the journal's table of contents) of authors who wrote for a local imagined public opened—without knowing or wanting it (that is, for conjunctural reasons of a particular, individual, and emotional nature)—lines of communication between the Souths. The ramifications of these connections remain to be explored, as for example in the case of the translation into Spanish and the publication in Bolivia, under the editorship of Rossana Barragan and Silvia Rivera, of selected Subaltern Studies.[2]

THE SPEEDY TRAVELER

For my part I concur with the appreciation that most South-South exchanges will pass at a light trot over a bridge extended by theoretical and methodological proposals, although I would add that these should be imbricated in historical ones, forming a single corpus. If there is anything in the short and fractional writings of those primogenial studies that appeared in the journal Subaltern Studies that could seduce the reader from the antipodes of the Latin American world, it is precisely the admiration that they excite in a desire to imitate a manner of proceeding in research. This manner consists in elaborating methods in relation to the documents, inventing concepts in relation to the processes, and contriving narratives in accordance with the concepts and methods. These three aspects—woven like a cloth of fine thread that shimmers with the contortions of the particular histories embedded in local processes—rebound in the narrative procedure that the author invents.

Perhaps this is something like the poetics (ontological indetermination) that Jacques Rancière poses between science and history, veracity and fiction. The idea is to provoke a tension, to create something indiscernible between the historical and the theoretical. This would be an oscillating indetermination that has repercussions in three poles—derivation, model, and invention—of both dominions. As for example when one proposes, at the same time in one telling and in only one modality of writing, a tension between processes and concepts that is a tension of problems and methods. The result is a state of instability in which an oscillation may rouse echoes and reverberations in the pragmatic imagination of other researchers distracted by other histories. The object would be to create a perpetual movement of disequilibrium between concepts and processes, analysis and narration; to generate an intensity of propositions whose potential creativity seduces to the point of provoking an effect of mimesis. Being a proposal of displacement, connection, and discompensation it could only become a model in order to create yet another state of instability.

To copy this model of instability, to attempt an idealization, to attempt the impossible repetition of the same (that impulse that is excited by the specific creativity that resides in the breast of the particular in a history, at a specific moment in the life of the historian, that of his interlocutors and in the questions that occupy them) it would be necessary to modify the conditions of reverberation (so that it should oscillate once again, like a Calder mobile) among the concepts and processes until the ties that bind them are, at one point or another, snapped. The act of creation, by derivation and failure, is that which retains only a certain *familial air* with the model. Perhaps it is in such a detour that something new may emerge.

Perhaps what was missing at the New Delhi conference organized by SEPHIS, to which Amin refers in his foreword, was that we did not arrive at a sufficient intensity of tensions, a disequilibrium of charges between problems of theory and method and those of history, and vice versa. Perhaps this would have facilitated an exchange among people from the four corners of the South, each impassioned with and engaged in his or her particular history.

TO MEASURE WHAT WE HAVE LOST

In the writings and readings of our pasts, when has there been any communication from the South to the South? As in the old days when, in the South, we read about the South via its rereading in the North? Perhaps the yardstick of the lack of communication is the best measure of what we have lost: the negation of organic historical hybridizations, the disappearance of linguistic contact zones. Histories coexist without cross-fertilization and without interference from one another; the echo of dialogical struggle among them is muffled.

The narratives that we tell of our histories do not create a *natural* dialogue when interlocutors travel from South to South or when, in that rarest of events, they get together for a few days to exchange ideas. I experienced this lack of communication firsthand at that SEPHIS conference in New Delhi. Each participant brought his or her particular history, that which was his or her plaything. None were indifferent to these histories; we all listened attentively to each other, and without further discussion we each went our way. No bridges were built—there was very little exchange and no debate to speak of. What were the causes of our mutual deafness?

I vividly recall an intervention at that meeting by someone from the second row of seats (reserved for privileged observers) who participated in the sessions. I believe that this someone was the director of the Nehru Center who earlier had so warmly received us. With the fine-tuned ear of he who may listen without being implicated, I believe he grasped what was going on. He tossed out an acute observation that at the time seemed like a provocation, an anachronism. Did he hope to incite debate? A dense silence installed itself in our midst—a silence bluntly cut off by the chair of the panel by passing on to the next subject. Still, I think I recall the words of that participant from the second row: it is impossible to engage in a dialogue about the particular histories of the South, he said, without at some point erecting the model from which to extend connections toward those particular histories. That is, it would be useful to reopen lines of communication via the figure of the zenith. At that moment I rejected the proposal, but his intervention continued to float in my being with the force of those words that, although obvious, are enigmatic because extemporaneous. I now wish to reconsider those words here.

In effect, yes, to create conditions for direct communication among the histories that before were known as mere variations on the mirror image of the model, it may be necessary to reinvent the figure of the triangle, the return of the same, albeit in another time and set in another, nonbinary configuration. It is necessary to close the vertex at the open side where the fragments of the South were incommunicable, to trace the *cathetus* (base of the triangle) that was ignored because it was considered useless or unthinkable. The model may be used as an indispensable fiction (an object of *thoughtful contemplation*) for constructing a triangular figure that communicates all the angles, each converted into a vertex, each made into models, all of which are derivations. The triangle turns around. It has not one apex but various temporal apexes, each dependent on the moment in which the gyration is detained. It requires a decision and the institution of a contingency. It consists in setting an imaginary point, an arbitrary referent for construction—like the imaginary line of sight and the vanishing point that together permit the tracing of rectilinear and orthogonal perspectives in a system of visual representation. The human eye cannot perceive the line of sight because it is double and because the retina is concave. Nevertheless, the cognitive faculty interprets the straight line, it *sees* the line. It utilizes the symbolic artifact to construct a three-dimensional representation of reality. From this point the vertex, being closed, becomes a triangle.

The South African apartheid system can serve as model (implicit or explicit, imagined or analyzed) of the *administration of populations* in the construction of regimes of citizenship in terms of thinking about the derivations of exclusion in the Andes with respect to indigenous and Afro-American populations. But the reverse is also true. The history of customary or *natural citizenship* in the Andes may be utilized as a model for the analysis of postapartheid forms of exclusion in South Africa or, from a postcolonial perspective, of citizenship in the United States. In turn those two vertices may not make sense without respect to a third: that is, the construction of the universal ideal of citizen equality as proclaimed by the liberal revolution in France or North America. Each vertex may become an apex depending on the rotational position of the triangle. The fragments are no longer defined in terms of their distance from the model (that unilateral and isolating link with an apex that used to be the norm through which the Souths communicated, which is to say, remained incommunicable). In the new figure the Souths connect directly by way of an act of institution in the imagination: the rotational triangle. Dipesh Chakrabarty reserved the homage for the last page in his book. Once Europe is made a province, one more vertex among several, we may all cry out with gratitude (and thus confront the great Lord of the Absolute, knowing that the master lies on his deathbed): Long Live Europe!

1 In this my countertext the notion of "the South" carries validity only to the extent that it engages in a dialogue with Amin's text. I am thereby able to enlist myself in a fictional unity, thus creating the imaginary or textual context in which to initiate a conversation among the antipodes.

2 See Rossana Barragan and Silvia Rivera, eds., *Debates Post Coloniales* (La Paz: SIERPE, 1997).

After Spanish Rule

Writing Another After

✳ One day in the life of this project, Andrés Guerrero and I made our way along the shady streets of the old anarchist, but now increasingly Morrocan, quarter of Madrid, here and there window shopping for Africanist, Native Americanist, and orientalist kitsch, mostly made in Indonesia or China. On this day our post-siesta perambulations lead to a pleasant outdoor café on one corner of the sun-drenched, seventeenth-century Plaza Mayor at the center of the old city. On the plaza our incessant conversation blends with the many hundreds of other such conversations that take place at so many *mesas* all around this oldest of convivial public spheres. We exchange remarks on the current news: the unspeakable fate of Africans drowned on Spanish beaches in failed efforts to cross the windy Strait of Gibraltar (Gibraltar remains, by popular vote of its settler-citizens, an English colony); Basque nationalist bombings in the city; the triumphs of the Royal Madrid football club; the rise of the racist, colonial Right in the French elections; Bush's redeployment, after Huntington, of the old imperialist discourse of "civilization" in the so-called global War on Terrorism. But then finally, like so many others on this savory afternoon, we settle into the intimate emotional details of our lives and intellectual projects "back home," in this case North and South America. As the sun sets behind the baroque arcade, gypsy (or are they French hippies?) and indigenous Andean (or are they Ecuadorian mestizos?) musicians begin to work the acoustical public space.

To wit: intensely local and relentlessly global, the Plaza Mayor was built by imperial Hapsburg Spain during the first great globalization of efforts of the early modern age, when the Spanish and Portuguese realms were united in world domination. It was said that "the sun never set" on the empire of Carlos V and Felipe II. This vast empire enlisted the native, enslaved the African, and bonded the Asian worker, displaced and resettled not only the European, and became all-too-entangled with the expanding dominions of the English and the French. As a result, what comes after Spanish rule now seems to us to be anything but predictable or contained, resisting any facile comparison with parallel imperial, colonial, and postcolonial histories. Yet there is also a palpable sense, lived and felt in our real and metaphorical Plaza Mayor, in which what comes after Spanish rule is, in a word, the predicament of the postcolonial world.

Spilling off that untidy mesa on the Plaza Mayor, atop a pile of newspapers, theater bills, and cheap paperback editions of Nietzsche and Borges, were some scattered notes for an introduction to a set of conference papers—the set that is now bound, marketed, and in your hands. The central question raised by *After Spanish Rule* is no more nor less than this: how to write the history and theory of Spanish America's postcolonial predicaments?[1] As a historical-anthropological "muddling" in the literary-critical waters of colonial and postcolonial studies,[2] our parasol volume opens modestly with the uncluttered temporal "notion of 'postcolony' [which] simply refers to the specific identity of a given historical trajectory," in the words of Achille Mbembe.[3] Thus, although the sun never set on the empire of Carlos V and Philipe II, we note that (post)colonial irradiations have not warmed all subjects and soils in quite the same way. For Mbembe's francophone Africa, for example, the trajectory of post-colony is one "of societies recently emerging from the experience of colonization and the violence which the colonial relationship involves."[4] Here, however, the "specific identity" of that trajectory is not so simply named, for Spanish American and Spanish societies not only began "emerging" centuries ago from under imperial rule, but they continue to emerge, and have not yet fully emerged, from colonial or neocolonial relationships that cannot be neatly separated into the "domestic" and the "foreign."[5] For although the Spanish American republics were—like the United States or Haiti, and as Benedict Anderson argues—gawking "pioneers" of the postcolonial national age, imperialism or colonialism in the world's vicariously Hispanic "contact zones" are palpably more than an antique object of and for reflection. *Manifesto americano:* The array of historical trajectories and lived critical predicaments suggests that colonialism and its after are not everywhere and at all times the same; that no "postcolonial theory" adequately accounts for colonial and postcolonial American histories; and that colonialism, although never identical with an essential image of itself, is not finished in the Americas.

A deeper temporality or historicity is obviously not the sole dimension of difference marking an elusive Hispanic postcoloniality; rather, structural and poststructural questions of power, discourse, and its critique are also implicated. Do discrepant histories necessarily imply different structures of power and language? Is it possible or desirable to translate different languages and discrepant histories into an (anglicized?) Esperanto of postcolonial critique? Jorge Klor de Alva has sensibly insisted that "Mexico is not another version of India, Brazil is not one more type of Indonesia"; but Klor de Alva's argument that "colonialism and postcolonialism as commonly understood today" are little more than a "mirage" or discursive "effect" of no historical relevance to "the Latin American experience" is wrong-headed.[6] What if we want to play somewhat (as history does, and in good faith) with time and space and face? And what if we see in the mirage not an illusion but a mirror? Not an effect but a reflection of the road we are on? What then? What if we feel at home in an *uncommon* understanding of colonialism and postcolonialism? Madrid today is not what London was or New York is. Is there then nothing to talk about, nothing to drink to? Might something important be gained by thinking about London in the nineteenth century in some imaginable relation to Madrid in the seventeenth century? Might it be useful to ask if early-nineteenth-century Creole patriots in the Americas wrote and thought in Spanish about the history of empire and nation "not quite like" the late-nineteenth-century Bengali nationalists did in English? Or to ask if later empires and nations took and take things (structures, histories, idioms, strategies) from earlier ones? Or that native subalterns negotiate such historical takes in just so many ways? What is at stake in thinking such transhistorical comparisons and connections? At what costs and under what circumstances may they be drawn?

Madrid has long been a postmetropole, a provincialized center. But there was a time (roughly, the sixteenth and early seventeenth centuries) when in the trained eyes of much of the colonial world (the Indies east and west) Spain was Europe (or, at any rate, Europe was unimaginable without the Spanish monarchy, its sword and cross, and its tall seafaring ships). Indeed, the Hapsburg Spanish monarchy then dominated much of Europe itself. But by the time of the American independence wars in the early 1800s Spain had been provincialized as a backward, second-rate power. In certain ways akin to the imaginary construction of the Ottoman Empire, Spain in decline was effectively "orientalized" by the northwestern European Enlightenment, by the rising empires of France and England, and by capital. Hispanic and Anglo-Creole patriots in the Americas finished the job by condemning monarchist Spain to a past provinciality, in effect declaring a universal, American future of new nations and citizen-states inspired by a classical republican imagination of recent colonial invention. Once the fulcrum of European world empire, Spain was subsequently thrown out of Europe by the Dutch, the French, and the English, and finally by the Americans. Recently, and particularly after the Columbian quincentennial commemorations of 1992, Spain has returned to the imaginary of Europe. In 2002 with the displacement of the peseta by the Euro, Spain has been brought back into the fold of a very real European economic community, if in a peripheral position. With such an in and out and in again history of metropolitanism, what could a project called "provincializing Europe" mean to postcolonial Spanish Americans?

If by provincializing Europe we mean, as Chakrabarty suggests, a project that might deconstruct, from peripheral points, the universality of European history, then the provincializing of the world's first Europe—chiefly "Spain"—was achieved long ago by the Enlightenment! It was then that another "Europe" took Spain's (and Portugal's) place—the modern northwestern Europe of the Enlightenment and modernity, history, and capitalism: Chakrabarty's Europe. But this modern imperial "Europe" of (modern) history would also be eclipsed in the twentieth century, in the case of Latin America, by the postcolonial global empire of the United States. And so the crass, unhistorical centers of New York, Washington, Los Angeles, or Miami might displace old Madrid or London or Paris. The West was no longer fully consonant with Europe. It was then that the postcolonial critic could claim to provincialize a Europe that was now merely a shadowy referent of the expanding extra-European (post)colonial West.

To put our (post)colonial Hispanic question another way: What does it mean to live precariously on an old postcoloniality spoken in the postimperial language of an orientalized postmetropole? To live in a double-post under the shadow or in the belly of a contemporary settler postcolony turned global hegemon—the imperial mother's tongue of which, as the lingua franca of global capital, now colonizes all discourse from the silver screen to cyberspace and the academy? Had not the Liberator Simón Bolívar once lamented the imaginary fact that South America had been dealt a bad imperial hand? To be colonized by the "despotic" Spaniard rather than the "enterprising" English? Had the Argentine liberal Domingo Sarmiento, to cite another canonical figure, not echoed his words when in Spain or on the Pampas? But there is no need to go hunting in nineteenth-century fiction for such lamentations: today one may hear the unmistakable echoes of the same sentiment among Latin American intellectuals. Then as now the unfavorable comparison among imperial patrons was and is drawn in unwavering reference to the overbearing vertex, the giant of the north: modular postcolonial Anglo-America. But if we turn the vertex toward another point of the British Empire at another moment in time, India also appears as an English colony, albeit of a very different kind. And so a new vertex, that of a postcolonial apex, comes into view. If only the intellectuals of the Latin American diaspora in the United States were latter-day English-speaking colonial subjects like the South Asians! Undoubtedly we/they would have dominated the formulation of "postcolonial theory" in the metropolitan academy!

Sitting at our *terraza* (outdoor café) in postmetropolitan Madrid (under the arcades of the imperial Plaza Mayor) such twilight thoughts incite throaty laughter and another round of *tinto* (red wine). But we also sit and have sat at other imperial cafés and cantinas: in Miami, Quito, Lima, or Mexico, or in an unnamed village *chichería* (pub) in the central Andean highlands. Things, of course, may be imagined differently from a Novo Latino café-bar in Miami. What is Miami becoming, and what does it mean? Miami cannot be mistaken for Madrid. Flying concrete spans, blue neon lights, the freight and cruise shipyards, skyscraper banks, and orthodox Jews and sunburned French tourists shuffling among the in-line South Beach set, "new immigrants" from every country in Latin America, everywhere anglicized inflections of Latin American national languages—variations of Spanish, Creole, Portuguese. But note that Spanish capital controls most of the skyscraper "Latin" banks. Miami is a new metropole for many, a steamy vacation spot for pleasure seekers, a great and sleazy entrepôt for North-South finance and commerce. Many of my Latino and Anglo university students call this place home. Are they provincializing the United States? Or are they making a once-provincial town metropolitan? But what kind of metropole would this be? In the genre of a Hong Kong or a Singapore?

Back at our mesa in the new Europe of postmetropolitan Madrid, we are not yet so drunk as to forget that the mere suggestion of the "postcolonial" in the Spanish American context raises blazing red flags for some of our colleagues. Still, we are more concerned with a deeper question. To wit: dissonance looms not only in the suspicion that Spanish America's and Spain's old clothes do not match very well with the latest postcolonial wardrobe (although black never goes out of style); lurking in our entrails is a deeper apprehension that globalizing the postcolonial so as to include Spanish American historicities would only contribute to a nauseating universalization or normalization of a postcolonial panopticon, thus closing the very critical slit that an edgy postcolonial heterodoxy from the fragments cut open in the first place.[7] The dilemma is only amplified by the avalanche of trenchant criticism—some justified, some not—that has come crashing down on at-large "postcolonialism."[8]

This dilemma inhabits the very name "postcolonial." At once temporal and critical, it "doubly inscribed" or contrapuntal inflection summons universal history only to deconstruct its universalizing effects. Postcolonial pasts are necessarily stamped by the derivative fragments of colonial projects; critical postcolonial histories of those present and future pasts would likewise dwell among the fragments, the absences, and the detours, implicitly recognizing the limits of its own "will to knowledge" and representation—yet that refusal to will and its representation is most eagerly consumed and distributed by the metropolitan academic machines. We step in and out of the machines.

Sara Castro-Klarén once complained that "the Post-Colonial perspective has come to be associated with the contemporary diaspora and dispersal of Post-Colonial intellectuals and academics. . . . This anxious subject of English speaking Post-Coloniality writes the world and itself without awareness of a previous, major, if not modular, colonial period and Post-Colonial experience which is enormously relevant to many of its concerns."[9] For others, however, this urgent anglophone worlding of the postcolonial amounts to rather more than benign neglect. As the observant Anglo-Australian critic Bill Ashcroft noted in a recent multilingual anthology on "the postcolonial question" in Latin America, there is a deep-seated fear that "Latin America is under threat from a new colonizing movement called 'colonial and post-colonial discourse,' yet another subjection, it would seem, to foreign formations and epistemologies from the English-speaking centres of global power." Not unsurprisingly, "there is considerable resistance to the idea of Latin American postcoloniality."[10] Our temporal/critical use of the "post" signals both the domestic resonance of this resistance and our unease with any universalist historicizing or flat "worlding" of "the postcolonial." At the same time, our parasol shades a desire for a positioned conversation among what Ranajit Guha has called the "small voices" of histories. Yet that twilight desire for lingering conversation at our small mesa of history recognizes the need for a historical and thus fictional common ground. In this volume the name of that ground is colonialism and its contemporary postnationalist fiction (mirage, mirror, plastic bag) of the postcolonial.

PROVINCIALIZING SO MANY EUROPES: POSTCOLONIALITY AND HISTORICAL DIFFERENCE

Gyan Prakash once noted that the South Asian Subaltern Studies project developed within a "catechrestic negotiation" of contradictory critical approaches—Gramscian, Foucauldian, Derridean—to South Asian colonial and postcolonial histories. Key to that catechresis or detouring and muddling of "original" significations were the transnational negotiations between the ostensibly demarcated, but necessarily complicit, "Western" and "Indian" historical fields. Given the historical discrepancies of those negotiations, Prakash warns that as "this project [of Subaltern Studies as postcolonial criticism] is translated into other regions and disciplines, the discrepant histories of colonialism, capitalism, and subalternity in different areas would have to be recognized. . . . Representing a negotiation between South Asian historiography and the discipline of history in the West, its insights can neither be limited to South Asia nor globalized."[11]

Although we like the tenor of Prakash's remarks, the wider project imagined for this volume would be unsatisfying if it merely sought to "translate" South Asian subaltern studies and postcolonial criticism into the received idiom of Latin American history. Rather, yet another "catechrestic negotiation" is at hand, this time between a universalizing "postcolonial theory" and an ongoing critique of the received idioms of Latin American history. Although many critical conversations unleashed by the Subaltern Studies project have proven inspiring for many of the contributors to this work, the volume reflects a necessarily fragmentary, temporally specific, and reflexive negotiation of Spain's and Spanish America's old haunts, via critical engagement with the historical field's own (domesticated and transnational) idioms of the colonial. Although these idiosyncracies may very well disappoint theory poachers and "homonym hunters," some consolation may be had in the theoretical realization that the "small voice of history" often makes big the repeating irony of the unexpected.[12]

In the last few years it has become proverbially evident, even among anglophone "postcolonial critics," that the history of colonialism and postcoloniality is heterogenous. As Robert Young notes: "South America, where many states achieved independence in the early nineteenth century, is only the most obvious example of a region where colonialism has a very different history."[13] But what would this different history mean in theory and for criticism? The question is not so much whether meaningful differences among the various colonial and postcolonial pasts and presents may be observed and lived, but whether those differences produced or produce notably distinct discourses and regimes of power and critique. May critics credibly speak of a universal "colonial discourse" and its derivative or reflexive "postcolonial critique" without considering the historical differences among the various colonial projects? Indeed, in the 1990s the vexing "question of historical difference" appears to have caused something of a "scramble" in anglophone postcolonial criticism.[14] From the history side of theory the question rang somewhat differently: How could one pose the question of historical difference in such a way as not to disable critical engagements with postcolonial histories and critical idioms elsewhere in the world?

For many Latin American observers, what passed for "postcolonial theory" or "postcolonial studies" in the late twentieth century was obviously inflected by different colonial histories and readings. Thus the recent preeminence of anglophone and francophone literary-critical readings of the textual traces of the modern British and, to a lesser extent, French empire in Asia, Africa, the Middle East, and their metropoles appeared to have several undesirable effects on the metropolitan academic "fielding" of colonial and postcolonial studies.[15] First, a certain poststructuralist style of critical reading whose academic home was in the English department or in cultural and literary studies, and that is often associated with the profiles of anglophone "Third World" intellectuals at private elite institutions of the metropolitan academy, became synonymous with postcoloniality.[16] And, second, there was "a noticeable geographical and historical homogenization of the history of colonialism,"[17] one effect of which was the subalternization of Latin America's colonial and postcolonial pasts. (Another effect was the sublimation of 1970s sociological readings of postcolonial states and societies, an objection to which was raised by Aijaz Ahmad in reference to Africa and Asia, but which also bears relation, as we shall see, to an incipient Latin American sociology of the postcolonial.) Thus, in the Latin American historical field questions about the postcolonial were often formulated in more or less reactive ways: "How and on what basis can we establish links between Latin America and other colonized regions?" and "Can a word such as 'colonialism' really refer to the historical experience of Latin America?"[18]

In an influential set of articles Jorge Klor de Alva responded to the latter question with a resounding *no*, declaring that "Mexico is not another version of India, Brazil is not one more type of Indonesia, and Latinos in the United States—although tragically opposed by a dominant will that has sought to exclude and disempower them—are neither like Algerians in France, Pakistanis in Britain, or Palestinians in Israel."[19] In short, Klor de Alva argues that "the Latin American experience" was unlike that of later, now modular colonialisms, and that as a result "colonialism and postcolonialism *as commonly understood today*" did not apply and, indeed, in this strange context was little more than an anachronistic "mirage" or discursive "effect."

Klor de Alva's insistence on difference is not unfounded, but as Peter Hulme observes it does not preclude the possibility of reading/living *historically different* (post)colonialities. In effect, Hume counters, Klor de Alva's "we are not the same as you" objections (which are fairly common in the Latin American literature)[20] "offer no compelling reasons why we should take that single, later definition [of modern French or British empires] as the model for colonialism and decide that since American countries do not fit we therefore cannot talk about decolonization or colonial discourse or postcolonial theory with reference to the continent. Spanish colonialism in America was undoubtedly different from British colonialism in India: to deny that one was colonialism at all takes away the ground that would facilitate understanding of the particular differences." Hulme insists instead that "the field of postcolonial studies *needs* to find a place for America; that the inclusion of America will, and should, affect the shape and definition of the field; and more positively, many of the misgivings about the role of America in postcolonial studies, on closer inspection, are misplaced."[21]

Many of these misgivings have been based on a number of dubious historical assumptions. As Javier Morillo-Alicea argues in this volume, the exceptionalist narratives that seem to cling to the Spanish empire and its Indies/Americas are founded both on significant historical differences and on a number of now questionable narratives, perhaps chief among which is the notion of the paucity (or illegitimacy) of modernity in the Hispanic world (i.e., Spain as the "backward sister of Europe," her colonies a bastard progeny). This governing assumption of a lackluster modernity lay at the root of notions of a wicked neocolonial hegemony practiced by the settler/Creole class in conjunction with complicit hybrid/mestizo populations (with the upper reaches of both colonial castes later converging as a "Westernized" *comprador* bourgeoisie) with their counterfeit version of modernity often dubbed, as it is in Peru, a "traditional modernity."[22] In certain Creole nationalist and social historical versions of the story, these quasi-Western colonial cultural configurations of power are responsible for interring the *profundo*—that which was authentically native, national, or "deeply indigenous" in the Americas. The received comparative wisdom that once gave weight to this storyline of Western deviance—namely, "that in Asia and Africa the difference between ruler and ruled was always stark and clear" or that British and French colonial regimes were infinitely more "modern"—no longer persuades as it once did, however.[23] Thinking otherwise, Morillo-Alicea notes in this volume that recent work suggests that "colonialism in many regions created interstitial categories of people whose very existence challenged easy dichotomies of colonizer and colonized."

As Hulme noticed, Klor de Alva's insistence that the Spanish Americas were not and are "not colonial or postcolonial *as commonly understood today*" is also informed by the notion (which has become nearly an article of faith, as it were) that the Creole-dominated movements for independence in the early-nineteenth-century Americas were uniquely unpopular, elitist, and Europeanizing, and that unlike Europe the middle and lower classes had not been "politically baptized" by the event,[24] and indeed were not "political" at all in the modern sense. (The political baptismal of the lower orders did not happen, in this standard narrative, until the arrival of the popular nationalist regimes of the early to mid-twentieth century.) But postcolonial America seems not to have been unique in this regard. That old, distinguished, and exceptionalist profile of American independence is now blurred both by recent thinking on colonial nationalisms around the globe[25] and by new Latin Americanist historical work (see Lasso, Guardino, and Thurner in this volume, and the historiographical discussion below). As the Peruvian novelist and cultural critic Alfredo Bryce Echenique reminds us, "control of postcolonial power was won by the conquerors' heirs, as much in Africa and Asia as in America."[26] But the "control" exercised by postcolonial nationalist elites was rarely absolute. Moreover, recent Latin Americanist research on the independence and postindependence eras also suggests that blacks, mulattos, Indians, and other colonized subalterns not only resisted or participated decisively both in the independence wars and in alternative nationalist projects but that, perhaps more profoundly, their silenced subaltern political practices shadowed, fractured, and at certain moments undermined Creole national projects.[27]

Also no longer taken for granted is Klor de Alva's enabling assumption that complicit mestizos were inevitably "sucked into the vortex of the West." In Peru, for example, recent research has argued that ambiguous postcolonial processes of "indigenization" or "Indianization" led many mestizos in what might be seen to be precisely the opposite direction, toward strategic native and nativist identifications.[28] In short, as historians and anthropologists of colonialism and the postcolonial "turn their gaze more onto the category of the colonizer," in the words of Javier Morillo-Alicea (in this volume), the colonial Creole, the hybrid middle sectors, and the subaltern native classes, "it is increasingly clear that although the ideology of empire always seems to suggest that the colonizer/colonized binary is absolute, in many contexts what constituted Europeanness—or rather, proper Europeanness—was always up for debate." Not only was Europeanness up for debate, however, but Creole, interstitial or hybrid, as well as "indigenous" or "native" subjectivities were also sites of conflict, subterfuge, invention, hybridity, and fluidity in the colony and postcolony, as Tom Abercrombie's contribution to this volume subtly demonstrates.

Despite the many complexities involved in speaking about the early modern universal Spanish monarchy as a particular form or moment in European colonialism,[29] Hulme's critique of Klor de Alva's exceptionalist stance is workable if the meaning of "colonialism" is left unsecured, genealogically specific, and contextually maleable.[30] Thus, it is not simply a matter of "including" the Spanish Americas in a normalizing metropolitan postcolonial studies with global pretensions, nor of posing a comparative question that "correctly" departs from early modern hispanophone rather than modern anglophone and francophone imperialisms and postcolonialities. The deeper problematic raised in this volume is somewhat more ambiguous and reflexive: how do we negotiate multiple projects—each proceeding from its postcolonial fragments—of provincializing the various Europes of our historical imaginations? This would obviously imply provincializing the postcolonial "in here" as well as "out there," making "it" recognizant that its very limits are also its deepest wellsprings of creative critical practice vis-à-vis modernity, coloniality, and globalization. In a word, if postcolonial studies would provincialize Europe it would first need to deconstruct and redeploy its historical provincialities in useful theoretical ways.[31] In any case, the anglophone provinciality of (an ostensibly universalist or at-large) postcolonialism as presently constituted may be seen to be derivative of the very universal modernity (enacted by colonialism) that postcolonial critique sought to contest, and so the irony of its universalizing effect should not be so surprising nor debilitating.

Interpolating this provinciality from the provinces of the Spanish Americas thus partakes of a spirit of deconstruction/reconstruction, in part because the region, in the words of Ashcroft, "has given ample evidence of its post-coloniality long before the emergence of 'colonial and postcolonial discourse' from the [anglophone] metropolitan academy,"[32] and in part because its particular negotiations of its own Europes are potential sources of critical theorizing. Along with the interpolation goes the postcaveat that provincializing the postcolonial in a globalizing anglophone world may be as impossible as provincializing Europe. Still, philosophical deconstruction or postcolonial criticism, as Spivak notes, consists in saying "an impossible 'no' to a structure which one critiques, yet inhabits intimately."[33]

Although the work of this volume may stand as an explicit or implicit critique of postcolonial universalism, it also suggests, with Chakrabarty, that critical rethinking of the colonial and postcolonial cannot hope to go very far as a nativist, *indigenista*, or area studies project. The historical heterogeneity of the postcolonial demands not only that in the words of Gyan Prakash "the discrepant histories of colonialism, capitalism, and subalternity in different areas [of the world] be recognized"[34] but also that historical criticism itself entertain a "radical heterogeneity" of narratives and subject positions in the discursive spaces between nativisms, area knowledges, and global universals.

It is not merely a question, then, of "recovering" the "subaltern pasts" of the colonial and postcolonial Spanish Americas (as social history "from below" and "minority history" have proposed in the past) in an effort to disavow the postcolonial historicism and "theory" generated elsewhere.[35] And it is also not a question of whether this or that region or country "is or is not" postcolonial. Rather, the challenge may lie in problematizing and rewriting master historical narratives in such a way as to render unnecessary both the liberal rhetoric of "recovery" with its power-hungry faith in, and will to, total representation, *and* the modernist binarism of (postcolonial) theory versus history—both of which are underwritten by a developmentalist historicism of absence that still inhabits receptions of and debates about "the postcolonial." The problem, which is also a challenge, then, lies neither in nativist exceptionalisms (falling back into the domestic comfort zone of area knowledge and populist patriotic epistemology) nor in the universal claims of a changing metropolitan academy, but in the deeply problematic historical discourses of "lack" and "recovery" and the critical subjectivities that must write them and in turn are constructed by them.

In *The Names of History* Jacques Rancière refers to this pitfall of modern historical discourse, in its "Marxist manner," as the determining "not yet." In Rancière's formulation it is the slowing of the future, the lack of maturation of the historical subject, that is made responsible in orthodox Marxist historical discourse for the continual regression to, or repetition of, the past. The "not yet" linked to the inevitable "one more time" always connotes the absence or anachrony of the present.[36] Arriving at a similar diagnosis, Dipesh

Chakrabarty more recently has developed a fuller critique of the founding "not yet" of historicism. In Chakrabarty's postcolonial critique, "historicism—and even the modern, European idea of history—one might say, came to non-European peoples in the nineteenth century as somebody's way of saying 'not yet' to somebody else."[37] In this colonial historicist discourse, India was not ready, it was necessary to wait, India was not this and it was not that. The well-worn historicist stance that says that Latin America is not this and is not that, and therefore cannot be "postcolonial," is rooted in structurally similar discourses of modernization and dependency—these latter two thought clichés having conspired in the constitution of the going metanarrative of the deficient, which continues to structure the master telling of Spanish American history.

THE EUROPES OF THE COLONIES, PAST AND PRESENT

Responding to the critical challenges posed by the discrepant histories and imaginaries of colonialism in the Spanish Americas, Walter Mignolo has recently proposed the concepts of "colonial difference" and the "colonial/modern world system." He notes that "the current and available production under the name 'postcolonial' studies or theories or criticism starts from the eighteenth century, leaving aside the crucial and constitutive moment of modernity/coloniality that was the sixteenth century."[38] Working entirely within this modern temporal province, South Asian subalternists and postcolonial theorists nearly always associate "colonialism" with capitalized notions of the Enlightenment, Capitalism, and Modernity. As Tom Abercrombie writes in this volume, "Spanish American countries have been marginalized in treatments of the postcolonial question because of their lack of fit with this historical schematic, having become independent during the nineteenth century from an empire forged in the sixteenth century, and having been shaped in ways that break the world historical mold created by postcolonialism's equations of modernity and colonialism, postmodernity and decolonization."

In short, Mignolo's critique suggests that the Europe of South Asianists is the (British and French) Enlightenment, Capitalism, and Modernity. Spanish America's Europe is different. Sixteenth-century imperial Spain was postcolonial Spanish America's first "Europe," but this Europe was later redefined as unenlightened, mercantilist, and "medieval." But early modern imperial Spain has not been Spanish America's only Europe. Another Europe appeared on the Spanish American cultural horizon in the eighteenth century. Recent historiography argues, however, that this new Europe of the Enlightenment, modernity, and capitalism was not just "foreign," as many contemporary Creole patriots maintained, it was also part of an emerging "us"—that is, it was "internal" to Bourbon colonial rule (not just an imposition of its metropolitan agents) and intrinsic to Creole nationalist projects within the Americas. Later still, other "Europes" and "neo-Europes"—those of British neocolonialism and French civilization, and then of the trend-setting and expanding republic of the United States—would populate the entangled genealogy of Spanish America's sedimented postcolonial imaginary. There is nothing simple or straightforward about disentangling the stretchy imaginaries of Europe that have been generated, at different historical moments, in the colonial Wests.

Not surprisingly, Mignolo finds little use for the patented chronology that underwrites anglophone and francophone postcolonial studies, and so for inspiration he turns instead to the 1970s "world systems theory" of Immanuel Wallerstein. This happy return to the heady "airport sociology" of the structuralist 1970s is not without pause, however. Wallerstein's "Eurocentric critique of Eurocentrism" needs tinkering, and Mignolo's toolbox includes Aníbal Quijano's notion of "coloniality" *as constitutive rather than derivative of* capitalist modernity. In Mignolo's long view, the "colonial/modern world system" *was enabled by* the sixteenth-century intersection of "the European system" and "Amerindian" or "Aztec" and "Inca" systems. Modernity, we might say, was inaugurated not by the figure of Columbus but by that of Malintzin (la Malinche), the native woman translator who (one should add, along with tens of thousands of her non-Aztec warrior kinsmen) mediated the encounter between Cortez and Montezuma. This moment could be written, as Marx and Engels did in the *Communist Manifesto*, as "the rosy dawn of capitalism" but it might also be written as the stormy daybreak of the twin figures of "Europe" and "the Indies" (later, "America"), those hyperreal historical inventions that have never lost their ability to signify a global modernity in coloniality.[39]

And so Mignolo's work must come to terms with two broad phases of a historically hinged "coloniality/modernity." The first phase runs from the sixteenth century to, or (if I read Mignolo closely) in some cases through, the eighteenth century, while the second phase runs from the Enlightenment, or in some cases the early nineteenth century, to World War II. By "colonial difference" Mignolo appears to mean at least two things. I make these out to be the different historical experiences and locations of coloniality/modernity in the distinct phases and under the various "national" regimes of colonial power around the globe,[40] and the different ways of thinking engendered by those experiences and locations.[41]

Despite an obvious contrast of style with Mignolo's work, Anthony Pagden's comparative inquiry into the languages and ideologies of the Spanish, British, and French empires during the early modern period (1500–1800) suggests a similar, albeit in this case openly Eurocentric, historical frame.[42] Following earlier writers, Pagden registers two long, yet interconnected phases in the history of European imperialism. In Pagden's scheme the global age of the "First European Empires" of Spain, France, and Britain (as well as other early powers, such as Portugal and the Netherlands) extends from the early 1500s to the late 1700s, while the more national age of the "Second empires" of Britain in India and of France and other European powers in Asia and Africa runs from the late 1700s to the late 1900s. For the most part the First empires of the early modern period imagined themselves to be "universal monarchies" inspired by the imagined legacy of Rome. In diverse ways these prenational empires attempted to establish settler colonies or provinces and kingdoms in distant lands among colonized populations. The Second empires were for the most part broadly modern in the sense that they were informed by the Enlightenment and by nationalism (an ideological narrowing of the ecumenical or universal empires of the pre-1800 period). In many cases the Second empires sought to exploit the colonized through commercial and extractive means while minimizing settler colonization and its attendant threat of Creole independence "from the mother country."

In its general outline Pagden's two-phase framework for historicizing the world history of European imperialism agrees with Mignolo's views. Taken together, these dissimilar texts provide some useful correctives to the "temporal provincialism" of much contemporary anglophone and francophone postcolonial theory. Ashcroft has written that "the antiquity and character of [Latin America's] colonization, the longstanding reality of its hybridized cultures . . . all radically widen the scope of postcolonial theory."[43] Perhaps. But it is also possible, as Mignolo suggests, that this deep history of colonization narrows the scope of "postcolonial theory," or at any rate pushes its limits in new directions.

The long view of coloniality may also have its shortcomings. If deployed baldly the very long and unbroken view of coloniality that Mignolo espouses—always viable and rhetorically seductive in the Americas—glosses over complicating colonial and postcolonial histories of class differentiation and cultural hybridity, thus subsuming to its master narrative more ambivalent local histories marked by engagement and disengagement between ethnically marked populations and class segments and the claims of colonial and national elites and states. Lumping together the long period of Spanish colonialism—or worse still, claiming an undifferentiated "coloniality" stretching from the sixteenth to the twentieth centuries—is simply no longer acceptable to many historians.

Broadly speaking, the first wave of colonialism in the Americas under the universal monarchy of the early modern Hapsburg dynasty suffered significant transformations in the seventeenth century, and in any case was quite unlike the centralizing, Enlightenment-inspired Bourbon rule of the eighteenth century, which, it is important to note, directly precipitated the Comunero Revolt in New Granada and the Tupac Amaru II insurrection in Peru, in effect conditioning the Creole independence wars across the continent. In turn, as Morillo-Alicea argues in this volume, the nineteenth-century Spanish colonial administration of the remaining island colonies (Puerto Rica, Cuba, the Philippines) differed in notable ways from late eighteenth- and early-nineteenth-century Bourbon imperialism. Then one confronts the rather distinct commercial neocolonialism of Britain, and finally the military interventionism and economic and cultural imperialism of the United States with the "close encounters of empire" it engendered and continues to engender throughout the hemisphere.[44] In the Americas, then, an unbroken and essentialized "coloniality" sounds as strangely out of place as the universal "postcolonial" of anglophone literary theory.[45]

Other problems would arise if Pagden's very broad contrasts between pre-1800 and post-1800 imperialism were taken too literally. These distinctions are useful reminders of major shifts in European imperial designs, but are less helpful for local historical analysis. In the Americas, for example, settler colonialism became the province of expanding postcolonial nation-states in the nineteenth century. The devastating consequences of Creole nationalist "internal" settler colonialism (which often invited land-hungry European peasants to do the settling for them) on native societies in the United States, Mexico, and the Andean and Southern Cone countries were in many cases more pronounced than during the formal colonial period of Spanish imperial rule from abroad. To simply call these nationalist settler colonialisms mere continuations of earlier imperial designs is to miss the profoundly different ways in which such projects were imagined, executed, and resisted.

Given the two-phase world historical framework for European colonialism, does it follow that a two-phase scheme is appropriate for the global postcolonial? That is, a modern postcolonial phase in the nineteenth-century Spanish Americas followed by a postmodern one in English and French Asia and Africa? There may be some quick advantages to thinking in this way, but a discreet division derived from the early-modern/modern colonial phases would tend to disable the connections between colonial and postcolonial regimes (an issue I will address further at the close of this essay). And there is also the problem of modernity after Spanish rule.

Perhaps it is Mignolo's polemical reclamation of an early Spanish American coloniality/modernity that leads him to repeat the well-worn narrative that "the second phase of modernity, the Enlightenment and the Industrial Revolution, was derivative in the history of Latin America and entered in the nineteenth century as the exteriority that needed to be incorporated in order to build the 'republic' after independence."[46] The narrative of an "external modernity" descending to Latin America rings familiar to historians of the period, because liberal Creole elites in the late nineteenth and early twentieth centuries readily espoused a variant of this view. Although the notion remains powerful in the Americas (it is in any case resonant with the foundational narrative that links Columbus with the arrival of modernity), it is now increasingly apparent that such a vision elides alternative and subaltern histories of modernity that in effect pluralize and/or destabilize the master colonial and national narrative of an external modernity defined by the negative indigenous status of the "not yet" modern.

Benedict Anderson's account of early Creole nationalism in the Americas broke decisively with the master narrative of an enlightened modernity from without, and much recent research by Latin Americanist social historians and historical anthropologists—although critical of certain aspects of Anderson's argument—tends to support the view that the "long nineteenth century" (1750–1920) produced its own (postcolonial) modernities in domestic cauldrons both political and cultural. Recent historical writing on the critical Bourbon period of enlightened liberal Franco-Spanish rule that forged modern notions of nation, state, and the indigenous subject; on the Spanish American or Creole patriotic enlightenment;[47] and on early-nineteenth-century nationalist experiments in the industrial and mining sectors of Mexico, Peru, and Bolivia has rendered dubious the narrative of an "exterior" Enlightenment or "imported" post-Enlightenment modernity.[48] Enlightened liberal rule during the national period is now as likely to be seen in the historiography as derivative of the colonial Creole enlightenment associated with the Bourbon state, when it was not inspired by its contemporary Spanish liberalism across the Atlantic, or when it was not developing in ideological confrontations with conservative nationalists, or in response to social conflict with subaltern classes on the domestic front.[49] Later in the nineteenth century, second-generation Creole liberals did look increasingly to "foreign" models of enlightened rule emanating from northwestern Europe (England, France, and to a lesser extent Germany) and the aggressively expanding United States, but it remains an open question as to the extent to which such North Atlantic "exteriorities" operated in the postcolonial Spanish American imagination.[50] But this line of questioning contemplates only elite histories. From the critical perspective enabled by recent histories of subalternity and state formation in the late colonial and postcolonial Americas, "the Enlightenment" looks ever less like an "exteriority" and ever more like a domestic point of contention, hybridity, and resignification. In short, there is no longer any pressing need in the historiography to look beyond the Americas for the formation of enlightened modernities, in part because the Americas themselves are products of global empire. The nationalist vocabularies of "foreign" and "domestic" or of "imports" and "exports" proves limiting in this historical context.

In the dynamic interdisciplinary subfield of colonial/postcolonial Latin American social history and cultural anthropology, William Taylor's notable historiographical essay published in the mid-1980s on global and local approaches to the past was perhaps at the time emblematic of the growing unease with "dependency perspectives." Taylor's call for an anthropological, or at least Wolfian, connected history of the state, society, and culture anticipated Dipesh Chakrabarty's argument that Third World histories tend to be variations on the history of Europe. Taylor argues that Latin American history in the dependency vein was often reduced to the history of European capitalism wherein "Latin America is treated as the underdeveloped West. . . . [Certain] dependency perspectives have promoted a new Black Legend [wherein] Europeans are the real subjects of history."[51] Taylor also criticized another historiographical tendency to view the long period before the supposed "arrival" of a dynamic commercial capitalism in the late nineteenth century as histoire immobile. The most immobile and understudied of all was the "orphan period" of the "first half of the nineteenth century." Thanks to new research, this critical postcolonial period is no longer the incognito backwater that it was in the 1980s, yet it is still most often represented in the teleological narrative of Latin American economic history as "the long wait" (la larga espera) or "the great delay" before the inevitable consolidation of the "neocolonial order."[52] It is hard to imagine a more archetypal "not yet" than this.

In another but equally significant vein, Florencia Mallon's call for more rigorous research into the pivotal "long nineteenth century" focused new attention on Latin America's postcolonial historical problematic. Critical Marxist historians were the first to point out that this great "not yet" of modernist and dependentista Latin American historical discourse obscured more meaningful local histories of class formation, agency, and resistance to capitalism and to Creole national projects.[53] Although many Latin Americanist Marxist histories were still held hostage to underlying metanarratives of the "transition" from feudalism to capitalism (if not to labyrinthine "articulations" of seemingly infinite modes of production), some Marxist social historians successfully shifted the terms of the historical conversation toward local actors and national contingencies.

At about the same time, in the South Asian project of Subaltern Studies Gayatri Spivak saw the potential for a break with the master narrative of transition. She argued that the South Asian group was beginning to deconstruct the narrative of capitalist transition "by proposing at least two things: first, that the moment(s) of change be pluralized and plotted as confrontations rather than transition . . . and secondly, that such changes are signaled or marked by a functional change in sign-systems."[54] Latin Americanist social history also developed plural plots of confrontation and resistance, but it was the historical anthropologists who were more likely to plumb the history of signs. Building on but also departing in critical ways from the Marxist tradition—which in the Latin American historical field shifted during the course of the 1980s from the master narrative of capitalist transition to that of domination and resistance—some historical anthropologists (and historians of culture and power) have turned to the less certain task of writing histories of subaltern subjectivity, social movements, and political formations in the Americas.[55] This new writing, a small sample of which is presented in this volume, is already generating alternative narratives which twist or suspend the inherited master tropes of Latin American history (the tragedy of the not yet, the romance of the revolution, the epic story of the authentic victim). It demonstrates that "the complexity of [Spanish] American post-colonial societ[ies], far from lending itself to the concept of some Latin American essence, provides the ground for an increasingly sophisticated understanding of post-colonial relations throughout the world."[56]

THE NAME ON THE GATE

In a short comment that appeared in 1997, Peter Hulme remarked that "like many of its critics, I am in favour of more and more analyses of the different forms of imperialism and colonialism, of more and more analyses of different local situations, and of determined efforts to avoid the ism-ization of the adjective 'postcolonial.' But if—as seems inevitable—'postcolonial studies' is the name that is going to hang over the gate, then let us use the word in a way that includes America."[57] The inevitable has come to pass—and not only in English departments and comparative literature and/or cultural studies programs and publications. The word "postcolonial" now appears with some frequency on—if not between—the covers of new books and in the titles of new articles in English dealing with some aspect of the nineteenth- and twentieth-century histories of Spanish America. The term also appears, although rather less frequently, in Spanish-language history writing published in Latin America or elsewhere (where it is also often rejected as "foreign" if not "neoliberal" or "imperialist"), and it is increasingly encountered in Spanish-language literary and cultural studies. What is the meaning of this new sign hanging over the old gate? Does it announce the imperial claim of Anglo-American academe? Is it the deceptive "mirage" that Jorge Klor de

Alva sees?[58] A mere passing fashion driven by editorial marketing trends? Or is there something newly old in the teaming forest beyond the gate and its keepers that the new sign brings into view?

First, it may be worth remembering that the sign "postcolonial" is not quite so new in the (Latin) American field as many suppose. In his sharp critique of late-twentieth-century anglophone "literary postcoloniality," Aijaz Ahmad points out that academic talk about the postcolonial was lively in the 1970s, when "a fulsome debate [took place] on the issue of postcolonialism, but with specific reference to the type of postcolonial state that arose in Asia and Africa after postwar decolonisations."[59] In referencing this earlier debate, however, Ahmad passes over the sociological series on the subject of race and ethnicity in postcolonial states that was commissioned by UNESCO and inaugurated in 1974. The series included volumes not only on the postwar "new states" of Africa and Asia but also on the Caribbean and the Americas. Of particular interest here is the second volume in the series, published in 1977 under the title *Race and Class in Post-Colonial Society: A Study of Ethnic Group Relations in the English-Speaking Caribbean, Bolivia, Chile, and Mexico*. A Spanish-language edition was also published. Edited by the comparative sociologist John Rex, *Race and Class in Post-Colonial Society* takes its subject to be "inter-ethnic relations" in Mexico, the Caribbean, and the South American Andes, respectively. There are chapters on Caribbean society by Stuart Hall, on Bolivia by Fernando Calderón, and on Chile by Wilson Cantoni, as well as four articles on Mexican "inter-ethnic and class relations," including one each by such figures as Arturo Warman and Roger Bartra. The volume is introduced by Rex in a useful essay titled "New Nations and Ethnic Minorities: Comparative and Theoretical Questions." This forgotten sociological precursor to the literary-critical "postcolonial reader" is worth a pause.

Race and Class in Post-Colonial Society harbors what Rex and Hall describe as "Weberian" or "historicist" and "classical-Marxist" or "structuralist" approaches to "post-colonial society." The counter-point makes for an uneasy but not unproductive tension. The Mexican "structural Marxists" see precolonial and early colonial ethnicity to be dependent on the mode of production; when this mode of production was destroyed so too was any meaningful ethnicity. Some readers may recall that 1970s Marxian structural-functionalism had unmasked "ethnicity" or "Indian identity" as merely vestigial and epiphenomenal, of some ideological service to capitalism's super-structure but otherwise "false" because immaterial. The correct line was that so-called Indians were in reality peasants or, more precisely, petty commodity producers, engaged in the corresponding petty commodity mode, which was a secondary mode temporarily sub-sumed under the dominant capitalist mode of production, which, given sufficient productive forces, would necessarily destroy the secondary mode.

The relative merits of 1970s Weberian and structural-Marxist sociologies of race and ethnicity aside, the example reveals that the rubric "post-colonial" could be enlisted in the 1970s as a comparative framework for discussions of race, class, and ethnicity in the various regions of the "Third World." Perhaps we should blame UNESCO, the Weberian comparative sociologists, and/or the messy inclusion of the English-speaking Caribbean for all this. What I found notable, however, was that the "post-colonial" sign served as an umbrella for sociological analysis of both the "plural society type" identified for the Caribbean new states (e.g., M. G. Smith, The Plural Society in the British West Indies) and the "system of stratification of the colonial type," which the authors identified with contemporary Spanish America. What these different "types" of social formations evidently had in common was the problematic coexistence of not fully "modern" ethnic or race-marked societies alongside "modern" national ones. This developmentalistic ethnic/national distinction appears to have been one of the defining characteristics of the comparative sociologist's "post-colonial society." "Post-colonial" denoted the politically independent state that was not yet fully "modern" in the social sense. It implied an intermediary station between "colonial" or caste-like societies and those fully "modern" or class-based societies. Notably, "post-colonial" appears to be used interchangeably with "neo-colonial" and "colonial," such that the sociological "post" did not necessarily derail analytical discussion of "colonial systems of stratification."

Rex notes in his introduction that the "colonial" adjective as applied to contemporary Spanish American society "was suggested by our Chilean colleagues." Rex also noted that Chile was probably the only society of those examined to clearly be of "the settler type," that is, demographically and otherwise dominated by the Creole descendants of white European colonial settlers. Cantoni's chapter on Chile argued that the "colonial type" of stratification was giving way to a "modern type of relation" wherein the Mapuche Indians would be "integrated" into national society as a "dominated group" rather than continuing to live "outside national society" as a "resistant ethnic group." It is both the dominant settler pattern and the "enclave" of "resistant" ethnic Mapuche that makes Chile "colonial" or "post-colonial" here. The Mexican Marxist social scientists, on the other hand, rejected the "colonial" label for society in their country, arguing that the "colonial type" of stratification no longer existed in Mexico because the capitalist mode had destroyed the material basis for ethnicity. Indeed, the capitalist mode and the postrevolutionary national state had combined to completely subordinate and integrate the former "Indian" as a peasant producer within the petty commodity sector of rural society.

Many of the obvious "pitfalls of the postcolonial" that Anne McClintock and Ella Shohat[60] pointed out in the early 1990s are clearly evident in the comparative sociology of development of the late 1970s. But this early sociological "post-colonial studies" also raised interesting questions that deserve to be revisited. In the hands of some historical and comparative sociologists, the "post-colonial" was a transitory station in a familiar teleology compatible with "modernization" approaches that were concerned with identifying the "obstacles" to economic development and liberal nation-building in the so-called new states with UNESCO membership. In this liberal-Marxist teleology, ethnicity was equated with tribalism and colonialism, class with capitalist modernity. But as Stuart Hall's essay in *Race and Class in Post-Colonial Society* demonstrates, one of the advantages of the sociological approach was its problematization of state-society relations and its incipient questioning of the viable routes to modernity. Indeed, the Caribbean detour in the sociology of decolonization and identity, associated with the magnetic figure of Hall, has contributed strongly to a multipositioned cultural studies of identity in Britain that appears to be rather more ecumenical than the variety found in U.S. English departments.[61] Perhaps unfortunately, and for reasons that deserve historical attention, this kind of comparative/historical sociology of the postcolonial does not appear to have fared well in the Latin American field. Still, one cannot help but wonder if this sociological postcolonial might have provided a more fruitful way out of the increasingly sterile structural-Marxist debates over mode of production that dominated Latin American treatments of the "agrarian question" in the late 1970s and early 1980s.

With one or two exceptions the operative "postcolonial" sign hanging on the gate of Spanish American historical studies today is no older than the early 1990s.[62] As I have noted elsewhere, it was in the post-1989 conjuncture of the "crisis of the Left" and the so-called crisis of paradigms that the "postcolonial" reappeared in North-South American conversations and histories. The reappearance of the "postcolonial" at this moment was not just about the transnational academic careerism of a voracious word, it was about the new and in many ways troubled transnational receptivity produced in intellectual circles by the post–cold war/post–liberation war or "postrevolutionary" historical moment in Latin America and the United States.[63] In addition, the prolonged crisis of, or at least ambivalence toward, a totalizing dependency theory as the master narrative or paradigm of modern Latin American history had led some historians and anthropologists to seek alternatives, in some cases building out inductively from microhistories, in other cases looking beyond European historiography to critical productions of history in other ex-colonial regions of the global south.[64]

An unscientific survey of 1990s publications suggests that the term "postcolonial" began to appear in Latin American historiography only rarely, and then most often as an underproblematized, modernist epochal name. At the same time the old standards of Latin American historical discourse, including epochal names like "post-independence," "neo-colonial," "national," "republican" and, the master sign of all, "modern"—each with its own history, each with its analytical pros and cons—remain firmly lodged in the historiography, not least in textbook and official narratives at all levels. In his probing and insightful introduction to *Close Encounters of Empire* Gilbert Joseph notes a reticence among Latin Americanist historians to use the term "postcolonial" in the "neocolonial" context of contemporary inter-American relations. Joseph reflected that this hesitance registered the temporal and contextual pitfalls of the term rather than any objection to the critique of modernist binaries otherwise associated with postcolonial theory. Joseph thus warns that "the historical rupture suggested by the prefix *post-* belies both the continuities and discontinuities of power that have shaped the legacies of the formal European . . . empires [in the Americas]. . . . [The term is] prematurely celebratory: when we consider the manner in which the region now confronts the colonizing of its markets, media, and cultures under the New World Order . . . there may be little 'post' about colonialism!"[65]

But when does the postcolonial begin? When does it end? Or does it ever begin and end as such? It should come as no surprise that these questions elicit as many responses as there are takes on the postcolonial.[66] In the globalized British excolonial world the temporal postcolonial is something like the dark, decolonizing side of the "postwar"—that is, a recent Commonwealth past and now "vanishing" present.[67] This will not do for Latin American pasts. As for the settler colony that became the United States, Hulme suggests that the temporal postcolonial as postindependence moment comes to an end around 1898—although 1848 seems like a better choice. In any case, Hulme argues that the temporal "post" is never perpetual but instead depicts a momentary condition, as in "postwar." But there are good reasons for thinking that "colonialism" is not as discreet an event as "war," and that its "post" is correspondingly indiscreet. Does the Spanish American postcolonial end in 1898? Certainly not for Cuba. On the Spanish American mainland, politically independent since the 1820s, when does the postcolonial begin and end? Is it dissolved by the twentieth-century advent of the Gramscian "national-popular," widely taken to be embodied by the Mexican Revolution and the populist regimes that followed? Or does it ever end? Is it an "ever after?" Or may the postcolonial (and the colonial) mark a condition other than, or in addition to, epochal time?

There can be little doubt that if "postcolonial" were read simply to mean "the end of colonialism" its utility for writing histories of the nineteenth- or twentieth-century Americas would be severely limited.[68] Moreover, there are strong reasons for thinking that the domesticated "neocolonial" gloss resonates more readily with populist, anti-imperialist political projects that oppose contemporary processes of globalization in the Americas. Still, a closer encounter with the writings on postcoloniality and empire suggests that "endist" or modernist readings of "the postcolonial" may miss the mark. Lyotard noted that any linear reading of epochal ruptures was necessarily modernist, inconsistent with the ambivalent relationship of the "post" to the modern and its wary stance toward closure. Hall insists that "what 'post-colonial' certainly is not [is] one of those periodisations based on epochal 'stages' when everything is reversed at the same moment, all the old relations disappear forever and entirely new ones come to replace them."[69] Peter Hulme, Gyan Prakash, and Ania Loomba, among others, have each suggested that if read contrapuntally rather than in a modernist fashion, the "post" in postcolonial may imply not only an ambiguous colonial "after" but also and at the same time a critical "going beyond" marked by its double relation to the colonial.[70] Hulme, for example, holds that the "post" simultaneously conveys a "temporal dimension, in which there is a punctual relationship in time between . . . a colony and a postcolonial state, and a critical dimension in which . . . postcolonial theory comes into existence through a critique of a body of [discourse deemed] at least implicitly 'colonial'—with the concomitant recognition that the critique in part is made possible by the object of the critique."[71] Hall explains that such a reading of the "post" does not mean that "the after-effects of colonial rule have somehow been suspended," and "it certainly does not mean that we have moved from a regime of power-knowledge into some powerless and conflict-free time zone." Rather, for Hall the going beyond "stakes its claim in terms of the fact that . . . 'emergent' new configurations of power-knowledge . . . are beginning to exert their distinctions and specific effects." He insists that the "post" be conceptualized "not as an epistemological 'break' in the Althusserian/structuralist sense but more on the analogy of what Gramsci called a movement of deconstruction-reconstruction or what Derrida, in a more deconstructive sense, calls a 'double inscription.' "[72]

Keeping temporality and critique on intimate terms, Ania Loomba has argued further that if "the word 'postcolonial' is . . . uprooted from specific locations, 'postcoloniality' cannot be meaningfully investigated, and instead, the term begins to obscure the very relations of domination it seeks to uncover."[73] Breaking with modernist readings of the postcolonial, the critical/temporal or contrapuntal postcolonial suggested by Hall and Loomba would foster a rooted intimacy of temporality and critique by approaching postcolonial predicaments in specific places, moments, and relations of domination, and in the multiple archives and social fields that write or perform that domination as history.

Such a reflexive locating of the "doubly inscribed" or temporal/critical "postcolonial" within the discourse of Latin American history inevitably raises disturbing—and for some, liberating—possibilities, including a certain "going beyond" or partial "negation" of the field's master narratives, modes of knowledge accumulation, and theoretical presuppositions. This contrapuntal postcolonial may usefully be deployed to problematize the received epochal signs of Latin American history and their underlying master narrative structures. Nineteenth-century "afters" of the Spanish colonial now may be named "postcolonial," not because "the after-effects of colonial rule have somehow been suspended"—that would be an epochal, nationalist, or modernist reading—but rather because " 'emergent' new configurations of power-knowledge [were beginning to] exert their distinctions and specific effects." This ambivalent but critical Latin Americanist usage of the "postcolonial" is not a "substitute" epochal sign but a problematizing supplement. The "postcolonial" here does the critical work of undermining the developmentalist teleology of the nation as the universal historical vessel of a transition from the colonial to the modern, a transition that in the dependency version is marked by "the long wait" or "great delay" which results in an inescapable "neocolonial order."

Thus, and at least in some post-1989 Latin American history writing, the hanging of the "postcolonial" sign or name over the old "postindependence" gate is more than the faddish consumption of "foreign theory" and not just a simple substitution.[74] Rather, the sign makes efforts to transgress inherited historiographical limits. Implicated here is the move beyond (Latin) American exceptionalism and its field-structuring metanarratives—a desire that shares in the mood of Chakrabarty's "provincializing Europe" in his work by that name—in this case by turning a provincial or parochial field (which has tended to mirror, albeit with a significant lag, master narratives and interpretive trends derived from European historiography) toward the project of provincializing those received universals. This move is driven first and foremost by new microhistorical research informed by critical poststructuralist turns—research that finds its "small" voices to be out of synch with the available master narratives and teleologies that structure broad understandings of modern Latin American history.[75]

Nevertheless, deploying the "postcolonial" critically and temporally, now as in the 1970s, does not mean that "neocolonialism" and "internal colonialism" are or should be discarded. As in the 1970s, there is no prudish law prohibiting cohabitation among neos and posts. This would simply be in keeping with the language of "postcolonial theorists" who for the most part have never stopped talking about the neocolonial, if only to trip up hurried modernist readings and political miscues.[76] Still, there is no denying that "neocolonial" has often been an appendage to a vague but omniscient dependency perspective wherein, as Taylor argued, all Latin American history tends to end up being a hinterland of European or U.S. history.[77] Any cursory survey of university course offerings and textbooks will reveal that "modern" remains the official epochal sign hung out on the gate of nineteenth- and twentieth-century Latin American history as written and taught in the United States—yet few "working" historians have bothered to ask when and why this "modern" sign got hung on the gate that semantically fences off the colonial from its after.[78] Among other things, the notion carried the same burden as it did in the sociology of the 1970s, with "modern" being a gloss for a developmentalist notion of "class," and colonial standing in for a stubborn "ethnicity" or "caste." The master epochal sign of textbook histories was also obviously tied up with the liberal teleology of the Europeanizing Third World nation-state as the exclusive vessel of modernity.

Because "colonial" reigns for the "preindependence" period and "modern" for the "postindependence" period (and those stubborn binaries and teleologies of tradition/modernity, continuity/change, and caste/class under them), "the postcolonial" sign, when deployed in its contrapuntal critical/temporal sense, signals a crack in the received master narrative of Latin American history. The colonial/ postcolonial medley resonates with something other than the colonial/modern developmentalist binary. The "post" problematizes "modernity" by raising the specter of coloniality in ways that do not lose sight of the important transformations of nation and subalternity that have taken place since the Spanish colonial period; it also retrains the critical eye to focus on the imperial-to-republican political and cultural mutation in a nonmodernist fashion. No longer the modernizing political history of elites and institutions or, conversely, the macroeconomic social history of "the great delay" that ushered in the "neocolonial order," a new postcolonial history is rewriting transfigurations of "the political" across the colonial/national divide —transfigurations that have not necessarily constituted radical epistemological breaks or "ruptures" for all those millions implicated by its history, but rather ambivalent "double inscriptions" of the colonial in the national.

Professional historiography everywhere has been predominantly if not exclusively national (even and perhaps especially when derivative of European historiography) since its institutionalization during the nineteenth century,[79] and there is no reason to suspect that Spanish America has been an exception in this regard. "National" or "republican" and not "postcolonial" are the master epochal signs of histories written within and addressed to the national readerships of the hispanophone postcolonies of America. Until recently, however, much history writing in Spanish American countries was confined to the national and the provincial, not for the lack of desire to write transnational histories but rather by virtue of the world capitalist maldistribution of books—a dire situation that has grown steadily worse under neoliberal regimes and globalization.[80] As early as 1976 the Peruvian historian Pablo Macera envisioned the outlines of a transnational history written from the "provincialized countries of the periphery." Macera noted:

> That, in principle, a broad historical perspective is easier to achieve when the historical process is viewed by historians who hail from [the metropolis]. [They may have] a more global vision than that elaborated by any historian [from the periphery]. In this sense, it would appear that Peru . . . should resign itself to practicing an ultra-nationalist, provincial, and isolationist historiography . . . [Nevertheless] there is an opportunity, indeed a probability that countries now provincialized will one day produce a historiography of transnational scope.[81]

Macera imagined a Marxist structural history of general processes; today that postponed opportunity presents itself anew in the promise of a postcolonial, transnational historiography from the provinces of the South. In sprawling megalopolises like Lima, with relatively good universities and libraries and vibrant intellectual communities, many if not most students simply do not have ready access to more recent books and articles. By and large, only "national history" (and its mirror image, "universal history") is taught and written in such places. Even "Latin American studies"—to say nothing of "postcolonial studies"—is nearly impossible to teach and extremely difficult to research or talk about outside elite institutions or NGOs in major metropolitan centers like Mexico City or Buenos Aires. Nevertheless, I want to argue here that transnational histories of the genealogies of colonial, national, and postcolonial discourse are likely to be written from worldly provinces like Peru, Ecuador, or Bolivia.

The first postcolonial national age in Andean South America transpired at a moment when across the South Atlantic a European "high imperialism" of the modern nationalist variety (albeit under the guise of reinvented and "ornamentalist" absolutist political forms)[82] was descending with greater violence on the peoples and landscapes of Africa and Asia. One textual consequence of the trans-Atlantic intersection of these distinct trajectories or genealogies was the Creole reception of new European colonial discourses. Despite the notable differences between the two broad phases of early modern and modern European imperialism (and these are critical differences that include contrasting regimes of power/knowledge and distinct modes of colonial and national administration), Anthony Pagden has suggested that "it is . . . in the domain of political and cultural self-imagining . . . that the most enduring historical link between the first and second empires is to be found."[83] Critical theorists have frequently identified this link as an essentially unchanging "colonial discourse."[84] Yet Pagden's history and Chakrabarty's critique both point to historical discourse or historicism itself as the key diachronic hinge between the political and cultural self-fashionings of empires and nations. It is for this reason that tracing the shifts in the historical self-fashioning of empires and nations (rather than "comparing" the empires and nations per se) is of critical use to the task of provincializing postcolonial theory.

My case in point is lifted from a text authored by Eugene Melchor de Vogue and published first in France in the notable Parisian journal *Revue des Deux Mondes;* it appeared abridged and in translation in the bulletin of Lima's National Geographic Society under the title of "Las Indias Negras," or "The Black Indies." Written on the eve of the Colombian quatercentenary, this travelling text suggests ways to write connected histories of colonialism and the postcolonial. Melchor de Vogue's "Black Indies" suggests, as Pagden and others have, that the heterogeneity of colonial pasts does not necessarily produce a corresponding heterogeneity in colonial language; but it also suggests that the reception and deployment of that language are anything but uniform.[85] "The Black Indies" is also a sobering reminder of the once obvious fact that the "new" colonialism of the so-called age of empires (in this case, the English and the French in Africa) could not have been the model for colonial discourse in 1891. Instead, the early precedent of Iberian "old colonialism" or "first imperialism" provided bearings and language for the emerging "new colonialism" or "second imperialism." Indeed, for Melchor de Vogue it was precisely the "fame" of Iberia's early colonial heroes that provided the necessary tonic for France's fin-de-siècle imperial blues:

> We commonly hear that the end of this century is devoid of interest, and that it will leave no significant mark on history . . . Is it not generally admitted that the great individualities of history have been declining, and that human activity itself has become ever more impoverished since the days of those geniuses who enlarged the world at the end of the fifteenth century? Nevertheless, history will establish a parallel between those times and our own. History will say that the explorations of Africa, realized largely by peaceful means, are deeds of such beauty and of such great consequence as the discovery of America with its procession of bloody episodes. History will establish a new era of Queen Victoria, of Wilhelm II, of Leopold and Umberto, just as it did for Isabella the Catholic [queen of Spain], Ferdinand the Conqueror, and Henry the Navigator. And if history does not assign a glorious place to M. Carnot it will, in the course of time, acknowledge the great role of France in the civilizing mission.[86]

For Melchor de Vogue history repeats itself in all things imperial, yet the progress of European civilization is also clearly evident. The "one more time" of the developmentalist narrative of progress—the telos of modern historicism—rescues the "not yet" colonial enterprise. In contrast to the Spanish conquest of America, here characterized as "a procession of bloody episodes," Africa is now explored and colonized "largely by peaceful means." The Berlin Conference of 1890 is thus likened to the famous papal bull issued by Alexander VI in 1493 (which anticipated the Tordesillas Line of 1494 dividing the still largely unmapped colonial world of "the two Indies" between Spain and Portugal). And just as the Atlantic had been a turbulent "Spanish Lake," the Mediterranean is now destined to become a tranquil "French Lake." And the glorious repetitions of imperial history would linger on schoolchildren's lips:

> The fame of the most glorious names stems from their constant repetition, from their passage over the lips of children in which they reach an extreme degree of idealization . . . as in the names of Bartolome Diaz and Vasco da Gama, Columbus and Magellan, Pizarro and Cortez . . . But the day will come when humanity pronounces with the same admiration the

names of Caillie, Barth, Gordon and Livingston . . . So let us civilize that land, subjecting it to our powerful material and moral forces . . . Africa shall be redeemed because of, more than anything, the sacrifices of great figures, and the abnegation of a Livingston.[87]

Spanish political theorists had cited a Roman precedent, the French now cited the Spanish. Shall we therefore name it "Latin" colonial discourse? That was one option among several, although for many reasons I prefer not to allow the repetition of the civilizational discourse of Latinism to pass over my lips.[88] But it was the circulating linguistic capital of the foundational figures (today reduced by virtue of twentieth-century schooling to the figure of Columbus), deployed in the fourth centennial as it was in the fifth, which lent and continues to lend resounding words to innumerable lips. This linguistic capital derives from a narrative of origins: that of modernity. One may also trace the Dutch, Anglo, and French imperialist redeployments of the myth of Spain's conquest and colonial misrule via the long road of the infamous "Black Legend."[89] But, old as it is, that is not the problem that I wish to accentuate here. Rather, the point I wish to make is this: what is now missing in the contemporary postcolonial criticism of colonial discourse was then central to Melchor de Vogue's colonial discourse. In a word, the current eclipse in "postcolonial theory" of nineteenth-century discourses like Melchor de Vogue's is at once symptomatic of the displacement of the Americas and of Spain in colonial discourse analysis and postcolonial criticism yet also of critical use to the project of provincializing postcolonial theory.

I confess that as a provincial Creole Latin Americanist I came across Melchor de Vogue's text only and precisely because "The Black Indies" appeared in abridged and translated form in the relatively obscure Boletín de la Sociedad Geográfica de Lima. On the eve of the fourth centennial of Columbus's maiden voyage, this seafaring French text did not—at least as far as I have been able to ascertain—elicit a public denunciation from the pens of Creole nationalists, although had it appeared, say, during the conflict-ridden 1860s when Spain (with support from France and England in that unholy Triple Alliance) seized Peruvian guano deposits (nitrogen fertilizer) and ports it most certainly would have.[90] Instead, Melchor de Vogue's translated text was consumed as scientific discourse (rather than imperial fabrication), and it found its place in the then current positivist conversations about the Peruvian nation's civilizing mission on its own Amazonian "frontier." French colonial discourse was useful here for racializing Amazonian peoples and for lending moral justification to the planned "conquest and colonization" of the "savage" who then inhabited the "virgin lands" of the republic.

But it would be a mistake to conclude that all Peruvian discourse about the exploitation of Amazonia was "colonial" in the same way of that of France vis-à-vis Africa. This is well illustrated by the case of the enterprising Englishman Sir Clements Markham, who spent many years as a colonial agent, explorer, and historian both in Peru and in British India. Markham was lambasted by Creole nationalists for taking Peruvian quinine plants from the Amazon region and transporting them to malaria-ridden India for cultivation. But in Markham's account of the quinine project, and in a subsequent history of Inca civilization, he argued, contrary to most contemporary European accounts, that the original founders of Inca civilization were indigenous to Peru (rather than migrants from Asian empires) and that Tupac Amaru, the "last Inca" who led a great insurrection in 1780 against the Spanish, had been Peru's "last great patriot." Markham's colonial career and patriotic historical discourse suggests some of the strange ways in which colonial, national, and indigenist histories became tensely intertwined.[91]

Self-evident proclamations to the effect that "Latin America is not another Africa or Asia" miss the historical connections made by the transatlantic traffic in colonial discourses that were evidently so useful to Melchor de Vogue's fin-de-siècle revival of France's imperial dreams for Africa, and to the Peruvian national campaign to bring "savage" Amazonia and its valuable resources under the civilizing sway of the republic, itself imagined in historical discourse to be the heir to Inca civilization. Was Melchor de Vogue seeing a "mirage" in Spanish conquest? Was Markham living a "mirage" when he compared and contrasted conditions in British India with those he found in Peru? Or do colonialisms and postcolonial nationalisms around the globe exhibit intersecting discursive histories deployed to different ends at different moments?

Tracing the transatlantic connections between colonial and national historical discourses and projects during the late eighteenth and the nineteenth centuries is incumbent to the task of negotiating discrepant (post)colonial histories and to writing "the global context of imperial knowledge exchange." As it turns out, the problematic of colonial/postcolonial hinges recommends transnational, trans-oceanic, and hemispheric research[92] of the kind that historians of Spanish Empire and of the postcolonial Americas are, by an accident of history, well-positioned to pursue.[93] Besides the colonial connections briefly mentioned above, connections between the older post-colonial world of the Americas and the newer postcolonial worlds of Asia and Africa are also not so hard to find. Travelers between the colonial and neocolonial or postcolonial-national worlds include not only Englishman of the ilk of Sir Clements Markham. The Peruvian statesman and "neo-Inca" revolutionary Juan Bustamante traveled around the globe, stopping in Calcutta and China. His views refract the "mirror-game of colonial meaning-making" that Mary Louise Pratt glimpsed in the writings of Humboldt and Sarmiento.[94] In Algeria and Mozambique, as in some other African new nationalist movements, allegiances were declared to the Caribbean examples of Haiti and Cuba. In this regard, Fanon, James, Rodney, Retamar, and Ortiz—intellectuals whose works and lives have been claimed by contemporary postcolonial criticism—were all "from" the Caribbean. Recently it has also been suggested that turn-of-the-century Chinese and Indonesian nationalists looked to late-nineteenth-century Cuba for inspiration and, on several occasions, to the early-nineteenth-century Spanish American independence movements for precedents in their own struggles against European imperialism.[95]

Beyond the "mirage" of the sameness of the coloniality of power, and beyond the insistence on an irreducible historical difference, is a Borgesian library of seemingly infinite corridors and chambers albeit with limited, or *periodic*, holdings.[96] We may call this library "history." And in the postcolonial American imagination, which muses at a mesa in Madrid's Plaza Mayor, this volume will be but one among the many such *periodic* holdings of this imaginary wing called postcolonial history.

NOTES

This essay has a longer history and carries more intellectual debts than I care to admit. Still, I want to take this opportunity to thank my graduate students at the University of Florida, particularly those in my seminars Postcolonial Spanish American History and Postcolonial History and Theory, who helped me think through the issues I discuss in this essay. The Postcolonial Theory and History faculty reading group at Florida also shaped my thinking about the postcolonial; among this faculty group I would like to single out the always stimulating critique and affectionate company of Maria Todorova. Also memorable for their insights were three rendezvous: one in Lima with Shahid Amin, another in Guadalajara with Gyan Prakash, and a third with Dipesh Chakrabarty in Gainesville. The comments of several participants in the Wenner-Gren workshop made me rethink key points in this essay, which was presented at that meeting as a position paper. Whatever the result, this essay's long history was made lighter by a constant dialog with Andrés Guerrero, when possible over *tapas y tinto*, and when not, over the Internet or the phone lines. All translations are mine unless otherwise noted.

1 In choosing this unambiguous title we hope to make absolutely clear from the outset that this volume does not pretend to treat that huge legacy of Portuguese rule in America named Brazil. Although the colonial and postcolonial histories of Brazil differ in certain key respects from those of Spanish America, we recognize that more ambitious projects that trace connections or draw contrasts between the two imperial linguistic regions of Latin America are both needed and welcome. One example of an anthology that deals intelligently with both of the Iberian imperial dissolutions in America is Antonio Annino, Luis Castro Leiva, and François-Xavier Guerra, eds., *De los imperios a las naciones: Iberoamerica* (Zaragoza: Ibercaja, 1994).

2 Clifford Geertz, "Blurred Genres," *American Scholar* 49 (1980) 167–79.

3 Achille Mbembe, "The Banality of Power and the Aesthetics of Vulgarity in the Postcolony," *Public Culture* 4.2 (spring 1992): 1–30. For a suggestive Latin American response to Mbembe, see Dain Borges, "Machiavellian, Rabelaisian, Bureaucratic?" on pp. 109–12 of the same issue.

4 Achille Mbembe, *On the Postcolony* (Berkeley: University of California Press, 2001), 102.

5 See Steve Stern, "The Decentered Center and the Expansionist Periphery: The Paradoxes of Foreign-Local Encounter," in *Close Encounters of Empire: Writing the Cultural History of U.S.-Latin American Relations*, ed. Gilbert Joseph, Catherine LeGrand, and Ricardo D. Salvatore (Durham: Duke University Press, 1998), 47–68.

6 Jorge Klor de Alva, "The Postcolonization of the (Latin) American Experience: A Reconsideration of 'Colonialism,' 'Postcolonialism,' and 'Mestizaje,'" in *After Colonialism: Imperial Histories and Postcolonial Displacements*, ed. Gyan Prakash (Princeton: Princeton University Press, 1995), 241–75; and "Colonialism and Postcolonialism as (Latin) American Mirages," *Colonial Latin American Review* 1.1–2 (1992): 3–23.

7 Commentary by Andrés Guerrero, plenary session, After Spanish Rule.

8 There have been many trenchant critiques of postcolonialism, and any such booklist is likely to include Arif Dirlik, *The Postcolonial Aura: Third World Intellectuals in the Age of Global Capitalism* (Boulder: Westview, 1996); Aijaz Ahmad, *In Theory: Classes, Nations, Literatures,* (London: Verso, 1992); and E. San Juan, *Beyond Postcolonial Theory* (New York: St. Martin's Press, 1998). Stuart Hall has observed, however, that such strident critique sometimes has the "whiff of politically correct grapeshot and the unwelcome glimpse it unconsciously affords into . . . the bizarre preoccupation of American-based critical intellectuals with . . . the 'ins' and 'outs' of American Academia" (Hall, "When Was the 'Postcolonial'? Thinking at the Limit," in *The Post-Colonial Question: Common Skies, Divided Horizons,* ed. Iain Chambers and Lidia Curtis [London: Routledge, 1996], 243). A critique from "inside" is Gayatri Spivak, *A Critique of Postcolonial Reason: Toward a History of the Vanishing Present* (Cambridge: Harvard University Press, 1999). In India, the Subaltern Studies group has also been criticized for its anglophilism (Hindi translations of these works have begun to appear, however). See Arvind N. Das, "The Poor Man's Subaltern Studies," *Biblio* (Delhi) 11.1 (February 1996).

9 Sara Castro-Klarén, "Writing Sub-Alterity: Guaman Poma and Garcilaso, Inca," in *Borders and Margins: Post-Colonialism and Post-Modernism,* ed. Fernando de Toro and Alfredo de Toro (Frankfurt am Main: Vervuert/Madrid: Iberoamericana, 1995).

10 Ashcroft's reference here is to the rancorous debate around Patricia Seed's brief review article, "Colonial and Postcolonial Discourse," which appeared in the *Latin American Research Review* 26.3 (1991): 181– 200; for the debate, see volume 28, no. 3 of *LARR*. Bill Ashcroft, "Modernity's First-Born: Latin America and Post-Colonial Transformation," in *El debate de la postcolonialidad en Latinoamerica,* ed. Alfredo de Toro and Fernando de Toro (Frankfurt am Main: Vervuert/Madrid: Iberoamericana, 1999), 13–29.

11 Gyan Prakash, "Subaltern Studies as Postcolonial Criticism," *American Historical Review* 99.5 (December 1994): 1490.

12 Jacques Rancière, *The Names of History: On the Poetics of Knowledge* (Minneapolis: University of Minnesota Press, 1994).

13 Robert Young, *Colonial Desire: Hybridity in Theory, Culture, and Race* (London: Routledge, 1995). Still, Young's more recent book on the subject, *Postcolonialism: An Historical Introduction* (Oxford: Blackwell, 2001), attempts to write a unified history of postcolonialism rooted in Third World or tricontinental anti-imperialist movements.

14 Steven Slemon, "The Scramble for Post-Colonialism," in *De-scribing*

Empire: Postcolonialism and Textuality, ed. C. Tiffin and A. Lawson, (London: Routledge, 1994), 17.

15 Peter Hulme, "Including America," Ariel 21.1 (January 1995): 117–23; Hall, "When Was 'the Postcolonial'?"; and Young, Colonial Desire. Several collected works in the anthropology and history of colonialism have notably skirted the problematic of Spanish Empire and/or Latin America by focusing only on the "modern" northwestern European colonialisms: see Nicholas Dirks, ed., Colonialism and Culture (Ann Arbor: University of Michigan Press, 1992); and Frederick Cooper and Ann Stoler, eds., Tensions of Empire: Colonial Cultures in a Bourgeois World (Berkeley: University of California Press, 1997).

16 Kwame A. Appiah has argued that "what we might ungenerously call a comprador intelligentsia: a relatively small, Western-style, Western-trained group of writers and thinkers, who mediate the trade in cultural commodities of world capitalism at the periphery," is at the heart of postcolonialism as migrancy (Appiah, "Is the Post in Postmodernism the Post in Postcolonialism?" in Contemporary Postcolonial Theory: A Reader, ed. P. Mongia [London: Arnold 1996]). But Appiah may exaggerate. The metropolitan-based intellectual rarely mediates at the periphery where she or he is in less demand but rather at the center because the periphery never, or almost never, gets the goods (only recently have Subaltern Studies works appeared in Hindi). Revathi Krishnaswamy also has a point: "Given that metropolitan attitudes towards the postcolonial are caught between Orientalism and nativism, between unmitigated condemnation and uncritical celebration of Otherness, identification with subalternity and commodification of the 'Third World' often seem the only assured means to authority for many 'Third World' intellectuals. The very modes of access to power are thus rife with the risk of reification and subordination under such currently popular theoretical categories as cultural diversity, hybridity, syncretism, and migrancy. However, if postcolonial politics is to retain its radical cutting edge, what 'Third World' intellectuals must confront is not our 'subalternity' or even our 'subalternity-in-solidarity-with-the-oppressed,' but the comparative power and privilege that ironically accumulate from our 'oppositional' stance, and the upward mobility we gain from our semantics of subalternity" (Krishnaswamy, "Mythologies of Migrancy: Postcolonialism, Postmodernism, and the Politics of (Dis)location," Ariel 26.1 (January 1995): 129–30.

17 Young, Colonial Desire.

18 Ashcroft, "Modernity's First-Born."

19 Klor de Alva, "The Postcolonization of the (Latin) American Experi-

ence," 241–75. This work is a revised version of "Colonialism and Postcolonialism." (The quotes here are from the former essay.)

20 Another variation on the Latin Americanist exceptionalist theme is the all too frequently heard objection that, in a phrase, "since your history has its own proper name our history cannot have the same." In this vein the normally more critical Peruvian sociologist Nelson Manrique inexplicably confesses that he would accept the notion of "postcolonial" only if the situation in Peru were "an exact parallel" of that in India (Manrique, "Modernity and Alternative Development in the Andes," in *Through the Kaleidoscope: The Experience of Modernity in Latin America*, ed. Vivian Schelling [London: Verso, 2000], 221–47).

21 Hulme, "Including America," 119.

22 Juan Carlos Callirgos, "Postcolonial Modernizations of the City of Kings" (dissertation research proposal, University of Florida, Gainesville, 2002).

23 David Cannadine's *Ornamentalism: How the British Saw Their Empire* (Oxford: Oxford University Press, 2002) questions the notion that the design and practice of colonial rule under British Empire in the nineteenth and twentieth centuries is best understood solely as a modernizing and orientalizing regime of power.

24 An argument that is reproduced in Benedict Anderson, *Imagined Communities: Reflections on the Origin and Spread of Nationalism* (London: Verso, 1991), as well.

25 See Anderson, *Imagined Communities*, and his "To What Can Late-Eighteenth-Century French, British, and American Anxieties Be Compared? Comment on Three Papers," *American Historical Review* 106.4 (October 2001): 1281–89; Nicholas Canny and Anthony Pagden, eds., *Colonial Identity in the Atlantic World, 1500–1800* (Princeton: Princeton University Press, 1987); Partha Chatterjee, *The Nation and its Fragments: Colonial and Postcolonial Histories* (Princeton: Princeton University Press, 1993).

26 "No debemos olvidar que el control del poder poscolonial fue ganado por los herederos de los conquistadores, tanto en África como en Asia o en América" (Echenique, "La colonialidad presente," in *Crónicas perdidas* [Barcelona: Anagrama, 2002], 157).

27 For some recent examples of research on popular and subaltern politics in the early nineteenth century, see the work of Peter Guardino, Florencia Mallon, Charles Walker, Cecilia Méndez, Sarah Chambers, Marixa Lasso, and Mark Thurner.

28 See Paul Gootenberg, "Population and Ethnicity in Early Republican Peru: Some Revisions," *Latin American Research Review* 26.3 (1991): 109–57; Marisol de la Cadena, *Indigenous Mestizos: The Politics of Race and*

Culture in Cuzco, Peru, 1919–1991 (Durham: Duke University Press, 2000); and Mark Thurner, From Two Republics to One Divided: Contradictions of Postcolonial Nationmaking in Andean Peru, (Durham: Duke University Press, 1997).

29 Several Latin American historians have argued that the words "colonies" and "colonialism" were not used in the Spanish Empire or in Spanish America before the Bourbon era, hence the Habsburg realm was not an empire and the Americas not colonial entities. Even if one accepts this line of reasoning there is plenty of early modern Hispanic language and political theory to counter it. The seventeenth-century Spanish political theorist Solorzano used those terms to refer to Spanish settlements in the "Provinces of the Indies," and Pagden has amply demonstrated the Hapsburg ideology and use of the classical concept of universal empire. But strict historico-lexicographic method also begs reflexive and comparative critique; strictly speaking, such a method would oblige one to exclude certain cherished examples of modern or "new" colonialisms, including the case of the French "provinces" of Martinique and Algeria.

30 Here I am arguing against the continuing effort in cultural studies, traceable perhaps to Said's approach, to "secure" the concept of colonialism in textual ways. See Slemon, "The Scramble for Post-Colonialism."

31 See Dipesh Chakrabarty, Provincializing Europe: Postcolonial Thought and Historical Difference (Princeton: Princeton University Press, 2000).

32 Ashcroft, "Modernity's First-Born," 13.

33 Cited in Prakash, "Subaltern Studies as Postcolonial Criticism," 1487.

34 Prakash, "Subaltern Studies as Postcolonial Criticism," 1490.

35 See Chakrabarty's Provincializing Europe and "Subaltern Pasts, Minority History," Perspectives 35.8 (November 1997):37–43.

36 Rancière, The Names of History, 31.

37 Chakrabarty, Provincializing Europe, 8.

38 Walter D. Mignolo, Local Histories/Global Designs: Coloniality, Subaltern Knowledges, and Border Thinking (Princeton: Princeton University Press, 2000), 37.

39 Ashcroft makes the same point in "Modernity's First-Born."

40 Mignolo accepts the older view that Spain was a "nation-state" in the fifteenth century, which then extended itself via imperialism. This view, associated with historians like John Elliot, has been challenged by more recent work on the history of nationalism and nations, particularly that of Hobsbawm and Anderson, and also by the more recent work of Hispanists like François-Xavier Guerra and Jaime Rodríguez. In the more recent view, "Spain" does not become a modern nation-

state until the early nineteenth century; the Spanish Empire was not "national"; and "Spain" was not a nation during most of the colonial period in Latin America.

41 Mignolo is particularly interested in what he calls the "subaltern knowledges" and "border thinking" that emerge in the cracks of "colonial difference."

42 See Anthony Pagden, *Lords of All the World: Ideologies of Empire in Spain, Britain, and France, c.1500–c.1800*, (New Haven: Yale University Press, 1995).

43 Ashcroft, "Modernity's First-Born," 16.

44 Although the global two-phase design of the history of imperialism and coloniality/modernity serves as a useful starting point for identifying certain of the discrepant elements of temporally and geographically distant colonialisms and postcolonialities, any history writing project that gets inside those discrepant elements quickly finds itself in need of sharper distinctions and problematizations, and this is particularly so in the new historiography and anthropology of the temporally deep case of the Spanish Americas. Steve Stern's three-phase periodization of "foreign-local encounter" in the Americas is a step in this direction because it responds more closely to the entanglements of the region's colonial and postcolonial pasts. Working out of a Latin Americanist social history framework, Stern outlines what he calls "three eras." In his scheme, the "first post-Conquest era" (circa 1540s to circa 1750s) is marked on the subaltern side by "reverse colonization" (by which he appears to mean the "colonization" of Spanish colonial institutions by Indian or native agents and cultural practices) and "massive social leakage" or strategies of avoidance that gave rise to the increasingly preponderant interstitial castes (mestizos, mulattos, and others) and to new, hybrid colonial cultural practices. Stern's second era of "colonial dismantling and national state formation" (circa 1750s to circa 1930s) is defined by the "struggle to remake the 'who' and 'how' that populated a triangle of interacting social forces." This triangle included the "unraveling of the Iberian colonial framework," the rise of "American-centered elites," and the "adaptation and resistance strategies of popular sectors" to Creole rule. In Stern's third era (circa 1930s onward), "the triangle of interacting social forces developed within a framework of overwhelming U.S. importance as the hegemonic external presence in the Latin American world." This most recent period has seen the paradox of a "massive expansion and diversification of direct [foreign-local] relationships, dependencies, and communications that turned [national] territorial boundaries and directions of control into an illusion" (Stern, "The

Decentered Center," 49). Each of Stern's three eras of "foreign-local encounter" carried civilizing and colonizing projects, the results of which were less than predictable. The gross discursive kinship among these projects, however, does not obscure the genealogical or historical differences. Instead, my reading of Stern's periodization would suggest the existence of shifting postcolonial predicaments under different historical regimes of cultural encounter and imperial power.

45 Solidarity with the indigenous nationalities movement whose quincentennial cry was "500 years of resistance" should not obscure the critical understanding that the colonial and postcolonial histories of those five hundred years are not all about, or perhaps even primarily about, an unrelenting "resistance." As Chakrabarty argues, subaltern histories are not so much histories of resistance as histories of negotiation *within* the cracks of capitalism, coloniality, nationality, and modernity.

46 Mignolo, *Local Histories/Global Designs*, 19.

47 J. Cañizares-Esguerra, *How to Write the History of the New World: Histories, Epistemologies, and Identities in the Eighteenth-Century Atlantic World* (Stanford: Stanford University Press, 2002).

48 On industrialization efforts, see Paul Gootenberg, *Imagining Development: Economic Ideas in Peru's "Fictitious Prosperity" of Guano, 1840–1880* (Berkeley: University of California Press, 1993).

49 See Charles Hale, *Mexican Liberalism in the Age of Mora* (Princeton: Princeton University Press, 1968).

50 On the economic and technological imagination of Peruvian elites, see Gootenberg, *Imagining Development.*

51 W. B. Taylor, "Between Global Process and Local Knowledge: An Inquiry into Early Latin American Social History, 1500–1900," in *Reliving the Past: The Worlds of Social History,* ed. O. Zunz (Chapel Hill: University of North Carolina Press, 1985), 125–26.

52 For the now canonical formulation, see Tulio Halperín Donghi, *The Contemporary History of Latin America,* trans. and ed., John Charles Chasteen (Durham: Duke University Press, 1993). The "not yet" narrative also structures Richard J. Salvucci's pocket-size catechism, *Latin America and the World Economy: Dependency and Beyond* (Lexington, Mass.: Heath, 1996).

53 Steve Stern, "Feudalism, Capitalism, and the World-System in the Perspective of Latin America and the Caribbean," *American Historical Review* 93.4 (October 1988): 829–72.

54 Gayatri Chakravorty Spivak, "Subaltern Studies: Deconstructing Historiography," in *Selected Subaltern Studies,* ed. R. Guha and G. Spivak (Delhi: Oxford University Press, 1988), 3.

55 See Gilbert Joseph, C. G. Grand, and R. D. Salvatore, eds., *Close Encounters of Empire: Writing the Cultural History of U.S.-Latin American Relations* (Durham: Duke University Press, 1998).

56 Ashcroft, "Modernity's First-Born," 16.

57 Hulme, "Including America," 122–23.

58 Klor de Alva, "Colonialism and Postcolonialism."

59 Aijaz Ahmad, "The Politics of Literary Postcoloniality," *Race and Class* 36.3 (1995): 1–19.

60 Ella Shohat, "Notes on the Post-Colonial," *Social Text* 31/32 (1992): 99–113; and Anne McClintock, "Pitfalls of the 'Post-Colonial,' " *Social Text* 31/32 (1992): 84–98.

61 See Paul Gilroy, Lawrence Grossberg, and Angela McRobbie, eds., *Without Guarantees: In Honour of Stuart Hall* (London: Verso, 2000).

62 The "postcolonial" sign does appear in some early 1980s anthropology, however. For one example of such an exception, see John Hawkins, *Inverse Images: The Meaning of Culture, Ethnicity, and Family in Postcolonial Guatemala* (Albuquerque: University of New Mexico Press, 1982).

63 Mark Thurner, "Historicizing 'the Postcolonial' from Nineteenth-Century Peru," *Journal of Historical Sociology* 9.1 (1996): 1–18. These trends are also discussed in Florence Mallon, "The Promise and Dilemma of Subaltern Studies: Perspectives from Latin American History," *American History Review* 99:5 (1994): 1491–1515. Andrés Guerrero has suggested that the end of "revolution" as the field-structuring keyword of Latin American political and historical discourse (despite, and because of, the Shining Path, Marcos, Gonzalo, FARC [the Revolutionary Armed Forces of Columbia], and Chávez) is partially responsible for this new receptivity.

64 See Frederick Cooper, et al., ed., *Confronting Historical Paradigms: Peasants, Labor, and the Capitalist World System in Africa and Latin America* (Madison: University of Wisconsin Press, 1993); and Mallon, "The Promise and Dilemma of Subaltern Studies."

65 Joseph, "Close Encounters," in *Close Encounters of Empire*, 31 n.30.

66 See Shohat, "Notes on the 'Post-Colonial' "; and Dirlik, *The Postcolonial Aura.*

67 See Slemon, "The Scramble for Post-Colonialism," 17.

68 This is also why Klor de Alva's "oppositional" or anticolonial definition of the postcolonial is of limited use. Ania Loomba writes: "If the term postcolonial is taken to signify an oppositional position or even desire, as [Klor de] Alva suggests, then it has the effect of collapsing various locations so that the specificities of all of them are blurred. Moreover, thought of as an oppositional stance, 'post-colonial' refers

to specific groups of (oppressed or dissenting) people (or individuals within them) rather than to a location or a social order, which may include such people but is not limited to them . . . Postcoloniality becomes a vague condition of people anywhere and everywhere, and the specificities of locale do not matter" (Loomba, *Colonialism/Postcolonialism* (London: Routledge, 1998), 253–54.

69 Hall, "When Was 'the Postcolonial'?" 247.

70 Among other works, this productive tension between the temporal and the critical has been noted in Gyan Prakash, "Can the Subaltern Ride? A Reply to O'Hanlon and Washbrook," *Comparative Studies in Society and History* 34.1 (January 1992): 168–84; Mallon, "The Promise and Dilemma of Subaltern Studies"; Loomba, *Colonialism/Postcolonialism*, 253–54; Hulme, "Including America"; and Hall, "When Was 'the Postcolonial'?"

71 Hulme, "Including America," 121.

72 Hall, "When Was 'the Postcolonial'?" 243.

73 Loomba, *Colonialism/Postcolonialism*, 19. Nevertheless, Loomba's survey houses a contradiction between the desire for location and heterogeneity and the ease with which the colonial and postcolonial are globalized in her unified, textbooklike discourse.

74 The venerable and "neutral" sign, "postindependence," much preferred by no-nonsense historians, does at first glance possess the advantage of clarity. One does not wonder why this "post" has not been derided like the others (although, come to think of it, the word might have possibilities!). It remains complicit with the liberal, modernization paradigm, however.

75 For an archival-based but respectful challenge to some of dependency theory's central assumptions concerning nineteenth-century Latin American history, see Paul Gootenberg, *Between Silver and Guano: Commercial Policy and the State in Postindependence Peru* (Princeton, Princeton University Press, 1989). See also M. Demélas, J. Piel, T. Saignes, and Y. Saint-Geours, "Informe Preliminar," in *Estados y Naciones en los Andes: Hacia una historia comparativa*, ed. J. P. Deler and Y. Saint-Geours (Lima: IEP/IFEA 1986), 17–23.

76 See Fernando Coronil, "Can Postcoloniality Be Decolonized? Imperial Banality and Postcolonial Power," *Public Culture* 4.2 (spring 1992): 89–108.

77 See Taylor, "Between Global Process and Local Knowledge."

78 A handful of Latin Americanist historians have broached the "early modern," but the big sign on the gate remains "colonial." "Early modern colonial" is probably better, at least until circa 1750.

79 Hayden White, *Metahistory: The Historical Imagination in Nineteenth-*

Century Europe (Baltimore: Johns Hopkins University Press, 1973); Anderson, *Imagined Communities.*

80 For one discussion of the problem, see Philip G. Altbach, "Literary Colonialism: Books in the Third World," in *The Post-Colonial Studies Reader,* Bill Ashcroft, Gareth Griffiths, and Helen Tiffin, eds. (London: Routledge, 1995): 485–90.

81 The original Spanish is as follows: "Que una perspectiva histórica ampliada resulta, en principio, más fácil cuando el proceso histórico es visto por historiadores que pertenecen a [la metrópoli]. [Pueden tener] una visión más global que la visión que elabora cualquiera de [las periferias]. En ese sentido parecería que el Perú . . . debería resignarse a practicar una historiografía aislacionista, provinciana y ultranacionalista . . . [Sin embargo] hay . . . una oportunidad, una probabilidad de que paises hoy provincianizados elaboren una historiografía de escala transnacional." Pablo Macera, "Explicaciones," in *Trabajos de historia: Teoría,* vol. 1 (1977; reprint, Lima: Herrera, 1988), 75.

82 In this regard, see Terrence Ranger and Eric Hobsbawm, *The Invention of Tradition* (Cambridge: Cambridge University Press, 1984), and Cannadine, *Ornamentalism.*

83 Anthony Pagden, *Lords of All the World: Ideologies of Empire in Spain, Britain, and France, c.1500–c.1800* (New Haven: Yale University Press, 1995), 9–10.

84 See Slemon, "The Scramble for Post-Colonialism."

85 This problem of the heterogeneity of colonial pasts and the apparent homogeneity in colonial discourse has been a concern in colonial and postcolonial studies. See Slemon, "The Scramble for Post-Colonialism," and Young, *Colonial Desire.*

86 The original Spanish is as follows: "Oímos decir comunmente que el fin de este siglo se encuentra desprovisto de interés y que no dejará en la historia sino insignificante huella . . . ¿No es acaso punto admitido que han ido decreciendo las grandes individualidades y empobreciéndose la actividad humana, desde aquellos genios que engrandecieron el mundo a fines del siglo XV? Sin embargo, la historia establecerá un paralelo entre aquellos tiempos y los nuestros; dirá que las exploraciones en el Africa, efectuadas en gran parte pacíficamente, son hazañas tan hermosas y de tan grandes consecuencias, como el descubrimiento de América con su cortejo de sangrientos episodios; ella fijará una nueva era de la reina Victoria, de Guillermo II, de Leopoldo, de Humberto; como fijó otra de Isabel la Católica, de Fernando el Conquistador, de Enrique el Navegante; y si no asigna a M. Carnot alguno de esos renombres, andando el tiempo, reconocerá a la Francia una

gran parte en la misión civilizadora" (Melchor de Vogue, "Las Indias Negras," *Boletín de la Sociedad Geográfica de Lima* (1.5 [August 15, 1891]).

87 The original Spanish is as follows: "La fama de los más gloriosos nombres nace de su constante repetición, de su paso por los labios de los niños en que llega a un grado extremo de idealización . . . tales como Bartolomé Díaz y Vasco de Gama, Colón y Magallanes, Pizarro y Cortés . . . También llegará día en que la humanidad pronuncie con la misma admiración los nombres de Caillie, Barth, Gordon y Livingstone . . . Vamos, pués, a civilizar esa tierra, sometiéndola a nuestras poderosas fuerzas materiales . . . y morales . . . que el Africa fuese rescatada, sobre todo, por el sacrificio de almas grandes, por la abnegación de un Livingstone" (Melchor de Vogue, "Las Indias Negras," 188–90).

88 In the middle decades of the nineteenth century, Latinism was critical to racially inflected imperial and national discourses of civilization in Europe and the Americas, and it produced such enduring transnational concepts as "the Latin Race" and "Latin America," as well as the somewhat less-enduring concepts of "the Anglo-Saxon Race" and "Anglo America."

89 See R. García Cárcel, *La leyenda negra: Historia y opinión* (Madrid: Alianza, 1992).

90 I base this counterfactual affirmation on the 1860s anti-imperialist critiques of the pioneering Peruvian sociologist Carlos Lissón; see especially his *La República en el Perú y la cuestión Peruano-Española* (Lima, 1865).

91 See Markham's *Travels in Peru and India* (London, 1862), and his *History of Peru* (Chicago, 1892), translated as *Historia del Perú* (Lima, 1895). See also Thurner in this volume (below).

92 Similar effects followed the passages of liberal discourses of nation-building between North and South America. Tocqueville's magisterial history of "democracy in America," widely read in francophone "Latin America," described the process of uprooting and exterminating the native population. Mexican, Argentine, and Chilean liberals took note of the example.

93 Macera's 1970s prognostication (cited in his "Explicaciones") echoes from the past.

94 Pratt, *Imperial Eyes.*

95 Anderson, *Imagined Communities*; Rebecca Karl, "Secret Sharers: Chinese Nationalism and the Non-West at·the Turn of the Twentieth Century" (Ph.D. diss., Duke University, 1997).

96 For an illustrated, English language version of Borges's fable, see *The Library of Babel* (Boston: Godine, 2000).

MAURICIO TENORIO TRILLO

Essaying the History of National Images

✳ "Imagine," said Marcel Schwob in Spicilège (1896), "that likeness is the intellectual language of difference and that differences are the sensible language of likeness." "Know," he added,
"that all things in this world are but signs, and signs of signs."
Likewise, I assume that the academic differences among today's
scholars are in truth the judicious language of our overwhelming
likeness. As any good post-this and post-that being, I recognize
that all things are signs and signs of signs. But I am merely able
to undertake what Carlos Pereda calls lecturas itinerantes of signs in
history. Scholars more acquainted with contemporary theoretical
paradigms are better fitted to engage in, to borrow Pereda's terms,
lecturas argumentadas (how truthful, how useful, how genuine is a
sign as a sign of something more important), and lecturas explicativas
(what makes possible the articulation of any given sign and why it
becomes readable).[1] However, I too have engaged in some form or
another of "post-imagining," although my current concern is with
both the post—today's omnipresent prefix—and our very capacity for
imagining.[2]

These lines offer some thoughts on our academic understanding of
nations, people, and identities. Through my specific and limited
research of the use of Mexican images in world's fairs I came to think
of nations and history, but what I have dealt with in fact are national
images. These images represent inherent parts of any kind of nationalism, but they are not the whole thing. Terms like nationalism
and identity have become such an academic industry that I do not aim
here to make a new contribution to their study. Rather, I will propose
general and provocative ruminations on the specificity of the crafting
of national images. If my contentions are either a part of, or anathema
to, any theory, it is merely a coincidence of which I am not aware.

Ernest Renan believed that a nation is a "soul," a "spiritual princi-ple."[3] Yet, if not for its face, its expression, its look, how would we be able to talk about any particular nation? Modern national images (i.e., commonplaces, stereotypes, the symbolism attributed to all nations) stem from the modern ideology of nationalism. Whether this ideology forms an intrinsic part of Western modernity is some-thing that I may believe but that many will debate.[4] What seems clear at least is that the voluminous production of national images is indeed a modern phenomenon. In modern times, these images be-came at once a national and unavoidable characteristic of any nation. In essence, nationalism was neither a purely domestic output nor a culturally productive force. It constituted an intricate global phe-nomenon, a molding power that, rather than giving rise to new and original cultural phenomena, instead reoriented, revitalized, and re-arranged existing cultural features, tailoring a comprehensive model that was assumed to be a unique and natural historical production.

For instance, practical and historical matters were at the roots of withdrawing the religious overtones of Mexico's national, civic im-age (the Catholic nation of a Jacobin elite that never resigned to religious myths and yet reinvented a civic religion over ancient be-liefs). Along similar lines, pragmatic and historical issues were at stake when a nation of immigrants, such as the United States, na-tionalized a universal republican discourse and made it into a na-tional common sense, full of earthly commands: ubi panis, ibi patria (according to Hector St. John de Crèvecoeur). As a result of the formation of all national images, we live in a world of nationalist portraits, in which each appears to be an exceptional and inimitable product of the same artist. This is not to say that there are not miscellaneous forms of national images and different nationalisms, but simply that historically there seemed to be no option but to craft a national image.

Once developed, national images became mandatory. A time and space with a "national" face became a sine qua non of modern times. These faces involved a process of cultural and political homogeniza-tion and centralization that often coincided within (or with the aim of achieving) the physical and historical boundaries of modern states. National images, state formation, and searches for national or ethnic identities have been concepts that have supported each other, *but they are not the same.* For instance, that modern Mexico had been defined according to the creed of *mestizaje* does not mean that, indeed, Mexico has been absolutely or uniquely mestizo, which is not to say that the *real* Mexico resides either in the mestizos or in those native groups that were not *mestizados.* Nor does it mean that an omnipotent state violently imposed mestizaje as the face of the nation. Mestizaje could be seen as a historical outcome that encompasses such undeniable facts as miscegenation, but also such realities as social arbitration, state legitimacy, and conflicts as well as agreements among different identities.

Modern national images could be seen as the arena, historically constituted, in which each new and old nation-state tried to develop a synthesis of history, culture, and traditions that could be presented as both unique and universal. The universal parameters are dictated, of course, by the model of a modern nation that has been in ascendance in Western history since the Enlightenment. Nonetheless, modern national images are far from being the product of a homogenous and stable "dominant" ideology. They form a complex arena in which all nations define each other by affirmations or negations, and in which modernity and tradition, features both popular and elitist, and inside and outside, must lose their crystalline distinctions.

When talking about the image or the idea of a nation, we believe to be referring to entire territories, cultures, and societies. This is an illusion. In fact, with the general term of nation we only refer to that central, intellectual arena in which modern nationalism has been debated, and which has undergone an impressive historical partition, giving rise to all modern national images. Therefore, by the early twentieth century the very idea of a nation, whether conceived by popular sectors or by an "enlightened bourgeoisie," had become inseparable from that same central arena. Even non-European or non-*criollo* (Creole) alternative geographical or cultural units, or popular alternatives to social organization had, and have, no other way to format their proposals but by referring to that central arena. Thus new nationalist movements, popular or indigenous, have rarely rejected the central idea of national images but rather have attempted to begin a new cycle of nationalism, a new partition. While popular nationalist movements aim to create a new historical unit as an alternative to old national images, they nevertheless hope to form what seems to our contemporary academic eyes a natural result: nation.

There is, however, the realm of the fragmented, domestic, traditional, and popular—that sphere in which local senses of belonging interact with the central images of nations—where alternative cultural views enter into conflicts and negotiations. This is the realm of the creation of different images, of the consumption and re-creation of broader national images at the local level.[5] Often there are difficulties in exploring this arena historically: first because of the problems in finding historical sources that portray the cultural and ethnic heterogeneity of the peoples who inhabit what we know as Mexico; and, second, because all too frequently in the Americas the indigenous past has been mythologized both by native nationalists and by contemporary scholars. That is, it is troublesome to "uncover" the "people without history" through the very use of concepts heavily loaded with the moral connotations associated with nationhood; for example, *"nuestros indios," "los desheredados,"* "the indigenous inhabitants," "the communities," or "the subalterns." Indeed, the purity and goodness of the noble savage that moved the consciousness of sixteenth-century friars may still be with us, albeit in different reincarnations. Nonetheless, it is fair to say that our understanding of the creation of national images would be insufficient unless we tell the story of how national images are defined, consumed, rejected, and transformed by various peoples within a nation.

The problem of sources and the very complexity of dealing with the abstract consciousness and identities of past peoples who left few records of their views has not hindered the realm of the popular from becoming the *terreno de la esperanza* (terrain of hope) of intellectuals and scholars who aim to save the historical and political likelihood of a real indigenous or popular nation. The considerations of nationalism often have been indistinguishable from the search for morally acceptable identities. Because the domain of the fragmented and popular is as much a part of modern nations as their central capital cities, we search for alternative real nations in this realm. It is as if in the midst of so much uncertainty and fragmentation the idea of the real nation ought to be rearticulated, safeguarded, and protected.

Power for inclusion, exclusion, and centralization, of course, always has been at play in the historical composition of national images. But the modernity of nationalism is in its comprehensiveness. If modern nations are, as we are consistently reminded, "imagined communities"—especially in regard to their historically visible images—it follows that the people who did not participate in the imagining may not necessarily possess the real image of the nation. The "falseness" of nationalism rests not in some or other form of "imagined community," but in the very attempt to come out with such a thing as a national image.

Debating the falseness or authenticity of nations resembles discussing what God really looks like. In our post-Nietzschean era God has died and we understand this, but we know that nevertheless he/she somehow exists and is part of our understating of the world. And yet we do not care to talk about the real and the fake God. Ironically enough, national imaginaries have become more real than ever, but they are not more or less genuine than they have ever been.

NATIONALISM: MODERN AND DEMOCRATIC?

Scholars have long debated the origins of the concept of nationalism, although its final genealogy is unattainable. When dealing with nationalism in the Americas we encounter the nineteenth-century nationalism of former European colonies. For this kind of nationalism, to talk about pristine origins is misleading because it was already a product of empires and globalization. Overall, what is generally accepted by scholars is that, at least in regard to national images, nationalism is an inherent outcome of modern phenomena, and that by the nineteenth century it was a comprehensive trend.[6] Yet do all good modern things come together? Are notions of social unity and solidarity at a national scale, and of republicanism and democracy, necessarily part of the same historical package?

Beyond theoretical and historiographical debates, the appraisal of nationalism has long maintained a sort of approving view of the "good type" of nationalism, either born in Europe, liberal and democratic, or "authentically" rooted in a community's tradition.[7] Some have argued that nationalism and democracy were history's twins, and thus democracy included a kind of "genetic" predisposition (having been born modern, as in the United States) or a "mutation" of national identity (e.g., a change in Catholic, patrimonial values).[8] Others have blamed America's nineteenth-century liberals for the destruction of "authentic" solidarities and values that resulted from the forced imposition of "artificial" Westernized concepts of nation. But liberalism, various forms of communitarianism, democracy, and nationalism have all followed different historical tracks, although at times crossing each other.

One would only need to survey the history of Europe's nineteenth century to see that what today is considered a democratic ideology was then deeply feared by liberal nationalists and monarchists alike. Out of the Enlightenment notion of sovereignty of the people grew such notions of national sovereignty, and these notions did not extend democratic rights to a country's nationals. Throughout the nineteenth century, nationalism was a strong tendency by itself—one that was capable of selecting its own ideological partners depending on the circumstances.[9] Liberals and republicans in the early nineteenth century, in Mexico or in the United States, were, rather than nationalists, strong advocates of their respective *patrias chicas* (local homelands). By the early twentieth century, Mexican nationalists were often either liberal Jacobins or progressive Catholics; at the same time U.S. liberals tended to be either community-oriented progressives or T. Roosevelt-like nationalists. There is no fixed marriage between nationalism and any particular political ideology. Not all "nice things" come together; indeed, those nice things (nation, democracy, authenticity, equality) were hardly ever fully achieved.

But can we detect in national images a "good nationalism" through its genuine rooting in real (cultural, popular) ground? How would this be done? Under the criteria of durability? (It has lasted, ergo it must have some popular content.) Or of consensus? (Not much conflict, so it must be the real thing.) Or of purity? (It is really out there, in the people, without having been polluted by the central, elitist idea of the nation.) Historians have shown that people can be *patriotes malgré nous* (patriots in spite of ourselves), as Josep Maria Fradera has sustained for Catalunya, where the bourgeoisie could not translate their great economic power into social control until it finally came up with a nationalist synthesis. But historians also have shown, as G. P. Thomson and Antonio Annino have for Mexico, that the articulation of local versions of the central national image meant both significant national incorporation and strong local power.[10] Somehow, however, many of today's historians seem to need to document the real nation sought by new nationalists (ethnic or otherwise), anthropologists, and global activists. To this I will return later.

For the specific case of the nineteenth-century nation-states of the Americas, the creation of national images included the discussion of citizenship and democratic representation insofar as these elements were part of the emerging global definition of nationalism. With a pragmatism of which history is replete, the elites of these new nations constructed both national images and stable states by political bargaining and negotiation in which democratic representation was used or abused according to the balance of power.[11] It could be argued that authoritarian rule has proven to be functional in defining comprehensive nationalist consciousness, as in Porfirian Mexico where the construction of nationality was believed to be the exclusive duty of the state. Democracy, one finds in history, is neither a natural popular outcome nor the monopoly of a particular ethnic or cultural identity. It is a process of political learning that has never had a fixed meaning and a pure expression, and as such it has (and has not) played a role in the definition of national images throughout the world. For the United States's national image (the presumably quintessential democracy) democracy was a foundational myth (with changing meaning and functioning) but not a condition that exempted the nation from establishing—often through undemocratic means—a homogeneity of language, culture, flag, symbols, heroes, and whiteness.[12]

Nonetheless, studies of nineteenth-century Mexico or Peru or Brazil have often emphasized the dichotomy between traditional and modern politics to explain either the failure of democracy in these countries or the continuation of a particularly Mexican, Peruvian, or Brazilian status quo that, although undemocratic, had nonetheless proven to be a workable political system. Such systems operated behind a series of complex democratic facades ("fictitious citizens," symbolic elections, and ideal—not factual—democratic standards) that in truth were more than mere useless forms.[13] In fact, one or another form of democratic creed—whether popular or statist—was always used by the different political factions for constructing a nationalist ideology. The term democracy has been for the definition of nationalist ideologies in the Americas what egalitarianism was for the U.S. democracy: a consistent point of reference in political rhetoric yet never the sine qua non for the existence of the nation and its symbolism. This is not due to Mexico's or the United States's seemingly undemocratic or democratic natures but rather to the utilitarian, subterfugelike, and changing nature of modern democratic thought. The last part of the twentieth century witnessed a unique lesson in the Americas. Nearly all the former "atavistic" dictatorships became formal democratic nations. Democracy—that old dream—has proven to be an intricate patchwork of political learning, negotiation, and struggle, by and large accomplished regardless of particular national histories.

POPULAR NATIONALISM, POPULIST NATIONOLOGISTS

Popular customs, beliefs, and claims always have been included in nationalist ideologies worldwide. A *national* image is necessarily inclusive and linked to often centralized (socially and/or geographically) interests, and it may interact with or oppose localized popular senses of belonging. Alternatives to the established national image were and continue to be present. These counterimages have influenced the creation of the national image depending on their economic or military strength, as well as on their articulation and social and political resonance within the only language that we—modern cosmopolitan observers—recognize: that of what we know to be nations and identities.

National images are often rooted, so to speak, in "spiritual" and domestic forms of authenticity. This is because modern nationalism requires both a globally recognizable uniqueness and domestic legitimacy. It could be argued that a national image could be more or less contested depending on its "authenticity" as an echo of a domestic spirituality. Yet all national images aim at comprehensiveness and stability in symbols and meanings. Thus, no national image could be spiritually faithful to all of its presumed constituency at all times. Indeed, national images cannot be measured vis-à-vis "authentic" identities because modern nationalism is not fundamentally about authenticity but rather is about efficiency defined as two mutually dependent goals. These goals are the maximization of domestic economic and political gains (always historically defined) and the achievement of and contribution to nationalism as an international, global phenomena. As long as we maintain the existence of good, popular, authentic, national images versus bad or fake nationalisms we keep company with a theoretical and political battle fought within the terms of nation and identity.

National images are only partially related to the excessively discussed issue of identity.[14] Various identities are affected inasmuch as homogenized, centralized, and powerful notions of nation are presented as an *official* and *exclusive* synthesis. Countless studies have shown that nationalism requires the constant influence, transformation, destruction, and reinvention of local traditions and identities. But the consideration of national images cannot contribute essentials to those who search for identities. National images help to ask questions related to identity, but not to affirm real or negate fake identities. In dealing with national images one does not ask, for instance, who were the genuine Peruvians and how they really thought and felt; rather, one aims to find out what part of some people's historiographically visible existence they believed to signify Peruvianness. All in all, the destinies of the various identities within a nation are constantly changing, challenging, and utilizing the nation according to specific circumstances.

It used to be that both liberal and radical thinkers either rejected nationalism as a "revolt against reason" (e.g., Karl Popper) or they simply did not take nationalism into account because class conflict supposedly knew no national frameworks. New forms of old understandings, however, have reconsidered nationalism more favorably. And for these new perspectives the authenticity of a national identity has become the criteria used to distinguish between "good" and "bad" nationalism.[15] These kinds of moral conclusions seem unavoidable as long as nationalism is attached to notions of authentic identities. One does not need to agree with the doggedly argued thesis of the "end of the nation-state," nor with the final reaching of a postmodern, postnational stage in the history of humankind to believe in the historiographical and political imperative of unloading the debate on nationalism of its heavy ethical content.[16] Allow me here to illustrate this point with some examples from Mexican history.

The interpretations of nationalism in Mexico have taken multifarious forms or tropes (comedy, tragedy, parody, epic). The revolutionary nationalism of the 1910s and 1920s inaugurated a new national epic in which the history of the nation unfolded as the path from darkness to light, from exploitation to freedom, from falsehood to authenticity. But the critical works of David Brading and Edmundo O'Gorman have opened the Pandora's box of the history of Mexico's nationalism.[17] Both historians have examined the many myths and historical reconstructions inherent to Creole patriotism as it emerged in the last part of the eighteenth century. The analysis of Creole or criollo patriotism has been the historiographical basis for many interpretations of twentieth-century Mexican nationalism, which often echo the tragi-comic drama of local and foreign intellectuals searching for Mexico's true identity. An emblematic example is the literature on things Mexican, or lo mexicano, which began to appear in the late 1930s—sometimes making use of history and at other times disregarding it. By the late 1950s, Mexico's nationalism was widely assumed to be the expression of a single and unique identity. More important, it was believed that it was possible to condense, extract, and know such an identity. The ideas of Bergson, Adler, Freud, or Ortega, among others, were useful in locating this essential Mexicanness. Historical memory and myths were extrapolated to identify Mexicans' atavistic characteristics.[18] These searches for lo mexicano portrayed Mexicans as, in Roger Bartra's words, "almas arcáicas cuya relación trágica con la modernidad las obliga a reproducir permanente su primitivismo" (archaic souls whose tragic relation with modernity obliges them to endlessly reproduce their primitivism).[19] Ironically enough, after many books on lo mexicano, Mexicans were portrayed by new poets, scholars, and intellectuals in a fashion startlingly similar to the stereotypical images served up by foreign traveler literature and film: fiesta, siesta, día de muertos, sombrero, and so forth.

The views of O'Gorman and Brading, as well as the industry of lo mexicano, underwent a reconsideration in the 1980s as official nationalism and the political system suffered another wave of a modernizing will. Roger Bartra's seminal study was the long-overdue parody of the foundational myths of Mexican nationalism and identity. The work showed how Mexico's apparently pristine, homogenous, genuine, and benign nationalism was yet another expression of Western intellectual trends. It also revealed how this nationalism had been used and abused by an authoritarian "revolutionary" and populist state. Bartra was, of course, accused of elitism, of Westernfilia, and of having a lack of sympathy for the real Mexico. For if all those alternative and beautiful things that are believed to be Mexican were but expressions of old European beliefs and traditions, from whence can the new indigenista intellectual, the alternative cosmopolitan scholar, or the new political strategist derive a sense of transcendental hope and inspiration?

In historiographical terms the 1990s saw the emergence of regional studies on the functioning of nationalism and identity. With a more or less disenchanted perspective (vis-à-vis previous political and epistemological explanations) historians studied how, at the local level, popular patriotism interacted with national "hegemonic" nationalism and international trends.[20] At times these insightful studies appeared to still be full of an epic spirit: the search for the true Mexico, which, to be sure, is indigenous, egalitarian, and tolerant. Thus the phantasm of the *real* Mexico reappears in the historiography, where Robert Redfield's eternal spirit is still with us.

Overall one can argue that the interpretation of Mexico's modern nationalism has completed a cycle, now that the country itself seems to be arriving at bizarre social and political scenarios that include all sorts of violence, democratic openness, and economic integration with the United States. Nationalism in Mexico reaches the twenty-first century as a seemingly insurmountable collective hallucination. It is still the ideological bedrock of a lasting domestic and foreign political culture, maintained the same by the official party, the leftist and rightist oppositions, guerrilla movements, and by sophisticated European and U.S. activists and intellectuals. We all want our real Mexico to be that of "under the volcano," although Mexico is more like the rest of the industrialized world than ever before.

The cycles of analysis of Mexican nationalism echo international debates over identities and nations. The term mestizaje—once again in vogue in academic and political circles throughout the continent— exemplifies these echoes. In essence, mestizaje as a historical, sexual, and racial miscegenation took place more or less everywhere in the world. To talk of racial or cultural purity is historically nonsensical. (By the same token, to talk of hybrid cultures as a post-NAFTA phenomena is likewise absurd.) But what is controversial about mestizaje is not its historical occurrence but rather what different national or regional ideologies have done with it. For instance, in postrevolutionary Mexico, mestizaje became an essential part of a nationalist project of social reform. In sharp contrast, in the United States mestizaje was by and large denied or masked under the term melting pot. In both countries mestizaje was a fact.

Today race and mestizaje represent once again a global intellectual challenge. In colonial times the Spanish Crown recognized mestizaje and developed a sophisticated institutional apparatus to deal with it. Such apparatus included the exclusion of blacks and Jews, the recognition of mixed marriages of any other ethnic or cultural group, and the acknowledgment and defense of the autonomy of Indian communities, if only to subject them better to the process of spiritual conquest under missionary Catholicism. In this way colonial times may seem closer to our postmodern, identity-conscious eyes. Modern holistic political and social ideologies like liberalism, socialism, Marxism, or indeed nationalism itself found no time to face mestizaje and multiple identities. After all, what was important was liberal citizenship, class consciousness, and national identity. Perhaps only anarchism and romantic socialist utopianism (as Marx dubbed it), with their emphasis on the small, the individual, the self, and nature, developed if not a concern then at least a certain respect for local identity. But even anarchism was imprinted by racial certainties. In Mexico, for instance, the Magonista program called for the expulsion and banning of Chinese immigration based on the anomalies of the Chinese race (as well as on the need to support small Mexican agricultural communities).

During the last two decades of the twentieth century—with the crisis of the Left and the collapse of former empires and nation-states—the fixation with identities and thus with mestizaje has reemerged. New forms of primitivism and liberalism have also flourished. Neoprimitivism can be found in many powerful NGOs, in anthropologists, and in radical activists throughout the world—all aiming at alternative social and spiritual scenarios through the poor, the native, and the ethnic minorities of the world. On the other hand, new forms of liberalism regain strength, seeking to finish the job begun by the nineteenth-century creation of homogenous nations and states, continuing the disregard for collective identities. Racism and all sorts of mestizajes and hybridities continue to be a fact everywhere in the world, but we have inaugurated a postproletarian, postcitizen way of referring to these issues.

Inevitably these identity "loops" are combined with the idea of modernization. For some, a truly modern Mexico or Peru will bring about a liberal, individualist, and responsible nationalism; for others, it would produce the end result of the *real* Mexico or Peru. In countries with large indigenous populations like Mexico, Guatemala, or Peru this marriage of modernization with nationalism has led to proposals for new quasi utopias, for the recovery of *México profundo* (deep Mexico) or the *país profundo* (deep country) (Jorge Basadre's Peru) of that country where *buscando un inca* (searching for an Inca) is a national pastime.[21] These nationalist reconsiderations of nationalism, I am afraid, could not take us out of the cycles of nationalism that the world began two centuries ago. Of course, those who are able to maintain new utopias deserve our full attention, and in that sense the intellectual search for postnational scenarios in countries like

Mexico or Peru would find great help in the utopias that militantly opposed and criticized powerful nationalist ideologies. But should we begin a new cycle of nationalism departing from these utopias? That would be, I believe, to betray the liberating spirit that guides the work of those such as Bonfil Batalla and Flores Galindo.[22]

But if not an identity, might class grant us a criterion by which to distinguish the good nation from the bad nation? It would be difficult to claim that the articulation of modern national images by elites possessed a class character in the strict sense.[23] Doubtless these images were maneuvered and reformulated according to the particular interests of those with political and economic power. But more than being the pure reflection of the character of a single class, national images were marked by the conditions of negotiation among and within the classes that articulated them. In other words, modern national images required multifarious domestic mediations among competing economic interests, political aspirations, intellectual views, cultural perspectives, and local social circumstances. Furthermore, these bargains always remain part of a larger discussion with international circumstances, pressures, intellectual influences, and cultural implications. The results of such negotiations were both intricate and provisional.

More than class in a Marxist sense, class as style—particularly the regional identity of the articulators—was surely stamped on the national image. The national image of Mexico was largely dictated by the collage of victorious economic and military elites who had Mexico City as their final destination. Just as Paris became France, and New England the United States, Mexico City gave shape to the nation by simultaneously ignoring and selectively appropriating features of its regional and social identities. In addition, the negotiated images of the nation included various aspects that were otherwise unquestionable. These included the accepted gender, racial, political, and cultural features of elites, which were rarely at stake. Mexico, Brazil, the United States, and France developed national images of both the "virile" exercise of conquest and sovereignty over nature and/or other nations and the female symbols of republicanism. More than class, these gender distinctions filtered up from the local institutions and icons to the larger national constitutions and more bellicose symbols. To appropriate one or another popular cultural feature was at least thinkable. To go against the virility of modern nationalism was not.[24]

Modern Mexican nationalism gave rise to a civic religion that was (had to be) not only secular but also laden with Jacobin hints donated from a history of popular-religious rebellions and from conservative-versus-liberal encounters marked by foreign interventions. The new civic religion required not that all persons in Mexican territory be Mexicans but that they become so only through incorporation into the environment of late-nineteenth-century national citizenship: cities and the market. However, throughout the nineteenth century foreign interventions and wars of liberation, together with local cultures and senses of belonging, originated various popular patriotisms.[25] But in wars and in discourses the articulators of nationalist ideologies readily used and abused those popular patriotisms. For their part people opposed, adapted, readapted, and learned to cope with the central notion of the nation. The national image officially created was indeed fake, but not because popular patriotisms could somehow form a real national image.

But class understood as an acceptable refined style, as éclat, played an important role in the formation of legitimate national images. In Mexico race, class, and gender differences varied depending on bizarre social linkages. In the nineteenth century one could be an Indian male and be powerful, as were Benito Juárez, Porfirio Díaz or Francisco Manuel Altamirano to name only the most notorious. One could be racially marked and powerful in a way unthinkable, say, in the United States. But that did not mean that there was not a "race problem" in Mexico. How were Indians accepted by an aristocratizing society? Who accepted whom? Did powerful Indians accept Mexican aristocracy or vice versa? These questions touch on class as controversial style, fought over by different sectors of society in complicated fashion. These fights over style are far from the conventional dichotomies of proletariat versus bourgeoisie, or subalterns versus the rest.

Estilo y Clase (style and class) did not often come together, however. When Victoriano Huerta reached power Mexico City's aristocracy supported him, but they did not accept him socially. He was un patán, un pelado, no gente como uno (a hick, a hobo, not like us). When Plutarco Elías Calles and Alvaro Obregón headed the victorious factions, their plans for the new revolutionary capital city were articulated by an unbearable aristocrat (Alberto J. Pani) who sought to continue the Porfirian city, although the revolution itself was a revolt against catrinura (aristocratic mannerisms). Indeed, during the late Porfiriato, éclat more than class marked the national image. Over the years of stability all forms of social arrangements (at the local, regional, and national levels) expressed economic interests, but the arrangements were ontologically cultural and based on affinities of ways of being, speaking, drinking, and feeling.[26] These kinds of hegemonic processes, so to speak, were extremely fragile not only because of the existence of "counterhegemonic" resistance, or because of the decline of the aging symbol of the state (Porfirio Díaz), but for the natural *acratinamiento* (elitism) of nineteenth-century politics and culture. (Indeed, Marx himself saw this: the bourgeoisie always aspires to the style of the aristocracy.) Therefore, it would be difficult to argue either that Mexico's Porfirian national image was simply that of the *científicos* (positivist circle of Porfirian advisors) or that the revolution was made by the proletariat *tout court*. What can be safely argued is that by the first decade of the twentieth century Mexico's national image—or for that matter that of the United States or France—had been *acratinada* (gentrified) by a Victorian aristocratic era that soon came to an end. By the same token, one could debate whether the Mexican Revolution was proletarian, *campesino* (peasant), or *ranchero* (small farmer), but what is clear is that it was the insurrection of the *peladaje* (hillbillies). And the plebeian revenge included such dissimilar characters as Francisco Villa and Plutarco Elías Calles.

All in all, once a national image has been more or less developed it will be used and abused by different factions, not always respecting class borders. In the very divided society of late-nineteenth-century Catalunya, nationalism essentially sought, as Joan Lluís Marfany has argued, "to control the Catalan society, rather than [to achieve] its own autonomy—and of course not [to gain] its independence." Thus, in Catalunya nationalism "invited Catalans to join a sort of a collective psychodrama that exorcizes them from their problems through the symbolic representation of the settlement of all social contradictions in the unity of the nation: hence, let us all bend for the motherland, let us all sing together in a single voice, let us all shake hands to dance a great *sardana*."[27] Similarly in Mexico the national flag served very different uses for two different movements. In 1915 the lawyer Antonio Díaz Soto y Gama, who formed part of the intelligentsia of Zapata's Indian revolution, was almost shot at the National Congress for dragging the flag and roughly calling it the symbol of "el triunfo de la reacción clerical encabezada por Iturbide" (the triumph of the clerical reaction headed by Iturbide). Certainly this is not the image of the nation that southern Mexican Indians supported. The love for the flag, common to all factions (Villistas, Carrancistas, Obregonistas), bonded all of them together in a collective effort to remove the flag from Soto y Gama in a scandalous performance of unified patriotism.[28]

Ironically enough, in 1995, as a token of a process of negotiation between a self-appointed Zapatista movement in the state of Chiapas and the Mexican government, a guerrilla commandant and an official emissary posed for the international media in a colonial church, each one pulling the Mexican flag at one end as proof of the consensus on the nation, despite violent discrepancies. To be sure, the new Zapatista leader was more astute than Soto y Gama, but he was also less politically and historically coherent. Soto y Gama was, historiographically speaking, accurate. The Mexico that the flag represented was painfully constructed by a Creole elite. In flamboyantly embracing the flag, the 1995 guerrilla commandant was either saintly forgiving or ignorant, if indeed what the movement he represented sought was to make la patria speak thus: "Hablando en su corazón indio, la Patria sigue digna y con memoria" (Speaking from its Indian heart, the Patria retains its dignity and memory).[29] In 1995, if one were to be politically and historically coherent, one would have to concede that someone was being controlled or fooled by the flag. But whom? The Mexican government? The guerrilla movement? The guerrilla commandant? An ambitious negotiator who gained notoriety in the name of the nation? A group of indigenous people represented by the commandant? All of them?

BETWEEN EAST AND WEST

The national images of the Americas are not all what we conventionally call Western, but they are very little else. Most countries of the Americas emerged out of a process of decolonization and arrived late to modern industrial development, thus nationalism acquired a specific feature epitomized by the inseparable link between nationalism and modernization. That is, nationalism for the new nations of the eighteenth and nineteenth centuries was an economic and cultural dictum. To be a modern nation meant to follow, ambivalently but constantly, the paradigmatic model of the European nation. The real progress and future of the nation was in modernizing the nation.

And modern values, capital, and technology were not inside but outside the country. Therefore, nationalism and modernization became interchangeable terms, and whenever one or the other had to be negotiated there materialized the dichotomy of a traditional, backward, and obstructing inside versus a progressive, modern, and accelerating outside.

But the outside was already domestic. The nations of the Americas were by and large nineteenth-century phenomena, products of globalization and economic and cultural integration. In this context inside and outside acquired a very different meaning than, say, the notions of inside and outside in such twentieth-century nation-states as India, for whom the nationalisms of the Americas constituted an inherent ingredient of modern Western nationalism.[30] For twentieth-century anticolonial Indian nationalists, it was clear, according to Partha Chatterjee, that "the greater one's success in imitating the Western skills in the material domain . . . the greater the need to preserve the distinctness of one's spiritual culture."[31] For late-nineteenth- and early-twentieth-century Mexican nationalists, the goal seemed to be to modernize both the present and the interpretation of the past, to acquire not only a national epic but a modern, cosmopolitan national epic.

It could be argued that nationalism was for the Americas a colonizing process, a case of "Creole nationalism."[32] In this sense, studies of India have been used as a point of reference because they reveal the dialectic of East and West in a complex power relation. For, as Chatterjee has maintained, nationalism as a modern, universalist, and Western phenomenon is indeed inescapable for both East and West. Modern nationalism has required a continual contrast with an Other to reflect itself; a mirror for Prospero, as Richard Morse once argued in commenting on U.S. views of the other ("Latin") Americas.[33] Without Ariel or Caliban there is no Prospero, a new cycle has to begin again and again. However, in dealing with the nationalism of the Americas one should not exaggerate the East/West dichotomy. This dichotomy did indeed constitute an intrinsic ingredient in the making of modern Western European nationalism.[34] But the independencies of the Americas were historical experiments in liberalism, nationalism, and republicanism. Although Europe and the Americas mutually shaped the origins of modern nationalism, the new countries of the so-called Latin part of the Americas were neither fully Western nor entirely non-Western. Neither the duplicate nor the radical Other of the West, the Americas became the forgotten constitutive structure of the West.

Therefore one could say that Mexico, vis-à-vis the West, is traditional, backward, and not fully Westernized. Nationalism, democracy, and modernization as a whole have been seen by Mexican elites in a sort of intersection of mirror images. Modernization is outside, and hence the country needs to reflect the image projected by Western modernization. But that large image is already a composition made of various mirror reflections of Europe's own historical play of tradition-modernity, progress-backwardness, self-Other. The mirror effects do not end there. What is considered Western modernity, reproduced by the elites of countries like Mexico, is in turn in the colonized country superimposed over many domestic mirrors that reflect both local images and their own versions of the large image of modernity. These multifarious refractions of mirror images shape the nationalism of a country like Mexico. Consequently, what emerges in view is a type of nationalism that is simultaneously cosmopolitan, parochial, modern, traditional, and, especially, elusive.

HISTORY AND NATIONALISM: NEWS FROM NOWHERE

At the end of the nineteenth century the great French geographer Elisee Reclus reproved the nonsense of national frontiers and stereotypes; these absurdities, he believed, would gradually be eliminated. Similarly, at the end of the twentieth century—and as the world underwent the post-1989 renaissance of nationalisms that, once again, produced numerous instances of ethnic, racial, and cultural massacres—Eric Hobsbawm hinted that all the talk about nationalism was a sign of the actual abatement of the importance of the nation-state. History, however, has not approached the twice-announced end of nationalism.

Beyond our current debates on nationalisms and identities is there a list of topics, advice, or notes of caution that we would like to bear in mind for future accounts? Within modern nationalism there is an inherent ambivalence that oscillates between rejection and total acceptance, between reason and passion, universalism and patriotism, hate of conformity and love of what is known. This ambivalence is intrinsic to current political or academic discussions on nationalism, for the world cycles of nationalism have known no finale. There is always a renewal of an old nationalism, or a new process, a new nation, and reconditioned national images. These phenomena enchant us with their liberating spirit, their authenticity and pureness, despite the hate-and-love inconsistencies inherent in any kind of nationalism. For the nation is an idea akin to those which made José Bergamín affirm "no es la idea la que apasiona, sino la pasión que idealiza" (it is not the idea that empassions, but the passion that idealizes).[35] I say let twenty-first-century historiography take advantage of the ambivalence of nationalism by pushing it to its extremes in a *reductio at absurdum*.

Historiographical and theoretical discussions will and must continue their pace, although at times academic trendiness prevails. However, one thing must be clear. In essence national images, nationalism, and identities are no longer mere historiographical or ethnographical issues, but important ethical challenges. That is why the academic literature on nationalism is full of (implicit or explicit) quasi-moral categories (e.g., good, authentic, real, fake, hegemonic, counterhegemonic, popular, liberating, dominant, empowering, agency, resistance). The time has come to launch another historiographical experiment—a rethinking of national images, nationalism, and identities in a disenchanted, nonnationalist, pragmatic, and yet wishful fashion.

To do this one needs to reduce nationalism to the absurdity of its own hate-and-love ambivalence. For historians this is a long-overdue assignment, for memory and oblivion have been the essential raw material of nationalism. "The essence of a nation," states Ernest Renan, "is that all individuals have many things in common and that all have forgotten many things."[36] Indeed, historians have been the main artisans in the crafting of common memories and collective oblivion. Patriotic historians wrote the epic of nations and created the symbols, while professional historians "uncovered" the "real" past of the nation, and still other professional historians found all that to be an invention. The time may have come for historians to consciously play again, with different objectives, the pragmatic and yet imaginative and far-looking task undertaken by the best of the nineteenth-century historians. They dealt with their circumstances, seeking to construct a nation for their present. Knowing that the nation did not exist, they hoped to shape a future that they were unable to fully imagine and manage. We may now reconsider the conventional combinations (as well as the all-too-standard "deconstructions") of memory and forgetfulness.

This reconsideration ought to depart from our current intellectual, historical, and political inventory (national images, nations, and identity problems are here to stay, at least as intellectual issues, for the foreseeable future). We should assume both the intrinsic ambivalence of nationalism and its ethical dimension. In what is possible (in research and analysis) we ought to essay a history of national images and nationalism that is not so heavily loaded with ethical content, a history of nations and nationalism that accentuates the many contradictions, nonsense, and ironies (including in this intellectual scrutiny our own national consciousness and political proclivities) of nations. This approach would be more than a matter of "postmodern" or "post-this and post-that" calisthenics; it would constitute part of the profoundly modernist duty of total, consistent, and ironic disbelief. In the final analysis we ought to try to balance so many epics and counterepics of nationalism with the mere comedy of nationalism and its surroundings.

However, this demoralization is not entirely possible. Therefore we ought to seriously assume the ambivalent ethical dimensions of these issues and thereby consciously afford them an open historiographical and political direction. That is, historians have long debated the good nation; yet it may be time—as in the classical ethical dilemmas—to opt for the right nation. Such a shift accepts the historical inevitability of nation-states, but considers them beyond the search for the good and the authentic. Nations-states thus become mere inevitable units of historical analysis and human coexistence, but not a moral imperative to either maintain or destroy.

I believe the time has come to talk about the nation without necessarily having to enter into a nationalist dispute. If the consideration of nationalism must have a moral content it ought to be the historical spelling out of its contradictions seen not through the glass of an ideal good, unconscious, moral nation assumed by the historian, but vis-à-vis the achievement of more or less visible human goals and rules of coexistence. This basic ethical criteria could be defined— granted, simplistically—according to what could be an epoch's consensus, historically and politically defined (such common things as, say, less killing, dying, and suffering, and as much freedom, comfort, equality, and opportunities as possible for more people).[37] And this is why these topics are an ethical challenge, because historians must consciously assume a minimum ethical dimension while striving for historical accuracy, and be ready and willing to use the historians' other resource: oblivion. Think, for instance, of the amount of memory and above all oblivion used by Truth and Reconciliation Commissions either in South Africa or Guatemala. Between memory and oblivion, for the historian the choice is, when conscious, ethical and political. But it is not a simple matter of objective knowledge or poetic justice, nor is it a question of mere scientific truth or unquestionable social redeeming.

This means that historians can research and imagine histories that could make conceivable nations and national images not as necessary or good but as inevitable facts. The task then would be to separate from this historical randomness any sense of pride and superiority, or any sense of sentimental betrayal. More specifically, the job would be to detach from the history of nations and nationalism any strong relation with the histories of personal or collective identities, which can be only partially studied or understood.

To the extent that a historian can talk about visible identities, he or she ought to gain access to this difficult terrain not by his or her default credentials (being white, Indian, woman, black, gay, Mexican, North American) nor by any particular passion for correctness. Even well-done nationalist histories of nationalism—the self-congratulatory history of one's identity—do not observe the intrinsic ambivalence and dynamism of identities and nationalism. These histories do not exercise the humor, irony, and disbelief required to effectively deal with these topics. One should undertake the study of these phenomena conscious of self-limits (in regard to our present politics, persona, and the availability and reading of historical records) and in total disenchantment. To write the comedy of these topics we must be capable of mocking ourselves.

Unhinged from its strong citizenship and identity connotations, the idea of the nation could become just another story. The nation as a sort of tangible and well-delimited unit that can be used as an administrative framework of historiographical utility, as well as a limited arena for the discussion of social, political, and economic problems. If we pursue this experimental way of thinking historically about the nation we may be able to furnish a historiographical infrastructure that would allow us to conceive of a world comprised not of nationalist nations or collectivities focused on their needs for authenticity and greatness but concerned instead with the solution of problems and with the well-being of their inhabitants or constituency. In this way we could intellectually make of nations a kind of serviceable "noble lie": an unfixed, dynamic, conflictive, absurd, temporary, self-destructive, and yet stable and useful framework of historical research and political action.

Identities will always be a historical *causa beli*. Yet if the history-wise nation holds no strong (either positive or negative) identity mandates, the borders of identity would become permeable. Many identities could be seen as coexisting or conflicting depending on specific circumstances. Moreover, identities would be able to overcome national constraints and move freely beyond anachronistic national frontiers.[38] In essence the problem with Manichaean histories of identities is not that there are not good and bad guys in history but that there are continual changes of characters, exchanges of roles and, as in a good Dostoyevskian plot, there is no way to find the same guys always on the same side of the equation. Histories of identities ought to keep this in mind, considering that actual national identities are not the final evil or good outcome of the ingredients historians analyze but rather the conjuncture of the many possible ones in a complex local, regional, national, and international interaction.

Historians would also have to be ready to take the historiographical and political risks entailed by supporting a particular interpretation, at a specific moment, given unique present conditions that require immediate and unambiguous positions. On those occasions the historian may postpone valuable skepticism and doubt, knowing that he or she eventually could be found on the wrong side of truth or hope. Perhaps in our current academic circles one rarely finds oneself in a position of having to risk one's reputation or life: we are safely guarded by our ivory tower.

To be sure, some histories are radicalizing the ambivalence of nationalism, furnishing nations with a new ethical dimension. This may be the case, for instance, of histories that document extranational pasts; of histories of ecological problems; of the global research and negotiation of science; of languages that simultaneously developed in various regions of the world; or of popular struggles that surpassed the traditional understanding of national borders;[39] these types of histories are undermining the overwhelming nationalist order of our historiographies. Indeed, a truly postnational historical consciousness would not emerge simply out of the nationalist counterstory of official nations, but from a gradual and painstaking challenge of the notions of time and space that order our lives and knowledge.

For the study of the nationalism of the Americas, including the United States, considerable research remains to be done to make the absurdity of nationalism emerge on the surface, although there still is much revindication to be done before undertaking any far-looking perspective. In the meantime, resistance, genuineness, authenticity, empowerment, agency, etc. are truly important categories for dismantling nationalist infrastructures. But unless these categories shed their pristine and naive ethical connotations they are unlikely to complete their dismantling work. If we were able to show how all hegemonic national images were created; if we were able to document all the potential "alternative" or defeated popular projects of nations; if we were able to write the full epic of "our" people; in all cases we would have neither a different debate about nationalism, nor a different world of nations. In the best scenario, our histories would serve to open the spectrum of current nationalisms to make them more inclusive, multicultural, and rhetorically plural. In the worst cases, our histories could be taken as epics for new racial, ethnic, or political nationalisms whose consequences we would not want to know. We need all the analytical categories plus a profound disenchantment and irony if we are to leave some hints for a new imagination.

Yet it could be argued that irony leads nowhere but to cunning cycles of erudition and cynicism. Certainly no academic rationale can be based on the serendipity of the emergence of Voltairean satire. Notwithstanding, no "unimagining" or "postimagining" is possible without an ironic imagination. And then again, an ironic imagination is not a substitute for a creative, serious, and well-structured forging of new ethical and political scenarios. Irony is merely indispensable, but it is not enough.

The current academic boom in studies of nationalism, in post-this and post-that, will certainly pass and, perhaps more surprisingly, return. Yet the relevance of these topics for the present, and the overwhelming complicity of historians in the whole matter, make us even more aware of our own temporal and political responsibilities. We cannot help to follow academic trends, but we must constantly check whether we are freely and rigorously anguishing within and between past, present, and future. Let us make the debate on nationalism crumble in its own ambivalence by imagining different combinations of memory and oblivion for the future. We are not to invent or imagine anything *ex nihilo*; we are just to meticulously furnish material to make possible a different imagination. And yet, as I will be reprimanded, to deal with the future is not the historian's business. And so I close with the words of that wise eighteenth-century Portuguese priest, António Vieira: "*Se já no Mundo houve um profeta do passado, porque não haverá um historiador do futuro?*" (If there has already been a prophet of the past in the world, why should there not be a historian of the future?)[40]

NOTES

I thank Charles A. Hale, Matt Childs, Anju Reejhsinghani, and Mark Thurner for their comments and help in thinking over various parts and versions of this essay. Note that all translations are mine unless otherwise indicated.

1 Carlos Pereda, "Hermenéutica, virtudes epistémicas y postcolonialismo," unpublished manuscript, 1999.

2 Mauricio Tenorio Trillo, *Argucias de la historia* (Mexico City: Paidós, 1999).

3 Ernest Renan, *¿Qué es una nación? Cartas a Strauss*, trans. Andrés de Blas Guerrero (Madrid, 1987), 59–68.

4 For a summary of the debate of the when of nationalism, see Anthony D. Smith, *Theories of Nationalism* (New York: Harper and Row, 1983).

5 There are a number of different approaches to this realm, from various academic perspectives (postmodern, postcolonial, cultural studies, etc.). In essence, what all these studies share is the urgency to study this area. Beyond any of the particular scholastic languages, Anthony Smith has articulated clearly this concern, see his *Nations and Nationalism in a Global Era* (Cambridge, Mass: Polity Press, 1995), 40. Mexico often has attracted attention as a uniquely "real" and/or "ideal" site to study nationalism from the standpoint of the popular and the fragmented. See, for instance, anthropological views, ranging from Robert Redfield's *Tepoztlán: A Mexican Village* (Chicago: University of Chicago Press, 1930) to Claudio Lomnitz's *Exits from the Labyrinth* (Berkeley: University of California Press, 1993). See also historical approaches such as Guy P. C. Thomson's "Movilización conservadora, insurrección liberal y rebeliones indígenas, 1854–1876," in *America Latina: Dallo stato coloniale allo stato nazione*, vol. 2 ed. Antonio Annino (Turin, 1987), 592–614, and his "Bulwarks of Patriotic Liberalism: The National Guard, Philharmonic Corps, and Patriotic Juntas in Mexico, 1947–1988," *Journal of Latin American Studies* 22 (February 1990): 31–68; Alan

Knight's insightful "Popular Culture and the Revolutionary State in Mexico, 1910–1940," *Hispanic American Historical Review* 74.3 (1994): 393–445, and his "Peasants into Patriots: Thoughts on the Making of the Mexican Nation," *Mexican Studies/Estudios Mexicanos*, 10.1 (1994): 135–62; and the provocative historical account by Florencia Mallon, *Peasant and Nation: The Making of Postcolonial Mexico and Peru* (Berkeley: University of California Press, 1994); and by Peter Guardino, *Peasants, Politics, and the Formation of Mexico's National State: Guerrero, 1800–1857* (Stanford: Stanford University Press, 1996).

6 Of course, there are authors who disagree on the modernity of nationalism: for an example, see John Breuilly, *Nationalism and the State* (Manchester: Manchester University Press, 1982). For studies that trace the origins of nationalism to the Middle Ages but agree that nations were especially articulated in modern times, see Smith, *Nations and Nationalism*, especially 29–50; and Josep R. Llobera, *The God of Modernity: The Development of Nationalism in Western Europe* (Oxford: Berg, 1994).

7 See, for instance, John Plamenatz, "Two Types of Nationalism," in *Nationalism: The Nature and Evolution of an Idea*, ed. Eugene Kameka (New York: St. Martin's Press, 1976); and Liah Greenfield, *Nationalism: Five Roads to Modernity* (Cambridge, Mass: Harvard University Press, 1993). For a view of "good nationalism" rooted not in invented *ex nihilo* traditions but in real (ethnic or otherwise) popular bases, see Smith, *Nations and Nationalism*. For an optimistic view of nationalism as a way to maintain "good communities of memory," see Daniel Bell, *Communitarianism and Its Critics* (Oxford: Clarendon, 1993).

8 See, e.g., Greenfeld, *Nationalism*.

9 See Wandeley Guilherme dos Santos, "A anomalia democrática: Adolescência e romantismo na história política," *Revista Brasileira de Ciencias Sociais* 13 (February 1998): 5–11; and Owen Chadwick, *The Secularization of the European Mind in the Nineteenth Century* (Cambridge: Cambridge University Press, 1975).

10 Josep Maria Fradera, *Cultura nacional en una societat dividida* (Barcelona: Peninsula, 1992), especially 108–27; for Thomson see, for instance, "Movilización conservadora, insurrección liberal"; and "Bulwarks of Patriotic Liberalism."

11 For the intellectual history of the idea of political representation in Spanish America, and for the way in which it was pragmatically maneuvered, see François-Xavier Guerra, "The Spanish-American Tradition of Representation and Its European Roots," *Journal of Latin American Studies* 26 (1994): 1–35, and his *Modernidad e independencias: Ensayos sobre las revoluciones hispánicas* (Madrid: MAPFRE, 1992). For important

insights on how the norms and laws were negotiated during the transition from colony to nation, see Antonio Annino, "Prácticas criollas y liberalismo en la crisis del espacio urbano colonial," *Quaderno Storici* 69.2 (December, 1988) and reprinted in *El águila bifronte: Poder y liberalismo en México*, ed. Enrique Montalvo Ortega (Mexico City, 1995), 17–63; and his "El pacto y la norma: Los orígenes de la legalidad oligárquica en México," *Historias* 5 (January–March 1984): 3–31.

12 See, for instance, two excellent studies of the impositions of a nationalist rhetoric in the United States: Cecilia Elizabeth O'Leary, *To Die For: The Paradox of American Patriotism* (Princeton: Princeton University Press, 1999), and David Waldstreicher, *In the Midst of Perpetual Fetes* (Chapel Hill: University of North Carolina Press, 1997).

13 For examples of this functioning of facade and institutions, see Fernando Escalante, *Ciudadanos Imaginarios* (Mexico City: El Colegio de México, 1992); Ariel Rodríguez Kuri, *La experiencia olvidada: El Ayuntamiento de México: Política y gobierno, 1876–1912* (Mexico City: El Colegio de México, 1996); Antonio Annino "El pacto y la norma," and his "Ciudadanía versus gobernabilidad republicana en México: Los orígenes de un dilema," in *Ciudadanía política y formación de las naciones: Perspectivas históricas de América Latina*, ed. Hilda Sabato (Mexico City: Fondo de Cultura Económica, 1999), 62–93; Carmen McEvoy, *La utopía republicana: Ideales y realidades en la formación de la cultura política peruana (1871–1919)* (Lima: Pontificia Universidad Católica del Perú, 1997); and Wanderley Guilherme dos Santos, *Paradoxos do liberalismo: Teoria e história*, 2nd ed. (Rio de Janeiro: Revan, 1999).

14 See Etienne Tassin, "Identités nationales et citoyenneté politique," *Esprit* (January 1994): 97–111.

15 See, for instance, the theoretical effort to unify liberal thought with what Yael Tamir calls "cultural nationalism" in his *Liberal Nationalism* (Princeton: Princeton University Press, 1993); and Smith's consideration of the real bases of nationalism in *Nation and Nationalism*. See also renewed radical suggestions for the study of popular "alternative" nationalisms in Latin America in Florencia Mallon, "The Promise and Dilemma of Subaltern Studies: A Perspective from Latin American History," *American Historical Review* 99 (December 1994): 1491–1516, and her "Indian Communities, Political Cultures, and the State in Latin America, 1780–1990" *Journal of Latin American Studies* 24, supplement (1992): 35–54.

16 For a contrast, see Fernando Savater's consideration not of good and bad nationalisms but of bad and grave nationalisms, in his *El mito nacionalista* (Madrid: Alianza, 1996).

17 See Brading's work, first published in Spanish as *Los orígenes del na-*

cionalismo mexicano (Mexico City: Secretaria de Educación, 1973). The English version was finally published as *The Origins of Mexican Nationalism* (Cambridge, Eng.: Cambridge University Press, 1985). For O'Gorman, see his lengthy introductions to the works of such authors as Carlos María de Bustamante and Fray Servando y Teresa de Mier, and his *México: El Trauma de su historia* (Mexico City: UNAM, 1977), and *Destierro de sombras: Luz en el origen de la imagen y culto de Nuestra Señora de Guadalupe del Tepeyac* (Mexico City: UNAM, 1986).

18 See Samuel Ramos, *El perfil del hombre y la cultura en México* (Mexico City: UNAM, 1934); Octavio Paz, *El labertino de la soledad* (Mexico City, 1959); José Vasconcelos, *La raza cósmica; misión de la raza iberoamericana; notas de viajes a la América del Sur* (Paris: Agencia Mundial, 1923); and Abelardo Villegas, *La filosofía de lo mexicano* (Mexico City: Fondo de Cultura Económica, 1960).

19 Roger Bartra, *La jaula de la melancolía* (Mexico City: Grijalbo, 1987).

20 See, for instance, Mallon, *Peasant and Nation*; Guillermo Bonfil Batalla, *México profundo: Una civilización negada* (Mexico City: CIESAS, 1987); and Peter Guardino, *Peasants, Politics, and the Formation of Mexico's National State*.

21 I do not seek to review the entire discussion—it is sufficient to recall these more recent emblematic examples: Bonfil Batalla for Mexico; Flores Galindo for Peru; and Jorge Basadre's afterword to *La multitud, la ciudad y el campo en la historia del Perú*, in which he passionately talks about the *país profundo*. See Bonfil Batalla, *México profundo*; Alberto Flores Galindo, *Buscando un Inca: Identidad y utopía en los andes*, 4th ed. (Lima: Editorial Horizonte, 1994); and Basadre's *La multitud* (Lima: Huascarán, 1947). I thank Mark Thurner for directing my attention to Basadre's work. See also Charles R. Hale's account of the potential of indigenous struggle in a transnational perspective, in "Indigenous Struggles against Marginality in Latin America: Beyond the National Phase," in *Margins of Insecurity*, ed. Sam C. Nolutshungu (Rochester: University of Rochester Press, 1996): 155–84.

22 Flores Galindo himself believed that the continuation of the Andean utopia would mean an upside-down type of genocide and exploitation. He proposed the elaboration of a new utopia by combining modern socialism with the old Andean utopia (see Flores Galindo, *Buscando un inca*, 344–46).

23 For an excellent consideration of class in nationalism, see Eric Hobsbawm, *Nations and Nationalism since 1780: Programme, Myth, Reality* (Cambridge, Eng.: Cambridge University Press, 1990).

24 See José Murilho de Carvalho, *Formação das almas* (São Paulo: Cia das Letras, 1990). For great insights on these unquestionable aspects of

nationalism, see Begoña Aretxaga, *Shattering Silence: Women, Nationalism, and Political Subjectivity in Northern Ireland* (Princeton: Princeton University Press, New Jersey, 1997); and Partha Chatterjee, *The Nation and Its Fragments: Colonial and Postcolonial Histories*, (Princeton: Princeton University Press, New Jersey, 1993). I thank Carmen Ruiz for having directed my attention to this literature.

25 There are various studies on the emergence of these popular patriotisms. For an excellent synthesis of these patriotisms, see Alan Knight, *U.S.-Mexico Relations, 1910–1940: An Interpretation* (La Jolla, Calif.: Center for U.S.-Mexican Studies, 1987).

26 This I further develop in *"An I Clipped from a We": A History of Mexico City, 1900–1930*, forthcoming.

27 Marfany et al., *La qüestió nacional: Un debat obert. Ponències presentades a les I jornades sobre la qüestió nacional, Barcelona 13–14 gener de 1996* (Barcelona, 1996), 26–27. See also, Marfany, *La cultura del catalanisme* (Barcelona: Editorial Empúries, 1995).

28 See A. Díaz Soto y Gama, *La revolución agraria del sur y Emiliano Zapata* (Mexico City: El Caballito, 1961). For an account of Soto y Gama's speech at the revolutionary convention, see Francisco Ramírez Plancarte, *La ciudad de México durante la revolución constitucionalista* (Mexico City: Botas, 1941).

29 Subcomandante Marcos's communiqué, January 1, 1996, reproduced in *Crónica: El Mundo* (Barcelona), August 4, 1996, 5.

30 See the controversial essay by Jorge Klor de Alva, "The Postcolonialization of the (Latin) American Experience: A Reconsideration of 'Colonialism,' 'Postcolonialism,' and 'Mestizaje,'" in *After Colonialism: Imperial Histories and Postcolonial Displacements*, ed. Gyan Prakash (Princeton: Princeton University Press, 1995): 241–75; and Guerra, *Modernidad e independencias*.

31 Chatterjee, *The Nation and Its Fragments*, 6.

32 Benedict Anderson, *Imagined Communities: Reflections on the Origins and Spread of Nationalism* (London: Verso, 1983).

33 See Richard M. Morse, *El Espejo de Prospero: Un estudio de la dialéctica del nuevo mundo* (Mexico City: Siglo Veintiuno, 1982).

34 François-Xavier Guerra, commenting on Spanish American countries, argues: "These are countries which belong in their own right—at least in term of their elites' origins and culture—within a European cultural area. Countries which were among the first within this cultural area to set up modern political regimes" (Guerra, "The Spanish-American Tradition of Representation," 1). Here I have benefited from Anju Reejhsinghani's comparison between Subaltern Studies in India and "Latin America," see his "Parallel Lives? Subalternity in the South

Asian and Latin American Contexts" (Master's thesis, University of Texas, Austin, 2000).

35 José Bergamín, *Aforismos de la cabeza parlante*, (Madrid: Ediciones Turner, 1983).

36 Renan, *¿Qué es una nación?*, 66.

37 I do not regard this as an homogenous and optimal set of values but, at least, as a general and inevitable framework for articulating social and political programs within modern Western countries. For a review of the complexity and diversity of the Enlightenment's modern proposal, see Daniel Gordon, *Citizens without Sovereignty: Equality and Sociability in French Thought, 1670–1789* (Princeton: Princeton University Press, 1994). For a different, if more friendly, proposal for a *historia para mañana*, see Josep Fontana, *La historia después del fin de la historia* (Barcelona: n.p., 1992).

38 See Hale, "Indigenous Struggles."

39 See ibid. See also the pragmatic proposal for a "post-ethnic" America in David A. Hollinger *Postethnic America: Beyond Multiculturalism* (New York: Basic Books, 1995), 1–17, 131–63.

40 António Vieira, *Historia do futuro* (1718; Lisbon, 1992), 53.

2. POETICA

Knowledges, Nations, Histories

JORGE CAÑIZARES-ESGUERRA

Postcolonialism *avant la lettre?*

Travelers and Clerics in Eighteenth-Century

Colonial Spanish America

The genre of travel writing is increasingly attracting the attention of scholars. Until recently, travel accounts were largely considered useful only as primary sources for reconstructing the nature of the societies that travelers had visited. As postmodern and poststructuralist sensibilities have gained ground, however, scholars have begun to read these sources primarily for what they reveal about "Western" colonial and imperial imaginings. For all the insights gained from this reorientation, the current new effort to deconstruct travel narratives is often afflicted by ethnocentricity. Western scholars study representations of the Other in travel narratives solely to understand how Western identities have been crafted. Fortunately, however, some academics have realized that these approaches are as colonial and therefore as impoverishing as the sources they allegedly set out to deconstruct. Mary Louise Pratt has suggested that students of travel narratives should also study the views of the intelligentsia of the places visited by the foreign observers. Local interpreters and intellectuals, Pratt argues, have offered critical and creative readings of travelers' views, as well as contributed to the conception of the narratives themselves.[1]

This insight has not fallen on deaf ears. Deborah Poole, for example, has explored the history of European visual representations of "Andean" peoples put in circulation by eighteenth- and nineteenth-century travelers. Yet she has also reconstructed the ways some mid-nineteenth- and early-twentieth-century Peruvian intellectuals critically engaged these visual languages. She argues that, particularly in

Cuzco, the local intelligentsia created highly original aesthetics. The ideas of the Cuzqueño intelligentsia surpassed in complexity and sophistication the naive and simpleminded approaches to identity often brought to bear by the European observers.[2] In line with Pratt's and Poole's insights, in this essay I examine a chapter of the long and complicated history of the reception of travel narratives in Latin America, with a focus on the late colonial period.

Notwithstanding repeated allegations throughout the seventeenth and eighteenth centuries that the Spanish Empire in America had remained sealed to foreign visitors and therefore unknown, many travel accounts by non-Spanish observers regularly did appear in the European presses. British and French writers who managed to visit the Spanish American colonies wrote dismal portrayals of the places they visited. Local peoples, they argued, were consumed by an effeminate idleness. The land itself, some maintained, was cursed. In the early seventeenth century the apostate Thomas Gage, for example, saw fit to warn prospective English visitors to New Spain that just as the local fauna and flora were deceptively wholesome on the outside but with "little inward virtue" so too were the people "false and hollow hearted."[3]

In 1716, after a brief stint in coastal Peru, the French engineer Amédée Frezier found all peoples in Peru to be wanting. Indians who were given to dissimulation and malice were said to lack ambition as they passively endured Spanish greed and cruelty. As puppets of their Spanish masters, blacks contributed to the morally unwholesome environment by exploiting the meek Indians. Finally, Creoles were fond of external displays of religiosity but with little inner spirituality; enamored of exaggeration and ridiculous metaphors; slothful and emasculated due to the lushness of their environment. Frezier found the Creoles promiscuous and oversexed, which in contemporary medical discourse implied impending sexual transformations.[4] In 1728, after a short visit to Lima, Le Gentil de la Barbinais concluded that "there is no country in the world where a vicious person can live more fully a life of vice and where the sage man can run the risk of forgetting his virtue" than in Peru.[5] Again in 1752, Abbé Courte de la Blanchardiere maintained in his travel narrative on the Southern Sea that "in no other place in the world [does] luxury and debauchery [rule] as much as it does in Peru."[6] Both Barbinais and Blanchardiere were simply echoing a trope first put in circulation in France at the turn of the century by the fake narrative of one François

Coreal.[7] Travelers kept this thesis alive well into the nineteenth century. Alexander von Humboldt and Fanny Calderón de la Barca argued that Latin American elites were indolent and effete owing to their lack of manly republican virtues or as the result of climatic influence.[8]

Spanish writers were no less critical of what they found in the colonies. Peninsulars referred condescendingly to Spanish America as a land where humidity and the stars had condemned Indians and European settlers alike to a life of corruption and idleness.[9] Such portrayals only got worse as the European Enlightenment unfolded. Reformers used baroque Spanish America as exemplary of the perils of disobeying the laws of nature and commerce. The anticlericalism of the eighteenth century also found in Spain's colonies illustrations of the follies of the human mind led astray by senseless superstition and powerful but ignorant priests.[10]

Spanish American intellectuals kept abreast of this travel literature. To be sure, they first sought to counter the European attacks by portraying their lands in lovely and often utopian terms and their people as morally upright and unusually accomplished. This much was to be expected from patriotic writers.[11] A closer look, however, reveals that the local intelligentsia did not rest satisfied with simply inverting European representations of Spanish America, they also sought to offer an epistemological critique of the limitations of the European observer. Take, for example, Juan José Eguiara y Eguren, the powerful rector of the University of Mexico, who along with scores of provincial collaborators compiled in the mid-eighteenth century the Bibliotheca Mexicana, an annotated bibliography of works (published or in manuscript) by Indian and Creole clerical authors written in the viceroyalty of New Spain since the conquest.

Eguiara y Eguren and his team embarked on this ambitious project with the main purpose of addressing the negative views of Spanish America harbored by two of the most important Spanish neohumanists of the late seventeenth and early eighteenth centuries, Nicolás Antonio and Manuel Martí. Antonio and Martí had published in 1735 and 1744, respectively, works in which Spanish America appeared as a land of material riches but also of extreme poverty when it came to matters of the mind. Although the Bibliotheca Mexicana sought to put these misconceptions to rest by compiling an extensive survey of local writers and their works, Eguiara y Eguren sought to do something else as well; namely, he wished to demonstrate that European travelers and armchair philosophers who relied only on the information quickly gathered by their senses or solely through reason were wrong because they bypassed the knowledge accumulated by the local Spanish American intelligentsia. Eguiara y Eguren argued that only travelers who spent a long time in America or who relied on learned local informants were reliable. He did not, however, elaborate on the epistemological reasons why this was the case.[12]

Later in the century other Spanish American intellectuals did address the epistemology of ethnographic and travel reporting, and they reflected at length on the reasons that rendered unreliable the knowledge of transient foreign observers. This late colonial concern with exploring the epistemological limitations of foreign observers resulted from efforts to stem a new tide of negative writings on Spanish America that appeared in Europe in the wake of the publication of the views of the French naturalist Georges-Louis Leclerc Buffon. Drawing on the authority of the new European sciences to support the old argument of America's organic degeneration, Buffon popularized the thesis of America as a humid and emasculating continent that had only recently emerged from the waters and where animals and peoples alike lacked organic potency. Enveloped by humid miasmas, America was a land in which everything was condemned to degenerate.[13] The earlier views of the French philosopher traveler Charles-Marie La Condamine—to the effect that the Indians of Spanish America were "stupid" not as result of brutal Spanish coercion, as had traditionally been alleged, but because of their innate organic disposition—only served to bolster the authority of the critics of America.[14]

In the following pages I examine the views on the epistemological limitations of European travelers held by four Spanish American authors who participated in the controversy outlined above. These writers, three of them exiled, explored the linguistic and sociological forces that rendered the foreign observer unreliable. By reconstructing these forgotten views, I seek to demonstrate the early modern roots of some aspects of both modern ethnography and postcolonial theory. This episode can also help clarify the role of exiles in the articulation of discourses of difference and identity.

Francisco Xavier Clavijero was a Mexican Jesuit who, while in exile in Italy, became one of the most active Spanish American critics of Buffon and his followers. In his writings Clavijero proved deeply skeptical of the knowledge produced by foreign travelers.

According to Clavijero, contemporary philosophical historians and travelers sought to pepper their books with fables to dazzle and entertain their audiences, and to do so they constantly drew generalizations on the basis of isolated observations.[15] For Clavijero the problem of foreign observers ultimately lay in their limited knowledge of indigenous languages. Clavijero, for example, argued that Buffon's analysis of the number of species in the New World was related to the French naturalist's failure to understand native taxonomies. Had Buffon known Nahuatl and, more important, had he spent time in Mexico, he would have realized that the species he placed into a single category were in fact separate and distinct. Buffon, Clavijero argued, reduced the number of species of quadrupeds in Mexico because by building on facile analogies from the comfort of his home he had sought to reorganize the works of Francisco Hernández, the sixteenth-century naturalist sent by Philip II to compile a natural history of America. Unlike Buffon, Clavijero insisted, Hernández spent many years in Mexico and used the taxonomic categories that the natives themselves had devised.[16]

According to Clavijero, linguistic limitations also bedeviled those who chose to visit the New World instead of speculating at home. For example, Clavijero considered that for all of La Condamine's prestige as a philosopher traveler, the French erudite was an unreliable witness because he had not spent sufficient time in the Indies and, worse, lacked a working knowledge of Quechua. During his trip to the Andes, La Condamine, like most travelers, had relied on interpreters, and this mediated perception had led to misrepresentations.[17] Long periods of residence in America and close contact with the natives through mastery of their language were, according to Clavijero, prerequisites for writing about the land and peoples of the New World.

Juan de Velasco was another Spanish American Jesuit who from exile in Italy sought in the 1780s to respond to the critics of America. Like Clavijero, Velasco became particularly interested in highlighting the epistemological limitations of foreigners. Falling back on early-modern idioms developed by Locke, Velasco held that the experience of the marvelous was only relative to the observer. Velasco took European readers to task for their exaggerated skepticism, which he considered a mask for narrow provincialism,[18] and therefore sought in his natural history of the kingdom of Quito to dazzle European readers with constant references to marvels and curiosities.[19] Velasco assembled a catalog of natural phenomena typical of the kingdom of Quito that in the eyes of Europeans could have been construed as fables.[20]

As for Clavijero, for Velasco the epistemological limitations of outsiders stemmed from their lack of mastery of Indian languages. Velasco offered Quechua taxonomies to catalog the flora and fauna of Quito using the same assumptions that had moved Clavijero to introduce Nahua taxonomies for Mexico, namely, to show that linguistic shortcomings lay behind the tendency of European naturalists to find fewer species in the New World.

Velasco also criticized the persona of the philosopher traveler on grounds of linguistic incompetence. For all their philosophical training and experimental instruments, travelers like La Condamine and Antonio de Ulloa, Velasco maintained, were ultimately unreliable witnesses.[21] Short visits to foreign places as well as linguistic ignorance, according to Velasco, made travelers dependent on informants. La Condamine, who did not know Quechua, had failed to realize that the natives liked to tailor their behavior to fulfill the foreigner's expectations, and he mistakenly concluded that the Indians were naturally stupid. Velasco, who was being raised by Indian wet nurses when La Condamine visited Quito, recalled how the Indians joked among themselves every time they deceived the French. In fact, the Indians thought that La Condamine was the naive and stupid one.[22] According to Velasco, La Condamine's linguistic and cultural ignorance made him easy prey to manipulation, leaving him without the critical tools to weigh the credibility of his informants.

Velasco presented himself as a follower of the epistemology of José de Acosta. The sixteenth-century Jesuit had set his writings apart from the existing corpus of books on the New World by emphasizing not only his learning but his firsthand acquaintance, based on his stay of long duration, with the land and peoples that he described, including the knowledge of Indian languages.[23] Acosta's emphasis on mastering Indian languages and living in close, intimate proximity to Indian communities led Velasco to privilege the religious over the secular priest and the lay observers. Although aware of the eighteenth-century critique of the biased missionary observer, he thought that only the religious were reliable eyewitnesses.[24] According to Velasco, the religious were learned and therefore able to fend off the tricks of self-delusion and superstition. They were also thoroughly knowledgeable of local languages and therefore able to gain the confidence of the indigenous peoples.[25]

JUAN IGNACIO MOLINA

Of all the Creole Jesuits who wrote natural and civil histories of their homelands in exile, Juan Ignacio Molina stood out for refusing to embrace the epistemological critique of the foreign observer. Unlike Velasco and Clavijero, Molina organized his history of Chile around the testimony of European travelers, for he was "not disposed to question the account of respectable writers, several of whom have been eyewitnesses of what they describe."[26] Drawing on his own personal experience, Molina also used the writings of travelers like Amédée Frezier, Louis Feuillée, Antonio de Ulloa, and Lord Anson to bolster his own credibility.[27] Molina's surprising departure from the Creole Jesuit critique of the epistemological limitations of the foreign traveler was related to the fact that Chile had traditionally fared well in most European travel accounts. The country had long been a peripheral colonial outpost sparsely populated by Spaniards, a land whose climate most learned travelers found benign and whose original Araucanian inhabitants were portrayed as courageous republican warriors. Unlike Peru or Mexico, Chile received positive reviews from European travelers. The early-eighteenth-century account of the Southern Seas by the French engineer Frezier typifies this tendency. Whereas Frezier portrayed Chile as an Alpine, temperate land with Araucanian republican warriors, he presented Peru as corrupting, a land of concupiscence, paganism, and effeminate idleness. It is understandable, therefore, that Molina did not choose to criticize "foreign" accounts. In fact, he deliberately cast his book as a learned complement to the early-eighteenth-century natural history of the Capuchin friar Feuillée.[28] His embrace of accounts by foreign witnesses, however, was tempered by his forceful critique of armchair philosophers and taxonomists. Throughout his history, Molina refused to consider "vague conjectures and hazardous hypotheses."[29] Like Clavijero and Velasco, Molina decried the tendency of European conjectural historians of America to generalize using isolated examples, particularly because they had never set foot in the New World.[30] Molina's contempt for systems caused him to only grudgingly introduce Linnean taxonomy in his work; such taxonomies, Molina argued, were artificial. Indeed, Molina followed Linnean classifications largely because they were popular, not because he thought they were useful.[31]

The growing literature on transnationalism suggests that identities are crafted as much outside as within the boundaries of nations. Communities of exiles and expatriates have played a critical role as cultural brokers between the societies hosting them and their homelands, easing processes of globalization. By the same token, these communities have also been instrumental in the fragmentation and atomization of identities. Amidst hardship and loss of status, as well as exciting new cultural stimuli, exiles turn nostalgia into a powerful creative force that generates discourses of identity and difference.[32] This might seem to be the case in the examples I have presented above: the Jesuits Clavijero, Velasco, and Molina endured exile, and their works (civil and natural histories) helped articulate distinct geographical and historical identities in Mexico, Ecuador, and Chile, respectively. But it would be wrong to attribute too much protagonism to the Jesuit exiles. The clerical critique of the foreign observer was as much homegrown as it was the product of the exile imagination. Not only exiles but also scholars who stayed home felt compelled to assume the role of interlocutors of metropolitan intellectuals. Eguiara y Eguren, as we have already seen, was, without ever having to leave Mexico City, the first to put forth a critique of the epistemological limitations of travelers. The case of José Antonio de Alzate is perhaps even more revealing.

More than any other Spanish American scholar, José Antonio de Alzate, a secular priest and a leading figure of the Spanish American Enlightenment, pushed to the limits the anti-European dimensions of the discourse of the epistemological limitations of the foreign observer. Unlike the Jesuits, Alzate developed all his work entirely within the confines of the Central Valley of Mexico. In 1788 Alzate inaugurated the periodical *Gacetas de literatura* with the intention, among other things, of subjecting to public scrutiny foreign accounts on New Spain. The reviews posted in *Gacetas de literatura* sought to demonstrate the epistemological limitations of outsiders to comprehend the nature and history of the New World.

Alzate's approach was typified by his criticism of the travel accounts of Laporte and Lord Anson and of the treatise on amalgamation by Count Ignaz von Born. In 1788 Alzate stated that in the compilation of travel narratives by Laporte, the French editor had treated the New Spaniards worse than Eskimo "savages." In particular, Alzate zeroed in on those passages by Laporte that presented colonials in New Spain as lascivious, corrupt, ignorant, and superstitious. Alzate also condemned the Frenchman's many factual mistakes concerning natural history and geography.[33]

As he sought to expose before the Mexican public the lies of travelers, Alzate also took on Lord Anson. Alzate was disturbed and angered that Anson had cast Spanish Americans as cowards, so incapable of defending the colonies that in Anson's estimation the entire viceroyalty of Peru could have been seized by a navy fifteen hundred strong. Alzate introduced evidence from an unpublished memoir describing the siege of Manila by the English where a contingent of Mexican commoners (the Philippines were economically and politically linked to New Spain) had outsmarted the aggressors. The testimony of Lord Anson notwithstanding, this episode showed that even the rabble of New Spain, the "feces" (*heces*) of Mexico, was capable of routing the English and that "even the rotten members of the Spanish nation maintained their noble lineage."[34] In 1790, Alzate blasted the history of silver mining as described in *New Process of Amalgamation of Gold and Silver Ores* by the learned German mineralogist Ignaz von Born. According to Alzate, Born's narrative was even more outrageous than those of Laporte and Anson because Born's account of the discovery of the technique of amalgamation (mixing mercury with silver ores) in Spanish America was deceiving. On the surface Born appeared to be praising Spanish Americans, but in fact, Alzate maintained, Born presented the discovery of amalgamation as a serendipitous breakthrough, the product of mindless chance. Because he argued that the inventors were mere empirical innovators, Born called on his peers to study the process rationally so it could be better used in European mines. Besides the numerous factual historical errors, including the name of the discoverer of amalgamation, Born described the colonists as rabidly opposed to the Crown's introduction of rational reforms in mining.[35] Alzate took issue with each and every one of Born's points.[36]

Alzate's criticism of foreign accounts was part of a critique of the epistemological limitations of travelers. In notes commissioned by the printer Antonio de Sancha for the failed Spanish edition of Clavijero's history, Alzate echoed the Jesuit's conclusion that travelers were linguistically ignorant and gullible, easily manipulated by the more savvy local populations.[37]

Alzate's critique of foreign accounts was also part of a larger critique of taxonomists. For example, Alzate put the natural and civil histories of the viceroyalty of New Granada, written by the Italian Jesuit Filippo Salvadore Gilij, under critical scrutiny.[38] Alzate cast Gilij as a follower of conjectural historians such as Buffon, who on the flimsiest evidence concluded that the New World had recently emerged from the waters and that the Indians were newcomers. These armchair travelers, Alzate contended, subordinated observations to their systems, and in the case of America the facts showed that Buffon was wrong. Indian monuments, Alzate argued, demonstrated that the natives had ancient roots. The higher mountain heights of America, on the other hand, indicated that the New World was geologically much older than Europe. Had Buffon limited himself to describing animal species, Alzate contended, his natural history would have avoided being characterized by future generations as a "physical romance." According to Alzate, Gilij belonged in Buffon's school: the many mistakes in the text, beginning with the geographical errors in the title, suggested that Gilij had never visited the territories of Panama, Colombia, and Venezuela that he pretended to describe. Moreover, Gilij's generalization of *castas* (mestizos and mulattos) as cowardly and of Indians as drunkards demonstrated his predilection for taxonomy. Gilij, Alzate maintained, was wrong to argue that all Indians and castas in America were alike.[39]

Having read Clavijero's analysis of the contradictions and inconsistencies in the writings of the likes of Cornelius De Pauw, Buffon, and William Robertson, Alzate firmly linked his attack on taxonomists to his patriotism. By so doing, he created a discourse that presented New Spain as a land whose natural wealth showed the folly of all philosophical generalizations. Like the Jesuit Velasco (whose work he did not know), Alzate insisted that patriotic natural historians should identify the "curiosities" of the land to debunk European taxonomists. Alzate made a career out of discovering natural phenomena that contradicted the natural "laws" devised by European naturalists, particularly by taxonomists such as Carl Linnaeus.[40]

Between 1788 and 1790, Alzate engaged Vicente Cervantes, a Spanish naturalist charged with teaching Linnaean taxonomy at the new botanical garden, which was opened by the Bourbon Crown to challenge the clerical-Creole control of the faculty of medicine at the University of Mexico. In a debate conducted in the pages of rival Mexican periodicals, Alzate derided the Linnaean classifications propounded by the newcomer Cervantes for their inability to capture the uniqueness of Mexican species; their tendency to group fauna and flora not according to "virtues" but according to misleading, even microscopic resemblances; and, finally, their corrupting influence on youth due to their inordinate attention to the sexual characteristics of plants.[41] Alzate used the singularities of the fauna and flora of Mexico to throw into disarray the neat logic of Linnaeus and his Spanish disciples in New Spain as he highlighted the incompetence of foreigners to ever comprehend Mexican reality.[42]

THE CLERICAL CRITIQUE OF THE TRAVELER AND MALINOWSKI'S "FIELD METHOD" IN ETHNOGRAPHY

In the late eighteenth century, Spanish American authors advanced a critique of the limitations of the knowledge compiled by travelers. Travelers, they argued, were helpless victims of cunning, savvy local peoples who did not hesitate to mislead and manipulate the linguistically ignorant outsider. The transient and necessarily mediated nature of their observations rendered travelers incapable of gaining deep insight into the behavior of local communities. Their short visits to the land greatly limited their understanding of those aspects of nature and human behavior that escaped the norm. The traveler lacked the linguistic tools, the time, and the inclination to develop a lasting attachment to communities; they therefore proved incapable of penetrating beneath the surface of local social phenomena. Travelers were at the mercy of communities that gulled the foreigners and laughed at their expense.

This epistemology resembles that put forth in the early twentieth century by Bronislaw Malinowski, the founder of modern ethnography. For Malinowski, "savages" had unfairly been cast in the Western imagination as lacking in social restrictions and regulations. The illiterate savage, it was widely assumed, did not have the tools to codify and articulate sociopolitical rules. Informed by such prejudices Western observers had never bothered to make inquiries, and their observations had remained shallow, biased, and therefore unreliable.

For Malinowski the time to survey and describe the nature of these long-neglected complex social structures had finally arrived. To do so, it was necessary for the anthropologist to observe all facets of native life firsthand, avoiding interpreters and mediators. In response to this issue, Malinowski introduced a methodological revolution in ethnography: the field method. Because for Malinowski the reconstruction of primitive social structures could only be done through Baconian induction (by drawing tables of absences and presences), he recommended that the anthropologist live in indigenous villages for relatively long periods of time, acting as "an active huntsman" who follows his prey, the native, "into its most inaccessible lairs."[43] Moreover, Malinowski considered that anthropologists needed to reconstruct the mental world of the illiterate natives that lay underneath their invisible yet dense social regulations. "The anthropologist," Malinowski argued in 1925, "must relinquish his comfortable position in the long chair on the veranda of the missionary compound, Government station, or planter's bungalow . . . Information, must come to him full flavored from his own observations, and not be squeezed out of reluctant informants as a trickle of talk."[44] Like Clavijero, Velasco, and Alzate, Malinowski thought that only those who had firsthand acquaintance of long duration with the natives and who mastered their languages were reliable observers.

For all the remarkable similarities between the epistemologies of the Spanish American writers and that of the modern professional ethnographer, the world of Malinowski was miles away from that of the eighteenth-century clerics. Indeed, Malinowski singled out missionaries for criticism, holding them responsible for having created the Western image of the "lawless," "noble" savage. By assuming that the savage was closer to nature and therefore governed by "unchecked passions," the missionary had introduced a distorting theoretical bias that rendered invisible all native systems of social control. For all their proximity to the natives, the missionaries had managed to remain blissfully ignorant and utterly uninformed. The ethnography of missionaries, along with those of "bureaucrats" and "planters," Malinowski argued, was unreliable.

There was a second way in which Malinowski considered the missionary the nemesis of the modern ethnographer. Intent on civilizing and disciplining the native, the missionary had been largely responsible for the destruction of the very systems of social control that the modern ethnographer was now seeking to describe.[45] The native, the raison d'être of modern ethnography, Malinowski complained sadly, was "melting away with hopeless rapidity." Precisely when anthropology was finding in field ethnography a method for understanding the natives objectively, they, in a "sadly ludicrous, not to say tragic" twist of fate, were disappearing.[46]

Malinowski's nostalgia for the disappearing native resembles slightly that of the Spanish American clerics described earlier. Just as modern ethnography sought to preserve the "real" native from the corruptions engendered by transculturation, Spanish American eighteenth-century clerics longed to arrest the corrupting forces of colonial history. According to the late-colonial cleric, the colonial regime had failed to preserve the strict social hierarchies that had characterized precolonial indigenous societies. The slow but steady elimination of the ruling elites, they argued, had rendered the natives into communities of slothful commoners. Due to this simplification and even elimination of indigenous social hierarchies, the Indians, just like the Greeks under "Turkish" rule, had witnessed the transformation of their great pagan civilizations into homogenous communities of emasculated commoners. The ancien régime logic of this discourse puts the views of clerics such as Clavijero, Velasco, and Alzate at loggerheads with those of modern investigators, for the latter operate within the principles of citizenship of the modern nation-state and condemn all forms of extraeconomic coercion. Our eighteenth-century clerics, however, aspired to return to the times when the now-absent, powerful Indian elites had disciplined their slothful charges through the generous use of forced labor, creating in the process well-regulated and exemplary polities.[47]

Despite these differences, our Creole clerics, like Malinowski, condemned cultural miscegenation, albeit differently. The Spanish American clerics discussed earlier praised the racial and cultural encounter that had first brought Spanish conquistadors and Indian elites together. Had this mestizaje remained restricted and limited to the elites, they argued, it would have created new Christian, virtuous polities. Our Creole clerics, however, condemned the mestizaje of commoners, which they argued had created large sectors of society at the margins of the traditional mechanism of hierarchical control and whose irreverent culture had corrupted the Indians.[48]

THE SPANISH AMERICAN CLERICAL EPISTEMOLOGY AS POSTCOLONIAL CRITIQUE?

One should recall that the epistemological critique of the foreign observer put forth by the Spanish American clerics was strongly anti-European. For clerical observers such as Velasco and Alzate, the New World appeared as a land destined to contradict laws and generalizations created by Europeans. In their writings, America came across as a continent whose many marvels and curiosities could only be comprehended by the local interpreter. These writers denounced Europeans as provincials who peddled their views as universal narratives.

From the description of the clerical epistemology I have offered it would be absurd to cast authors such as Clavijero, Velasco, Molina, and Alzate as forerunners of postcolonial theory. Postcolonial epistemology encompasses areas and theories that our clerics would have found preposterous and would have rejected. Among other things, postcolonial epistemology includes a commitment to a deconstructive reading of texts (that reveal in the "surpluses" of writing silenced voices and unstated and/or unconscious assumptions);[49] a belief that the identities are contingent, socially constructed, and hybrid (against the colonial construction of identities as oppositional binaries: colonized vs. colonizer, Indian vs. European);[50] a notion that asymmetric relations of power are usually imagined in gendered terms;[51] an understanding that the histories of metropolises and peripheries cannot be treated in isolation and that they are the product of their mutual interaction;[52] and a vision that the narratives of the nation are teleological and exclusionary.[53] There are, however, two areas in which postcolonial critics and the clerics overlap.

Postcolonial critics have shown that, for all their claims to objectivity, both travelers and ethnographers are hopelessly biased, having more to say about themselves and the lands from where they hail than about the communities they purportedly seek to describe. Rather than being detached contributors to the making of a perspectival knowledge, travelers as well as ethnographers like Malinowski have been deeply enmeshed in the history of North Atlantic colonial expansions.[54] This postcolonial critique has led some scholars to privilege local, non-Western ethnographic observers.[55] This resembles some of the positions taken by the Creole clerics.

The late-colonial clerical authors saw themselves as "native" ethnographers with greater authority to speak for the land and peoples of America than the foreign European visitors. Our prevalent historiographical wisdom would maintain that such self-representations are untenable, that the clerics were in fact "Creoles," whites of European descent born in America. The historiography on Creole identity would have us believe that the Spanish American elites stood separated by an unbridgeable cultural chasm from the Indians (and blacks) and that the claims of the clerics to speak for the Indians was, at best, self-delusion or, at worst, cynical manipulation. Yet the historiography on the Creole clergy is urgently in need of some revision. As William Taylor has shown for late-colonial Mexico, clerics hardly saw themselves, nor did rural communities see them, as "foreigners." Clerics and Indians created an inextricably religious culture that modern historians have sought to rend asunder. Clerics acted condescendingly and often brutally toward their charges, yet they also saw themselves as the natural leaders of Indian communities. Indians, in turn, could harbor both hatred and love for the clerics, yet they saw them (many of whom were indeed "Indians") as powerful intermediaries of their deities.[56] The clerics discussed above had a point when they presented themselves as "native ethnographers."

The epistemologies of the late-colonial Creole clerical authors and today's postcolonial critics find yet another commonality in the efforts of both groups to undermine the normative character of Western narratives. Postcolonial critics have persuasively argued that historical narratives that interpret changes in North Atlantic societies have become normative for the rest of the world. Historians from India to Mexico, therefore, have sought to apply North Atlantic categories and paradigms to their own societies, producing as a result narratives of failure. These historians seek to explain why, for example, industrialization and modernization failed relative to that in the North Atlantic.[57] Spanish American clerical authors challenged as normative the nature narratives of the West. Velasco and Alzate in particular sought to provincialize the views of the West and turn the natural history of America into the norm.

The critique of the universalizing tendencies of North Atlantic narratives of nature and history, I suspect, continued after the wars of independence among the post-colonial (in the temporal sense) Latin American intelligentsia. Criticism of the reliability of the European observer in America, for example, exercised the imagination of Peruvian intellectuals like Manuel Atanasio Fuentes, whose *Lima: Esquisses historiques, statistiques, administratives, commerciales et morales* (1866) repeated the late colonial complaint that European travel accounts of America were untrustworthy.[58] Were post-colonial (in the temporal sense) Latin American intellectuals also postcolonial critics (in the epistemological sense)? As the work of Paul Gootenberg so clearly illustrates, the history of ideas in nineteenth-century Latin America is still terra incognita.[59] The shibboleths that have passed as the history of the nineteenth century are fortunately now being cast aside.[60] Historians should not be surprised to find that (temporally) postcolonial Latin American intellectuals were also epistemologically aggressive postcolonials. Paradoxically, it is the very field of postcolonial studies that is getting in the way of this recognition. As Mark Thurner suggests in the opening pages of this volume, postcolonial theory seems to be suffering from the same universalizing, normative impulses that it ascribes to the narratives of the West. Most postcolonial theorizing nowadays remains narrowly parochial, solely interested in British and Commonwealth texts and traditions.[61] The work in this volume should open the gates to a more catholic, generous understanding of the postcolonial, and it has been my intention here to call attention to its "prehistory"—one located in Mexico or Peru not India.

NOTES

I wish to thank Mark Thurner for his numerous suggestions for improving earlier drafts of this essay. Note that all translations are mine unless indicated otherwise.

1   Mary Louise Pratt, *Imperial Eyes: Travel Writing and Transculturation* (London: Routledge, 1992). Pratt uses Humboldt as an example, see 135–37, 172–97.
2   Deborah Poole, *Vision, Race, and Modernity: A Visual Economy of the Andean*

Image World (Princeton: Princeton University Press, 1997), see especially chapter 7.

3 Thomas Gage, A New Survey of the West Indias, or, The English American, his Travail by Sea and Land, 2nd ed. (London, 1655), 42–43.

4 Amédée François Frezier, Relation du Voyage de la Mer du Sud aux côtes du Chily et Pérou fait pendant les années 1712, 1713 et 1714, rev. ed. (Paris: Nyon, Didot et Quillau, 1732), 210–31, 240–47.

5 Le Gentil de la Barbinais, Nouveau voyage autour du monde, 3 vols. (Paris: Briasson, 1728), 1:149.

6 Abbé Courte de la Blanchardiere, Nouveau voyage fait au Perou (Paris: Delaguette, 1751), 126–27.

7 François Coreal, Voyages aux Indes Occidentales contenat ce qu'il y a vu de plus remarquable pendant son sejour depuis 1696 jusqu'en 1697, 2 vols. (Amsterdam: Frederic Bernard, 1722), part 1, ch. 10–11, 147–65; part 2, ch. 12, 324–32; part 3, ch. 1, 1–33.

8 Alexander von Humboldt, Briefe aus Amerika 1799–1804, ed. Ulrike Moheit (Berlin: Akademie Verlag, 1993), 155–56; Fanny Calderón de la Barca, Life in Mexico, ed. Howard T. Fisher and Marion Hall Fisher (Garden City, N.Y.: Doubleday, 1966), 286.

9 Jorge Cañizares-Esguerra, "New World, New Stars: Patriotic Astrology and the Invention of Indian and Creole Bodies in Colonial Spanish America, 1600–1650," American Historical Review 104 (February 1999): 31–68.

10 Typical of this approach was the secret report to the Spanish Crown penned by the philosopher travelers Jorge Juan and Antonio de Ulloa. It was only made available in the early nineteenth century, but it circulated widely within official circles in the mid-eighteenth century: Noticias secretas de América sobre el estado naval, militar y político de los reynos del Peru y de las provincias de Quito, costas de Nueva Granada y Chile (London: R. Taylor, 1826).

11 On the genre of "Creole" patriotism, see David Brading, The First America: The Spanish Monarchy, Creole Patriots, and the Liberal State, 1492–1867 (Cambridge, Eng.: Cambridge University Press, 1991); and Bernard Lavallé, Las promesas ambiguas: Ensayos sobre criollismo colonial en los Andes (Lima: Pontificia Universidad Católica del Peru, 1993).

12 Juan José de Eguiara y Eguren, Prólogos a la Bibliotheca mexicana, ed. and trans. Agustín Millares Carlo (Mexico City: Fondo de Cultura Económica, 1944), 82–83, 115, 165–66, 169, 193, 221.

13 Antonello Gerbi, La disputa del nuevo mundo: Historia de una polémica, 1750–1900, 2nd ed. (Mexico City: Fondo de Cultura Económica, 1982).

14 Charles-Marie La Condamine, Relation abrégeé d'un voyage fait dans l'interiur de l'Amérique méridionale. Despuis la côte de la mer du Sud, jusqu'aux côtes

du *Brésil et de la Guiane en descendant la rivière des Amazones* (Paris: Veuve Pissot, 1745), 52–53.

15 Francisco Xavier Clavijero, *Historia antigua de Mexico* (Mexico City: Editorial Porrua, Colección "Sepan Cuantos," 29, 1945), diss. 5, sec. 1, 508.

16 Ibid., diss. 4, sec. 1, 477–49, 500 (n.66). On the same theme, see diss. 5, sec. 1, 506.

17 Ibid., diss. 5, sec. 2, 521; and diss. 6, sec. 6, 545.

18 Juan de Velasco, *Historia del Reino de Quito en la America Meridional; Vol. 1: Historia natural* (Quito: Editorial Casa de la Cultura, 1977–1979), bk. 2, ch. 8, 158.

19 Ibid., bk. 2, ch. 8, 158–62, and ch. 9, 163–67; bk. 3, ch. 6, par. 2, 222–24; bk. 3, ch. 7, par. 2, 230–32; bk. 3, ch. 5 par. 4, 209–12; bk. 3, ch. 3, par. 7, 191–92; and bk. 3, ch. 9, 252–55.

20 On this aspect of early-modern epistemology, see Locke, *Essay Concerning Human Understanding*, ed. A. C. Fraser (Oxford: Oxford University Press, 1984), bk. 4, ch. 15, sec. 4. See also Lorraine Daston and Katharine Park, *Wonders and the Order of Nature, 1150–1750* (New York: Zone Books, 1998), 250.

21 Velasco, *Historia del Reino de Quito*, bk. 1, ch. 3, par. 8, 74; bk. 3, ch. 5, par. 17, 212; catálogo, 434.

22 Ibid., bk. 6, ch. 8, par. 23, 342.

23 José de Acosta, *Historia natural y moral de las Indias*, ed. José Alcina Franch (Madrid: Historia 16, 1987), 56–57; Velasco, *Historia del Reino de Quito*, bk. 4, ch. 9, 331.

24 Velasco, *Historia del Reino de Quito*, bk. 4, ch. 7, par. 14, 307.

25 Ibid., bk. 3, ch. 9, par. 12, 222; bk. 3, ch. 9, par. 15, 224; bk. 4, ch. 3, 192–93; bk. 4, ch. 9, par. 1, 331, par. 24, 342–43.

26 I use here the English edition of Juan Ignacio Molina's *Saggio sulla storia naturale del Chili* (Bologna, 1782) and *Saggio sulla storia civile del Chili* (Bologna, 1787), together published as *The Geographical, Natural, and Civil History of Chili*, 2 vols. (London: Longman, 1809), 1:46.

27 Ibid., 1:xiv–xv. On this, see, for example, his use of travel accounts to support the assertion of the great agricultural productivity of Chile (1:45–46).

28 Ibid., 1:x–xi.

29 Ibid., 1:xiv.

30 Ibid., 1:xv–xvii, 73.

31 Ibid., 1:xiii–xiv.

32 On transnationalism and national identities, see Prasenjit Duara, "Transnationalism and the Predicament of Sovereignty: China, 1900–1945," *American Historical Review* 102 (October 1997): 1030–51. For the

role of exiles and expatriate communities in the elaboration of identity discourses in Latin America, see the collection of primary and secondary sources edited by Ingrid E. Fey and Karen Racine in *Strange Pilgrimages: Exile, Travel, and National Identity in Latin America, 1800–1990s* (Wilmington: Scholarly Resources, 2000).

33 José Antonio de Alzate, "Historia de la Nueva España por el abate La Porte," *Gacetas de literatura* 1 (January 31, 1788): 5–12.

34 Alzate, "Falsedades vertidas por Jorge Amon [sic] en la descripción de su viage al rededor del mundo," *Gacetas de literatura* 1 (May 10, 1788): 40 (Alzate described the Mexicans in Manila as commoners of Indian descent).

35 Ignaz von Born's treatise first appeared in Vienna in 1786 under the title *Über das Anquicken der Gold und Silberhaltigen Erze, Rohsteine, Schwarzkupfer und Hüttenspeise.* It was then translated to English by R. E. Raspe under the title *Baron Iñigo Born's New Process of Amalgamation of Gold and Silver Ores, and other Metallic Mixtures, as by his late Imperial Magesty's Command introduced in Hungary and Bohemia* (London, 1791). The fact that Alzate reviewed the treatise in 1790 indicates the dynamism of the public sphere and the book market in New Spain.

36 Alzate, "Traducción de algunos artículos del estracto del caballero Born acerca de la estracción de la plata y oro con su correctivo," *Gacetas de literatura* 2 (December 30, 1790): 84–90.

37 The notes are housed in two different repositories: those corresponding to Clavijero's books 1 and 2 are in MS 176 at the Archive of the Museo de Antropología of Mexico (hereafter AMNA). The notes for books 6–10 are in MS 1679 at the Biblioteca Nacional of Mexico (hereafter BNM). The notes for books 3–5 are missing. Roberto Moreno de los Arcos has made available a critical edition of the notes in *Estudios de Cultura Nahuatl* 10 (1972): 359–92, and *Estudios de Cultura Nahuatl* 12 (1976): 85–120. Note 55 to book 7 (BNM, MS 1679) reiterates Clavijero's critique of the epistemological limitations of the philosopher traveler.

38 Filippo Salvadore Gilij, *Saggio di storia americana o sia storia naturale, civile, e sacra de regni, e delle provincie Spagnouole di Terra-ferma nell'America meridionale,* 4 vols. (Rome: Luigi Perego Erede Salvioni, 1780–1784).

39 Alzate, "Noticia del viage en la America por el Abate Gilli y repulsa de sus falsedades," *Gacetas de literatura* 1 (January 10, 1790): 246–54.

40 His research program is laid out in "Ajolotl es muy eficáz su jarabe para la tisis," *Gacetas de literatura* 2 (November 16, 1790): 52–53. On this aspect of Alzate's work, and in general on this dimension of Creole patriotism, see Jorge Cañizares Esguerra, "Nation and Nature: Patriotic Representations of Nature in Late Colonial Spanish Amer-

ica," working paper no. 93031 of the International Seminar on the History of the Atlantic World, 1500–1800, Harvard University.

41 The many essays by Alzate and Cervantes that appeared in *Gaceta de México* between 1788 and 1790 have been reproduced by Roberto Moreno in *Linneo en México: Las controversias sobre el sistema binario sexual, 1788–1798* (Mexico: UNAM, 1989). For an interesting account of the controversy over the reception of Linnaean taxonomies in late-eighteenth-century Spain from the perspective of the resistance of the traditional corporate university to the opening of new alternative institutions, see Dorothy Tanck de Estrada, "Justas florales de los botánicos ilustrados," *Díalogos* 18.4 (1982): 19–31. See also Xavier Lozoya, *Plantas y Luces en Mexico* (Barcelona: Ediciones del Serbal, 1984), ch. 2.

42 For examples of this aspect of Alzate's patriotic epistemology, see "Botánica," *Gacetas de literatura* 1 (February 15–April 8, 1788): 20–27. For an example that carries the paradigm into the law of physics, see "Continua la descripción topográfica de Mexico," *Gacetas de literatura* 2 (October 4–8, 1791): 274–75, 278.

43 Bronislaw Malinowski, "Introduction: The Subject, Method, and Scope of This Inquiry," in *Argonauts of the Western Pacific: An Account of Native Enterprise and Adventure in the Archipelagoes of Melanesian New Guinea* (London: George Routledge and Sons, 1922), 8. On Malinowski and his brand of functional anthropology, see George W. Stocking, *After Tylor: British Social Anthropology, 1888–1951* (Madison: University of Wisconsin Press, 1995), 233–97; and Henrika Kulick, *The Savage Within: The Social History of British Anthropology, 1885–1945* (Cambridge: Cambridge University Press, 1991), 182–241.

44 Malinowski, "Myth in Primitive Psychology," (1925) in *Magic, Science, and Religion and Other Essays* (New York: Doubleday, 1954), 146–47.

45 Malinowski, *Argonauts*, 6–7, 10.

46 Ibid., xv.

47 For a more detailed account of the politics and historiography of the Spanish American clerics, see my *How to Write the History of the New World: Historiographies, Epistemologies, Identities in the Eighteenth-Century Atlantic World* (Stanford: Stanford University Press, 2002).

48 Ibid.

49 Gyan Prakash, "Subaltern Studies as Postcolonial Criticism," *American Historical Review* (December 1994): 1475–90; Gyan Prakash, ed., *After Colonialism: Imperial Histories and Postcolonial Displacements* (Princeton: Princeton University Press, 1995); Robert Young, *White Mythologies: Writing History and the West* (London: Routledge, 1990); Stuart Hall, "When Was 'the Post-Colonial'? Thinking at the Limit," in *The Post-*

Colonial Question: Common Skies, Divided Horizons, ed. Iain Chambers and Lidia Curtis (London: Routledge, 1996), 242–60.

50 Kwame Anthony Appiah, In My Father's House: Africa in the Philosophy of Culture (Oxford: Oxford University Press, 1992); James Clifford, The Predicament of Culture: Twentieth-Century Ethnography, Literature, and Art (Cambridge, Mass.: Harvard University Press, 1988).

51 Anne McClintock, Imperial Leather: Race, Gender, and Sexuality in the Colonial Contest (New York: Routledge, 1995).

52 Frederick Cooper and Ann Laura Stoler, eds., Tensions of Empire: Colonial Cultures in a Bourgeois World (Berkeley: University of California Press, 1997); Ann Laura Stoler, Race and the Education of Desire: Foucault's History of Sexuality and the Colonial Order of Things (Durham: Duke University Press, 1995).

53 Prasenjit Duara, Rescuing History from the Nation: Questioning Narratives of Modern China (Chicago: University of Chicago Press, 1995); Partha Chatterjee, The Nation and Its Fragments: Colonial and Postcolonial Histories (Princeton: Princeton University Press, 1993).

54 The first to call attention to the colonial roots of anthropology were the French in the 1950s; see Robert Young, White Mythologies, esp. 119–26; and James Clifford "Introduction," in Writing Culture: The Poetics and Politics of Ethnography, ed. James Clifford and George Marcus (Berkeley: University of California Press, 1986), 8–9. In Anglo-America the trend began later with Edward Said, Orientalism (New York: Vintage Books, 1979); and the essays of Bernard Cohn, compiled in Colonialism and Its Forms of Knowledge: The British in India (Princeton: Princeton University Press, 1996). See also Talal Asad, ed., Anthropology and the Colonial Encounter (London: Ithaca Press, 1973).

55 Hyssein Fahim, ed., Indigenous Anthropology in Non-Western Countries (Durham: Carolina Academic Press, 1983); and Emiko Ohnuki-Tierney, " 'Native' Anthropologists," American Ethnologist 11.3 (1984): 584–86.

56 William Taylor, Magistrates of the Sacred: Priests and Parishioners in Eighteenth-Century Mexico (Stanford: Stanford University Press, 1998).

57 See Dipesh Chakrabarty, "Postcoloniality and the Artifice of History: Who Speaks for 'Indian' Pasts?" Representations 37 (winter 1992): 1–26; and Steven Feierman, "Colonizers, Scholars, and the Creation of Invisible Histories," in Beyond the Cultural Turn, ed. Victoria Bonnell and Lynn Hunt (Berkeley: University of California Press, 1999), 182–216.

58 Poole, Vision, Race, and Modernity, 142–44.

59 Paul Gootenberg, Imagining Development: Economic Ideas in Peru's 'Fic-

titious *Prosperity' of Guano, 1840–1880* (Berkeley: University of California Press, 1993).

60 For an egregious example of the Manichaean narratives that plague the historiography of this period, see E. Bradford Burns, *The Poverty of Progress: Latin America in the Nineteenth Century* (Berkeley: University of California Press, 1980).

61 See, for example, the collection of readings on postcolonial studies in Bill Ashcroft, Gareth Griffiths, Helen Tiffin, eds., *The Post-Colonial Studies Reader* (London: Routledge, 1995), which completely overlooks Spanish and Portuguese America. With the exception of a token entry on Haiti (5 pages out of 514), it is entirely devoted to the British colonial experience. For a somewhat muted criticism of the provincialism of contemporary postcolonial theory, see Walter D. Mignolo, *The Darker Side of the Renaissance: Literacy, Territoriality, and Colonization* (Ann Arbor: University of Michigan Press, 1995), vii–xvii, 1–25.

JAVIER MORILLO-ALICEA

"Aquel laberinto de oficinas": Ways of
Knowing Empire in Late-Nineteenth-Century Spain

It was a long time before we saw that blessed report on the office renovations; but alas it returned from Madrid fat . . . and grown, as if the trip had been good for its health. The twelve parchments it had consisted of had become at least fifty, and it was something to be seen, the look of glee on my uncle's face as he contemplated the numbers of eyes that had set sight on those many letters he had written with his own hand.
—Ramón Meza, Mi tío el empleado

★ Spain in the nineteenth century was far from being the backward, medieval ruler of the sixteenth-century conquest, as described in U.S. narrative after its imperial takeover in 1898. Although it is easy to see today how the countless North American descriptions of Spaniards as cruel masters and evocations of the conquest served the political purpose of rhetorically justifying U.S. overseas expansion, it is a more difficult task to explore how these stereotypical images of Spain have nonetheless pervaded scholarly representations since that time. Although we no longer see such explicit depictions of a Spain caught in its sixteenth century, historian Richard Kagan notes that, "Spain remains something of an Other, a nation synonymous with the ominous figure of Tomás de Torquemada and connected, inextricably perhaps, to Columbus, to Cortés, and the other Conquistadors."[1]

Kagan's analysis of "Prescott's Paradigm" limits itself to surveying the scholarship of the Iberian peninsula, but we can extend his concerns about the historiographic depiction of the metropole to the portrayal of its nineteenth-century empire. Spain and its colonial possessions of the nineteenth century are, if even present, but a footnote in what has come to be known as the colonial and postcolonial studies of the "age of empire."[2] The dramatic loss of empire in 1898 has carried so much historical and historiographical weight, both inside and outside of Spain, that it is extraordinarily difficult to represent the nineteenth century as in any way "modern." The empire, which encompassed Cuba, Puerto Rico, the Philippines, Guam, and the Mariana Islands, as well as Spain's African possessions, for years has been described as but a pathetic remnant of the once-glorious Spain of Charles V. In this narrative, 1898 merely saw an end to the centuries-old process of Spanish decline.

The weight of this historical narrative has been lightened somewhat in recent years by a revisionist historiography about Spain's nineteenth-century empire, coming largely, but not exclusively, from Spain. As Christopher Schmidt-Nowara notes, in this revised view the Iberian empire "in the Caribbean and the Pacific was not the empty shell of a great imperial past but rather a new colonial project unprecedented in the history of Spanish colonialism."[3] As he and others have pointed out, Spain in the nineteenth century sent more soldiers and other émigrés to its possessions, particularly Cuba, than it had to its colonies in America during the previous three centuries. As the Iberian metropole adjusted to its status as a modern empire in the nineteenth century, after the loss of the mainland American colonies, Spaniards created a new, elaborate imperial system that linked the possessions to the peninsula.

As an economic, military, and cultural project, the late-nineteenth-century Spanish Empire was administered and conceived of bureaucratically through the Ministerio de Ultramar, founded in 1863 as Spain reformed its colonial system to adapt itself to the world of modern colonialism and imperial competition. The ministry handled all of the affairs of the colonies in a wide bureaucratic umbrella that managed justice, budgets, and government. While in the peninsula, for example, all criminal matters were handled through the Ministerio de Gracia y Justicia, criminal matters of the colonies were handled in the Dirección de Gracia y Justicia within the Ministry of Ultramar. While its library collected printed works about its colonies as well as those of its neighboring empires, the ministry's archive processed and eventually stored mountains of paper coming from the colonies on matters big and small.

The creation of the Ministry of Ultramar was a culmination of a long history, dating from the Latin American independence movements, of discussions about how to reorganize the remnants of the empire. Historian Agustín Sanchez Andrés has taken an in-depth look at these debates throughout the nineteenth century, stressing the political and administrative history of the various groups and institutions that participated in them from 1810 to the end of the century.[4] While various liberal governments starting with the first Cortes (Parliament) of Cádiz attempted to centralize the government of the colonies, this was not achieved fully until the creation, in 1851, of the Dirección General de Ultramar, a bureau within the Consejo de Ministros (ministerial cabinet) but not a separate ministry in itself. A commission created to study the problem of colonial administration and the chaotic state in which financial matters were handled stated that "es una convicción general y profunda que todos los asuntos de Ultramar no están manejados en la metrópoli con todo el lleno de atenciones que se merecen" (it is a widely held and deep conviction that the affairs of the colonies are not managed in the metropolis with the full attention that they deserve).[5] It was not until 1863, however, that matters of the overseas territories came to be handled at the ministerial level. In the debates surrounding the ministry's creation, a recurring theme was the need for Spain to establish a colonial office in the manner of rival powers Britain and France.

The vast bureaucratic web centered in Madrid was so central to the workings of empire that when Cuban novelist Ramón Meza set out to criticize Spanish colonial order, it was the bureaucracy on which he chose to focus his satirical novel. In 1887 Meza published *Mi tío el empleado*, the story of a young man and his uncle who leave their small provincial town in Spain to do what so many had done before them: *hacer las Américas*, to *make* and make it in the Americas.[6] The two depart for Cuba with the expectation that a relative prominent in the island government will be able to place them as employees of the state. Meza, who himself served as a government bureaucrat in Havana, tells his story through the eyes of the young nephew, poking fun at the state by playing up the absurdity of the jobs they eventually land through their corrupt relative, don Genaro. As bureaucrat-turned-novelist Meza paints a picture of the colonial state as a paper empire where the movement of documents, their constant shuffling, per-haps even more than the information contained within them, main-tained the empire's control through the appearance of efficiency.

Once placed in their jobs, uncle and nephew are assigned to dust stacks of documents and move them from one side of the room to the other. They are then ordered to read the documents, although it is never quite clear what they are meant to be doing by their reading. Indeed, the novel's audience is never told what branch of the bureaucracy the two work for, or of what exactly their jobs consist. The reader only knows, as the characters only know, that these mountains of documents are highly important. In this absurdist world of bureaucratic entanglement, don Genaro decides, with the help of his two new subordinates, to submit a petition to the Ministry of Ultramar in Madrid. Before the proposed project can be sent to the ministry, however, the uncle first has to take the request around his office to get the appropriate approval signatures, which proves to be an exhausting task:

> He had been lost in that labyrinth of offices. It was altogether impossible for him to recall the number and order of offices that his report had reached. First, it went to the gentleman subinspector, and then to the gentleman inspector, who studied it in minute detail. Later, it was taken to a gentleman who cut off an edge of the document; a little further down, someone else punched a hole in it; then it was sewn to other papers. It was rolled, copied, logged in four or six registers . . . in a word, my uncle took his report to so many people and places that he was dizzied and could not find the exit door.[7]

In his attempts to find the exit the uncle is ridiculed by employees, some of whom purposely confuse him by yelling "Over here! Over there!" Lost and wearied, he finally makes it back to his own office, where he arrives out of breath.

The reality of this labyrinthine bureaucracy that through paper united colonies and metropole is where I would like to center my analysis of Spanish colonial knowledge and power. The fact that Meza chose the bureaucracy as a focal point for satire and criticism, as opposed to any one of the other Cuban institutions he might have chosen (a slave plantation, for example), is telling. In the world of the novel, the power, and absurdity, of the colonial state lies in its control of the systems of information. Using Meza's fictional world as a starting point, I will analyze Spanish colonial knowledge by turning attention to the trade in bureaucratic paper—the paper trails of the Spanish Empire.

Just as colonial critics like Meza focused on administrative bureaucracy, the state itself saw this site as central to its authority, and the ideal of morality in administration was deeply entrenched and defended. Although colonial nationalists like José Rizal in the Philippines and Eugenio María de Hostos in Puerto Rico criticized the immorality of public administration in the colonies, the state defended itself against such claims by prosecuting officials who were found to have profited from their offices. Local bureaucrats accused of the crime of *falsedad en documentos*, (falsifying state documentation for personal profit) often received harsh treatment from the Crown when they appealed for pardons or clemency.[8] The state's interest in presenting a moral face is obvious: if the sanctity of the paper trails of Spanish Empire were publicly upheld through this kind of policing, then the colonial relationship itself was moral.

By focusing on the ministry and, specifically, on its archive, I would like to suggest an archive-centered approach to understanding colonial knowledge. This means making the archive itself an object of analysis rather than simply using it as a source of information. Anthropologist and historian Ann Laura Stoler has recently called for students of colonialism to analyze carefully the functionings of the colonial archive, the manners and institutions through which colonial powers collected and created information about their possessions.[9] By asking historians to read the archive "with the grain," Stoler suggests that interrogating the logic of the archive will enable us to better understand not only colonial situations but also how it is that our very epistemologies for interpreting them are deeply embedded in the forms of knowledge that colonialism itself produces.[10]

Interrogating the logic of the archive offers us a unique window into empire, and the reason for this is the organizational schemes under which archives have operated historically. European archival arrangement of textual materials developed according to two guiding principles: provenance and original order. The principle of provenance "provides that records should be grouped according to the nature of the institution that has accumulated them" while the standard of original order requires "that archives should be kept in the order originally imposed on them."[11] Unlike library methods of classification, where new materials are grouped according to a preexisting code of subject indexing, archives, in principle, file materials according to the logic, random though it might have been, given to them by those who produced and originally preserved the information. This means, in theory, that the form of the archive can allow us to glean some information about what historical actors thought were meaningful, or perhaps just logistically useful, forms of classification.

In proper archival form, the documentation created by the Ministry of Ultramar exists today at the Archivo Histórico Nacional in Madrid, preserved in the original order in which the materials were collected. In what follows, I will discuss the ministry through this archive, because it is through the bureaucracy and its archive that empire can be said to exist. The ministry was the only place where information from all corners of Spain's Empire was housed in one specific location. Although to someone living in Puerto Rico or the Philippines this may have seemed a distant place of little or no relevance, in the metropole the same bureaucrats who filed *expedientes* (case files) coming from the Pacific also handled those of the Caribbean. The wide-angle view of the empire afforded to the ministry's bureaucracy is thus also afforded to us today. Then, the archive managed the empire; today, the archive is the empire.

The royal decree that established the ministry also gives a detailed description of its hierarchy. In addition to describing the jobs of the upper echelons of the bureaucracy, the decree offers details about the role of lower-level employees who worked in the archive as well as those hired as scribes and porters. It is these employees, the ones who in Meza's world did all the stapling, stamping, and binding, who are of interest to me here. These bureaucrats were the men Max Weber described when he wrote: "In the great majority of cases he is only a small cog in a ceaselessly moving mechanism which prescribed to him an essentially fixed route of march."[12] I take seriously Weber's contention that it is all of the individuals working in conjunction that give the modern bureaucracy its power. Together, those who wrote out reports, punched holes in documents, and carted paper were the archive and the empire.

The bureaucracy that created and moved all of this paper had to run in an orderly fashion. The rules outlined in the decree described in detail every employee's job. Documents were prepared and copied by officially certified scribes. According to the rules that governed the ministry, the head scribe had to "ensure that in the office assigned to the Scribes the greatest order, silence, and composure be maintained, absolutely forbidding entry to anyone who does not belong to the Ministry." The archivist, the scribes' supervisor, must "satisfy as quickly as possible requests made by the Subsecretary, Chiefs of Section, Officials, or Auxiliaries of the Ministry." In addition, the Archivist absolutely must not "1. Certify any document nor put an official seal on any paper without a written order from the Subsecretary. 2. Make available to the Ministry any document without a request signed by the Subsecretary, Chiefs of Section, Officials or Auxiliaries." Additional rules demanded that only eyes meant to see certain documents did so, and they strictly policed who could request a document, who could be present when scribes produced documents, and who could handle them. They note even that "doormen are forbidden from reading documents they are given to handle or that are on tables in the Ministry."[13] The care with which these rules are laid out suggests an important manner in which the state was defining documentary truth. Just as the content of a document would be judged, so too would the process through which it was handled. What Meza presents as farce—the need for every inspector, subinspector, and so on, to view and approve the document—was in reality a practice, if not a goal.

The actual functioning of an archive was much more complex than these simple rules might imply. In the case of the reorganized empire of the late nineteenth century, before order in an archive could be maintained, an archive had to be created for the new empire. In Madrid, the task of creating this archive fell to one José Arias Miranda, the head archivist during the first years of the ministry's existence.[14] In a petition to the queen for funds to travel throughout the region to assemble the documents needed for this new archive, Arias Miranda describes the chaotic state of imperial record keeping and storage before his taking the post:

> Don José Arias de Miranda, . . . expresses: that from the day that he took possession of the office that Y.M. saw fit to confer upon him, he put all the effort and assiduousness of which he is capable to come to an indepth understanding of the state in which the Archive was, and to study the means that could appropriately be adopted, so that it might serve the important function for which it was created and could benefit from all possible improvements. It is easy to understand how the repeated transfers the archive has suffered, with sometimes its papers being distributed among the various ministries . . . has created disorder and wreaked havoc on the methods adopted for cataloguing the files.[15]

Arias Miranda makes reference here to the bureaucratic uncertainty that befell the overseas territory until the creation of the Ministry of Ultramar. At times documents pertaining to the colonies were scattered about the various ministries according to their subject matter. It was not until the creation of the ministry that documents from and about the colonies were permanently archived in one central location, thus remedying what he deemed "la dislocación general de los papeles" (the general dispersement of documents).

In the petition, Arias Miranda states that despite the best efforts of the archive's employees, the fact that papers related to colonial administration were scattered across many ministries meant that the task of assembling the new archive was immense. In order to bring the archive up to par, as archivist Arias Miranda would have to ensure that "all papers relevant to the government of the Overseas provinces in its different branches be accumulated, for they are disseminated and hidden among the papers of the rest of the kingdom despite the fact that they are needed a thousand times over for matters of currency." He proposes to use the funds he is requesting to travel the Iberian peninsula, "visiting the Archives of the Kingdom belonging to the State, and some of those beyond, like those of Lisbon and Paris, if he is granted the very small amount that he believes indispensable for the trip to be fruitful." Not only is Arias Miranda building an archive, he is rebuilding it in a specifically Spanish context. Having lost most of its overseas possessions, the nineteenth-century empire was not "new," but it was reconfigured. Spain was in need of a new archive for the new ministry that reflected and named this reality. Arias Miranda's archive research trip was necessary so that he, as the person most knowledgeable on the subject, could decide what materials in other archives were relevant to the present-day concerns of the overseas office. The rest could safely remain in those other state archives as history. The disorganization of the papers themselves reflected the fact that for several decades there was no consensus in broader imperial policy about how the remaining possessions should be managed. With the creation of the ministry and the archive that Arias Miranda helped found, this chaos gave way to order. An elaborate system was established to manage correspondence coming from the farthest reaches of the empire.

The document quoted above is just the first in a thick employee dossier for Arias Miranda, one that spanned his entire career as an employee of the empire. From this file we learn not just about the archive Arias Miranda helped create but about his personal life as well. Arias Miranda had already published one general history of Spain's early empire, and he also appears to have been a very sickly man. The dossier is filled with numerous requests for leaves of absence so that he might travel to northern Spain to bathe in the hot springs there. Answering on behalf of the queen, one official finally expressed exasperation with Arias Miranda, suggesting tartly that he should perhaps take fewer leaves of absence for illness and instead complete the second history book he had been promising the Crown for some time.

In his initial request for travel funds, as well as in other documents, Arias Miranda explains that he is working on a history that would serve to defend Spain's role in the colonization of the New World, "a work that has a purpose of vindicating the conduct of Spaniards in their overseas conquests." The archivist, then, in addition to ordering the documents needed to administer the present, would vindicate the nation's past. This effort by Arias Miranda was not simply nostalgia, but rather a reality of contemporary imperial competition. The so-called Black Legend about Spanish conquerors in the New World was still used by imperial competitors, particularly Britain, to portray the Spain of the nineteenth century as the same brutal empire described by Bartolomé de las Casas. It played a prominent role in anti-Spanish rhetorical struggle as Britain worked toward abolishing the slave trade in the Americas.

Arias Miranda therefore saw himself as a vindicator of the old empire, a role perfectly in line with his job as "middle manager" of the new. While as the archivist he supervised scribes writing away in the halls of the ministry and helped to ensure that no unauthorized people read what they wrote, in his life as an intellectual he supervised the reputation of the empire and kept its secrets. Max Weber wrote, "Bureaucratic administration always tends to exclude the public, to hide its knowledge and action from criticism as well as it can."[16] José Arias Miranda is just one person, one of many who worked as keepers of the state's secrets and, in this case, keepers of the empire.

Using Arias Miranda's description of the archive, we can add some nuances to the impression of the archive given in the royal decree's description of the archive and its employees. Although it implied that the state had an interest in maintaining a strict order in the archive, the reality of actually creating and maintaining an archive for rule was a bit more complicated. But whatever the problems, it had to be done—the archive was a necessity. Arias Miranda must collect all documents he deems pertinent, not simply to claim ownership but because, in order to *govern*, everything relevant to the present empire had to be centralized.

Private matters affecting the lives of colonials found their way through the webs of the ministry. But this kind of private or secret knowledge is not the only kind of knowledge that empires produce about themselves. Although bureaucratic archives used for the purposes of administration were not open to the public, an official, public narrative of the empire was presented by the colonial powers. To explore one such narrative, let us now turn to the ministry's library, founded in 1887.

WAYS OF KNOWING: THE LIBRARY

On June 30, 1887, Spain's Minister of Ultramar, Víctor Balaguer, stood with the young King Alfonso XII and his mother, the Queen Regent María Cristina, as she officially inaugurated Madrid's first-ever Philippine Exposition. Organized by Balaguer through the Ministry of Ultramar and its officials in the metropole and in the Philippine Islands, the exposition was meant to showcase for the metropolitan capital the agricultural and economic potential of that faraway archipelago that so many knew so little about. The exposition opening, described contemporaneously as a lavish event, was attended by the city's best: "All of Madrid's press, men of all political persuasions and all classes have celebrated . . . and applauded the act warmly."[17]

The ceremony also inaugurated, in the same buildings, the Museo-Biblioteca Colonial de España, or as it was later known, the Museo-Biblioteca de Ultramar. The royal order that established the library read: "Using as a foundation the collections and other objects owned by the State in the present Exposition of products from the Philippine Archipelago, this Court will constitute a Museo-Biblioteca de Ultramar under the direction of the Ministry, which will be designated to exhibit permanently the objects and products remitted by the Ultramar provinces."[18] Long after the Philippine Exposition closed, the building that housed it continued to serve as the ministry's library, as well as the repository of the printed works and some manuscript collections and exhibition objects about and from Spain's late-nineteenth-century colonies. Although the library itself closed its doors after the 1898 loss of the island empire, its published catalog can be used to peruse its collection, which was transferred to Spain's Biblioteca Nacional.

Because the purpose of a library is different from that of a bureaucratic archive, it follows that a library would have a different system of classification. Whereas the bureaucracy's archives, as we have seen above, collected information for the purposes of administration and cataloged them accordingly, the library was to be explicitly a site of public knowledge of empire. This library, according to the documents pertaining to its foundation, was designed to hold all materials relating to the nineteenth-century empire, but it was also meant to hold materials "that might aid the conservation of the historical memory of the overseas countries discovered by Spain, or which at any point in history had belonged to our Nation."[19] Whereas the archivist Arias Miranda had been assigned the task of creating an archive that would exclude areas that no longer "belonged to the nation," the library was to collect and display materials that placed the nineteenth-century possessions in a broader context of Spain's imperial history. The catalog of the Museo-Biblioteca de Ultramar cannot recreate for us the physical space of its halls—we cannot see how books were organized in stacks or what categories were used for their display. What we have instead, however—one hundred years after the library closed its doors—is the alphabetical listing of materials it held.

Looking at this collection and knowing that the nineteenth-century empire revolved for so long around the "Cuban question," it is somewhat surprising to see the extremely large quantity of materials held about the Philippine Islands. This was due, in part, to the fact that the library owed a large part of its collection to the Philippine Exposition, but it is also indicative of a general scientific impulse toward the study of that archipelago. As historian of Spanish geography Horacio Capel has shown, in the nineteenth century Spanish geographers set to the task of applying their knowledge in the service of empire. After the loss of the American mainland colonies, it was with renewed interest that Spanish geographers began to chart the Philippine territories in particular, with the explicitly stated aim of increasing knowledge about these lands so that they could be more efficiently governed.[20] Although, as we shall see, state officials in the Philippines complained constantly about the lack of scientific knowledge about the archipelago, many were working to correct that lack.

While in imperial matters Spain's world seemed to revolve around the "Pearl of the Antilles," it is the Philippines—the "forgotten" corner of empire—that becomes the center of its public representation of empire to the world. Minister Balaguer, who saw the exposition develop from the king's personal vision to reality, would later lament, in his memoirs about his time at the helm of the ministry, his inability to do more on matters concerning the archipelago. He wrote, "But then there is Cuba, Cuba, which since 1870 has monopolized all of the hours of the minister, taking control of him body and soul. That is, after all, how it is. . . . Cuba, with its complications, its disturbances and its subversiveness, always active or in wait, leaves the minister with not a minute of rest and even absorbs, attracts, and captivates all of his attention and all of his time."[21]

And so, when it came to explaining the empire publicly, what made sense was to draw attention to its vastness, to the possessions that not only were lesser known but that needed the economic boost that a colonial exposition might provide. Whereas Cuba was widely known as a "problem," showcasing the agricultural products and cultures of the Philippine archipelago would give a different sense of the empire and its breadth and, it was hoped, strengthen the economic stability of the Pacific islands as its export products became known.

In what follows, I will go into some detail about the preparations for the Philippine Exposition, using documents from the private archive of Minister Balaguer.[22] In preparing for the exposition, Balaguer corresponded extensively with the archbishop of Manila, Pedro Payo, who headed the Comisión Central de Manila para la Exposición General de Filipinas, the local commission charged with gathering materials to be exhibited in Madrid. Useful for analyzing the public library and the exposition that prefigured it as sites for the production of a particular kind of colonial knowledge, this correspondence highlights some of the problems encountered when the state sets out to export information about a colony for public metropolitan consumption.

In his first letter to the minister on this matter, Payo detailed the obstacles that he faced in trying to prepare for this event. He complained of the short time given for preparations and of the general difficulties of getting Filipinos involved in any significant way in "one of the most recent practices of modern life." In this and subsequent letters, Payo faulted the "nature" of the Filipinos and their unwillingness to participate in "modern" practices like expositions.

He wrote: "The inhabitant of these islands, as a general rule, is of an excellent condition, submissive to authority, with great abilities in the arts, and prone to following good examples where he sees them; but whether it is due to the climate, or as a trait of his race, the truth is that he lacks initiative and is inactive, not easily stimulated into action, except only when he can see immediate results coming from little effort."[23]

But indigenous backwardness alone, according to Payo, does not explain the enormous difficulties of putting together exhibits. Like many Spaniards familiar with the Philippine Islands, Payo lamented the lack of scientific knowledge about the archipelago and the difficulties in trying to produce a global knowledge for consumption in the metropole when locally so little scientific exploration had been undertaken: "The day when we have complete statistics for all of its branches is still far away."[24] Payo insisted in several of his letters to the minister that with only limited political control over the archipelago there was not enough basic knowledge to be able to put together an appropriate exhibition. Finally, Payo listed the islands' economic problems as an obstacle in motivating individuals to participate in the project.

In a second letter sent before Balaguer had responded to the first, Payo adds to the list of obstacles the lack of adequate communication between the islands. Organizing the exposition was, he wrote, "an immense job here where communication is extremely difficult and where only the Isle of Luzón has telegraph."[25] In this letter he also underscored the lack of funding available to the commission for purchasing objects and transporting them to the peninsula. In addition, he sustained, he was being granted very little time to put together materials for the event: "You are aware, Sir, of the amount of time that went into preparations for the Colonial exposition celebrated in England, and it cannot be logically expected that in the Philippines, with less time and fewer resources, we accomplish as much or more than the British empire."[26]

In his response to Payo's worries, Balaguer did little to address the concrete matters that the archbishop raised, but rather he stressed the absolute necessity of opening the exposition because the queen saw it as the "sacred legacy of her deceased husband." The government had to follow through on its commitment to the event, "for to the contrary we would play an extremely sad role before the world. . . . In a word: we must do the impossible before retreating."[27]

The financial constraints of the commission would be taken care of, he assured the archbishop, and everything would be done to aid him in his effort.

Through this initial exchange we begin to see some of the layers involved in creating a public knowledge of empire. First we have the colonized who are, in effect, a problem, a nuisance. Between them and the metropolitan state is Payo, who must solve the local difficulties of collecting information and, in addition, satisfy the Crown's desire to work quickly. How could Payo, as the state's representative in this endeavor, make those not well-versed in the "practices of modern life" understand the benefits of participation? He describes himself as being at a loss as to how to inspire poor people to take the project as a personal goal unless he were to "exercise pressure and violence," which, he says, would probably have no effect anyway.[28] Minister Balaguer does not offer much by way of response. He promises to take care of the one thing he can, the commission's finances, but with respect to everything else he simply reiterates to Payo that the exposition must occur, and he expresses his and the queen's confidence in Payo's abilities.

And thus we have the first issue of producing this kind of colonial knowledge for show: the indigenous people as a problem. But colonialism is about more groups than the ministry, the crown, the commission, and local inhabitants. In a subsequent letter, Payo lays out a different explanation of the problem of native "lack of initiative" when he characterizes it as something that implicates the Spanish officials charged with governing the colonized. Here, "docility" is used to make natives innocent of any blame, which is to be placed instead on the representatives of the state: "The docility of the inhabitants of these islands, and their respect for the counsel and decisions of their authorities, makes one think that if the Exposition is not more successful than what is to be expected, we must not lay blame on the producers but rather on the lack of zeal on the part of those who have the moral obligation of leading them."[29]

Whereas previously, the indifference of the natives led them to be blamed, now it exculpates them. While this might seem somewhat of a shift on the archbishop's part, it is also indicative of the malleability of terms like "docility," as well an indication of the moral logic of colonial administration. A moral administrator is one who thinks *for* his charges, who in turn would follow correct paths if only they were given a good example. The fact that the administration was not moral in this respect leads Payo to become colonial critic: "The lack of experience and knowledge about the country on the part of some governors, the insecurity that all [state employees] have about their jobs, and many other reasons that would be too tedious to enumerate, keep the provincial chiefs from taking interest in a country where they will live very little time and to which they do not feel tied by the affect that longtime residence inspires."[30]

Using the occasion to criticize the way he saw the state functioning in his corner of the empire, Payo moves beyond blaming individuals and criticizing the system itself, writing: "Neither the Ministry nor any one person can be blamed for these faults, which are the product of our depraved social organization and of the injection of politics into matters that should be kept far from it."[31]

The colonial system as it exists is thus what makes it nearly impossible for the colony to represent itself properly to the metropole. The archbishop's criticism adds another layer to what we can observe from this instance of colonial knowledge production: a new "tension of empire."[32] The problem for Payo moves from the colonized to the colonizers. For this moment he stands outside of the system he is representing to criticize the state's organization. The system's inefficiency and the manner in which jobs are so tied to politics ultimately means that people who could otherwise be encouraged to lead productive lives are left to their own indolence. The local bureaucrats are the source of the problem and they, too, must be properly disciplined if the state is to carry out this and, by implication, any other project.

Payo states in his letter that he is forwarding a published announcement he sent out to the provincial chiefs, "in which I have tried every means, from persuasion to threat, and attempt to dissipate all objections or protestations that could be made in favor of not participating as exhibitors."[33] Whereas previously in regard to producers Payo had mentioned the futility of force or threats, regarding officials he uses it freely. The problem in presenting the Philippines to the metropole comes principally from the inept bureaucrats who are running the Crown's colonies in the Pacific. It is important to note that it is the language of morality that guides these assertions of Payo's: if the system were working correctly, these administrators would take on their moral responsibility and lead the natives by good example. Because they do not, Payo implies, the colonial administration is, in fact, immoral. The natives of the islands cannot help their faults—the administrators can.

And the natives do, in the end, participate in the exposition, as producers of exhibit objects and as exhibited objects themselves. As the date of the event approaches, Payo notifies Balaguer of shipments of objects being sent from the port of Manila to the port of Barcelona. One of the final shipments was to include natives who would construct "typical" homes on the grounds of the exposition, in Madrid's Parque del Retiro, and inhabit them as exhibits for as long as its doors were open. Balaguer writes to Payo to advise that they arrived well: "I have heard that they are drawing much attention because of the variety of their types, and they will draw much more attention when they are seen engaging in their everyday practices."[34] In a subsequent letter Balaguer complained that a shipment of plants did not arrive in good condition. The Filipinos arriving with them, however, were well-received by the minister: "The two *moros* from Mindanao are superior to the ones from Joló, and they are drawing much attention."[35] The minister goes on to say that all of the snakes and many of the birds sent had died due to the cold. The losses, however, were not limited to plants and animals: "Among the personnel, we have not had to suffer more losses than of the poor *mora* Basalia. Today we have one Igorrote ill with a high, eruptive fever that should not be dangerous but will be difficult to cure . . . I would regret deep in my soul if we suffered a second misfortune."[36]

By the end, however, there were two more such misfortunes. Balaguer thought that the family of Dolores Neissern, a woman from the Caroline Islands who died after the Exposition had opened, should receive some kind of government pension. This, he said should be done "with the aim of demonstrating the interest of the Patria in all of its children. I believe it is something that should be done if we are to preserve our good name and increase our prestige."[37] He also advises that in the same shipment carrying his letter he is sending along some of the indigenous personnel. He lists the persons remaining in Madrid, who they have decided to keep longer "as we consider that the exposition would lose much without the indigenous personnel."[38]

It was common practice in colonial expositions to have "live exhibits."[39] People being sent as exhibits participated in the representation of the colonies they inhabited. But their participation is extremely circumscribed according to the narratives that arise from these kinds of knowledge production. While Payo complained about the administration and its ability to adequately represent the colony, he is nonetheless a part of the process through which decisions were made. Although I seek here to analyze the representations of Filipinos in this exposition, my focus is less on the content of the exhibition and more on the channels used to put it together. Seen from this perspective, if we follow the hierarchy of knowledges from the colony up to the metropole, the important thing to note is not that indigenous people did not participate but that they participated within a framework set up by the state. The power of the state rested not just on the ability to define the content of colonial knowledge but rather more so on its ability to control the mechanisms through which that knowledge is produced.

As the exposition came to an end, the ministry officially announced that the grounds of the exposition would become the permanent Museo-Biblioteca de Ultramar. Balaguer then wrote to Payo to inform him that most of the submitted artifacts would be kept in Madrid for their permanent exhibition. The museum will be, in Balaguer's words, "a constant advertisement for the products of those provinces."[40] Payo, in turn, expresses satisfaction with the establishment of the permanent museum and library: "Only in this way can we defeat the natural apathy of these *naturales* and the repugnance they feel toward getting involved in matters whose usefulness is not clear, easy, and immediate."[41] With the exposition now organized and out of Payo's hands, the natives once again become the problem and the explanation for the lack of knowledge about the Philippines.

This particular kind of library, the exposition that inaugurated it, and the world of colonial exhibitions of which it was a part all produced very particular kinds of colonial knowledge, related to but distinct from the kinds of knowledge produced by bureaucratic archival systems as described above. The Museo-Biblioteca de Ultramar was set up to showcase the colonies to the world and, very importantly, to the metropole itself. It heaped attention on the Philippine Islands precisely because, Minister Balaguer and others felt, Spaniards did not know that corner of their reign well enough. In this representation of the empire designed for wide consumption, various levels of knowledge had to be negotiated. The ministry and the Crown might decide that an exposition was necessary and set a date for it, but it was at the level of the colony where the physical task of putting the work together saw its difficulties: from the inhabitants of the islands who Archbishop Payo saw as too "indolent" to want to participate on their own initiative, to the local bureaucrats he saw as being unqualified and unable to "inspire" the so-called *naturales* to work, to the ministry itself and the queen as she presided over the exposition's opening.

The library, in addition to being the site where the knowledge of empire was exhibited was also a site of nostalgia. Its mission was to showcase the present-day colonies *and* to preserve the memory of Spain's imperial past, and as such it was a site of nation and nostalgia. The strength of the nation's present and the resolve to remember its illustrious past guided the desire to establish the library. Although it existed from 1887 until the fall of the empire, the Museo-Biblioteca de Ultramar's catalog was finally published only in 1900—*after* there was no longer an "Ultramar" to exhibit.

BEYOND COMPARISON:
PLACING SPAIN IN THE "AGE OF EMPIRE"

In the preceding sections I have been discussing the Spanish Empire largely in isolation. It is important, however, to cast a wider net in order to understand the phenomena discussed here in a global context. The exposition, the Museo-Biblioteca de Ultramar, and the bureaucracy of the ministry, show us an empire firmly anchored in the age of modern empire. The Spain that exhibited itself in the Philippine Exposition actively participated in other international affairs and explicitly compared itself to other empires. Archbishop Payo, when trying to convince Minister Balaguer that he was not given enough time to prepare for the exposition, compares his efforts to the extensive preparations that went into a British colonial exposition.

According to contemporary accounts, the very idea behind holding the exposition came after Spain had been represented at the Philadelphia Centennial Exposition of 1876, where its contribution was well received by the press. Spain later participated, as well, in the Chicago World's Fair of 1893. Recent scholarship on colonial expositions has shown us how these events served as sites for information exchange: empires showcased their possessions to the world and they learned about each other's lands. The Ministry of Ultramar, meanwhile, owed its very founding in part to an awareness on the part of certain Spanish political sectors that in order to be competitive with other European powers, the state would have to centralize its administration of the colonies and make government more efficient.

Despite this history, recent scholarship still only rarely treats the

Spanish Empire on the same analytical or chronological plane as other empires in relation to the global colonial processes that were occurring simultaneously in the rest of Europe and its colonies. Frederick Cooper and Ann Laura Stoler, in their preface to their edited volume *Tensions of Empire*, describe their project as the exploration of nineteenth- and twentieth-century tensions "between the universalizing claims of European ideology and the particularistic nature of conquest and rule." The authors go on to explain that "to better focus on this question, we have narrowed our scope to areas of European colonial initiative during this period. This leaves out, most notably, Latin America, where the colonizing impulse occurred earlier and which was decolonizing itself during the nineteenth century."[42] This notion—that chronologically speaking, Spanish Empire does not fit into the age of modern empire—is an example of a common rationale for excluding the Spanish Empire from the purview of colonial studies.

The chronology here, seemingly straightforward, is actually quite slippery on further examination. The Spanish Empire did indeed begin much earlier relative to elsewhere in Europe, but the "colonizing impulse" of other powers also occurred before the nineteenth century. The British and French arrived in the Caribbean in the seventeenth century, and the first important colonizing impulse in India occurred in the late eighteenth century. Exploring the tensions within European liberalism is fruitful to Cooper and Stoler and the contributors to their volume; however the British colonial project of the late eighteenth century, like that of the French in the Caribbean or the Dutch in Indonesia in the seventeenth century, did not begin as a liberal movement, but rather only became one later. Rather than serving to justify the exclusion of Latin America from colonial studies, a focus on Liberalism should be a call for research on the internal transitions from "old" to "new" forms of empire. Thomas Richards has written: "Unquestionably, the British Empire was more productive of knowledge than any previous empire in history."[43] I would suggest here, however, that we rethink this notion. We have much to learn about the transition, if we may call it that, from "preliberal" colonialism to "modern" colonialism. The Spanish case is essential to understanding this transition precisely because the country reorganized its imperial possessions, practices, and understandings along these lines. Although peninsular debates about liberalism did indeed take place in a specific Spanish context, it is not a context incommensurably different from those of France, Britain, or the Netherlands.

This periodization of colonialism and its modern forms works because it recalls an image of Spanish Empire as being that of the conquests of the Aztec and Inca Empires and their aftermaths. This, then, equates the category "Latin America" with Central and South America and elides Spain's continuing and continuous presence in the Caribbean. Second, Spain's empire not only did not cease to exist in the Americas following the Bolivarian wars of independence, it continued to be a global one. The academic category of "Latin America" does not include the Philippines, suggesting perhaps that our unit of analysis at times might be better served by the term "Spanish empire."

The change in our unit of analysis allows us to engage differently with the period after the independence of Central and South America. To begin, it moves us beyond the Western hemisphere and into the Pacific. While Cuba and Puerto Rico are often discussed historiographically in relation to each other, and while they both are generally considered a part of "Latin America," in present-day area studies relatively little scholarship has examined the ways in which the Caribbean was connected—through military, economic, and bureaucratic circles—to Spain's possessions in the Pacific. From there we can begin to move beyond these internal circuits to the global context of imperial knowledge exchange. Although the nineteenth-century possessions were not newly incorporated, the earlier colonial losses meant that the metropole had to refocus its energies onto the remaining, previously neglected territories. This occurred in a process that, especially for the Philippines, meant practically a new conquest. And although historians like Josep Fradera, Ángel Bahamonde, and José Cayuela have already taught us much about the imperial economy and how to *hacer las Américas* helped to create the industrial metropole, we still have much to learn about the relationship of knowledge and rule (a central focus of contemporary colonial studies as defined by volumes like *Tensions of Empire*) in the nineteenth-century empire and how Spain adapted to its new imperial reality. The focus here on two of the ways of knowing that empire—the public and the secret state knowledges of rule—is but one attempt to remedy this lack.

Nineteenth-century Europe saw the rise of the field of statistics and the perfection of censuses and geography; social science became the means for quantifying and categorizing different groups and individuals.[44] Historian of colonial India Bernard Cohn has analyzed the ways in which the British colonial project was made possible precisely through these new methods of information gathering.[45] Horacio Capel has shown that, similarly, in the nineteenth century Spanish geographers set to the task of applying their knowledge in the service of empire. The loss of the American mainland colonies did not signify diminishing metropolitan concern with collecting information about colonial possessions.[46] To the contrary, after the 1820s it was with renewed interest that Spanish geographers began to chart the Philippine territories in particular, with the explicitly stated aims of increasing knowledge about these lands so that they could be more efficiently governed. Other historians have also pointed to some of the ways in which Spanish projects in one area became models for others elsewhere. When General Valeriano Weyler was summoned to put down Cuba's rebellion in 1896, he had already gained a reputation as a skillful strategist in the Philippines. In Cuba he implemented his infamous policies of *reconcentración*, a military tactic he had already rehearsed in the Philippines.[47] Knowledge and experience gathered in one area of empire could and did travel to other parts.

As we have seen with regard to Spain's own Philippine Exposition and its participation in other such international fairs, the Spaniards knew of and learned from other European empires. In 1876, for example, Madrid's Sociedad Geográfica participated in the Brussels conference that established the International Association for the Exploration and Civilization of Central Africa, and, as Capel writes, "the participation gave them direct knowledge of European plans for the penetration and partition of Africa."[48] Although Spain did not eventually become a heavy player in the "scramble for Africa," there is ample evidence that there was indeed interest in further colonial expansion and that at least some in Spain saw the country as being in competition on the global stage of modern colonialism.

The exclusion of Latin America from colonial studies, however, is not simply a matter of chronology. For Jorge Klor de Alva, colonial studies should have nothing to do with Latin America, and vice versa, because the region is *fundamentally* different from other areas deemed "colonial." Latin America, according to Klor de Alva, is simply incomparable to the rest, and he states: "In short, the Americas, as former parts of empire which, after a series of civil wars, separated themselves politically and economically, but not culturally or socially, from their metropoles, cannot be characterized as either another Asia or Africa; Mexico is not another version of India, Brazil is not one more type of Indonesia."[49]

Few would argue the opposite: that Mexico *is* another version of India, for example, or that India, Africa, and Indonesia all had identical colonial experiences. For Klor de Alva, the radical difference that Latin America demonstrates is not simply due to the chronological issues raised by Cooper and Stoler. He maintains that because the Creole and Hispanic-identified sectors that led the revolt against the Spanish Crown were never truly colonized, and that because indigenous groups of the Americas were never truly decolonized, that the labels "colonial" and "postcolonial" are inappropriate when applied to the region.

Klor de Alva investigates the genealogy of our current use of the term colonial and argues that our understanding of it is based on a northern European experience. For this reason, he states, we must therefore question its applicability to Latin America. This argument has two major flaws. First, Klor de Alva's genealogy of the term "colonial" is limited; indeed, the term "colonial" was explicitly used—the Museo-Biblioteca de Ultramar was originally called the Museo Colonial. The second, more fundamental, problem is that this limited genealogy leads Klor de Alva to argue *against* comparative work—the Spanish Empire becomes a case of European exceptionalism. The logic rests on the assumption that, unlike other colonial experiences, in the Latin American case rulers and ruled were not *different* enough from each other for the relationship to qualify as colonial; the difference between a Spanish-speaking mestizo and a Spaniard or between a Creole and a Spaniard was simply not as great as the difference between a British colonizer and an Indian.

This assumes that in Asia and Africa the difference between ruler and ruled was always stark and clear. In Dutch Indonesia, for example, the creation of the category "mixed bloods" caused metropolitan and colonial discussions of what it meant to be truly "European."[50] As historians of colonialism turn their gaze more onto the category of the colonizer it is increasingly clear that although the ideology of empire always seems to suggest that the colonizer/colonized binary is absolute, in many contexts what constituted Europeanness—or rather, proper Europeanness—was also always up for debate. Colonialism in many regions created interstitial categories of people whose very existence challenged easy dichotomies of colonizer and colonized.

From within the Spanish experience we can also challenge the suggestion that colonizers and colonized were simply not different enough from each other. I would argue that we should try to complicate our notion of what constituted racial and other differences in the Spanish colonies. First, the nineteenth-century situation cannot always be described as merely a struggle between Creoles and peninsulares or between Hispanic-identified people and Spanish masters, and, second, this should lead us to a more nuanced model for understanding cultural and political conflict during that period.

Although here I have argued against Klor de Alva's anticomparative approach, I do so in the service of actually moving beyond a comparative model altogether. In his approach, one category (Mexico and Brazil, standing in for "Latin America" as a whole) is measured against another (India and Indonesia, standing in for the "age of modern empire") and is found to be lacking. Instead of comparing two supposedly distinct entities, however, I argue that we should look to the circuits of global markets, travel, and information that binds them. In an important essay Frederick Cooper has warned of the "perils of comparative history" in precisely these terms.[51] If we view the Spanish Empire as an entity tied to other modern empires through ties of trade and information sharing (of which colonial expositions are only the most obvious sites), then we alter the terms of argument. This does not mean that we abandon the search for historical specificity—and comparative history—altogether, but merely that we look for global connectedness as well. As Cooper writes: "A global, interactive approach to history needs comparison, and comparison needs interactive and global analysis."[52] Viewing nineteenth-century Spain within the context of the age of modern empire, our findings will be not only relevant but essential to colonial studies.

If we assume, as I believe the historical record suggests we should, that nineteenth-century Spain was not extraneous to the age of modern empire but rather played an active role in its development, we will make an essential contribution to colonial studies. The Spanish case as described here tells us much about two different forms of colonial knowledge, secret and public. Heretofore I have treated the two institutions of the archive and the library as analytically separate: one governs while recording the practices of governance, the other collects and displays.[53] While the library produced knowledge for public consumption, the archive, as an arm of bureaucracy, produced knowledge that was strictly for the eyes of officials—that is, secret. Weber's description of the bureaucrat as a keeper of secrets is essential to understanding his position as a "cog in the machine," according to Weber.

But there is no strict dividing line between the "private" and "public" workings of the state. The same officials and bureaucrats producing knowledge for the ministry's archive put together the Philippine Exposition and later collected materials for the Museo-Biblioteca de Ultramar. And, as scholars working in the present, in terms of our understanding of colonial knowledge we might do well to explore at great length the idea of "bureaucratic secrets."

Secrets of the nineteenth-century empire, closely guarded at the time by the colonial bureaucracy and classified in a secure, hierarchically organized archive, become available to researchers and the public in the twentieth century, once the state's past is safely behind it and the paper trails no longer describe matters of current import. Eventually the archive becomes public or, we might say, more librarylike. When the Ministry of Ultramar ceased to exist after 1898, its archive was dismantled. Although documents from the defunct ministry's archive were originally slated to be taken to the Archivo General de Indias, the same archive that today holds the paper trails of Spain's pre-nineteenth-century empire, space limits impeded the move. They were sent, at first temporarily, to the Archivo Histórico Nacional and were made a permanent part of the archive's holdings in 1916, where they remain today.[54] Thus even in its afterlife, the paper trails of the nineteenth-century empire exist apart from the empire that existed from the sixteenth-century conquest to the Spanish-American independence movements. Similarly, after the Museo-Biblioteca de Ultramar no longer represented an existing empire, its holdings were transferred to the Biblioteca Nacional, again, with the empire now firmly in the nation's past.

And now that this history is past, let us imagine, for a brief minute, that the events of 1898 had never occurred and that Spain had instead ceded its empire to Britain or France in the nineteenth century, rather than the United States. We would surely thus have much more scholarly debate about the coloniality of Cuba, Puerto Rico, and the Philippines than we do today. At the risk of being polemical, I venture to make the case here that the exclusion of Spain and its continuing nineteenth-century empire reflects an unquestioned acceptance of the narrative of U.S. colonialism. First, this narrative held that Spain was an unchanged, absolutist colonial power for four hundred years, and, second, that U.S. expansion abroad was not itself colonial. As we look into our archives, libraries, and our own ways of knowing empire, we would do well to reflect on the ways in which we may have fallen prey to the continuing power of this story that the post-1898 U.S. empire told itself and the world.

NOTES

This essay has benefited enormously from the comments of the participants of the "After Spanish Rule" workshop, especially from Fernando Coronil who served as a panel discussant. Some of the ideas in this paper were presented at the meeting of the Society for Spanish Historical Studies in Minneapolis, Minnesota, in 1997. I would like to thank panel discussant Josep Fradera for his insightful comments. I would also like to thank the close readings and generous suggestions given by Ann Laura Stoler, Mónica Torres, Elyse Carter-Vosen, and especially John T. Stiles. This essay is part of my dissertation, "The Paper Trails of Empire: Bureaucratic Knowledges of Spanish Colonial Rule, 1863–1900." All translations of texts in Spanish are my own.

1 Richard L. Kagan, "Prescott's Paradigm: American Historical Scholarship and the Decline of Spain," *American Historical Review* (April 1996): 444.

2 See Eric Hobsbawm, *The Age of Empire: 1875–1914* (New York: Pantheon, 1987); the concluding section of this essay addresses the exclusion of the Spanish Empire from colonial and postcolonial studies.

3 Christopher Schmidt-Nowara, "Imperio y crisis colonial," in *Más se perdió en Cuba: España, 1898 y la crisis de fin de siglo*, ed. Juan Pan-Mantojo (Madrid: Alianza Editorial, 1998). See also Ángel Bahamonde and José Cayuela, *Hacer las Américas: Las élites coloniales españolas en el siglo XIX* (Madrid: Alianza América, 1992); José G. Cayuela Fernández, *Bahía de Ultramar: España y Cuba en el siglo XIX: El control de las relaciones coloniales* (Madrid: Siglo Veintiuno, 1993); and Christopher Schmidt-Nowara, *Empire and Antislavery: Spain, Cuba, and Puerto Rico, 1833–1874* (Pittsburgh: University of Pittsburgh Press, 1999).

4 A detailed overview of this history is beyond the scope of this essay, but more detail is given in Agustín Sánchez Andrés, "La política colonial española (1810–1898): Administración central y estatuto jurídico-político antillano" (Ph.D. diss., Universidad Complutense, Madrid, 1996). For metropolitan debates about how best to manage the

nineteenth-century empire after the loss of the American colonies, see Schmidt-Nowara, "Imperio y crisis colonial."

5 Quoted in Sánchez Andrés, "La política colonial española," 89.

6 The nineteenth-century phrase *hacer las Américas* is used by Ángel Bahamonde and José Cayuela in their *Hacer las Américas* to represent the importance of the economic elite created by Cuban sugar production and the political history of the metropole.

7 Ramón Meza, *Mi tío el empleado* (Madrid: Ediciones de Cultura Hispánica, Instituto de Cooperación Iberoamericana, 1993), 125–26.

8 See, for example, "Denegación de indulto a Mariano Iglesias, condenado en Puerto Rico a la pena de veintisiete meses de prisión e inhabilitación perpetua especial para cargo público, por delitos de fraude y falsedad en documentos oficiales," Archivo Histórico Nacional (hereafter A H N) Ultramar, Legajo 2069, expediente 38. The larger study looks at a group of cases of "falsedad en documentos," focusing principally on the case of the one nonstate employee charged with such a crime.

9 Ann Laura Stoler, "Unpacking Colonial Archives: New Movements on the Historic Turn," Lewis Henry Morgan lecture, University of Rochester, April 22, 1996; cited with the author's permission. Along a different vein, Nicholas Dirks looks at the role that native informants play in the creation of a colonial archive, especially in the early years of British colonial rule in India, in his "Colonial Histories and Native Informants: Biography of an Archive" in *Orientalism and the Postcolonial Predicament*, ed. Carol A. Breckenridge and Peter van der Veer (Philadelphia: University of Pennsylvania Press, 1993), 279–313. For the perspective of a literary critic who posits interestingly, if too anglocentrically, the question of the imperial archive, see Thomas Richards, *The Imperial Archive: Knowledge and the Fantasy of Empire* (London: Verso, 1993). For the case of Latin America, Roberto González Echevarría has analyzed the origins of Latin American narrative as being intimately linked to the archive as metaphor and practice in the early colonial period; see his *Myth and Archive: A Theory of Latin American Narrative* (Cambridge, Eng.: Cambridge University Press, 1991).

10 This is different from the work of, among others, Ranajit Guha, who has suggested that colonial archives require readings "against the grain" to find resistance embedded within them. However, I would argue that the two approaches are reconciliable because their object of inquiry is different. While Guha focuses on reading *documents* against the grain, Stoler is addressing the *process* of information collection—reading the archive, and not the content of the documents, with the grain. See Ranajit Guha, "The Prose of Counterinsurgency" in *Cul-*

ture/Power/History, ed. Nicholas Dirks, Geoff Eley, and Sherry Ortner (Princeton: Princeton University Press, 1994), 336–71.

11   See T. R. Schellenberg, "Archival Principles of Arrangement," in *A Modern Archives Reader: Basic Readings on Archival Theory and Practice*, ed. Maygene F. Daniels and Timothy Wlach (Washington, D.C.: United States National Archives, 1984), 150, 151. For a historical overview of the history of European archival administration, see, in the same volume, Ernst Posner, "Some Aspects of Archival Development since the French Revolution" (3–14). Some have claimed that the principle of original order was first used at the Archivo de Indias in Spain: "These antecedents give Spanish archive sciences a notable primacy in matters of archive ordering that have only been acknowledged much later in countries where the archive sciences are most developed" (*Guía del Archivo General de Puerto Rico* [San Juan: Instituto de Cultura Puertorriqueña, 1964], 11). I explore some of these issues in the context of the U.S. colonial bureaucracy in "Looking for Empire in the U.S. Colonial Archive: Photos and Texts," *Historia y Sociedad* (fall 1998): 23–48.

12   Max Weber, *Economy and Society*, vol. 2, ed. Guenther Roth and Claus Wittch (Berkeley: University of California Press, 1968), 988.

13   All decrees from "Cuidar de que en la pieza destinada á los Escribientes se guarde el mayor orden, silencio y compostura, no permitiendo la entrada á nadie absolutamente que no pertenezca al Ministerio" (*Ministerio de Ultramar: Reales Decretos de su Creación y Organización y Reglamento Interior del Mismo* [Madrid: Imprenta Nacional], 1863, 23).

14   All of the quotations from Arias Miranda and about his work on the archive are from "Expediente personal de José Arias Miranda, Archivero de la Dirección General de Ultramar," AHN, Ultramar, Península, Legajo 2427, Exp. no.6, doc. 5, 1858.

15   "Don José Arias de Miranda, . . . expone: que desde el día en que tomó posesión del destino que V.M. se dignó conferirle, puso toda la asiduidad y esmero de que es capaz para conocer a fondo el estado en que se encontraba el Archivo, y para estudiar los medios que convendrá adoptar, á fin de que correspondiese al importante objeto para que fue creado y pudiese recibir todas las mejoras de que es susceptible. Compréndese fácilmente que las repetidas traslaciones que ha sufrido distribuyendo unas veces sus papeles entre los respectivos ministerios, y volviendo otras a concentrarase en la Dirección de Ultramar, habían producido el desorden consiguiente y trastornado el método adoptado en la colocación de los expedientes."

16   Weber, *Economy and Society*, vol. 2, 992.

17   *Boletín de la Biblioteca-Museo Balaguer* 1.1 (October 26, 1884): 1.

18   Royal order of October 17, 1887, quoted in *Museo-Biblioteca de Ultramar*

en Madrid: Catálogo de la Biblioteca (Madrid: Imprenta de la Sucesora de M. Minuesa de los Ríos, 1900), iv.

19 Ibid., v.

20 Horacio Capel, "The Imperial Dream: Geography and the Spanish Empire in the Nineteenth Century" in *Geography and Empire*, ed. Anne Godlewska and Neil Smith (Oxford: Blackwell, 1994), 58–73.

21 "Pero ahí está Cuba, Cuba, que desde 1870 viene monopolizando todas las horas del ministro, apoderándose de él en cuerpo y alma. Porque es así. . . . Cuba, con sus complicaciones, sus turbaciones y su filibusterismo, siempre en acción ó en vela, no deja al ministro un momento de reposo, y absorbe, más aún, atrae y cautiva su atención toda y todo su tiempo" (Victor Balaguer, *Islas Filipinas* [Madrid: R. Angles, 1895], 4–5).

22 I say "personal archive" because although the Museo-Biblioteca de Balaguer is dedicated to his life and work, before his death Balaguer ceded it to the city of Vilanova I la Geltrú in Cataluña, his hometown. In terms of the larger argument being made here about the role of state archives, this is an interesting case. While this archive is not strictly "private," it does cause us to think about the role that personal archives (be they of politicians, merchants, travelers, etc.) might be seen to play in the creation of the global knowledges of empire being treated here. While it is beyond the scope of this essay to explore in detail these other forms of knowledge production, it would be worth exploring the manners in which these smaller institutions both coincide with and differ from the archives and knowledges produced by the state.

23 "Es el habitante de estas islas, por regla general, de condición excelente, hospitalario, sumiso a la autoridad, en grandes aptitudes para las artes, e inclinado a seguir los buenos ejemplos allí donde los encuentra; pero bien sea por razón del clima, ó como carácter de raza, ello es que carece de iniciativa y de actividad bastante, obedeciendo poco al estímulo, del interés al cual atiende únicamente cuando ve un resultado inmediato a costa de poco esfuerzo" (letter from Archbishop Pedro Payo to Minister Víctor Balaguer, September 27, 1886, Museo-Biblioteca de Víctor Balaguer [hereafter M BVP], Exposición de Filipinas: Correspondencia [hereafter E FC], doc. 1).

24 "se halla distante el día en que se tengan completas estadísticas de todos los ramos" (ibid).

25 "un trabajo inmenso aquí donde las comunicaciones son dificilísimas y en donde no hay telégrafo, mas que en la Isla de Luzón" (Payo to Balaguer, October 16, 1887, M BVP, E FC, doc. 2).

26 "No desconoce V. el tiempo que ha durado la preparación de la exposi-

ción Colonial celebrada en Inglaterra, y no puede esperarse lógica-
mente que hagamos en Filipinas en mucho menos tiempo y con
menos recursos, tanto ó más de lo que ha hecho el Imperio Británico"
(Payo to Balaguer, October 30, 1886, MBVP, EFC, doc. 8).

27 "pues de lo contrario haríamos un tristísimo papel ante el mundo en-
tero . . . En una palabra: hay que hacer [lo] imposible, antes que retro-
ceder" (Balaguer to Payo, November 17, 1886, MBVP, EFC, doc. 4).

28 "de no ejercer una presión y una violencia" (Payo to Balaguer, October 16, 1887, MBVP, EFC, doc. 2).

29 "La docilidad de los habitantes de estas islas y su respeto por los con-
sejos y decisiones de sus autoridades hace pensar que si la Exposición
no tiene mejor éxito del que fuera de desear no será por culpa de los
productores, sino por falta de celo de los que tienen la obligación
moral de dirigirlos" (Payo to Balaguer, October 30, 1887, MBVP, EFC,
doc. 8).

30 "La falta de experiencia y conocimiento del país de algunos Gober-
nadores, la inseguridad que todos tienen de sus destinos y otras
muchas causas que sería prolijo enumerar, impiden el que los jefes de
las provincias se tomen interés, por un país en el que han de vivir
escaso tiempo y con el que no se hallan ligados, por el afecto que
inspira la larga residencia" (ibid.).

31 "No puede culparse el Ministerio ni a nadie de estos defectos, que son
hijos de nuestra viciosa organización social y de la ingerencia de la
política en asuntos que debían hallarse muy apartados de ella" (ibid.).

32 Frederick Cooper and Ann Laura Stoler, eds., *Tensions of Empire: Colonial
Cultures in a Bourgeois World* (Berkeley: University of California Press,
1997).

33 "en la cual toco todos los resortes, desde la persuasión hasta la ame-
naza y procuro desvanecer cuantas objeciones y protestas pudieran
aducirse para la no concurrencia de expositores" (Payo to Balaguer,
October 30, 1887, MBVP, EFC, doc. 8).

34 "Oí que están llamando mucho la atención por la variedad de tipos y la
llamarán mucho más cuando los vean ejercer sus oficios" (Balaguer to
Payo, May 18, 1887, MBVP, EFC, doc. 14).

35 "Las dos parejas de moros de Mindanao son superiores a las de Joló, y
están llamando mucho la atención" (Balaguer to Payo, June 15, 1887,
MBVP, EFC, doc. 16).

36 "En el personal no hemos tenido que lamentar más pérdida que la de
la pobre mora Basalia. Hoy tenemos enfermo a un Igorrote con una
fiebre eruptiva, que no es de peligro pero sí de difícil curación . . .
Sentiría en el alma que tuviéramos una segunda desgracia" (ibid.).

37 "con el fin de demostrar el interés de la Patria por todos sus hijos. Yo

creo que algo debe hacerse si hemos de conservar nuestro buen nombre y aumentar nuestro prestigio" (Balaguer to Payo, July 27, 1887, MBVP, EFC, doc. 18).

38 "por considerar que la Exposición perdía mucho sin el personal indígena" (ibid.).

39 See Robert W. Rydell, *All the World's a Fair* (Chicago: University of Chicago Press, 1984).

40 "será un anuncio constante de los productos de dichas provincias" (Balaguer to Payo, November 16, 1887, MBVP, EFC, doc. 26).

41 "Solo de esta manera podría vencerse la natural apatía de estos naturales y su repugnancia a mezclarse en negocios cuya utilidad no vean clara, fácil, é inmediata" (Payo to Balaguer, October 15, 1887, MBVP, EFC, doc. 25).

42 Cooper and Stoler, "Between Metropole and Colony: Rethinking a Research Agenda," in *Tensions of Empire*, ix.

43 Richards, *The Imperial Archive*, 3–4.

44 Ian Hacking, "How Should We Do the History of Statistics? in *The Foucault Effect: Studies in Governmentality*, ed. Graham Burchell, Colin Gordon, and Peter Miller (Chicago: University of Chicago Press, 1991).

45 Bernard Cohn, *Colonialism and Its Forms of Knowledge* (Cambridge: Cambridge University Press, 1996).

46 Capel, "The Imperial Dream, 58–73.

47 See Louis Pérez, *Cuba Between Reform and Revolution* (New York: Oxford University Press, 1988).

48 Capel, "The Imperial Dream," 66.

49 Jorge Klor de Alva, "The Postcolonization of (Latin) American Experience: A Reconsideration of Colonialism, 'Postcolonialism,' and 'Mestizaje,' " in *After Colonialism: Imperial Histories and Postcolonial Displacements*, ed. Gyan Prakash (Princeton: Princeton University Press, 1995), 247.

50 See Ann Laura Stoler, "Sexual Affronts and Racial Frontiers: European Identities and the Cultural Politics of Exclusion in Colonial Southeast Asia," in *Tensions of Empire*, 198–237.

51 Frederick Cooper, "Race, Ideology, and the Perils of Comparative History," *American Historical Review* (October 1996): 1122–38.

52 Ibid., 1135.

53 Although I have presented the question of colonial knowledge through these two institutions of the state, I do not mean to suggest that these are the only two forms of understanding the problem. We can think of other spheres as sites of knowledge production, particularly if we move beyond the state into family, business, and personal archives.

54 Luis Sánchez Belda, *Guia del Archivo Histórico Nacional* (Madrid: Dirección General de Archivos y Bibliotecas, 1958), 173.

MARK THURNER

Peruvian Genealogies of History and Nation

Genealogy does not oppose itself to history . . . It opposes itself to the search for "origins."—Michel Foucault, *Language, Counter-Memory, Practice*

⁜ Spanish America's "ex-colonial" age was colored by the hazy dawn of a double artifice: "national history."[1] In the decades after independence "Creole pioneers" (but not only Creole pioneers) had turned to the century's bold new patriotic science.[2] Postcolonial Creole histories of *patria* (the homeland or country) and *nación* (nation) built on the venerable *crónica* (chronicle) and *historia* (history) traditions of the early Spanish colonial period, as well as on the enlightened philosophical histories of the (late-colonial) eighteenth century,[3] but the new work of "national history" was to narrativize pasts for the civico-political task of turning "ex-colonial" subjects into republican citizens with a national future.

In this essay I want to develop two notions concerning the genesis of certain iconographic and narrative motifs in the postcolonial national historical imagination. The first notion is that a fractured or schismatic inscription of the native past and present was foundational both for "patriotic" and imperial historical narratives of "Peru."[4] Simply put, the master narratives of Spanish imperial and Peruvian national history were underwritten by a colonial schism in native historicity that in effect severed the "glorious" native past from the "miserable" native present. In itself, the notion of "glorious" Incas and miserable "Indians" was not new, however. Scholars have pointed out that in the early seventeenth century distinctions between Inca or Aztec nobles and Indian commoners corresponded to the rigid hierarchies of the Spanish social imagination; the "miserable" condition of Indians, also common to the rhetoric of colonial authorities, referred to the childlike, slothful, ignorant, idolatrous, and otherwise uncivilized condition of impoverished commoners. But with the rise of the modern historical imagination these baroque social hierarchies underwent a mutation: temporal distances and mortal understandings supplanted the static imaginary of social caste.

By the late eighteenth century the temporal distancing of Incas from Indians had become a hallmark of the Creole patriotic historical imagination. This distancing had the great virtue of resolving an uncomfortable Creole predicament vis-à-vis "the West" and the "indigenous nation" or "indigenous race" that Creoles aspired to rule. Elsewhere I have argued that the Creole inscription of the native past and present under *historia patria* effectively displaced the colonial and postcolonial coevality of the colonized by, on the one hand, depositing him in the national museum of the precolonial and, on the other, postponing her return to the present by means of a patronizing displacement into the promise of the ever-receding republican future.[5] Although for want of space I do not develop this point here, I have also suggested that ethnohistorical writing on the Andes today is not entirely immune to the residual effects of this foundational schismatic inscription of the native.[6]

The second notion I want to develop here is that the republican revolution in the regime of political representation was also realized in the regime of historical representation. In the broad scheme of words and things, history writing in the enlightened liberal eighteenth- and nineteenth-century Spanish Americas charted the sea change from *history of and for kings* (that is, history in the dynastic mode, Spanish and/or in the Peruvian case Incan) to *history of and for nations*, which, in any given national instance, became an embedded *history of country* (*historia patria*, in this case *historia peruana*). In this new kind of history of the landed nation that emerged by the middle decades of the nineteenth century, the transhistorical subject "us" (a sovereign *nosotros* constituted by the communion of the patriotic author, the history of the patria he writes, and his imagined community of compatriot readers) was naturalized in and made coeval with a timeless place with a proper name—in this case, "Peru."

Taken in tandem these two notions suggest that the republican "we" of Peruvian national histories—the imagined national historical community—was constituted in the national landscaping of the violent split in native historicity. Further, I want to note that the "naturalization" in narrative of a violent colonial splitting in native historicity is probably not unique to the historical subject named Peru.

AN ANTIQUITY FOR CREOLE AMERICA

In the 1850s Peruvian natural scientist and museum director Mariano de Rivero lamented the "centuries [that had] passed before Peru possessed a collection [of artifacts] drawn from her ancient archaeological monuments." For "these mute yet eloquent witnesses reveal the history of past events and they demonstrate to us the intelligence, power and greatness of the nation ruled by *our Incas*" (emphasis added). In the very same breath Rivero added that "the history of nations . . . is not of interest merely to know what stage of power and culture was attained . . . but rather to instruct us in their progress . . . and to prepare the people for the enjoyment of national liberty . . . Babylon, Egypt, Greece and Rome are not the only empires worthy to serve as nourishment for a generous imagination."[7] Rivero was by no means alone in his historical sensibilities. In *Historia Antigua del Perú*, Sebastian Lorente pronounced that although the "ancient civilization of Peru . . . offers something of general interest to men of all countries, *for us* it is of special interest for the present and future [emphasis added]. This ancient civilization is personified in monuments which still stand, it lives in our customs, and it influences the march of our daily social and political life; whoever ignores it cannot comprehend our situation, nor can they lead our society with confidence . . . In the greatness of the past we shall find presentiments of the future."[8]

Who is Lorente's "us?" How is this "us" constituted in history? And how is it that, for Rivero, the Incas are "ours?" Let us begin to respond to these queries, which can never be raised by national history itself, by simply and half-erroneously saying that "our Incas" were nineteenth-century receptions of *crónica* narratives, most notably the Inca Garcilaso de la Vega's renaissance exegesis of dynastic oral tradition, *Los Comentarios Reales de los Incas*. That is, we are dealing with liberal-national readings and redeployments of the notion, at the time most readily associated with the bestselling Garcilaso, of a civilizing Inca dynasty that had carried out the Herculean task of unifying an Andean Babel in the extremely mountainous and far-flung territory called "Tahuantinsuyu" and "Peru."[9]

Lorente's narrative echoes Garcilaso's in granting foundational status to a precolonial classical age when the original Inca launched "Peru" on its "long career of civilization."[10] But the echo bounced between the walls of centuries and so Lorente would write, in the national-historical spirit of his liberal excolonial age, that "the vast Empire of the Incas laid the indestructible bases of the national unity of Peru."[11] With minor modifications, Lorente had redeployed the patriotic *garcilasista* narrative of Inca foundations in sophisticated turns of national historical rhetoric—and he was by no means the first postindependence historian of Peru to do so. Although born in Murcía, Spain, Lorente was easily the most prolific and intellectually adventurous historian working in nineteenth-century Peru. He was also an active educator and influential public figure. Contrary to the noisy pronouncements of a handful of xenophobes and political enemies who attacked him as a Spanish spy and an apologist for conquest,[12] Lorente should be thought of as the official historian of second-generation Peruvian liberalism.[13]

But what makes Lorente of particular interest here is that the past, present, and future are united in his pocket-size instructional histories or "catechisms" as a national "us" whose magical name is "Peruvian." We could even say that Lorente's language[14]—if not "the author" himself—knew that among national history's most formidable tools was its power to name, its authority to inscribe, and finally its ability to persuade itself, by the power of its own narrative, of the veracity of its own inscription. The desired poetic effect was the sweet unisonance of people and place: "Peruvians" and "Peru" forever made for each other.

This topological unisonance of names was key to excolonial nineteenth-century patriotism and its national historical discourse. Its refrain was sounded across the Americas in now classical pronouncements, from the Morelian "America for Americans" (1813) to the Martinian "Our América" (1891). The referents of "America" in these larger-than-life patriotic inscriptions were several, but the notion that "Americans" should *not* be consonant with "America" was in the nineteenth century becoming both unthinkable (unpatriotic) and manifestly true. Such was not the case one hundred years earlier when "Americans" (often modified by "Spanish," as in "Spanish Americans") most often denoted persons of European descent born in the colonial Indies, that is, Creoles. It is precisely the expansion of the name of "American" to include non-Creoles that is most notable in nineteenth-century historical discourse.[15]

José Martí's canonical lines on the pedantic value of Inca history, forever inscribed in his iconic "Our América," still resound on the lips of thousands of pedants, and are duly repeated by millions of schoolchildren: "La historia de América, de los Incas a acá, ha de enseñarse al dedillo, aunque no se enseñe la de los arcontes de Grecia. Nuestra Grecia es preferible a la Grecia que no es nuestra. Nos es más necesaria." (The history of America, from the Incas to the present, should be taught in perfect detail, even if it means not teaching the history of the archons of Greece. Our Greece is preferible to the Greece that is not ours. It is more necessary for us.)[16] Read from a Peruvian genealogy of history, however, these lines from "Our América" do not ring original. Martí's rhetoric fits in a deep patriotic lineage cultivated by generations of Creole republicans. Like their Anglo counterparts in New England,[17] Spanish American (and Peruvian) Creoles imagined and defended their new republics against the disparaging attacks of monarchists by turning to the authority of "ancient history." The ingenious move to "ancient history" reached back to the pure, premonarchical authority that beckoned from the mythical "republican" origins of the West. Contradictions notwithstanding, in the postcolonial Spanish Americas such classical republican claims on the originary West could merge in the national historical imagination with an "ancient" American dynastic narrative, which in effect provided a perch for Creole nativist claims to "our" original Incas, Aztecs, and Toltecs.

It is well known that in the late eighteenth and early nineteenth centuries Creole patriots repeatedly noted the parallel between American history and that of the ancient and modern Romans and Greeks.[18] What is perhaps less noticed is that as late as the 1860s, and for subsequent decades, influential Creole writers repeatedly recurred to the Greek analogy to score national points. One example is the 1868 anonymous member of the Peruvian "Society of Friends of the Indians" who—much in the fashion of the colonial Creole patriotic epistemology described by Cañizares-Esguerra in this volume—proclaimed that

various travel writers, above all the likes of Robertson, Pauw, Raynal and others, have popularized in Europe the idea of the extraordinary stupidity of the Indians . . . which renders them incapable of civilization. This is the place to say that those travelers did not study the character of the Indians, in part because they were ignorant of their language, and in part because the Indians became taciturn and reserved when dealing with the white race after the horrors of the Conquest. An American writer observed the tendency among Indians to deceive the whites in everything by way of a feigned ignorance, after which they congratulated each other for having misled the travelers in their researches . . . But *among us* it cannot be defended that stupidity should be the characteristic trait of the Indians, nor that they are incapable of civilizing themselves [emphasis added]. Vestiges of the civilization of this race remain . . . in the monuments and . . . eloquent ruins which bear witness not only to the civilization of the [Inca] Empire but to the barbarism of the Conquistadors. No, that race so great then as it is degraded today cannot have had stupidity as its characteristic trait. The same character may be atributed today to the modern Greeks, in whom servility has caused them to lose even the memory of their past greatness.[19]

José Martí's patriotic pen was dipped in the dark ink of this Creole rhetorical brew. The anticolonial Martí demands that "we" Americans cultivate "our" American history "from the Incas to the present" because this history is both preferable to Europe's and "more necessary for us." Martí's foundation here is the Peruvian "among us" of a Creole patriotic epistemology established, as critique of European knowledge, as early as the eighteenth century and carried, via historia patria, through the nineteenth. Whatever we may think about the correctness of the anti-Anglo Creole cultural politics of Martí, the point to be made here is this: that an exiled Cuban Creole residing in New York should fix the origins of "our America" in "our Incas" rather than in the Greeks was by the late nineteenth century becoming—and today generally remains—not only unproblematic but revolutionary and deeply patriotic for the Cuban nationalist and Latin Americanist historical imaginations. Nor did "race" throw up a barrier to this historical "us" of the patriotic imagination. In the realm of historical rhetoric the Creole epistemology of "spiritual mestizaje" had by the late nineteenth century largely swept aside the earlier objections of conservative Hispanists. The biting critiques of a Lucas Alamán or a Bartolomé Herrera—who in the 1840s had decried the hypocrisy of such "white" liberal hijackings of the legacy of precolonial native states—no longer packed any venom.

What were some of the effects of the republican inscription of this patriotic "our" in an invented "American" or "Peruvian" antiquity? By claiming the Incas as "our Greece," Martí's rhetoric availed itself of that familiar European historical alchemy that since the Renaissance has cast classical Greece as its first golden age and origin myth. The narrative of Hellenic origins and fall had endowed European national elites with an "ancient" pedigree and an imperial "Western" mission in the face of the modern historical fact that they (and the civilizing mission) were of recent invention. To claim in contestatory fashion from the location of the excolonial Americas a Greece of one's own naturally affirmed, in an operation of the simulacra, the hyperreal West's stakes in the "real" Rome or Greece. In this and other ways the Creole national historical imagination evidently contributed to the multisited historical invention of "the West." But this American-projected "West" was necessarily Janus-faced. The imagined originary Greece of Europe becomes "for us" a simulacrum in a history of the nation whose deep origins are to be found in the necessary historical study of "our Incas." (All of this should point to the strategic nature of the transatlantic project of the double simulacra, advanced during this same period, to rename "Our America" as "Latin America.")

Depending on political persuasion, today this move is readily enlisted as anti-imperialist Pan-Americanism or Creole internal colonialism, but underlying both readings lies a deeper effect. By means of the national conscription of classical Inca origins, the Americas are inscribed in the master historical narrative of the Western world. This inscribing tendentiously dissolves the Creole predicament in the Americas: to be of European descent "and law" but to claim native status in a colonial land with another genealogy. As we shall see, certain Peruvian narratives operated an ingenious Creole synthesis: classical genealogies of the Inca were made to merge with the dynasty of Spanish kings and Creole liberators, only to end, perhaps, with the historian himself.

A NARRATIVE STRUCTURE
FOR PERUVIAN NATIONAL HISTORY

Lorente contributed strongly to the unification of "Peruvian" history, but he did not invent its master narrative structure. Although the "ancient" segment of the narrative of Peru was taken mostly from Garcilaso de la Vega's *Los comentarios reales de los incas* (the classic seventeenth-century text had been published in a new edition in 1723) and from some of the early Spanish chroniclers like Pedro de Cieza de Leon, the three-part story of national history would have to await a postindependence historian. Perhaps it is not surprising that this historian should be a clerk with privileged access to dusty files. Once imagined, national history must have national archives and national libraries. In addition to officially renaming the natives as "Peruvians," it was the liberator San Martín who had the distinct honor of founding the National Library (it had been Jesuit property). And it was Lorente's powerful patron, the liberal caudillo Ramón Castilla, who created Peru's National Archive. Thus, it was *before* the national archive's foundation that José María de Córdova y Urrutia's paperwork had linked the foundational age of the Incas to the present independent Peru in a unified narrative structure.

As the late Franklin Pease noted in his pathbreaking survey of republican historiography, Córdova y Urrutia's rather meager *Las tres epocas del Perú o compendio de su historia* left its imprint on subsequent history writing in Peru.[20] This clerk's "compendium" of "Peruvian rulers" distributed the story of Peru in three epochs. The epochs were linked by the unbroken thread of rulers enumerated in a list that began with the original Inca, Manco Capac, and then, after the Inca dynasty, inserted all the colonial viceroys of Peru, followed by the liberators San Martín and Bolívar, and finally the presidents of the republic of Peru. Córdova y Urrutia's annal expressed that ingenious move by which the Spanish viceroys sent to govern Peru were "naturalized" as "Peruvian rulers" in postindependence historiography.[21] More important, the tripartite structure of the history gave "Peruvian history" its necessary beginning, middle, and end.[22] The first epoch was named "Foundation of the Inca Empire," the second the "Ultramarine Dynasty," and the third was called the epoch of "Independent Peru." The tripartition anticipated the contemporary textbook trinity of the pre-Hispanic,[23] colonial, and national periods. Significantly, there are no ruptures in this epochal political history. "Independent Peru" is the logical and moral progression from the previous two epochs. And the reason for this progression is self-evident: "el Altísimo" (God Almighty) oversees the course of history.

The invisible hand of God left its indelible trace on national history. His hand, for example, could provide Córdova y Urrutia with an ingenious solution to the national dilemma posed by the unsavory execution in 1532 of the "Inca Atahualpa" at the hands of the Spanish captain Francisco Pizarro. Creole patriots and other critics swayed by the Black Legend had developed a strong historical critique of the legitimacy of Spanish rule, based in part on the idea that the Inca

Atahualpa had been a legitimate monarch (or at least heir to the "Peruvian" throne). There were basically two patriotic responses to Pizarro's supposed regicidal act,[24] although both shared the conviction that Pizarro's actions had rendered illegitimate the imperial succession from "Peruvian" to "Ultramarine" (Spanish) monarchs. The first of these responses, which I will name here the Incaist response, and which actually had two distinct branches,[25] dreamed of returning an Inca to the "Peruvian" throne. The second response, which I will call the Creole republican response, was exemplified by Bolívar and the Bolivarian liberals who, in contrast, did not seek to place an Inca on any throne. The Creole republican response, however, did often portray the struggle for independence as a righteous avengence of Pizarro's odious crime of conquest, at moments specifically invoking the "disgraced name of Atahualpa" in the service of American liberty.

For the faithful clerk-historian the solution to the dilemma posed by the events of 1532 was to call Atahualpa's trial by Pizarro unjust, while maintaining that the death sentence passed was not. The ultimate penalty, Córdova y Urrutia reasoned, had been God Almighty's all-knowing way of punishing Atahualpa for having plotted to kill his rival "half-brother" Huascar. In short, it was the Inca Atahualpa's immorality (fratricide and regicide) and not Spanish conquest that had brought an end to the Inca dynasty. Spain's intervention was thus ordained by God. Only an ingenious nationalist turn of hand could then inscribe the "Dynasty from Abroad" in the framing master narrative drawn by the succession of "Rulers of Peru."

ANCIENT RUINS, INCA GENEALOGIES, AND THE HISTORICAL IMAGINATION

In the excolonial Spanish Americas the romantic and scientific imagining of the precolonial antique was expressed in several genres, from poetry to historiography to travel writing, and from iconography to dynastic genealogy to the landscape. The tableau of the ancient was constructed of all of these elements and more, but in the iconographic inscription of ruins it found the primal substance of a durable past.[26] Peru is a land of ten thousand ruins, but a handful of these have attained something like oracular status. In the nineteenth century the Andean pilgrimage of foreign savants and Creole *pensadores* (thinkers) often lead to the luminously ruinous Puerta del Sol

(Gateway of the Sun) at Tiahuanaco (Macchu Picchu had not yet been "discovered").[27] Standing among a complex of ruins near the shores of Lake Titicaca in what is now Bolivia, the monolithic Gateway of the Sun lured French, Austrian, Anglo, and Creole travelers and natural scientists. As in so many other imaginative enterprises in the postcolonial Spanish Americas, it was the baron von Humboldt who pointed the way (or at least he is credited by later visitors for having done so)—taking his cue from the early colonial chronicles of Cieza de Leon and Garcilaso.[28] In *Vue des cordilleres* Humboldt expressed the wish that "some learned traveller would visit the borders of the lake of Titicaca, the district of Callao, and the high plains of Tiahuanaco, the theatre of the ancient American civilization" so that the misty origins of that civilization might be revealed once and for all.[29]

Responding to Humboldt's romantico-scientific call to explore the high plateau of the southern Andes, the Yankee antiquarian Ephraim George Squier—following in the footsteps of the French savants Léonce Angrand and Alcides Dessalines d'Orbigny—made the trans-Andean trek in the 1870s to "this celebrated spot." As U.S. commissioner to Peru, Squier was charged to settle guano accounts (the bird-dung nitrogen fertilizer was Peru's leading export commodity); apparently he sought the post because it would present an opportunity to research firsthand the great Peruvian antiquities. Squier had been an aspiring student of William Prescott, and he was the author of notable books on Mississippian Indian mounds and Nicaraguan antiquities; for him, Tiahuanaco was nothing less than "the Baalbek of the New World."[30]

One-upping his French predecessors, Squier made sketches of the ruins based on what may be the first photographs of the place. Significantly, Squier's photographic drawings of the Gateway of the Sun include a native man dressed in rags who slouches at the base of the monument (figure 1). In his travel account Squier devotes several pages to the mysterious old man: "On our first day among the monuments, and within an hour after we had pitched our photographic tent and got out our instruments, we became aware of the presence of a very old man, withered, wrinkled, and bent with the weight of years. His hair was scant and gray, his eyes rheumy, and his face disfigured by a great quid of coca that he carried in one cheek." Squier is curious; he continues: "I prevailed on one of our [mule drivers], who could speak Aymara, to ask him what was his occupation. He got the curt answer from the old man, that he was 'cutting

FRONT OF GREAT MONOLITHIC GATE-WAY.

1. Gateway of the Sun in ruins. From E. George Squier, *Peru: Incidents of Travel and Exploration in the Land of the Incas* (New York, 1877), 288.

out a cross'" from an ancient stone slab that he held in his lap. Squier notes that "every morning he was at the ruins before us, and he never left until after we did at night. . . . After a time we came to look upon him as an integral part of the monuments, and should have missed him as much as the great monolith itself."[31]

The increasingly suspicious Squier then turned to the parish priest of the nearby village of Tiahuanaco, who

> explained in whispers, heavy with fumes of [cane liquor], that the old man was nothing more or less than a spy on our doings, and that we made no movement in any direction that he did not carefully observe. "He is . . . more than a hundred years old. He was with Tupac Amaru when he undertook to overturn the Spanish power, and he led the Aymaras when they sacked the town of Huancané, and slew every white man, woman, and child that fell into their hands. He is a heathen still, and throws coca on the *apachetas* [heap of stones]. Ah! If I only knew what that old man knows of the [buried treasures], *señor* . . . I should not waste my life among these barbarians! You can pity me! And for the love of God, Sir, if you do come across the treasures, share them with me! I can't live much longer here!"[32]

Squier then confirms his suspicion that the old man has been spying on him. He notes that his predecessor, the Viennese linguist and antiquarian Jacob von Tschudi, "when he was at Tiahuanaco,[33] found or obtained some ancient relics—small stone idols, if I remember rightly—but had not proceeded many miles on his way to La Paz before he was surrounded by a party of Indians from the town, and compelled to surrender them. We suffered no molestation, although there is no doubt we were closely watched, and that the deaf and apparently almost sightless old stone-cutter was a spy on our actions."[34]

The interlude of the native spy in Squier's illustrated travel narrative reveals some of the patent ways in which the suspicious, shadowy native could draw "the imperial gaze."[35] Although Squier's inscription of the old man in the sketch of the gateway ruins and in the narrative aroused the tropes of suspense and danger so common to the travel genre, nationalist texts harbored this very same danger embodied by the living native. Creole nationalists, however, would domesticate this dangerous native in his native land, turning him and her to the glowing promise of the patriotic history of "us." In short, imperial and national eyes shared the panorama of the native but turned it to slightly different purposes.

The national turning of the native was done early in the budding history of the republic. Fully twenty-five years before Squier gazed with suspicion on the old Indian at Tiahuanaco, the Creole antiquarian Mariano de Rivero had inscribed him in an elaborate, patriotic representation of the same Gateway of the Sun. Rivero's representation was also intended to capture the attention of imperial eyes abroad but more important, it wanted to entice the Peruvian national imagination. On the cover of the elegantly produced second volume of *Antigüedades Peruanas* (*Peruvian Antiquities*; hereafter AP),[36] the Gateway of the Sun beckons as a splendorous frame for the discerning national eye, an in situ museum for the "generous imagination" (figure 2). Commissioned by the Peruvian Congress and duly dedicated to the cause of "National Sovereignty," AP was authored principally by Rivero, with two short technical chapters by "Dr. Don Juan Diego de Tschudi." The creolized coauthor don Diego otherwise went by the name of Jacob von Tschudi—the very same Viennese anthropologist mentioned in Squier's travel account. Tschudi had made the artful publication of the illustrated second volume technically possible through his connections to the Royal Viennese Academy of Science and its state-of-the-art lithographic press. Rivero was

2. Gateway of the Sun in the generous imagination. From Mariano Eduardo de Rivero and Juan Diego de Tschudi, *Antigüedades Peruanas*, vol. 2 (Vienna, 1851), frontispiece. Photographic reproduction courtesy of the Library of Congress, Rare Book and Special Collections Reading Room, F3429.R54 1851.

the founding director of Peru's National Museum in Lima,[37] yet he sought to establish more than a national house for artifacts. At the time, many of the artifacts depicted in the frontispiece of volume 2 of AP were in fact on display in the showcases of the National Museum in Lima. Indeed, some are pictured in individual color plates in AP. But perched atop the exalted Gateway of the Sun, itself set in the sweeping, iconographic landscape of the high Andes, the artifacts take on new dimensions. In the romantico-scientific tradition then being invented, Rivero sought to create an exalted abode for artifacts in the Peruvian historical imagination.

The frontispiece of AP allegorized three primal aspects of the master text of historia patria. The patriotic trinity of icons is evident in the superimposed relief of the Inca dynasty on the "reconstructed" gateway itself; the natural landscape seen through and at the base of the gateway; and the diminutive native standing at the threshold, pictured as a benignly nuclear Andean pastoralist family with the Indian man pointing to the emblem held aloft by the mighty condor in flight. This holy trinity of secular icons seductively allegorized the schismatic inscription of the glorious native past and diminished native present in the landscape of the Peruvian national historical imagination.

The line of vision between ancient Inca glory (here represented in the iconical inscription of the Inca dynasty on the face of the gateway itself) and future national fulfillment (allegorized in the abundant natural resources of the land) is both drawn, and potentially interrupted, by the living Indian. More than mere "reference of scale" in pastoral pose (such posing as both perspectival and authenticating device remains familiar; today's postcards and tourist snapshots may still seem incomplete without "the native" presence. Today she may be the clever, fee-charging Indian woman in costume, llama on leash, ready to pose for the snapshot at Tiahuanaco, Sacsahuaman, or in the stone-paved plazas of Cuzco), the pointing native in this 1850s lithograph is none other than that inscriptive device that is so "necessary" for Creole national history. The pastoral scene is tranquil and the native man points upward and onward. "Our" national gaze is directed to the condor's banner while the eye, perhaps, gently drops to scan the Humboldtian landscape (conical volcanos, the high plateau, tropical montane flora and fauna) majestically framed by the nation's originary threshold.[38] It is a heavenly indigenist vision, transported to the timeless Peruvian land for the present and future of the secular nation.

The colonial predecessors of AP's allegorical arch may be found in eighteenth-century viceregal representations of ceremonial arches and of Inca and Spanish dynasts. Indeed, the nationalized ancient of AP's arch makes several direct references to imperial "ephemeral" arches.[39] The colonial design that perhaps best illustrates the genealogy of dynastic images was apparently the work of the Limean priest and historian Alonso de la Cueva. Cueva seems to have made the first Inca-Spanish iconographic genealogy for the ceremony in Lima in 1725 commemorating the coronation of King Luis I, although it appears that the letters of Nuñez Vela, written in the 1690s, exercised a strong influence on his design.[40]

As Gustavo Buntinx and Luis Eduardo Wuffarden note, Cueva's and subsequent geneologies, which depict the Spanish kings as the legitimate successors of the Incas, were not just imperial appropriations of the Inca mantle. Rather, these geneologies may also be seen to represent the Creole domestication or naturalization of the Spanish kings as Incas or "Peruvian emperors." Departing somewhat from the reading offered by Buntinx and Wuffarden—whose work follows in the interpretive path blazed by John Rowe, Manuel Burga, and Alberto Flores Galindo—here I prefer not to read this colonial domestication of the Spanish kings as the camouflaged expression of a utopian Inca nationalist movement associated with the native or mestizo nobility and supported by patriotic Creole conspirators. Rather, I wish to emphasize here that the Inca-Spanish genealogy also represents viceregal Lima's hegemonic pretensions as the place that synthesizes the two dynasties (Cuzco's and Madrid's) as one.[41] Read thus, Cueva's genealogy anticipates subsequent Limean Creole nationalist claims on the Incas,[42] including iconic representations like that which adorns the frontispiece of AP.

Cueva's iconography of Inca and Spanish dynasts was the model for José Villanueva y Palomino, who apparently first placed the portraits of the dynasts against an imperial arch. Published in Jorge Juan and Antonio de Ulloa's official Spanish travel account, *Relación histórica del viaje en América meridional* (1748),[43] the iconographic portraits of the fourteen "Peruvian monarchs" in the Villanueva y Palomino rendering of 1748 are identical with those on the frontispiece of AP (figure 3). The most notable differences between the arches that provide the allegorical background for the portraits are seen in the architectural style and in the setting. The eighteenth-century arch is rendered in the baroque style and was probably drawn from a model used for the ephemeral arches erected for regal and viceregal entries and religious processions in major "imperial" cities like Madrid, Lima, and Potosí.[44] In contrast, AP's arch is a modern neoclassical rendering of an "ancient Peruvian" ruin. The misty and ancient origins of the nation acquire, in the style of natural supernaturalism, the classical solidity of Roman inscriptions on a triumphal arch. The AP arch is necessarily set in a stylized Peruvian landscape likely influenced by the Humboldtian ideal. The imperial arch, in contrast, does not require an earthly landscape: Spanish Empire was universal.

In Villanueva y Palomino's representation of the dynastic arch printed in Juan and Ulloa's travel account, the Spanish monarchs succeed the Incas. In contrast, by pruning the successor Spanish monarchs from the Inca geneological tree and inscribing the Incan dynasty in an archway of ancient stonework set in a timeless Peruvian landscape, the frontispiece of AP resonates with the modern aesthetic archaism named "ancient Peru." Peruvian dynastic history is thus

3. Inca/Spanish dynasty of Peru. From Jorge Juan and Antonio de Ulloa, *Relación histórica del viage a la América Meridional* (Madrid, 1748). Photographic reproduction courtesy of the Library of Congress, Rare Book and Special Collections Reading Room, F2221.U45 1748.

"nationalized" and "naturalized" in graphic splendor: the Spanish kings are banished (indeed there is no iconographic space for them to occupy in the graphic field), the free land of Peru beckons, the glorious Inca past frames the Indian present and heralds the future of the nation.

According to Teresa Gisbert, the deployment in Spanish historical discourse of Incan dynastic iconography (which may have prehispanic origins) dates to the first official imperial history of Spanish deeds in Peru.[45] The frontispiece to court historian Antonio de Herrera's *Historia general de los hechos de los castellanos en las islas y tierra firme del mar oceano* (1615) differs from the two images discussed above, however. Herrera's graphic artist placed Manco Capac at the top center. In all, only thirteen Incas are represented. The "missing Inca" is Atahualpa, "bastard" son of Huayna Capac. Atahualpa is banished because in the Spanish imperial (but also Cuzco) version of the history of conquest and kingly succession, the "last Inca" was portrayed as a "tyrant" and king-killer who "usurped" the dynasty of Cuzco when he ordered the death of his half-brother, Huascar, the supposed "legitimate" heir to the throne. Having punished Atahualpa for the unspeakable act of regicide, in this official version of events Pizarro is credited with avenging the Inca dynasty of Cuzco and saving "Peru" from Atahualpa's impending reign of tyranny. Pizarro's execution of Atahualpa in Cajamarca is, therefore, not regicide but the administration of justice. Pizarro's intervention paved the way for succession from the late Huayna Capac, via the prematurely deceased prince regent Huascar, to the benificent and magnificent Carlos V, holy Roman emperor and (Carlos I) of the Spains, and soon "of All the World." Notably, this narrative of conquest was kept alive in Madrid at least as late as the 1780s, when it was dramatized in officially sponsored theatrical performances for the monarchs.[46]

Pizarro's deeds at Cajamarca were the object of diverse interpretation in Spanish and Creole historical writing, particularly in the seventeenth and eighteenth centuries.[47] Pizarro was variously accused of deceit, greed, and/or grave misunderstanding, even of murder and regicide. In Villanueva y Palomino's Inca-Spanish genealogy, for example, Atahualpa is restored as the "Fourteenth Emperor of Peru" while Carlos V occupies the fifteenth slot. This Creole patriotic solution to the dilemma of Atahualpa appears to find its textual echo in Córdova y Urrutia's history, discussed above.

As several scholars have noted, some early postcolonial-nationalist representations of the dynastic line of "Peruvian emperors" erase King Carlos III from the central medallion or oval frame and substitute an image of Bolívar or San Martín. Villanueva y Palomino's imperial arch remains as the necessary genealogical architecture (AP's ancient national arch was still improbable).[48] At first glance the view of a republican liberator portrayed in an imperial dynastic frame invites irony. Bolívar had assumed the liberation of Peru from San Martín and, although he had read his Garcilaso and his Las Casas (author of the foundational Black Legend text, *Brief Relation of the Destruction of the Indies*), in things political he was more persuaded by Rousseau. Hailed as an Inca by some, the Creole republican from Venezuela proceeded with haste to abolish all Peruvian aristocracies and dynasties.[49] Yet it should be noted that Bolívar's republican abolition did little to deter certain Peruvian Creoles from investigating Inca origins and representing Inca dynasts in historical narratives of the nation.[50]

Like many Peruvian histories written in the nineteenth century, *Las tres epocas del Perú o compendio de su historia* was deeply indebted to the *Comentarios reales* of Garcilaso de la Vega. In Córdova y Urrutia's foundational national history, physical "Peru" itself was the work of giants who had separated the land from the water, extracting the Andes from the Asiatic archipelagos sometime after Hercules had opened up the Mediterranean. *Las tres epocas* also confirms the civilizing and Christianizing mission of the Incas (the apostles Thomas and Bartholomew had "announced the Holy Scriptures in these regions" centuries before the arrival of the Spaniards) in Peru. And in Córdova y Urrutia as in Lorente, the original "son of the Sun" who laid the "indestructible foundations of the national unity of Peru" had a proper name: Manco Capac.

Blazing the path of historia patria, Córdova y Urrutia had rejected the scientific speculations of certain European savants and Creole pensadores who suggested that the mythical founder of the Inca dynasty was probably not "Peruvian" at all. In fine patriotic style, Córdova y Urrutia indignantly exclaimed that "this [speculation] has reached the extreme of depriving us of the glory of Manco Capac's being born in our country, persuading [us] instead [to believe] that he came from some foreign land."[51] The Peruvian historian desists from Humboldt's suggestion that Manco Capac's laws were "Asian," and he finds Ranking's claim that Manco had been a "son of the Gran Kublai Khan"[52] equally wanting. Instead, Córdova y Urrutia cites a version of the Ayar Brothers myth and insists that both Manco Capac and Mama Ocllo (the original Inca queen mother) undoubtedly "came from a small island in Lake Titicaca" (figure 4). Thus Córdova y Urrutia takes an early patriotic stand in a heated historical debate that would rage off and on for the duration of the nineteenth century: Who was the founder of "Peruvian" civilization? Was he Peruvian, Aryan, Chinese, Hindu, or perhaps Mongolian? Was Inca civilization derivative of some "foreign," probably "Asiatic" or "Oriental," civilization? Or were the Incas "indigenous" to "Peru?"

The Manco Capac question was informed by the schism that imperial and national histories had opened between the "glorious" native past and the "miserable" native present, but as the century pro-

MANCO CAPAC y MAMA OCLLO

4. Manco Capac and Mama Oclla. From Mariano Eduardo de Rivera and Juan Diego, de Tschudi, *Antigüedades Peruanas*, vol. 1 (Vienna, 1851), frontispiece. Photographic reproduction courtesy of Library of Congress.

gressed the schism and the origin question it raised were increasingly answered in the racialist terms of the new sciences of "comparative lexicography" and "anthropology." The question of Inca origins occupied many nineteenth-century minds. Learned books and reports pursued the original Inca via a variety of methods, including lexicography, comparative anatomy, and archaeology. Scholars with and without academic credentials published evidence that argued for the Aryan, Chinese, Japanese, Hindi, or Peruvian origins of Manco Capac (and of his Quechua language).

In the 1840s the Anglo-American physician and craniologist Samuel G. Morton proposed that two "races" had once inhabited ancient Peru. For Morton, one race was superior (undoubtedly the Inca) while the other was "common" Quechua, or Indian. Morton's work on Egyptian and Peruvian skulls appears to have circulated widely, and his views apparently exercised some influence in Peru.[53] Nevertheless, Peruvian Creoles like Mariano de Rivero favored the views of the versatile Jacob von Tschudi. An early Peruvianist in the round sense of the term, Tschudi had carried out extensive field and linguistic researches in Peru. In contrast to Morton, he argued that skeletal and lexicographic evidence suggested that not two but three, more or less equally endowed, "races" (which, being the linguist that he was, he named "Aymara," "Quechua," and "Chincha") had populated ancient Peru.

In 1890, Manuel García y Merino and Teodorico Olacchea published a pamphlet under the title *Antigüedades nacionales* (*National Antiquities*, henceforth AN).[54] This publication was a collection of previously published field reports. Among these was a report from an 1866 archaeological excavation in the south-central coastal region of Ica. The Ica report boasted an illustration of an unearthed *huaca*, or idol, inscribed with Chinese characters (figure 5). The character inscriptions on the Buddha/huaca supported the theory that Manco Capac had been Chinese. Notably, the faulty Chinese inscription on the Buddha/huaca of Ica evoked the notion of oriental despotism then associated in the Western scholarly imagination with centralized control of irrigation.[55]

Whatever their scientific standing, such reports resonated with the Creole-dominated postcolonial order. Peru's coastal planters were then engaged in a raging national debate over immigration. Liberal elites wanted to restrict immigration to white Europeans so as to "improve the race" and foster "civilization" in frontier regions of the republic. Facing the decline of slavery, Peru's coastal sugar barons needed *brazos*, or fieldhands, and that meant Chinese bonded laborers. Ica was the first plantation region in Peru to import Chinese bonded laborers (and, one must now assume, Buddhas and Chinese characters). Although further research is required to resolve the suspicion, the archaeological "discovery" of the Buddha/huaca of

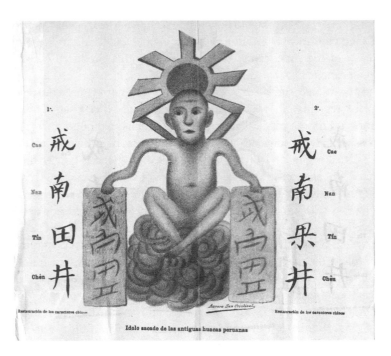

Idolo sacado de las antiguas huacas peruanas

5. The Buddha of Ica. From Manuel García y Merino and Teodorico Olaechea, "Relaciones entre los antiguos peruanos y los chinos," in *Antigüedades Nacionales: Recopilacion de los articulos publicados sobre esta materia en la "Ilustracion Americana"* (Lima, 1890). Image courtesy of Latin American Pamphlet Collection, Manuscripts and Archives, Yale University Library.

Ica may well have been intended to lend support to planter arguments that the Chinese were not the "undesirable" immigrants that Lima's racialist liberal elite supposed. No dusty pamphlet emblazoned "Manco Capac, First Chinese Immigrant" has yet emerged in Peru's archives—but my surprise would not be too great if it did.

The Creole desire to find legitimate historical precedent for their postcolonial rule was not universally felt in literate Peru, and it does not by itself explain the demise by the close of the century of the various foreign-origin hypotheses among serious intellectuals. Strong arguments against foreign origins were made throughout the nineteenth century, both by Peruvian and foreign intellectuals. Among the foreigners, perhaps the Englishman Sir Clements Markham made the Americanist or indigenist argument for Inca origins most forcefully, first in the 1860s and then at greater length in his classic *History of Peru* (1895).[56] In any case, any residual hope in the idea that Manco Capac (and Inca civilization) was "foreign" would fade in the rosy dawn of the Americanist twentieth century that produced Martí's "Our America."

The national sun of the Peruvian dawn has not yet set. "Ancient Peru" remains on proud exhibit at the rites of official nationalism and in the generous imaginations of Peruvians, although today the artifacts of the ancients are just as likely to be drawn from the so-called regional civilizations ("Mochica" or "Huari" or "Tiahuanaco") of the pre-Inca periods (or "horizons"), perhaps representing the new "multiculturalism" and the ever-stronger presence of Limeans with roots in the provincial elite. Thus, the recently excavated, two-thousand-year-old "Lord of Sipán" was warmly greeted in 1997 by government officials in the central plaza of Lima, with the familiar eulogy: "If the past was grandiose, the future will be ours." The festive event was reported by Lima's leading daily, El Comercio, as "the rediscovery of national identity by way of the millenarian Mochica culture . . . The central plaza [of Lima] was the scene last night of an encounter of Peruvianness between the man of today and the northern ruler [of Sípan] of eighteen centuries past . . . a dialogue in song of the millenarian riches of our country, the love of the land, and the many legacies of our ancestors."[57]

The eighteen-century-old Peruvian lord has had a remarkable diplomatic career on the international circuits. Christened "Peruvian ambassador to the world" he toured the world's museums, and on his return he was received by President Fujimori at the Jorge Chávez International Airport with all the official ceremony of a former head of state. What has become unthinkable in the historical imagination and profitable in the political sphere (and, thankfully, illegal under international law) is a past for "Peru" that should not belong to "Peruvians." National history thus effaces its finitude in the topological unisonance of names. Archaeology's artifacts can only confirm the unisonance. This unisonance of names is the true "patrimony" of the nation.

IMAGINING THE LEGACY OF THE INCA STATE

Parallel to the race-influenced debate on Inca origins ran another, related discussion on the nature of the precolonial Inca political system and its legacy. In 1847 the influential Anglo-American historian William H. Prescott published a short essay on the Incas as foreground to his *History of the Conquest of Peru*.[58] Prescott's two-volume work was quickly translated into Spanish and soon gained a place on the bookshelves of the Peruvian intelligentsia. Prescott blamed the decline of Peru not only on Spanish misrule, as any good nineteenth-century liberal would, but more profoundly on an abiding legacy of Inca despotism. Parting with Garcilaso's utopian vision of Inca civilization but maintaining a sense of wonderment, Prescott's protestant liberalism viewed the "semi-barbarian" Inca state as a totalitarian system that had left a deep imprint on the Indians, in effect squelching the indispensable "individual energies" otherwise necessary for progress.

Prescott was physically blind but that did not stop him from imagining the ancient ruins of Peru in terms that mixed wonder with dismay. For Prescott the so-called Inca fortress at Sacsahuaman (which he never visited) told an astonishing history of despotism:

> We are filled with astonishment when we consider that these enormous masses were hewn from their native bed and fashioned into shape by people ignorant of the use of iron . . . without the knowledge of tools and machinery familiar to the European. Twenty thousand men are said to have been employed in this great structure, and fifty years consumed in the building. However this may be, we see in it the workings of a despotism which had the lives and fortunes of its vassals at its absolute disposal, and which, however mild in its general character, esteemed these vassals, when employed in its service, as lightly as the brute animals for which they served as a substitute.[59]

Prescott could also not resist commenting on Tiahuanaco and the fabled "ruins around Lake Titicaca." For the Yankee skeptic, Manco Capac was merely a "figment of the vain imagination of Peruvian monarchs." Yet his dismissive stance does not keep Prescott from upholding Morton's finding that the Incas were indeed "a superior race" that once inhabited the imposing ruins of the Lake Titicaca basin. But Prescott the historian is not interested in the origins of this superior race—that is a matter for "speculative antiquarians" not real historians. Inca origins, Prescott noted, lie in "a land of darkness that lies far beyond the domain of history."[60]

As we have seen in the cases of Córdova y Urrutia and Lorente, Prescott's forbidden "land of darkness" necessarily fell very much *within* the domain of national history.[61] Prescott's liberal Protestant reading of the enduring effects of an Inca despotism became respectable currency among Peruvian writers, particularly during and following the plutocratic 1870s. Following the orthodox liberal-nationalist narrative of the Black Legend, in 1885 Peruvian journalist and would-be ethnologist Luis Carranza argued that Spanish conquest and the Catholic Church had "atrophied our indigenous race" like "the mammoths of Siberia" in an "Ice Age" of prerational "sentimentalism" and "servility." After Prescott and the positivist currents of the day, Carranza also admitted that Inca rule had "predisposed our indigenous race to servility."[62] By calling Inca rule despotic and "communist" (rather than classical and utopian, as in the garcilasista tradition), Carranza sounded a theme that was increasingly resonant in Peru by century's end, when visions of an archaic and glorious Inca past gave way to more resigned judgments regarding the long-term effects of a deeply rooted indigenous despotism. In Carranza's liberal-positivist narrative,[63] the Inca past was no longer severed from the indigenous present. It had a dreaded and dragging hold on the present that hindered Peru's progress. Both the Inca and "the indigenous race" they ruled were now, for better or for worse, "ours."[64]

CLOSING REFLECTIONS ON THE RUINS

As Anderson and Bhabha have noted, the ambivalent cultural temporality of the nation "always loom[s] out of an immemorial past and . . . glide[s] effortlessly into a limitless future."[65] But between the immemorial and the limitless lie the genealogical structures of national historical narratives. These structures are not unique to Peru. In Mexico, the inscribed gulf between the "glorious" native past of Toltecs and Aztecs and the "miserable" native present of Indians was tactically deployed by Creole patriotic clerics to lend historical legitimacy to the cause of independence.[66] By citing the present "miserable" condition of the "Indian" as living proof of the cruel exploitation and "despotism" of Spanish rule, Mexican Creoles staked out the high ground for the liberation of the vanquished native land named "Anahuac." Similar inscriptions of the native past and present are found in Argentine, Venezuelan, and Chilean independence narratives—to name only those with which I have some familiarity.[67]

Such narrative structures appear not to be unique to Spanish American histories. In the civilizing discourse of British colonial rule in India, for example, the "archaic" and glorious past invented by European orientalist scholarship was also severed from the decadent or "primitive" native of the colonial present, thereby justifying British rule in the name of civilization.[68] Nor was the colonial schism entirely banished in the "Indian history" written by the culturally Creole "Indian" nationalists. As Partha Chatterjee has argued, the narrative structure of modern, postdynastic (or post-Puranic) "Indian history" in the late nineteenth century was largely derived from European schemata. Indeed, colonial European historiography could applaud the new nationalist narrative of "Indian history" because it generally agreed with a European master narrative and periodicity. "India" thus found its "classical past" in a Hindu golden age that produced the first "national" unification of the subcontinent. India's classical age was then eclipsed by the "medieval darkness" of the Musulman "invasion." Later, this "dark period" was transcended by a nationalist renaissance under British rule that eventually generated a "critique of illegitimate Company rule." The nationalist critique was led by colonially educated "Indian" elites who claimed to simultaneously represent material modernity and a "spiritual" return to the "golden age" of subcontinental unity, thus heralding the break with British rule. Chatterjee also notes that Bakimchandra's national history was made "Indian" by virtue of the naturalization of an "us" in a timeless geography with a proper name: "India." This Indian "us" was the subject of a temporally schismatic, ostensibly all-indigenous formula: "ancient glory, present misery."[69]

In Peru, the imagined "us" of national history was more ambivalent. The Creole "us" was haunted by a domestically distant and sometimes threatening indigenous "them," a compatriot subaltern condemned by liberal history to inhabit the nation's prehistorical golden age. But this dead golden age that was the future promise of national history would reemerge in the scientific (langu)age of race as the living legacy of indigenous despotism, the Creole burden of "our indigenous race."

If history "in the ordinary sense is a series of events that happen to subjects who are generally designated by proper names," per Rancière, then in the writing of Peruvian history, as in the writing of the history of, say, France, "the king" was conceptually dethroned (after the event) by "the native land" whose same-named subject—the national Peruvian "us"—was bound in territorial nativity to her name.[70] But in the nineteenth-century American historical imagination "Peru" was not merely one more metonym for "France." Nineteenth-century European history, and indeed the discipline of history in the West, was typically either the "history of country" or kingly imperial history, or both. Postcolonial national histories were this and perhaps something more in the Spanish Americas, where authors negotiated the ambivalent relationship/descent of the Creole to the classical "Latin" West. The kingly imperial logic of the subject named "Peru" thus suffered, after the political rupture of independence, an ambiguous theoretical death that facilitated the gestation of a republican "history of country." This regicide in the domain of history was postponed and mediated by the Creole nationalist conjuring of "our" precolonial Incas in the dynastic mode of historical representation, perhaps because this mode had the great advantage of providing a deep temporal continuity for the precarious new nation. The republican embrace of *patria* eventually naturalized the history of the nation, however, dethroning kings and Incas in the harmony of the native land and its native-born inhabitants.

This historical harmony of the "Peruvian" was not deaf to the droning dissonance of colonial contradictions, which under the postcolonial Creole republic was eventually recast by the positivist discourse of race. Under the discourse of race the colonial schism in history was threatened with an extinction: the native past would meet the native present on the grounds of an indigenous despotism. The scene was set for the embattled emergence of complicit twentieth-century contestations. In the 1930s indigenist anthropology would take up the redemptive task of linking a glorious native past to a revivalist native present. The new "ethnohistory" of the 1950s would continue this work under more scientific auspices. It would be another beginning in an as yet unacknowledged genealogy of history—the ending of which has only recently become imaginable.[71]

NOTES

I wish to thank Andrés Guerrero and Alejandra Osorio for critical readings of this essay. I also wish to thank the Wenner-Gren workshop participants for many useful comments. The research for this essay was carried out with support from the Social Science Research Council and the American Council of Learned Societies, the National Endowment for the Humanities, the Fulbright-Hays Program of the U.S. Department of Education, and the University of Florida. I gratefully acknowledge each of these funding agencies. Note that all translations are mine unless indicated otherwise.

1 The term used in the early 1820s by the Liberator of Peru, José de San Martín and by other Creole patriots was not postcolonial but "ex-colonial." Likewise, the colonial subject was initially dubbed the "ex-Indian" in Peru.

2 This new science was literary, political, and pedagogical, and its Latinate homonym was, and remains still, "history." On "history" as homonym, see Jacques Rancière, *The Names of History: On the Poetics of Knowledge* (Minnesota: University of Minnesota Press, 1994). Benedict Anderson, in *Imagined Communities: Reflections on the Origins and Spread of Nationalism* (London: Verso, 2nd ed. 1991), accents the coevality of the nation and of history as institutional sites of vernacular knowledge.

3 On the eighteenth-century philosophical histories, see Jorge Cañizares-Esguerra, *How to Write the History of the New World: Histories, Epistemologies, Identities in the Eighteenth-Century Atlantic World* (Stanford: Stanford University Press, 2002).

4 Cecilia Méndez argues that the split or schism in native antique (Inca) past versus native Indian present emerged in Lima's 1830s Creole nationalism, particularly vis-à-vis Santa Cruz and the Peru-Bolivia Confederation, but it is now clear that the 1830s episode was preceded by earlier ones; see her "Incas sí, indios no: Notes on Peruvian Creole Nationalism and Its Contemporary Crisis," *Journal of Latin American Studies* 28 (1996): 197–225. Franklin Pease also points out the schism between the glorious Inca past and the miserable Indian present in nineteenth-century travel and history writing on Peru (*Peru: Hombre e Historia: La República*, vol. 3 [Lima: EDUBANCO, 1993]). In *From Two Republics to One Divided: Contradictions of Postcolonial Nationmaking in Andean Peru* (Durham: Duke University Press, 1997) I point out the presence of the schism in mid-1700s discourse, drawing on the works of Anthony Pagden and David Brading. J. Rabasa has pushed the splitting of preColombian pasts from Indian presents further back still to Carlos Siguenza y Gongora's account of the 1692 riots in Mexico City, if not earlier; see his "Precolumbian Pasts and Indian Presents in Mexican History," *Dispositio/n* 46 (1996 [1994]): 245–70.

5 See Thurner, *From Two Republics to One Divided*.

6 Mark Thurner, "Después de la etnohistoria," in Franklin Pease, ed., *Actas del IV Congreso Internacional de Etnohistoria*, vol. 2 (Lima: Pontificia Universidad Católica del Perú, 1998), 459–85.

7 Mariano de Rivero and Jacob von Tschudi, *Antigüedades Peruanas*, vol. 2 (Vienna, 1851), iii.

8 Sebastian Lorente, *Historia antigua del Perú* (Lima, 1860), 7–9.

9 On Garcilasco de la Vega's exegesis *Primera parte de los comentarios reales de los incas* [1609], see Margarita Zamora, *Language, Authority and Indige-*

nous History in the *"Comentarios Reales de los Incas,"* (Cambridge: Cambridge University Press, 1988).

10 Lorente was only doing what most nineteenth-century liberal-nationalist historical narratives did: narrativize the precolonial as a lost golden age of classical antiquity (e.g., Garcilaso had compared Cuzco to Rome). For Lorente not all was golden in this age, however. Working in the liberal Spanish tradition, Lorente rejected the more facile and patriotic versions of the Black Legend narrative of Spanish misrule, and he made the standard liberal critiques of Incan "communism." Nevertheless, Lorente's liberal history was a far cry from the apologetic and reactionary history of such figures as the Spanish Hispanist R. Cappa, who drew the wrath of such Peruvian liberals as Ricardo Palma.

11 Lorente, *Historia Antigua,* 4.

12 See, for example, the diatribe signed "Los Peruanos" in the August 7, 1867, edition of *El Comercio.* These rival "Peruvians" objected to Lorente having landed the government contract to publish the *memorias de los virreyes* (official reports of the viceroys) as well as other documents in his possession.

13 Lorente was the favorite of Peru's powerful caudillo and liberal state-builder Ramón Castilla and his education minister Saavedra, who commissioned Lorente to produce histories and memoirs.

14 In eighteenth-century French travel writing "Peruvian" was commonly interchanged with "Incan" or *indigene.* The latter term was apparently first used by the French to refer to colonized native peoples. Excolonial national historians like Lorente drew on early colonial chronicles and eighteenth-century French and Anglo historical and travel writings. Unlike most of his Peruvian contemporaries—most of whom wrote biographical sketches or chronological, duly footnoted political annals of the independence wars and elite political intrigues—Lorente wrote in a critical, didactic, and "philosophical spirit," sweeping across nearly the entire storied human past in the fabled land named Peru, from "primitive" pre-Incan peoples to the present Peruvian republic. Lorente himself referred to his philosophical mode of history as *historia crítica*—an antipositivist, liberal mode of history writing that openly and stylishly drew moral lessons for the present and future of its intended readership. As rector of Lima's leading liberal private academy and as the favored historian of the liberal and rich-by-guano Castilla regime, Lorente wrote and published voluminous tomes as well as pocket-sized "catechisms" for Peruvian schoolboys. For this he was taken to task in subsequent decades by Peru's positivist and neopositivist historians, many of whom considered Lorente's work

too vulgar, unsubstantiated, and dangerously close to plagiarism. In the early twentieth century Lorente was virtually expunged from the list of serious Peruvian historians.

15 The name "Peruvian" was not invented by postcolonial-national historiography. Rather, it appears to have begun its career in the conquest chronicles. As such, José de San Martín's famous decree of 1821— which abolished the "degrading sign of empire" which he took "Indian" to be and declared all "Indians and Naturals" to be "Peruvians"—is not quite the "neologism" that Anderson imagined (except in the limited sense that it was a new deployment of the term in official political discourse, albeit one with unimagined consequences). "Peruvian" as applied to "ex-Indians" faded in official Peruvian political discourse after San Martín's pushy successor, Simón Bolívar, officially displaced it with the enlightened colonial francophile term "indigene." But "Peruvian" could live on in national historical discourse as the name of the native inhabitants of Peru. The historical referent of the word "Peruvian" often included an "us" that went beyond the native, however, to include the imagined compatriot everyman from precolonial Incas to contemporary Creoles and lowly "indigenes." It is ironic and perhaps telling that twentieth-century anthropological (ethnohistorical and indigenist) discourse embraced Bolívar's "indigenes" and eventually introduced the archaeo-topological and *annaliste* notion of "the Andean," but found it unseemly to labor under the colonial/excolonial national names of "Indian" and "Peruvian."

16 José Martí, *Nuestra América* (Havana: Centro de Estudios Martianos/ Casa de las Américas, [1891] 1991), 18.

17 See Eric Wertheimer, *Imagined Empires: Incas, Aztecs, and the New World of American Literature, 1771–1876* (Cambridge: Cambridge University Press, 1999).

18 See Anthony Pagden, *Spanish Imperialism and the Political Imagination* (New Haven: Yale University Press, 1990).

19 The probable author of this anonymous commentary, which appeared in the October 23, 1868, issue of *El Comercio*, is either Lorente or Luis Carranza.

20 Pease, *Perú*, vol. 3, 93–128. José María de Córdova y Urrutia, *Las tres epocas del Perú o compendio de su historia* (Lima, 1844).

21 The state-sponsored publication of the *Memorias de los Virreyes* was key to this project. Sebastian Lorente had edited, albeit controversially, the first collection of *Memorias*.

22 Subsequently a fourth period was added by Lorente and others; this was the "formative" or "pre-Inca" period, which is also present, although in somewhat different language, in Garcilaso.

23 As noted, subsequently subdivided into "pre-Inca" and "Inca" periods. Today the "pre-Inca" is subdivided by archaeologists in various "horizons" and regional cultures.

24 The primal scene of the "Death of Atahualpa"—previously thought to have disappeared from the scene in the postindependence period—appeared regularly in the arts of the nineteenth century, particularly as the subject of Creole figural painting but also in history writing. At the height of liberal indianism, Luis Montero donated his romantic painting *The Funeral of Atahualpa* (1868) to the Peruvian Congress. Today it hangs in the stairwell of the Museo de Arte in Lima. Popular dramatizations of the "Death of Atahualpa" in Andean villages were also not expunged in the nineteenth century.

25 These two branches of patriotic Incaism in Peru have often been overlooked by historians who tend to conflate the Atahualpa and the Huascar lineages. In certain versions the Cuzco-centric lineage passed from Huascar via Pizarro to the neo-Incas of Vilcabamba and Tupac Amaru and then to the Spanish kings, who in fact were key to its maintenance. The Atahualpa lineage—considered illegitimate by those who favored the Huascar line—did not necessarily require the Spanish kings because of the obvious problem presented by Pizarro. Further research is needed, for example, on the different meanings of Pizarro's encounter with Atahualpa as enacted in the "Death of Atahualpa" dramatizations. The fact that in many such dramatizations Atahualpa triumphs over Pizarro may not necessarily have meant that the dramatization was pro-Tupacamarista, but rather quite the opposite. Another question to consider is if different genealogical readings of conquest and revindication were implicated in the Juan Santos Atahualpa and Tupac Amaru II insurrections.

26 Humboldt's romantico-scientific tableau of Mexican pyramids set in an iconic tropical landscape had stimulated the visual emergence of the ancient in the Creole historical imagination.

27 That these ruins lie on the then occasionally disputed Bolivian side of the border is another story I will leave for another time.

28 Cieza was of the opinion that the ruins at Tiahuanaco were "la mas antigua de todo el Peru" (the most ancient in all Peru). Pedro de Cieza de Leon, *Crónica del Perú*, ch. 105 [1533; reprint, Lima: PUCP, 1984].

29 Humboldt had sojourned to Cajamarca in northern highland Peru—the primal scene of Atahualpa's execution at the hands of Pizarro—but he did not travel to the southern highlands. See his *Vue des cordilleres*, 199.

30 Baalbek is on the site of Heliopolis, the ancient Phoenician city.

Ephraim George Squier, *Peru: Incidents of Travel and Exploration in the Land of the Incas* (New York: Harper, 1877), 272.

31 Ibid., 302–3.

32 Ibid., 303.

33 Tschudi had not visited Tiahuanaco during his first stay in Peru (1838–1842). Thus, he had not actually seen the Gateway of the Sun before the publication of his and Mariano de Rivera's *Antigüedades Peruanas* in 1841. See fig. 2. He appears to have visited Tiahuanaco at some point during his second trip to South America in 1857 to 1859.

34 Squier, *Peru*, 303–4.

35 D. Poole, "Landscape and the Imperial Subject: U.S. Images of the Andes, 1859–1930," in *Close Encounters of Empire: Writing the Cultural History of U.S.-Latin American Relations*, ed. Gilbert Joseph, Catherine C. LeGrand, and Ricardo D. Salvatore (Durham: Duke University Press, 1998), 106–38.

36 The first volume of *AP* was published by Rivero in Lima in 1841.

37 Peru's Museo Nacional was founded in Lima in 1825 but not installed until 1836. In the museum, Rivero noted in *AP*, "one [could] encounter an immense number of Indian antiquities which demonstrate the Culture of our ancestors."

38 On the Humboldtian trinity, see Mary Louise Pratt, *Imperial Eyes: Travel Writing and Transculturation* (London: Routledge, 1992).

39 The Museo de America in Madrid holds Melchor Perez Holguin's painting of the viceregal entry of Archbishop Morcillo to Potosí in 1716, which depicts an imposing ephemeral arch at the far right. At the top of this arch stands the figure of an Inca brandishing the imperial Spanish flag of the cross. The architecture of this ephemeral arch is more ornate than the one depicted in Juan and Ulloa, but in other ways it exhibits many standard features. Seven gilded frames are hung on the face of the Potosí arch, but the pictures in the frames cannot be made out. There also appears to be a large bird, possibly an eagle or condor, in roughly the same position as in the Rivero imaginary ancient arch. Standing in the threshold of the arch, but facing the rear of the viceregal procession that has already entered the city, are what appear to be two Inca subjects, possibly *doncellas* (virgins), in festive costume.

40 See Gustavo Buntinx and Luis Eduardo Wuffarden, "Incas y reyes en la pintura colonial peruana: La estela de Garcilaso," *Margenes* 8 (Lima, 1991): 151–209.

41 My reading is based on arguments presented by Alejandra Osorio in "Inventing Lima: The Making of an Early Modern Colonial Capital, ca. 1540–ca. 1640" (Ph.D. diss., Ann Arbor: UMI, 2001).

42 On Lima's Creole nationalist claims on the Incas in the 1830s, see Méndez, "Incas si, indios no."

43 Teresa Gisbert, *Iconografía y mitos indígenas en el arte* (La Paz: Gisbert, 1980).

44 Unfortunately, few paintings or descriptions of these ephemeral arches in Peru have been preserved. There are several paintings, however, that include ephemeral arches used in Cuzco's religious processions, and some descriptions for viceregal entries in Lima (Alejandra Osorio, personal communication).

45 Gisbert, *Iconografía y mitos*, 118. Spanish historian José Antonio Maravall, in *Carlos V y el pensamiento político del Renacimiento* (Madrid: Instituto de Estudios Políticos, 1960) has argued that Philipe II invented the royal genealogy as an emblem of power. The notion of dynastic genealogy evidently infused historical apprehensions of Inca rule in the early postconquest chronicles, but the source of those apprehensions is subject to scholarly debate. In *Reading Inca History* (Iowa City: University of Iowa Press, 2000) Catherine Julien argues that the official dynastic genealogy of Manco Capac was invented in precolonial times as a means for controlling succession among the various *panacas*, or "royal" lineages of Cuzco.

46 The proposed program and script for the dramatic performance of the Death of Atahualpa drama in Madrid in 1784 is described in Christoval María Cortés, *Atahualpa: Tragedia premiada por la Villa de Madrid . . . con motivo de los festejos publicos que executa por el feliz nacimiento de los serenisimos infantes Carlos y Felipe y ajuste definitivo de la paz* (Madrid, 1784). Consulted in the Sala de Investigación de la Biblioteca Nacional del Perú (hereafter B N P / S 1).

47 For one reading of three such views, see Patricia Seed, "Failing to Marvel: Atahualpa's Encounter with the Word," *Latin American Research Review* 26 (1991): 7–32.

48 Gisbert, *Iconografía*.

49 See Tristan Platt, "Simón Bolívar, the Sun of Justice, and the Amerindian Virgen: Andean Conceptions of the *Patria* in Nineteenth-Century Potosí," *Journal of Latin American Studies* 25 (1993): 159–85.

50 Most notable was Justo Apu Sahuaraura's self-promoting *Recuerdos de la monarquía peruana* (Paris, 1850), drafted during Santa Cruz's Peru-Bolivia Confederation of the late 1830s. Sahuaraura, prebendary in the cathedral of Cuzco, doctor of theology, and general inspector for the bishopric, decorated with the medal of the liberator Simón Bolívar, was, like Santa Cruz himself, something of a liberal Incaist (indeed, if we are to accept his geneological claim to being the last living descendent of the Incas, a "liberal Inca").

Liberal-nationalist Incaism in the Bolivarian vein appears strongest in the southern sierra of Peru and in northern Bolivia under Santa Cruz, and may be seen as something of a highland nationalist discourse that rivaled coastal Lima's Creole Incaism. It is ironic that this highland liberal Incaism, associated politically with Santa Cruz's Bolivarian project of Andean unification, was racialized as "Indian" (not Incan) by Lima's Creole elite, who thereby laid claim (or rather reasserted, since this claim was made long before), as Cecilia Méndez as argued in "Incas sí, indios no," to the nationalist mantle of "Inca" identity for itself.

Despite the fact that Sahuaraura's ancestors sided with the king of Spain and fought against the rebel Tupac Amaru II in 1780, the prebend appears to be the first notable Peruvian intellectual to have championed Tupac Amaru as "precursor" of independence, as evidenced by a manuscript submitted to Cuzco's journal *Museo Erudito* in 1837 and now held in the BNP/SI. In this manuscript Sahuaraura transcribes Spanish General Inspector Areche's "barbarous" decree ordering the execution of Tupac Amaru and the suppression of hereditary chieftaincies. In the preamble, Sahuaraura claims to have adhered to the *sistema de patria* (patriotic system) in 1814 (Pumacahua's revolt) and to have contributed to the war effort of the *Ejercito Libertador* in the Ayacucho campaign of 1824. Sahuaraura's Cuzco-centric dynastic representation logically excludes Atahualpa (who must be illegitimate) and adds the sometimes rebel neo-Incas of Vilcabamba who followed from Huascar: Sairi Tupac, Manco Inca, and Tupac Amaru I (from whom Tupac Amaru II claims descent). Notably, the prebend also pictures Francisco Pizarro, who was key to the succession of the line and, of course, himself.

51 Córdova y Urrutia, *Las tres épocas.*

52 John Ranking, *Historical Researches on the Conquest of Peru . . . by the Mongols* (London: Longman, 1827), 170.

53 Samuel G. Morton, *Crania americana* (Philadelphia, 1829).

54 Manuel García y Merino and Teodorico Olaechea, *Antigüedades Nacionales: Recopilacion de los articulos publicados sobre esta materia en la "Ilustracion Americana"* (Lima: Escuela de Ingenieros, 1890).

55 My thanks to Rebecca Karl for translating the characters, flagging the errors of script, and pointing out their contemporary meaning.

56 Clements Markham, *History of Peru* (Chicago: Sergel, 1892). Markham argues the indigenous side in his *Travels in Peru and India* (London: J. Murry, 1862).

57 *El Comercio*, July 6, 1997.

58 W. Prescott, *History of the Conquest of Peru*, vol. 1 (1847; Philadephia: Lippincott, 1874).

59 Ibid., 20.

60 Ibid., 14.

61 Lorente, in seeming reference to Prescott, writes: "Pudiera inferirse . . . que los antiguos tiempos del Peru en parte tenebrosos y en parte fabulosos estan fuera del dominio de la historia . . . No podemos renunciar a una historia tan instructiva como interesante" (One could infer . . . that Peru's tenebrous and fabulous ancient past lies outside the domain of history . . . [But] we cannot renounce a history that is so instructive and interesting). (*Historia Antigua*, 15–16).

62 Luis Carranza, "Apuntes sobre la raza indígena—condiciones físicas e intelectuales del indio—indole artístico." *El Comercio*, May 29, 1885.

63 The complex Luis Carranza (who was probably mestizo but denied it) also wrote far less pessimistic narratives of the indigenous future. On these more optimistic forecasts, see Paul Gootenberg, *Imagining Development: Economic Ideas in Peru's "Fictitious Prosperity" of Guano, 1840–1888* (Berkeley: University of California Press, 1993).

64 It was not, as previous arguments have it, the indigenists of the 1930s who abolished the schism between the native past and the native present. Rather, indigenists made the link positive but also archaizing, because the living natives were valued only to the extent that they carried the legacy of the glorious Inca past. See Frank Salomon, "The Historical Development of Andean Ethnology," *Mountain Research and Development* 5.1 (1985): 79–98.

65 Homi Bhabha, "Introduction: Narrating the Nation," in *Nation and Narration*, ed. Homi Bhabha (London: Routledge, 1990), 1. See also Anderson, *Imagined Communities*.

66 Pagden, *Spanish Imperialism*; and Brading, *The First America: Spanish Monarchy, Creole Patriots, and the Liberal State, 1492–1867* (New York: Cambridge University Press, 1991).

67 Mark Thurner, "Los indios y las repúblicas, 1830–1880," in *Historia de América Andina; Vol. 5: Creación de las repúblicas y formación de la nación*, general ed. Enrique Ayala Mora (Quito: Universidad Andina Simón Bolívar, in press). Brading argues in *The First America* that the presence of a subordinate but insurrectionary native elite in and around Cuzco (Tupac Amaru and company) made Peruvian Creoles hesitate at the prospect of an Inca heritage for the new nation they would rule. But this threat that the Tupac Amaru insurrection represented, which in any case only involved a fraction of the indigenous elite, was soon domesticated by those indigenous elites who had opposed it. Among them was the Cuzco prebend Justo "Apu" Sahauraura, who made Tupac Amaru a "precursor" of Peruvian independence. Tracing the multiple routes of historical invention by which Tupac Amaru became

the "last great patriot" lies beyond the scope of this note. Accounts written in Buenos Aires, La Paz, and Cuzco immediately after the 1780 insurrection, the compilations of Pedro de Angelis, the manuscripts given to General Miller in 1833 and published in his Memoirs, are all part of this "patriotic reinvention of Tupac Amaru II."

68 See B. Cohen, "Anthropology and History in the 1980s: Toward a Rapprochement," *Journal of Interdisciplinary History* 12 (1981): 227–52.

69 See Partha Chatterjee, *The Nation and Its Fragments: Colonial and Postcolonial Histories* (Princeton: Princeton University Press, 1993), 75–115.

70 Rancière, *The Names of History*, 1.

71 Ethnohistory of the 1950s and indigenist anthropology of the 1930s congealed in the figure of Luis Valcárcel, the institutional founder of modern Peruvian anthropology. See, for a preliminary discussion of the complicity of ethnohistory and indigenism in Peru, my "Después de la etnohistoria."

THOMAS A. ABERCROMBIE

Mothers and Mistresses of the Urban Bolivian Public Sphere

Postcolonial Predicament and National Imaginary in Oruro's Carnival

✳ In this essay I have two aims: First I seek to question the applicability of postcolonial theory to the Spanish American (and in particular, Bolivian) case by historicizing the phases of the latter's colonial and postcolonial (for the moment, equivalent to "postindependence" or national period) existence, regarding its processes of colonialism and decolonization in a comparative framework. Second, I wish to query the particular forms taken by nationalism's postcolonial predicament in Bolivia (and by extension, in other Spanish American countries), giving special attention to folklorizing public festivals, now a privileged arena for the gendered construal of Indianness, and for the cultural construction and contestation of the parameters of citizenship.

I take advantage of one of the most productive insights of Benedict Anderson's *Imagined Communities*, to treat nationalism, in the words of Claudio Lomnitz, "not as an ideology but rather as a hegemonic, commonsensical, and tacitly shared cultural construct,"[1] a product of an array of techniques for subject formation. But while Anderson holds up the rise of print capitalism to explain the emergence of new publics, I find more fertile ground for investigating the transition from Old Regime to postcolonial imagined communities and processes of subject formation in the arena of public performance. On this staging ground, not constituted by vernacular print capitalism but through music, costumed dance, and pageant allegories of subjectivity, communities inclusive of nonpatrician, even nonliterate subalterns have long been not only imagined, but embodied. And in the era of electronic communication, such sounds and images, since 1992 broadcast on country-wide live television, enable the country's major cities to vie for pride of place as locus of the most "authentic" festive citizen factory.

At the same time, I take up one of the least discussed of Anderson's assertions, that rather than being a residual product of borrowed European ideas, the Spanish American nation-state and nationalism were the original creation of Creole pioneers, who then exported their innovations from imperial periphery back to the metropole. Following a line of argument developed by Ann Laura Stoler, I suggest that the coimplicated schemas of race and class also emerged under colonial conditions, becoming the necessary foundation of national projects.[2] Rehearsed in practice as much as in policy, techniques of "cultural hygiene" were applied from above to police the faltering late-colonial boundary between colonizer and colonized,[3] their preferred object of attention being the sexual body. Swinging wildly between fear of contamination and transgressive desire, Creole elite ambivalence toward cross-class, cross-race (and one might add, cross-gender) cultural *alters* (intimate others) found expression in public performance in venues such as Oruro's carnival.

When Creole nationalist pioneers set out to forge their republics full of homogeneous citizens, invidious colonial distinctions became an obstacle. Although they risked contamination of class privileges now based on bourgeois notions of respectability and decency, the fantasy, at least, of transgressive romance between Creoles and colonial subalterns provided a way of underwriting patriotism with the passion of transgressive love. Taking a lead from Doris Sommer, I suggest that the national romance evident in Latin America's "foundational fictions," romance novels published from the 1840s through the 1940s that include, in the United States, James Fenimore Cooper's *Last of the Mohicans*, found a staging ground in the old tropes of the conquest and conversion plays of processional pageantry.[4] Such public rituals, from Corpus Christi to carnival, had always provided a stage for commenting on the relationship between the sovereign and the people; now it would become an arena for mimetically enacting theses on the social and sexual correlates of popular sovereignty.

Taking up, in part, Joseph Roach's approach to the analysis of circum-Atlantic performance, I argue that the specific forms taken by gendered, raced, and classed cultural alters in festival dance are granted ancestral warrants by the dead generations who are reembodied in performance by living surrogates. Such pageantry, I assert, is a privileged arena for study of the national romance, and for assessing the cultural construction of citizenship as a triangulated relation—mediated by what might be termed postcolonial desire— among individual bodies, the body politic, and the nation's colonial heritage. And because, as an indigenista pageant, carnival's transgressive romance reflects, in the main, the concerns of elite nationalists, as well as the bourgeois success that is an express wish of so many participants, including those of humble means, I will argue that it is construed as a particular sort of family romance, eminently about the internalization of colonial kinds of powers by subjects thus made capable of presiding over the model successful household, the racially stratified one.

Like the costumed performance of patron saint feasts in other Bolivian towns, that of Oruro's carnival—recently named one of UNESCO's exemplars of "World Cultural Patrimony"—has been critical in providing techniques through which to overcome, on behalf of the nation, the central predicament of postcolonial citizenship. I argue, however, that this predicament takes a special form in the countries wherein it first emerged, making the Spanish American cases distinct from those later nation-states (products of later empires) more often addressed by postcolonial studies.

I begin with a brief inquiry into the postcolonial predicament in countries deriving from imperialism's first wave. I then provide a thumbnail sketch of a carnival complex in Oruro, providing an ethnographic context for further analysis. Next, I historically contextualize festivals like carnival to make explicit the kinds of meanings they have carried as varieties of social drama, techniques of social memory, and rituals of religious devotion. Turning then to ethnographic accounts of carnival's most recent incarnations, I evaluate efforts over the past decade to resignify its dances. Throughout this essay I pay particular attention to the gendered nature of such representations, and I seek to account for the curious fact that while male costumes today clothe dancers in a wide variety of transgressive and wild, id-like versions of Indians, Africans, and devils, female costumes are for the most part modeled on those of the domestic servants and market vendors wearing *pollera* skirts and bowler hats, who are known by the usually insulting term *chola* (urban Indian woman).

To conclude I explore more fully what makes the Spanish American, and specifically the Bolivian, postcolonial predicament distinct from that faced by countries more recently independent of later empires, and hence perhaps I can account for the general poor fit between the problematic of Spanish American nationalisms and the concerns of "mainstream" postcolonial studies.

AN AMERICAN POSTCOLONIAL PREDICAMENT

By postcolonial predicament, I refer to a phenomenon that in Bolivia (as in other American countries) is doubled in its effect. On the one hand, like the former colonies of nineteenth-century imperialisms, the elite Creole architects of the postindependence republic of Bolivia sought simultaneously to distance themselves from their former imperial metropole, and to emulate it, depending on an imperially educated minority to build progress-oriented institutions for a new kind of nation-state. Along with the new republic's inherited and borrowed institutions came the very techniques for demarcating and defending regimes of privilege that had been used to subjugate both colonized peoples and Creole colonials. In the aftermath of independence they would be used by a new and national Creole elite to maintain power (and the proprietous respectability on which citizenship now depended) while gradually entraining the unschooled masses—that is, Indians, Africans, and mixed castas (castes)—to the subjectivity of progressive republican citizenship.

The first, and virtually universal, sort of postcolonial predicament set in when nation-building elites privileged themselves by their strong affiliation with European traditions, distancing themselves and the "modern" institutions and values of the new state from the "original citizenship" enjoyed by the relatively more "native" masses. This predicament, of course, is general to all nation-states of the post-imperial age, including those of Europe. There, nostalgia for disappearing authentic "folk" traditions in which to clothe uniquely English, French, German, and Spanish national subjects led to the invention of folklore as a discipline and as a means of rescuing a peasant "national soul"[5] even as peasantries were to be entrained as citizens. In Europe, the transnationally homogenizing forces of urbanism, mechanized progress, and capitalist modernity were counterbalanced through the discovery of the nation's folk roots. But in Europe's former colonies such forces were far more suspect precisely for their insistently European traces, while at the same time searches for the "authentic folk" led nationalist elites to the colonized subalterns they otherwise disdained. This kind of postcolonial predicament is characteristic of the twentieth-century nation-states that arose in the wake of the nineteenth-century empires of Africa and Asia. But in New Delhi, postindependence elites may have forged a nation in part through colonially problematic language, ideas, and institutions, but they did not distance themselves from the populace by claiming to be English.

In the first-wave nation-states of the Americas—nineteenth-century republics carved out of sixteenth-century empires—this postcolonial predicament was redoubled. For there nation-building elites were not only schooled in Spanish traditions, but had been privileged above the native masses by being Spaniards, if suspect Creole ones, tainted by their tropical environs and by the milk of their Indian or African wet nurses. Even while they bridled at the insults that peninsular Spaniards heaped on them, Creoles struggled for recognition of their rights as Spaniards.[6] Independence and its associated revaluation of the meaning of "nationhood" then definitively orphaned Creoles from membership in this privileged early-modern and metropolitan form of nationality. Finding the basis of their former privilege negated, Creoles then discovered, first, that the only "natives" with unimpeachably "primordial ties" to the country's soil were Indians, and second, that to retain their privileged status they had to embrace the theory of race and become whites, thus hauling themselves out of the mire of colonial hybridity into which their Creoleness had dragged them.

Even when the egalitarian principles of republican popular sovereignty erased racial language from censuses and voting rights laws, Creoles remained white and culturally figured Indianness remained the principal criterion for the exclusion of Indians from the rights of citizenship. This was possible through a crucial trick, by which enactments of status are taken as indices of essential difference. As we shall see, the workshop for learning this trick, and for forgetting its basis in artifice, was (in Joseph Roach's term) the process of surrogation in festive play.

The twentieth-century movement known as indigenismo turned such evaluations upside down (without thereby undoing the criteria of difference underpinning them), when they aimed to recapture Indianness to grant themselves, and their nation, non-European ancestral warrants. Seeking to solve the postcolonial predicament by attacking the racial scheme on which the nation-state had been erected, indigenistas also inverted other liberal tenets. Striving for a dignified imperialism-resistant basis for a new kind of patriotic nation building, they revalued "native" collectivism as a pre-Columbian forerunner to socialism. Drawing on anthropology and folklore (making tradition-bound virtues of the orality of nonliterate speakers of Quechua or Aymara; collective relations to productive resources; non- or precapitalist kinds of exchange and labor relations; and ancient cuisines, drinking practices, textile traditions, and sartorial styles), they effectively euphemized both race and class in the notion of "essential cultural difference." Celebrations of cultural difference must, then, be inspected for covert forms of the colonially constructed kinds of racism that might lurk therein.[7]

Indigenismo has been challenged by other identity discourses in countries like Bolivia, where indigenous movements now intersect with populist politics and collide with the exigencies of transnationally enforced neoliberalism. But the kinds of "cultural hygiene" by which the colonial metropole policed the boundary between colonizers and colonized remain patent in the anxieties of postcolonial desire. These are clearly traceable in pageant dancing and in other public discourse about private passions and transgressive sexuality.

To treat such issues I turn to a relatively old Bolivian pageant that has become a model for other, newer pageants for performatively enacting and striving to resolve the postcolonial predicament: the costumed dances and dramas performed during carnival time in the city of Oruro.[8] I also make reference to analogous festive sites of the national imaginary in other cities founded as Spanish enclaves during colonial times in the region that became Bolivian territory.[9]

In seeking to discover what it is about the costumed roles and festival frame of Oruro's carnival that has made it so adaptable and useful in so many places where politics, religion, and "the Indian question" merge in public pageants, I dwell particularly on the shifting relationship to such representations of the country's evolving, but always "raced," social classes. All may be drawn into a cross-ethnic national romance capable of underwriting patriotism, but it is important to explore the distinct meanings conveyed by embodying alterity when dancers are mestizo-cholo artisans expressing the Indianness they wish to shed; Creole indigenistas aiming to "revindicate" a past indigenous heritage (without themselves becoming Indians); or "neo-cholo" populist politicians striving to index their humble origins.[10]

I draw out of this analysis an insight owing much to the work of Doris Sommer,[11] who, using theses of Michel Foucault and Benedict Anderson to supplement one another, speculates that in the Latin American literary canon, heterosexual erotics and patriotic politics come together: "There . . . passion between the sexes and patriotism across national sectors were helping to construct one another, as if one kind of love were assuming a mandate from the other."[12] Here I seek to extend Sommer's thesis into the realm of performance, and to read the nationalist romance not only in reference to a fantasy of patriotically bridging divided social sectors, but as a family romance about conflicted relations within the racially stratified bourgeois/ elite household.

In performance, high romance may underwrite emancipatory aims, but such emplotments may also be read as adventures in sexual slumming: the beloved is exciting because she is prohibited; patriotic, dangerous, and also class-denying because she is rough and from the soil; easy because she is powerless; forbidden by a colonialist patriarch because she is pseudokin. She is, in brief, the domestic servant who in elite households stands in both for the rural Indian and for the mother, and who mediates not only parents to their children but the household and the realm of peasant production, thus deeply entangling class within the power struggles of family, forever tying race to desire and linking patriotism to exoticism.[13] Hence the carnival struggle to overcome colonial barriers to postcolonial desire can be read as oedipal fantasy, by which an upwardly mobile adolescent ego, aiming for autonomy, slays his colonialist father not to possess his mother but his Indian or cholita nursemaid.[14]

Foundation-narrative romances—which, as Sommer shows, play out as tragedies—have served to libidinally motivate the role-playing nationalist heritage pageantry that makes elite class- (and race-) crossing possible without the encumbrance of losing one's class- (or race-) based privileges. For the Bolivian kind of folkloric pageant, set always in the context of a patron saint festival but with overtones of carnival license ending in Lenten contrition, frames carnivalesque transgression within pilgrimagelike penitential processions. Such performances invariably index the relationship of the contemporary citizen to the colonial and pre-Columbian past, constructing the former by gaining access to the powers resident in the latter. Pageant dancing, that is, constitutes a form of social memory but is also a technique of structured forgetting.[15]

By engaging in an eminently embodied form of postcolonial "discourse" participants become "Indians" temporarily, thereby becoming bodily surrogates for kinds of alters usually relegated to the past, to the rural soil, and to the satanically inspired, id-like interior space of suppressed transgressive desire.[16] As Peter Stallybrass and Allon White put it, "the result is a mobile, conflictual fusion of power, fear and desire in the construction of subjectivity: a psychological dependence upon precisely those Others which are being rigorously opposed and excluded at the social level."[17] Dancers give sway to their "inner Indians" within the liminal space and "empty time" of ritual confines. Ritual poetics then enable dancers to domesticate Indian powers before (in Marisol de la Cadena's term) "de-Indianizing" themselves, returning from temporary role to everyday identity, in time for Lentenlike contrition.

Diverse emancipatory and revolutionary possibilities draw many different sorts of Bolivians to join the dance; here I seek to portray those possibilities as well as their limits. For regardless of the laudable ends to which it is put, the pageant romance of Indianness is also the pursuit of transgressive individual desires and sorceries that are set up as the antisocial (and sinful) antitheses of the expressly collective and patriotic (and redemptive) goals of the festival. Nowadays, indeed, festival dancing and the celebration of difference it appears to support seems to express a paradoxical effort to build a fraternal and equitable nation while underwriting the goals of the ideal neoliberal citizen subject, which depend precisely on reinscribing into social life and into the successful household colonially derived regimes of privilege.

A THUMBNAIL SKETCH OF ORURO'S CARNIVAL PAGEANT

Every year in Oruro during carnival—the short span of time preceding Ash Wednesday and the penitential fasting of Lent—between five and ten thousand dancers, members of more than fifty organized dance groups, dress up as Indians, devils, and African slaves (and as conquistadors, archangels, and slave drivers) in order to dance in procession from the outskirts of the city toward the city center. There, after passing the review stands in the plaza and proceeding through an arenalike "plaza of folklore," they end their dancing at the temple of the patroness of Oruro, the Virgin of the Mineshaft.

The patroness is an advocation of Mary deriving from the commemoration, eight days after the birth of Jesus, of her purification at the temple on February 2, for which reason she is also called Candelaria, because Candlemas is celebrated on that day. As the same advocation of Mary as the patronness of Bolivia, the Virgin of Copacabana, Oruro's celebrated purification/Candelaria is called the Virgin of the Mineshaft for the mine tunnels near her shrine, where according to folkloric tradition the painted Mary miraculously appeared to a dying, repentant thief in the late eighteenth century. In her honor, dancers move mainly to the sound of brass band marches in choreographed and practiced leaps and flourishes, bedazzling the eye in a carnival of bright colors, face paint, feathers, baroquely ornamented masks, and gleaming silver accessories. Devotees perform dances brought to the Andes by Spanish priests in the sixteenth century as well as recently revived versions of costumed dances performed in Inca days and carefully rehearsed representations of local and exotic Indians copied from life in "ethnographic realist" fashion. Each of up to a hundred groups fields hundreds of identically costumed men and women, who wend their well-choreographed way through town from morning until well past dark.

Notably, male costume (sometimes heavy and body-concealing, accompanied by elaborate masks, and now sometimes worn by groups of cross-dressing women who have eschewed the race and class associations of female costume) varies widely among dance types, but female costume (worn mainly by women but also, formerly generally, and infrequently still, by cross-dressing men) seems all of a piece. Male devils, African slaves, slave drivers, jungle Indians, and highland tinku (ritual battle) warriors seem always accompanied by women wearing tall boots; short, pleated skirts and low-cut blouses; mini-shawls; rounded, derbylike hats; and very often a pair of fake hair braids, looking every bit like salacious, sexualized versions of the cholita costume (full ankle-length pollera skirt, high-necked blouse, shawl, and bowler hat) worn by provincial women, marketeers, and domestic servants.

All dancers move along an established processional route through streets and plazas named to commemorate patriotic persons and the momentous dates of Bolivian independence. Like a canalized river, the procession runs along a narrow asphalt and cement channel, urged along by brass bands and held to its course by embankments of reviewing stands packed to impenetrability with the spectacle's enormous public. Among the tens of thousands of spectators are several hundred foreign tourists. Most of the audience, however, is Bolivian, both locals from Oruro itself (cheering on dancing family members) and "heritage tourists" from the nearby cities of La Paz and Cochabamba who come to witness Oruro's famed Carnival, long considered the pioneering and preeminent event among the country's religious-folkloric pageants. It is not for nothing that Oruro once earned the title "Folklore Capital of Bolivia."

Cheap seats can be had near the beginning of the parade route, far from the center of town, in neighborhoods where Quechua and Aymara are spoken by the city's majority of laboring people. Hours after beginning their danced procession the performers may be exhausted, but they make a special effort to brighten their performances when they reach the mostly Spanish-speaking and elite city center, near the procession's end. There, arrayed in high bleachers around the Plaza 10 de Febrero (named in honor of a proto-independence Creole rebellion in 1781), spectators who have been able to afford the expensive seats witness dancers as they pass the seat of city and departmental government. A few blocks up the hill against which the city nestles, performers dance through the final reviewing stands on each side of the long Plaza of Folklore, passing in review before judges and accompanied by loudspeaker commentary by folklore experts, who pepper their comments with advertisements for the soft drink or beer companies who are the corporate sponsors of the event. A few dance groups here present brief versions of old sacramental plays.

Of the up to one hundred dance groups (each comprised of a few hundred member dancers) are one or two small groups of "Incas" who perform a dance of the conquest that dramatizes the Inca Atahualpa's defeat by Pizarro and his followers.[18] Among the larger dance groups (some with several hundred dancers) several "Diabladas" groups depict the confrontation of Satan and his demons (along with the seven deadly sins) with the archangel Michael and the seven cardinal virtues.[19]

Starting in late morning and continuing until well after dark, phalanx after phalanx of different dance fraternities, representing twenty or so distinct sorts of dances, set out on an exhausting parade route that takes them several kilometers to the heart of the old city.

Cheered along the way by an audience in the tens of thousands, dancers and musicians stream past the review stands, sometimes jostled at the outer edges of the flow by passers by. Try as they might, police officers positioned along the route cannot always clear the way of vendors of food, drink, film, and programs, and everywhere are the photographers and video camera operators who, with or without the licenses that festival officials insist they buy, descend from the bleachers and move against the current of dance seeking a good shot.

Observers of the spectacle come from near and far, not to passively observe but to be active participants in the event. They enliven dancers with cheers and applause when they pass by, seeking to tweak from them a peak performance. But during the lulls that pass between groups of dancers and musicians the audience also entertains itself by retreating to the back of the bleachers where hot food and cold drinks can be bought from "popular-class" vendors, or by regaling each other with explanations of particular dances taken from memory or experience or guidebook.

Cognoscenti explain the dances to "outsiders" (from La Paz or Cochabamba, France or the United States), while among themselves they also debate the merits of novel dance steps, costumes, masks, and music. Given the representational nature of dancing, much discussion turns on the relative authenticity of different types of dances, and comparisons are made among dance types old and new and among the multiple fraternities performing each particular kind of dance. Some prefer to see resolutely colonial dances or those with clear religious playscripts, while others applaud dances typical of provincial towns or purporting to be based on "ethnographic realism," or those dances dating to the 1960s and 1970s that are favored by private high schools and university students, such as the Negritos, Sambos, and Caporales, and are held to require a high standard of athleticism.

Given the occasional ogling and teasing of spectators by leering devils or salacious *china supays* (temptress consorts of the devils, formerly danced by men in drag but more often in recent decades by women), it is not surprising that some spectators seem to most relish ogling the pretty girls, especially the cheerleader-style *walipoleras*, dancing in tight thigh-high boots, the shortest mini-polleras, and the most deeply cut blouses. Standing out among the latter are the *predilectas*, winners of intrafraternity beauty contests who proudly wear sashes announcing their victories. All dancers belong to organized clublike brotherhoods, each with its own internal hierarchy of authority that often includes president, secretary, treasurer, dance instructor, folklore specialist, and an altar guild to maintain a small image of the Virgin. Some groups own or rent their own quarters for their meetings, parties, and prayer sessions. Brotherhoods have begun as neighborhood associations, residents' clubs of migrants from particular towns or provinces, trade guilds (including butchers and bootblacks), industrial labor unions or management associations, university and high school clubs, ballet schools, or simply clubs of aficionados, some from the most elite social sectors of the city.

The dance groups of carnival encompass a wide range of social sectors, motives for dancing (with politics, religion, family tradition, peer pressure, and fun blended in various ways in the programmatic aims of all groups and individuals within them), but all groups nonetheless have something in common apart from their shape as brotherhoods. They process in an orderly way, following the route and rules of conduct established by the city's Association of Folkloric Groups, which licenses participation and requires entrance fees of each participant. The groups are comprised of individuals with sufficient economic resources to pay the entrance fee and fraternity dues and to buy or rent their sometimes very expensive costumes and masks from one of the impressive array of artisans and shops specializing in their manufacture. With extraordinarily few exceptions, the members of these groups are urbanites not members of rural "indigenous" communities or Afro-Bolivians from the tropical Yungas region, as the roles they embody purport to be.

In addition, participants carry out their processional dance as a form of penitence, in fulfillment of a formal promise to the Virgin, seeking her intercession before God to aid in the remission of sins and the delivery of blessings. Between November 1 (All Souls Day) and this carnival performance, members of each dance group engage in weekly practice sessions and prayer meetings before a miniature image of the Virgin of the Mineshaft in their dance group's headquarters. Between collectively intoned prayers of the Rosary it is not uncommon to hear testimonials to the miracles wrought by the Virgin in participants' lives. Each member, however, makes private requests in silent prayer, and thus dancing is done as a form of penitence, perhaps for kinds of sinfulness expressed by the figures that dancers represent in their performances. The dance is also, of course, a kind of bodily offering to the ancestral dead, signaled in the framing dates of the carnival season that begin in conjunction with the recollection of the dead and of the past more generally.

Throughout their procession, Incas swagger, "wild Indians" threaten, black kings menace, slave-driving *caporales* (overseers) lash their whips, and devils haughtily taunt and tempt until the final moment, played out before the temple of the Virgin of the Mineshaft, when Spaniards and archangels triumph. As each group enters the holy precinct, dancers remove their masks and shed their dance personas, fall to their knees, and, teary-eyed, approach the altar in order to receive the Virgin's blessing and once again enter a state of grace. Thus the public spectacle becomes enmeshed in larger ritual frames, deeply inflected by a historical discourse that stresses the continued relevance of the colonial past to national life.

COMMEMORATIVE HISTORIES AND COLONIAL SORCERIES IN A SERIOUS CARNIVAL

Given popular hagiography well known throughout the city (summarized in the programs, published in many folkloric books and pamphlets, and even sold in comic book form), Oruro's Virgin is especially attuned to such sins. Two very distinct accounts date her initial, miraculous appearance to preconquest times, and the appearance of the painting that is her current incarnation is dated to the late eighteenth century, before a repentant thief known as Nina Nina or in another story Chiru-Chiru.[20] Neither account is given any official weight by the church, although here, as in all apparitions and miracles that have acquired a following, documentation is of little consequence. During pre-Columbian times, the earlier story goes, the Virgin appeared in the form of a sword-wielding ñusta (a Quechua term for an Inca princess) seeking to draw the Uru inhabitants of the village on Oruro's later site away from the evil influence of the earth deity Wari. After convincing the Urus to cease their human sacrifices to Wari, this Virgin or ñusta then came to the Urus' defense when an angered Wari, seeking revenge on the Urus for abandoning him, set loose a series of monstrous creatures: an army of giant ants, an enormous frog, a huge lizard, and a kilometer-long snake.

The monsters threatened to devour the Virgin's new Uru devotees, but as each approached the village she descended from the sky with her sword of flame. Slashing at the ants she turned them into grains of sand, which formed the dune that at one time lay to the south of Oruro (before being used up in cement manufacture). She turned the frog into a large stone that once stood on the north side of town (until a military official dynamited it to pieces in a past decade). The lizard that came from the east was beheaded, leaving its hill-sized stone remains (still intact) some distance from town. And the snake that had menaced from the west was likewise beheaded, leaving behind a sinuous hill "body" separated slightly from a hillock "head" (a stony promontory, also intact), where a shallow cave is said to be the serpent's gaping mouth.

At one or another of these petrified monuments to pre-Columbian miracles, the people of Oruro carry out less-official acts during massive "public secret" events on the days preceding and following the central carnival procession. There, especially on the Friday before the carnival procession, one may contract a Kallawaya *curandero* (shaman) to help prepare offering-bundles to be burnt before the rocks in which these "chthonic" powers are thought still to reside.

Kallawayas, or persons claiming to be Kallawayas, perform a blessing ceremony over the burnt offering as well as over a fetish bundle tailored to the needs (and requests) of each devotee and prepared during the days running up to carnival. Alongside the bundle, miniature representations of desired outcomes help both underworld beings and the Virgin understand what is being asked of them.

In preparation for their visit to their chosen shrine to underworld powers, each family purchases miniatures (and beer, alcohol, firewood or charcoal, incense, and confetti) at a concurrent fair called *alasitas*, where a dizzying array of miniatures are offered for sale. Whether the offering bundle contains miniature tin or plaster kitchen appliances, a suburban bungalow, a jeep, or the implements of one's trade (tools, market stall, truck laden with goods, etc.), it is certain also to contain miniature bundles of cash (in dollars and/or bolivianos), and sometimes a miniature passport, U.S. visa, and airline ticket. The bundle may also include tiny savings-account passbooks, college degrees, marriage certificates or divorce decrees, and the title to the house of one's dreams.

Participants, which include great numbers of Orureños of all social backgrounds, describe desired outcomes to the Kallawaya, who then tailors his prayers of invocation and blessing to fit. Kallawayas perform an amalgamated rite, suited to the bivalent structure of carnival proceedings writ large. Each Kallawaya will ring a little bell, asperse fetishes with alcohol or beer, and recite a peculiar mix of Catholic prayer and invocations to the *sapos* (as the teluric rock monuments are collectively called) or to the *dios de las tinieblas* ("god of darkness," a reference to the devils of carnival, to Wari, and to the sculpted demons called *tios* who inhabit the mineshafts and receive from miners cult offerings this day and every Friday). Those who participate in this rite are also expected to carry away a little pile of stones hewn by sledgehammer from the living rockface of the serpent's mouth. As Wari's "silver," the stones are to be given as cult offerings on the first Fridays of each month, and returned to the mountainside the following year.

Not only does this peripheral urban space with its monuments to a founding war of the gods serve to open carnival; it also becomes the arena for enacting carnival's end. On Temptation Sunday following carnival, the "adios" to the carnival season, the city's inhabitants return to the serpent's head en masse. Strewn over the hillsides, now wearing the everyday clothing that marks their social standing through its differentiation from Indian and "chola" styles, family groups of participants in the earlier center city events now partake of a picnic meal and build small houses of stone into which their miniature goods are placed. Just below the snake-mouth cave, a veritable tent city of food and drink vendors serves a large crowd of revelers. Beer freely flows, as does *chicha*, the fermented corn beer of rural festivals.

On this day, too, part of the city's laboring population, excluded from the city-center procession by relative poverty or social discomfort, perform their own dances. Proceeding from a peripheral market down an avenue filled with automobile repair shops and open-air *chicherías* (taverns on the outskirts of town frequented by the "popular classes" and associated with prostitution, gambling, and violence, where "slumming" elites can freely mix with "more-Indian" laborers in order to imbibe Bolivianness and experience a transgressive frisson), they move from urban periphery to the serpent's mouth on the outskirts of town, dancing to marches played by the same bands that recently played for city dance-brotherhoods. Yet their costume is utterly distinct from that of carnival proper: they do not dress as Indians or devils or Africans but rather wear gala versions of their own everyday wear. Men in suits accompany women in extravagant cholita costumes (many-pleated ankle-length pollera skirt, shawl, apron, and bowler derby).[21] Covered in confetti, the only elements of "disguise" are small masks covering the eyes, like those at a costume ball. What is more, their dance is done pair by pair, in a *comparsa* (masquerade) style associated with the *vecinos* ("non-Indian" store-owning notables) of larger provincial towns.

In the vendors' tents at the end of the route, marketeers mix with the middle class and elite of the city, drinking chicha in stands set up by Cochalas, the chicha-vending cholitas of the Cochabamba valley. For this part of carnival alone they set up barrels full of chicha brewed in their valley towns and shipped in by truck, as they do for pilgrimage festivals and associated fairs elsewhere in the highlands. Famous for their shorter polleras and scooped-neck blouses and for barmaid ribaldry, they contribute to the transgressive, fairlike atmosphere in this most liminal space within the carnival frame, in which postcolonial desires are given full expression.

As with Bolivia's other highland urban pageants, the totality of events is highly complex. Likewise the range of participant motives and interpretations of festival meanings cover a broad array, more variable even than the number of confraternities, the breadth of participation among the country's social sectors, and the spread of associational practices through which they are organized.

My rough sketch here of the festival frame writ large highlights certain coordinates in space and time that mark divisions of class and race. Wealthier folks, including the city's uppermost classes and political elites, dance in costumes of cultural alters from the northeastern outskirts of town into the city center—that is, from the places of underworld gods into the Christian temple. Apart from their participation in the almost-universal framing events before and after the danced procession, poorer folks are but the audience of these events, although some among them have the opportunity to dance in their own clothes from urban periphery to the western outskirts of town. The social distinction thereby marked overlays the spatial divide between pre-Christian Indian periphery and Christian civilized center, while the framing narrative locates the former in a living past that in a modernist spectacle is briefly exteriorized and celebrated before being disavowed and sublimated to make way for the national future.

As with all of the saints and advocations of Christ and Mary that are the focus of this kind of processional pageantry, the account of the Virgin's pre-Columbian and colonial apparition links her critically to an eminently colonial narrative of conquest and conversion, which provides the overarching narrative frame for the procession itself and the accessory rites linked to it. So too do the dances and dramas of carnival respond to such a conversion frame. We cannot be surprised by this because most were introduced in the sixteenth century by Spanish priests as tools of evangelism in their crusade against devil-inspired Indian idolatry. More surprising is that the dances that least well fit this colonial conversion story are those of the poorer marketeers of the Temptation Sunday procession and of the rural people called Indians whose representation in dance is so central to the event as a whole.

Since perhaps the mid-eighteenth century, and until the 1990s, the farming and herding people that colonial Spaniards, "non-Indian" city folks, and anthropologists have called "Indians" have been excluded from these urban pageants, even as they have become the arena through which to romance the indigenous past required by the twentieth-century national imaginary. Since 1992 they have begun to insist on being included, and at the end of this essay I will address the 1990s "Indian invasion" of Oruro's carnival and the incorporation of rural people into Potosí's San Bartolomé festival, and the implications for rural people and the nation of the adoption in the countryside of the folkloric spectacle frame.

A HISTORY OF CARNIVAL

Hybrid Festive Genre:
Carnival vs. Penitential Pilgrimage in Pageants

Carnival calls to mind the carnivalesque and the ritualized transgressions and "world-turned-upside-down" inversions of social order that have been a hallmark not only of Victor Turner's brand of ritual theory, but also of a great deal of cultural and historical analysis of the 1980s and 1990s that draws on Mikhail Bahktin's reveries on Rabelais.[22] Here I do not mean to dismiss the degree to which all festive contexts enable a degree of transgression and contestation, but Oruro's carnival so lacks in the jibes against political and economic elites and the forces of order (whether of church or state), and is so generally bereft of outright licentiousness and vulgarity, that it has been lampooned in truly carnivalesque parody called "anti-carnival." Carrying placards with centerfold "virgins,"[23] legions of university students cross-dressed as cholitas but with large fake phalluses protruding below their polleras, put on a vulgar and contestatory display that lampoons not only politicians, the U.S. drug war, and carnival itself, but carnival's obsession with cholitas. Such contestations of carnival's messages, like those of the rural communities who have since 1992 sought to "invade" Oruro's procession, are not, however, admitted to the actual event, where such indexes of disorder and vulgarity, typical marks of indecent "Indianness," would sully carnival's sober display of indigenous heritage.

The blurring of festive genres evidenced in a carnival now imbued again with the emphatic orderliness and piety of Corpus Christi is of course a product of colonial and postcolonial entanglements, of the projection of symbolic power relations of a racially stratified polity onto the liturgical calendar and the coordinates in space and time to which belong temptation and sin as well as penitence and redemption. It is perhaps this hybrid quality in which transgression and contestation are admitted in carefully regulated form, and where interethnic or cross-class antagonism can be marshaled into the service of homogenizing nationalism, that has made Oruro's carnival so useful as a model for patriotic pageantry. Discovering how this came to be requires an examination of the long-term historical shifts in the nature of public festival in the Andes, shifts that owe much to the successive changes of heart of the state and of the powerful toward the disempowered and their entertainments.

The First Two Centuries of Colonial Festival:
1550s–1750s

The oldest of extant fraternities in carnival are (or were) artisan guilds, and their favored dance genres (Incas, devils, and Morenadas) are those attested in the earliest extant colonial documentation of urban festive dance. These derivatives of sacramental plays also trace back not to pre-Columbian origins but to the theater of evangelization of medieval (and reconquest) Spain, carried to the Indies as an evangelical tool and as a way of marking out the relationship there between Old Christians (in the Indies, Spaniards) and the newly converted. Neither in Iberia's Muslim territories conquered by Christians nor in the postconquest Indies, however, were such performances pegged to carnival. Instead, they were the dramatic spectacles of that church-militant festival par excellence, Corpus Christi.[24]

As a weapon against heresy, Corpus Christi demanded subordination to the central tenets of Catholic Christianity and transformed the populace into a moving image of the body of Christ, his church on earth, as it wound its way from the outskirts of town to the public plaza and church at the center. Often coinciding with the initiation of pogroms against Jews and Muslims (and later, against *conversos* and *moriscos*, their converted descendants), Corpus Christi was also emblematic of the homogenizing forces of the universal monarchs of the Spanish Empire.

A measure not only of faith and of submission to the two sovereigns (king and pope), Corpus Christi was also a totalizing rite that enforced social transparency. It was the vanguard of early modernity. From an archimedian view (as such festivals are depicted in panoramic paintings of the sixteenth century), the social body as a whole became visible and representable. In the later sixteenth century of Philip II, the king's endeavors to gain such a totalizing vantage on his realm led to both Herculean efforts to transform its social geography by rebuilding it for transparency and to efforts to record its human and natural features through census taking, map making, and bureaucracy building.[25]

Thus did Viceroy Francisco de Toledo undertake a "general visitation" of Peru in the early 1570s, demolishing the hamlets in which Indians lived scattered and hidden from view and laying out a much smaller number of carefully planned new *reducción* (resettlement) towns, each with its own set of ordinances for the maintenance of *buena policia*, the Spanish-style municipally based "good customs" on which the project of Christianization (and orderly collection of tributes) depended.

The plans of these new towns explicitly oriented Indian houses and activities toward the gaze of the colonial observer, so that behavior regulated in new ways could be monitored, by the priest and *corregidor* (magistrate), but also by the appointed members of the town council, who were to go out on scheduled circuits of the town to keep the curfew and guard, mostly, against idolatries, public drunkenness, and sin, especially of the sexual sort.[26] Colonial discipline was to be internalized within indigenous bodies in the form of mechanisms for social control oriented toward acts defined by new logics of "wrong," and also as conscience to be activated in confession and directed into penitential acts in public processions.[27] The confessional emphasized vigilance and discipline in the exteriorization and

194 Thomas A. Abercrombie

public correction of sin, located primarily in the sexual body. But Indians were also taught to regard sinfulness as originating not only in inner desire but also in their devil–inspired past and in their attentions to it. Thus a term for a category or aspect of preconquest dead, supay, was used to translate "devil," and the shrines to earth deities, deeply associated with cults to the dead, became temples of idolatry. The new regimes of surveillance were meant not only to reform Indians' bodily praxis but also to distance them from the bodies of the pagan dead and the commemorative monuments that kept their past alive.

As with rural Indian towns, so with the neighborhoods of urban laborers. The "two republics" policy aimed to separate Spaniards from Indians and created separate settlements for Spaniards in which Indians were not to dwell. Yet colonial Spaniards, who acquired many of the privileges of Spanish aristocracy (freedom from tributes, etc.) merely by being in the Indies, had also to avoid the stain of manual labor that had in Spain served to stigmatize the plebeian *pechero* (tributary).[28] This meant that every Spanish town and city was soon full to bursting with Indians and Africans, who were needed not only in the mines and in other types of manual labor (artisan trades, etc.) but also for domestic work in every would-be Spanish (and Creole Spanish) household. Prohibited from living in the central *traza española*—the part of town characterized by stone wall and tile roof—non-Spanish workers (Indians, imported Africans, mestizos, mulattos, etc.) were settled into neighborhoods on the periphery.[29]

Such urban *rancherías*, as they were called, were organized as parishes, each with its own church, priest, and festivals; such neighborhood festivals were then orchestrated together in the context of Corpus Christi. Taking part in dance dramas that reenacted the Spanish conquest of the Incas (in Incas plays); that replayed the "reconquest" victory of Christians over Muslims (in the Moros y Cristianos play); and that linked both conquest and reconquest to the defeat of Satan and the seven deadly sins by St. Michael and the seven cardinal virtues (in the Diablada dance and drama), Indians marked the Christian calendar by publicly embracing their conversion to Christianity and acknowledging, along with the rest of the colonial hierarchy, their willing subordination to God, king, and pope. They also thereby marched in tune to this Spanish imperial version of modernity.[30]

Organized simultaneously as confraternities and artisan guilds, Indian labor conscripts, "mixed-caste" free (that is, wage) laborers, and artisans, all of whom lived in peripheral parishes, were the main protagonists in the theater of evangelization, performing the well-known *autos sacramentales* (sacramental acts) from which derives Spanish golden-age theater and Oruro's carnival dance. Documentation of their performance from the sixteenth century is conclusive but sketchy and without the details that we might like. The seventeenth-century chronicler Ramos Gavilan describes a military parade of "Incas" during celebrations in 1614 honoring the opening of a new temple for the Virgin of Copacabana in her namesake pilgrimage town.[31] The Potosí chronicler Arzáns describes an Easter procession of "Incas" in 1555, including the production of eight "comedies"—four of which represented Inca history from its origins to its "ruin."[32] The performance history of such dance-dramas in Oruro is less certain for the colonial period but the wide distribution of these dances in, especially, mining centers of the region suggests that they probably have a long history in Oruro as well.[33]

Arzáns also provides a review of Potosí's analogue of Oruro's miraculous virgin, Saint Bartholomew, who is said to have imprised an indigenous "satan" within a cave on the outskirts of that city, a cave that still figures as an object of magical practices on the periphery of the folklore festival of San Bartolomé. Ultimately, then, a "pagan Indian" underworld full of chthonic demons was built into every new Spanish town by the very practices meant to exterminate it. Recalled in the dramatic processions of the church militant, such beings persist as evidence of their miraculous defeat, as critical elements in an allegory of the struggles of conscience. Once taken up by elites as a pilgrimage site in their patriotic project, the Indian past wells up at a fraught conjuncture. It becomes a vehicle for harnessing the lucre of neoliberalism's private interest, kept ritually in check by an enframing Christian devotion expressing the collective aims of fraternal dance and of patriotism.[34]

From soon after Spanish cities were first founded until the end of the Habsburg dynasty in the early eighteenth century, Corpus Christi and similar processions were a matter of universal participation, with Spanish city officials leading the way and Indians bringing up the rear. But over the course of those two centuries the composition of urban populations changed dramatically. Initially, perhaps, Spaniards could envision a social order neatly divided into two large blocks: the Spaniards of the city center and the Indian laborers brought from their rural nations into the urban periphery. But the chasm between these two kinds of peoples was by the end of the seventeenth century nearly filled in by a great assortment of hybrid kinds of persons, for whom the colonial project had made no provision. Increasingly upwardly mobile and dominating the urban crafts, mestizos, free blacks, mulattos, and urbanized Indians—known in Potosí as *indios criollos*, in Oruro as *indios forasteros*, and in Central America as *ladinos*—began to encroach on the privileged space of *españoles criollos*. Threatened from below by passing social climbers, and from above by the stigma of being suspect as to their Spanish nationhood, Spanish Creoles embraced a host of reforms enacted by Bourbon kings during the eighteenth century. Among them was a raft of new laws, many of which were meant to restructure the state apparatus and increase the efficiency of taxation, but also many of which were aimed at constraining the unruliness of the urban plebe and strengthening the barriers between dangerous urban multitudes and the aristocratic elite.

Decency, Propriety, and the Invention of Popular Culture, 1750–1780

By the mid-eighteenth century, the mixed "nation" of craft-guild/confraternities of the Indies had clearly become a serious threat to the Spanish/Creole aristocracy's symbolic regimes of privilege. In the Lima of 1750, one such processional dance—most likely a Seven Deadly Sins or Moors and Christians drama, as it was to take place on the feast of St. Michael—was to be the Trojan horse through which (probably guild-organized) Indians and mestizos sought to introduce an insurrectional army into the center of town.[35] The following year, panicky officials in Potosí called for reinforcements from the Audiencia capital when a carnival procession of a guild of categorially hybrid "unofficial miners," which also involved the use of arms in a dramatized battle, looked like rebellion to the city's elites.

The Q'aqcha guild, as it was called, with a membership drawn especially from the ranks of mulattos, mestizos, and Creole Indians, engaged in the activity of "weekend mining," although they were simply thought of as thieves to mine-owning elites.[36] By electing their guild leaders through the sponsorship of processional rites to miraculous crosses kept in the vicinity of the mines, their ritual activity had become an early form of organized labor, mostly outside of official control. When this *vulgo* (as elites called them) took to the streets for their devotions, "decent people" withdrew into their houses.[37] Spanish and Creole elites sought to clarify the situation by strengthening the enforcement of "two republics" policies, prohibiting the performance of processional dramas, circumscribing for themselves an autonomous arena of "high culture," and striving to eliminate the fuzzy social space between Spanish and Indian categories by turning mestizos back into indios and sending them back into the countryside (except when "invited" back by levy).[38]

Yet efforts at suppression only served to send mixed casta ritual activities further underground, into the mineshafts and out to the periphery of town and the now-prohibited rituals of rebellion like carnival. Even the efforts of Oruro's Creoles to ally themselves with rebelling Indians in 1781 in order to claim independence from the Spanish Crown backfired under these circumstances. On February 10, as it happened, in carnival season, the Creoles of Oruro called on rebellious Indians of the provinces to join them in an alliance of "Americans," asking them to invade the city and kill the Spaniards. The Creole heroes of this ill-fated revolt have given their names as revolutionary patriots to the city's streets, and the date of their plot to its main plaza, but they gave their lives to Indians (who did not make overly fine distinctions between peninsular and Creole Spaniards). Some managed to escape (only to fall into the hands of the king's men) by donning the clothes of their Indian servants to slip away from the carnage. Although not recalled in Oruro's patriotic programs, this may have been the first dance of "carnival Indians" through the city's streets.[39]

Sarah Chambers, for Arequipa, and Juan Pedro Viquiera-Albán, for Mexico, have documented the efforts of "middle-period" (1780s–1850s) urban elites to apply measures of cultural hygiene by which more readily to distinguish *gente decente* (decent people) from the vulgar masses.[40] Not only did carnival come under fire, along with the processional plays of baroque Catholicism, but so too did churchyard cemeteries and chicherías (bars serving corn beer and spicy food), both soon banished to urban peripheries. No longer would elites sit down in lowly chicherías and drink cheek by jowl with their social inferiors. At base, the unease with "popular culture," which just then came into existence (as the vulgar foil to refined "high culture" events and locales),[41] signaled the stark insecurity of Creole social position, highlighted too by new sumptuary laws and strictures on marriage choice, permitting parents to block marriages between their children and those considered their social inferiors.[42] Conditioned by the repressive surveillance of elite authority, the urban plebe, whose Christian practices as well as persons were marked "Indian" by their peripheralized occupations and residences, were in a position to develop the conversion allegories of their dramas in a quest for their own destinies and identities, in the space between Spanish god and Indian devil into which they had been cast.

Race, Class, and the New Nation, 1780–1920

While the Spanish early modern usage had assigned sovereignty to the *pueblo*, quite literally the town,[43] and in the Americas had limited citizenship rights in towns to those of Spanish nation, while assigning tributary plebeian (or pechero) status to Indians alone (providing the Spaniards of the Indies with a kind of second-class, de facto aristocracy),[44] the new popular sovereignty extended itself to include "the people" as a whole.[45] Creoles would have been electorally swamped by the masses had they not had recourse to a new regime of difference, the eminently colonial theory of race, which was invented already coupled to newly conceived parameters of class, decency, propriety, and property.[46] The language of color and race in something close to its current form emerged in Spanish America in the same decades during which Creole independence projects were shaped.[47] Indeed, without being able to envision the deployment of race, however covertly, to secure their privileges as *blancos*, Creole elites may not have been able to conceive of nation-state and popular sovereignty.[48]

The almost-universal reach of citizenship's charter within liberal republicanism made it impossible to limit the vote to blancos, as Creoles were calling themselves on the eve of independence, but Jim Crow-type laws requiring literacy and private titles to property gave self-styled whites a monopoly on the state and on the "civilized" cores of its metropolitan centers. Such laws, which came into being very shortly after initially expansive constitutions were promulgated, made the supposed (nonliterate) traditionalism and communitarian ways of Indians into targets of liberalism's ethnocidal policies.[49] Indians were to be forcibly converted into citizens by invalidating collective colonial land titles and encouraging the development of private property and wage-labor regimes. So as Creole and mestizo appropriations of Indian lands grew, continued opprobrium toward Indian illiteracy and traditionalism kept them laboring as *peones* (peons) on Creole and mestizo haciendas. From the mid-nineteenth century to the 1930s, the only Indians to be found in the cities were those who labored as dependents in the city homes of their hacendados, and recently arrived and often short-term migrants working in mining, markets, and as *cargadores*, bearers of heavy loads. The remaining members of the non-Creole (now nonwhite) population understandably sought to distance themselves from Indian status. And the processional dances of the mestizo-cholo artisan guilds, already structured as allegories of cultural conversion, became a useful tool in marking out that social distance.

By the late nineteenth and early twentieth century, when tin was king in Oruro and its rail link with La Paz and the coast had renewed both the "working class" and an increasingly foreign-dominated elite, there were two carnival processions in Oruro: one belonged to the elite, who on carnival Saturday carried out a short procession, dressed in a variety of orientalist visions (like sheik and harem-girl outfits) and ended up in gala balls; and the other belonged to the "vulgar Indian masses," who in carnival Sunday's procession (which successive municipal ordinances sought to prohibit), replayed the old themes of colonial theater.

Oruro newspapers of the late nineteenth century to about 1940 describe elite carnival balls in great detail, along with histories of carnival going back to Roman and Greek sources, but bypassing colonial Spanish ones. A 1924 notice typifies references to "Indian" carnival: "As usual the workers' groups of Diablos, Incas, Sicos, Tundikis [?], Llameros, etc. etc. will continue dancing through all the streets of the city. These uncultured customs persist again this year, but we shelter the hope that by next year they will have been abolished."[50]

As this formation of political economy teetered toward collapse (and revolution) from the 1920s to the 1940s, rural Indians as living bearers of pre-Columbian (and precapitalist) traditions became a magnet for indigenistas' folkloric searches for more authentic ways of being Bolivian, even as being labeled Indian remained a virtual decree of banishment from national life.

Only in the twentieth-century republic, with the rise of indigenista thinking almost always tied to socialist visions—have living "Indians" and their supposed primitive communism been extolled as models for the nation. Achieving its first great rise in the 1930s and 1940s, during a period of increasing preoccupation with labor movements and a strong antioligarchical bias among a formerly abhorred urban "mestizo-cholo" laboring class (members of which had become indispensable and influential in the lower bureaucratic and industrial administrative strata, especially after the massive mobilizations of the Chaco War), indigenism found its political strength in the Movimiento Nacional Revolucionario, which came to power in 1952.[51]

The period from the 1930s to the 1950s saw the confluence of indigenismo, labor movements, and fascist, military socialist, and populist politics, and renewed efforts by longstanding rural movements to consolidate indigenous land claims against usurping *latifundistas* (big landlords) by using the very arguments of liberalism to assert a new "social contract" with the state.[52] This same period saw a new wave of rural to urban migration; mainly of former hacendados (Creoles and mestizos) and ex-vecinos displaced from privileged positions in rural towns by agrarian reform, but also a technocratic mestizo elite, children of former mine foremen and the mestizo officer corps of the Chaco War. This was the seed bed of indigenismo.

Bound up with unionism and communitarian ideals and often with idealized visions of primitive communism, indigenista interest in things "Indian" was still focused on the most "ancient and authentic," which is to say the least colonial, aspects of rural culture, and was tied to a paradoxical demeaning of "mestizo-cholo" culture per se.[53] But by eliding cultural differences between rural "Indian" and urban "cholo" cultures, by relabeling "cholo" belief systems (such as those involving the earth mother Pachamama and the *tíos* [devil idols] of the mines) as authentically ancient and "Indian" ones, and by Indianizing both the provenience of urban dance-dramas and their representational content, the predominantly urban mestizo-cholo dance-drama and religious complex could be made to stand in for that of the rural "Indian." If the most auspicious forms of indigenous culture for the purposes of indigenista Creole nationalism were those with pre-Columbian pedigrees, these could by such sleights of sign be found in the barroom, the marketplace, and perhaps even in the kitchen.

Carlos Medinaceli was an influential indigenista ideologue and the author of one of Bolivia's indigenista "foundational fictions," *La Chaskañawi* (first published in 1947).[54] By casting the politics of racial, ethnic, and class intolerance as a conservative obstacle to a romance between lovers from distinct backgrounds, novels like *La Chaskañawi* urge the reader to support a politics of class leveling as both the precondition and result of the lovers' success in reaching their goal. In that novel, an elite Creole-Spanish college student named Adolfo pursues a cholita barmaid named Claudina, whose part-Indian ancestry gives her a robust sensuality that Adolfo is unable to see in the women of his own class. That same ancestry, and the honest laboring life that it condemns her to, also provides Adolfo (and the reader) with the basis for an authetic natural form of citizenship.

> Claudina . . . was not a Western soul transplanted from the high spiritual culture of theologically restless Medieval Spain to the telluric rusticity of the American landscape: she was the spontaneous fruit of this landscape, through which the ebullient and joyful current [of life] freely runs, full of the gaiety of creative power, . . . rich and swelling with sap; her soul was maternal, not ascetic. Just for that, Adolfo was for her the dehumanized man of the civilization that submits to the omnipotent female, eternal ally of life and nature. Once more matter triumphed over spirit, blood over idea. Eternal struggle. Source of all tragedies. Cruel perverter of souls.[55]

Adolfo's path to Claudina is blocked by a series of obstacles, including not only a host of colonially derived social conventions of class bounding but also a retrograde conservative political putsch that threatens to carry Claudina's male cholo peers into power. As Sommer surmises of the nationalist canon, Adolfo's libidinal attachment is at once sexual and patriotic. In sustained allegory, cross-class and cross-race romance, sanctioned by the liberal political goals of creating a homogenous nation of citizens, provides patriotism with the passion it requires. But even as it does all of this, *La Chaskañawi* also serves as a cautionary tale. As the elite Adolfo gives up his university education to possess the earthy and fertile, natural citizen, Claudina, his friends see him slide rapidly into the drunken apathy they associate with cholos, the men of his paramour's part-

Indian working class. They also see him feminized, his will sapped by the seductive but manly (autonomous and strong) Claudina.

In *La Chaskañawi*, Adolfo is lured into his first public acknowledgment of his submission to Claudina when, unable to resist her seductive dancing during carnival, he leaves the scornful Creole audience and joins in with the dancing cholada. Although it is set in the 1920s, the novel here recaptures a turning point in Oruro's carnival, when in 1940 a few elite indigenistas first expressed their solidarity with the "Indian" working class by joining the Diablada dance organized each year by the predominantly mestizo butchers' union.[56] But this sort of direct challenge to ethnic/class barriers did not last long. In 1944, elite dancers withdrew from the butchers' group to start their own dance group, with their own miniature image of the Virgin of the Socavón, weekly prayer sessions, and charter. In that same year, the ill-fated reformist president Gualberto Villarroel invited the butcher's group to give a command performance in La Paz, marking the beginnings of an explicitly politicized promotion of "folklore."[57] Since Villarroel's time it has, however, been the elite group that has moved to the center of the national stage. With a high concentration of Oruro's doctors and lawyers—whose wives would not be caught dead, outside of their carnival dances, in the cholita outfits worn by their maids and by marketwomen—even this group's weekly practice and prayer meetings, which may include lessons in folklore, receive attention. It has been elite "Indian devils" and "cholitas" who have traveled most widely abroad to represent Bolivia's national heritage (appearing, for example, in an Iowa City Fourth of July parade, in the French Revolution bicentennial festivities, and in Expo 92 in Seville), and who have become most fully emblematic, not only of Oruro but of the nation, as a quintessential icon of "Indian" Bolivianness.

Since indigenista elites first joined in the dances of urban working-class guilds in the 1940s, their vision of carnival dancing as a unifying tradition within which a national identity might be staged has become generalized. Nonetheless, at the same time that mestizo-cholo urban artisans' traditions about the relationship between "Indian" heritage and the "civilized life" have been adopted for nationalist purposes, and even as the pageant "cholita" becomes a key figure in carnival narratives, "cholos and cholitas" themselves have been marginalized from the patriotic and devotional core of the spectacle. Oruro's Adolfos may have been drawn into the dance by its original Claudinas, but the cholita roles in the dances in which they participate are, today, played by decidedly *de vestido* ("Western" dressed) women who employ *de pollera* cholitas as their maids. No doubt for them, as for their elite male peers, such transgressions add a certain frisson to the courtship that ensues in the truly carnival-esque private parties held at carnival time, but those parties, like the fraternities that sponsor them, tend to exclude "real" Indians, Africans, or cholitas.

*Populist Cholas and Rural
Invasions of Urban Pageantry, 1980–1990s*

In 1988, a new dance style (which since has become more generalized) burst onto the scene. The style originated with a group, called Ayllu Sartañani, made up of the university students who are children of *residentes* (migrants from towns of the Carangas region). Ayllu Sartañani is not only a dance group but an activist political and research organization as well. They have opted for a less "folklorized and styled" dance done to "represent" real Indians, and they have struggled to learn the actual dances and performance styles characteristic of Carangas towns during carnival in an effort to recapture their own recent heritage. There, carnival is associated with the end of the rainy season and the beginning of the harvest season, and is also a time when visiting spirits of the dead (called to earth during All Souls Day) are asked to depart. For this event rural men of Oruro's hinterlands play a recorder-style five-tone flute known as a *t'arka*, and dance in circular and serpentine patterns, sometimes in formation as couples. To achieve the authenticity they desired, Ayllu Sartañani worked with a campesino music master and sought to incorporate rural people into their dance group. Their activism and ethnographic practice, however, has aims far beyond carnival dance; they have produced valuable ethnographic works on the political organization of their towns, as well as position papers on the impact on the towns of neoliberal state-reorganization.[58]

Far more typical and popular among the new dances are the Tinkus dances that have become the rage since 1980, especially in working-class neighborhoods and within indigenista university circles. Because they are committed more to an effort to revalorize their own identities and to find their own political voice as urbanites than they are to projects aimed at rural communities, members of Tinkus groups seem to be engaged in a project to undo the disparagement, to which they are subject from above, for their presumed closeness to rural life and to Indianness.

Wearing stylized versions of the campesino dress of particular rural regions, Tinkus dancers have insisted on representing rural peoples themselves. In a kind of ethnographic realism, their organizers have made forays into the countryside to buy a sample of rural costume (later copied and "improved on" by specialist tailors) in order to represent what they take to be a characteristic form of customary indigenous festival practice, ritual battles, or *tinkus*.

The Tinkus group with which I worked in my 1988 research— a breakaway fragment of the very first such group (organized in 1980)—was another association of residentes, migrants (and their children) who came to Oruro from the provincial town of Bolívar. As former vecinos, dominating mestizo traders privileged by the patrimonial politics of prerevolutionary Bolivia, these migrants had been forced out of the countryside between the mid-1950s and the early 1980s. In that former vecino status, they would have detested being confused with Indians. Now, however, the paternalist ties they maintained, as truck drivers and intermediary commercializers of rural produce, with the peasants of Bolívar, gave them access to insider "ethnographic" knowledge of that region's traditional clothing styles and ritual forms. From that knowledge they forged a new dance, with an accentuated stooping lunge thought to be characteristically Indian,[59] representing an indigenous ritual battle.

In striving to offer an explanation for the violence they portray, they invented a playlet depicting a jealous struggle between rival men over a paramour. Meeting for their practice sessions in a chichería located in a peripheral neighborhood, and celebrating there a miniature image of the virgin dressed in Tinku costume, members of this group strove to organize its resources and distribute its obligations using the kinds of reciprocal aid characteristic of the countryside, *ayni* and *padrinazgo*. The relatively marginal status they now endured in the city as migrants at risk of being labeled "cholos" for their continued association with rural life, was aptly indexed in their name, Tinkus Huakchas, "orphan" or "poor" tinkus. Indeed, this group had in 1988 just parted ways from its parent group, Tinkus Tolkas, "son-in-law tinkus."

Tinkus groups of the 1980s were a vanguard of a new kind of populist politics emergent in that decade and ascendant in the 1990s. In that politics, subtly analyzed for the Cochabamba town of Quillacollo by Robert Albro, claims of "humble origin" must be backed up by demonstrations of affinity with stereotypically rural Indian or vecino kinds of practices, such as the pouring of chicha libations and use of cogodparenthood to forge a clientage network. Actualizing such networks has swept populists into power over the last decade, especially in municipal office. Such aims have not, however, prevented the female Tinkus costume from shifting progressively toward stylized piquant cholita dress; indeed, the chicha-bearing cholita figures for Tinkus dancers and populist politics alike as a signally important root metaphor.[60]

In *La Chaskañawi* "native cultural" *debits* are attached to the threatening and brutish masculinity of laboring-class urban male Indianness, "mestizo" or "cholo" men, while the (ambivalently) valued but alluring *strengths* of "native culture," linked through maternal bonds to the national soil, are projected onto the "domesticated," marketeering, and serving urban variant of female Indianness, de pollera cholas like Claudina.[61] Laboring men, unable to cloister their women; and cholita daughters and wives, ensconced in market stalls and elite households under the *patria potestas* (patriarchal power) of elite men and the state's "hygiene police,"[62] inherited the faults imputed to the vulgar estates and lower classes of Spain: an absence of ennobling honor and shame.[63] But they also inherited by their Indianness a tie to the homeland coveted by Creole indigenistas, and more recently by migrants' associations and populist politicians, and in this the wanton accessibility of the cholita as mistress or perhaps adoptive mother is revalued as a vehicle to patriotism.[64]

Through metonymies that let one social category, and one story, stand in for another, the surrogated narratives of carnival dance are able to recast the colonial asymmetry of power into a tragic transgressive romance, one located squarely within elite households. Initially, perhaps, the shape of that romance was exclusively a Creole manner of enacting love of country while preserving a privileged place within it, but it has since become more general, associated with entry into a particularly urban form of national life. In it we may see at work Sommer's double allegory, where through repeated metonymic association, a romantic love that needs the state's blessing and a political legitimacy that needs to be founded on love mutually motivate one another.

But there is also another allegorical connection proper to the saints' festivals in which such stories are so often played out in pageantry. The initial ardor that attracts an elite romancer to a lower-class and Indian object of desire is attributed not to nation, but to Satan, resident in the tempting body of the sensuous Other. In this allegory, consummation is the fall into sin, and ultimate renunciation—at pageant's end when the costumes come off—becomes redemption. Costumed elites, and increasingly the upwardly mobile progeny of mestizo-cholo migrants and old-style laboring guilds, play out a dangerously passionate story not only for the patria, but for the sake of piety that would ultimately civilize the beast that surges upward when patriots dig deep into their psyches in search of their native roots.

The nationalist romance may appear to bridge national sectors with a passion that constructs patriotism. But the source of its transgressive desire turns out to be not only erotics but an "antisocial" lust for lucre and the patriarchal potencies by which social divisions are produced and maintained. In the end, elite privilege (sought by the ideal neoliberal citizen-subject) still depends on control of the "Indian" labor power that magically produces lucre, and of feminine Indian domestic power that reproduces the urban elite household. Together these two figures "libidinally" motivate displays of transgressive patriotic passion, but fear of contamination and diabolical excess require renunciation of those same transgressions along with whatever revolutionary possibilities they may have implied. It is not for nothing that both the literary romances of the national canon and the nationalist heritage pageants are ultimately plotted as tragedies. Even so, they are subject to contestation, most effectively by those whom the dances are purported to represent.

Indigenous Activism and the Spectacle of Modernity, 1993–2000

Beginning in 1993 a "call to arms" by the departmental peasant union brought contingents of dancers and musicians from rural communities to Oruro in an effort to "invade" carnival. Unlike the new (since 1989) festival of Chutillos in the city of Potosí, which devotes a full day to the dances of that department's indigenous communities (separating them from the procession of the city's own dance troupes), Oruro's carnival made no room for actual rural people in its nationally famous pageantry. Their boisterous performances in local homespun clothing to the tune of the traditional carnival period t'arka flutes, carried out without a parade permit, have so far taken place only during one of the days running up to the main event. In 1993, their procession was headed by a car from which hostile invective blared from loudspeakers, proclaiming (in Aymara) that the q'aras (literally "naked" or "culturally peeled" people) who played at being "Indians" in their carnival should take a lesson from the authentic possessors of the national heritage. Asserting their rightful place in national consciousness, these dancers sought recognition as well as to win the prize offered by the union for the best dance group.

In 1995, on the day before the "official" procession, rural dance groups, again intent on "invading" Creole carnival, obtained a police escort into the center of town. An impromptu crowd gathered to watch the poorly advertised affair, and the Aymara loudspeaker commentary was more polite and muted than in the 1993 event. There was also innovation: each group had been asked (again by the union) to practice their performance in provincial capital rehearsals, and only the best were allowed to continue on to the department capital of Oruro. All had also been enjoined to carry out a costumbre, to perform a carnival ritual "typical" of their community. So after representing themselves in dance from a peasant market on the outskirts of town into the city center and the Plaza of National Folklore (already decked out with national brewery advertisements in anticipation of the next day's massive crowds), each group "represented" their "local culture and customs."

All of the groups demonstrated ch'alla sessions and the burning of q'uwa incense bundles; some included long invocations by hometown shamans, or yatiris. Led by their actual community leaders carrying staffs of community office and wearing vicuña-wool scarves, two groups performed mock llama sacrifices, balking at the actual bloodletting that might have on the one hand offended urbanites (and in any case is illegal outside of the slaughterhouse), yet on the other hand, in the proper context, would have made the ritual effective. Another group's dancers chalked out their community's name in large letters in front of the reviewing stand. Some of the groups performed dances and played instruments (such as the pan-pipe siku) that would have been completely out of place as parts of carnival-season rites in their hometowns.[65]

Members of these groups told me that they had chosen their costumes and instruments "to make a better impression" on city folks. But this was not a cynical effort to win the cow offered by the peasant union as first prize. Three women from a community a few hours north of Oruro explained that while they hoped to win the cow, they had come to demonstrate their pride in their local customs. One handed me the translated, typed, and photocopied lyrics to the carnival song they would sing in their costumbre—it was a paean to the beauty of their hometown. She then added that she was a fan of Oruro's carnival dances, and for the patron saint festival in her home community she much preferred to see a Morenada, Caporales, or Tinku dance (performed to brass-band marches in rented costumes, including the piquant cholita outfits) than the local dance styles of bygone years. As one jilaqata (alcalde or local official) from yet another town told me, they had come to demonstrate to city people the "authentic original" on which poor urban copies of "indigenous" dances were based. They had come, in other words, to teach city folks what national culture actually was, and at the same time to more fully participate in that national culture. In part, too, their efforts were aimed at being recognized as authentic rural "base communities," of a sort that since the passage of the 1994 Law of Popular Participation can petition for development money and hope for a more direct form of representation in national politics.

So far, such groups have not been admitted to the main event, and in any case they did not participate in the wider frame including offerings at rock shrines and mass before the virgin. But that day may come. They have appropriated the essence of public spectacle and have objectified a slice of practice as differentiating "custom." Both moves are now necessary in order to enter the arena of national cultural politics, where display of a sanitized and objectified emblem of cultural difference within a ritual frame that subordinates separate or private interests to patriotism now makes them legitimate interlocutors with the state. Likewise, as the urban appetite for "Indian" customs waxes, drawing the rural people called "Indians" into their pageants as once they only invited them into their markets (and, as maids, into their homes), so does the rural "Indian" appropriation of urban folkloric Indianness, which from the countryside looks like cosmopolitan progress. Through such convergences, a homogenous national "indigenous culture" is being generated in mimetic spectacle, an array of signifying practices that is, perhaps, an authentic way of being Bolivian. It remains to be seen, however, how rural communities will appropriate or revise the urban family romance of which such pageants also serve as allegories.

CONCLUSION: POSTCOLONIALITY, BOLIVIAN STYLE

Spanish American countries seem marginal to "the postcolonial question" because of their lack of fit with its historical schematic, having become independent during the nineteenth century from an empire forged in the sixteenth century, and having been shaped in ways that break the world historical mold created by postcolonialism's equations of modernity and colonialism, postmodernity and decolonization.

To consider Spanish America within the same purview requires us to problematize "modernity" so as to encompass the sixteenth-century project of Philip II. It requires, too, that we abandon old certainties deriving the rise of popular sovereignty and republicanism from late-eighteenth-century French epistemologies and political economies (in which the individual citizen-subject is mediated to the state by the confluence of Enlightenment positivism and the "bourgeois public sphere"). This is a tall order, difficult especially due to the continued stranglehold on academe of a "rise of the West" narrative that bypasses Iberia in its march from Mesopotamia to Greece, Jerusalem, Rome, and Paris to London and New York, and hence to New Delhi, Lagos, Manila, and Oruro and that has both underwritten and survived the heralded death of derivative "master narratives."[66]

To be sure, the Spanish American nations also fell under the domineering influence of other kinds of empire—notably British and American venture capitalism and the subsequent political, economic, and military pressures designed to preserve such interests—and in large measure those are the empires from which a Latin Americanized subaltern studies seeks to be decolonized. When Latin American intellectuals and activists decry imperialism, it is the last hundred years of U.S. imperialism, and the intellectual marginalization of Latin American traditions, that they have in mind, not the previous four centuries of Spanish domination.[67] Without questioning such positions, however, I have preferred here to consider the lasting import for Spanish America's nations of that first colonialism, and to plumb the contradictions within the national project left intact as a result of the manner by which those nations achieved their independence.

What I have suggested is that such elites have, since the 1940s, used the ritual tropes of carnival, still enframed within a colonial political theology, to carry off a singular bit of identity magic, which has since become useful in populist politics and in the efforts of rural peoples to claim their rights as Bolivian citizens. Becoming Indians on the stage of heritage pageantry fixed within the penitential processional of pilgrimage festivals, city folks nonetheless still make Indianness into a kind of sinful national id that is conveniently repressed at festival's end. Such indigenista-inspired activities enable participants to partake in their county's indigenous heritage, giving themselves bona fide "original citizenship" while simultaneously entrenching their differences from Indians, preserving the privileged paternalism monopolized since independence by self-avowed "non-Indians," in the interest of national progress.

One irony here is that the apparently "modern" form of subjectivity made possible through the medium of spectacle[68] is everywhere, in country and city alike, derived from very old colonial processional forms. They may now carry messages of pan-Bolivian resistance to U.S. imperialism and to neoliberalism, and like the festival of the Virgin of Urqupiña near Cochabamba that styles itself the "Festival of National Integration," serve as a vehicle for the coalescence of a truly national identity, but they carry signs of colonial difference that hinders "national unity." Through the overarching sixteenth-century tropology of such festivals, they also channel diverse goals into a common purpose that, today nationalist (but also always regionalist and municipal), was once an effective measure of imperial and monarchical hegemony.

Along with many of its dance and dramatic genres, the processional frame of Oruro's carnival derives directly from totalizing imperial rituals such as Corpus Christi processions, through which the inhabitants of Castilian and then Peruvian towns, as municipally organized publics, symbolically reenacted a rite by which sovereignty delegated to the monarch was claimed as the original property of el pueblo (in Spanish, both "people" and "town"). No wonder participation in such rites has today become a de rigueur exercise of would-be politicians, a means by which everyone can feel both patriotic and "more Andean," and also a vehicle through which rural communities can now seek greater inclusion within the state.

The colonial heritage still recalled in the spatial and temporal coordinates of festival seems to sabotage participants' transgressive or contestatory aims. Although cultural difference may be symbolically blurred, it seems that the festival frame reentrenches the divisions that were to be overcome, enchaining picturesque ethnic diversity to the service of the postcolonial, and neoliberal, state. And neoliberalism's celebration of pluriculturalism seems here to reinvest in culturally differentiated *alters* all the stigma formerly attached biologically to Indians (and Africans) by now-discredited theories of race. As Marisol de la Cadena has shown for Peru, such agendas use anthropologically informed theses about cultural difference to perpetuate covert forms of racism, even as they denounce overtly racist practices.[69]

Carnival also aligns the primary polarity (between what is Spanish, white, and Christian and what is Indian, African, and pagan) to schemas of space and time critical to the national project. The first is the nation's (and "indigenous peoples' ") historicity: in the "time out of time" of ritual, thoroughly urban and modern participants festively give sway to premodern and heterogeneous traditions deriving from the prenational past, but they do so in order to construct a particularly Bolivian form of modern citizenry. Perhaps heritage pageants always reembody the past in order to more effectively abolish it. Here, at any rate, Indians (and their customs) are condemned to the past even as they are constructed in dance. Festival done, they are then abolished from the national public sphere. Like fallen angels, they and the past they embody may be cast out from decent public space, but they do not cease to exist. They and the colonial past are projected beneath the surface, into earth shrines and mine tunnels, and through practices articulated in this temporalized space, into the psyche of the citizen who struggles to tame them, now in the shape of unruly desires.

The patriotic procession of folkloric Indianness may aim to domesticate those desires, but the never-ending search for the "most authentic" alter, always receding farther away into the past or into the countryside, perpetually diverts attention from the true locus of the predicament dancing aims to solve, the class- and race-stratified household of the ideal, patrician-bourgeois Bolivian citizen. Iconic indexes of that status (large house, car, money, bank account, professional title, passport, and plane tickets) are by far the most popular fetishes purchased by festival participants to be empowered by forces of the demonic Indian underworld. As embodied surrogates of such powers, dancers submit to the Virgin, who is capable of converting these powers into moral authority and civilizing patriarchy. The production of social privilege, in this scheme, hinges on interning dangerous and seductive Indian powers in the household as labor power and as surrogate mothers. Creoles were disinherited by mother Spain on suspicion they had been "Indianized" by the land of their birth and the milk of their Indian wet nurses. It seems, then, that the elite and upwardly mobile heirs to their privileged way of life may in this festive frame truly have found a way to express and even reproduce their Bolivianness, although it also endlessly reproduces their redoubled postcolonial predicament and poses the pursuit of self-interest (a definitive characteristic of the ideal citizen-subject in the early liberal republic as in the neoliberal one) as the antithesis of patriotism's "deep, horizontal comradeship."

Perhaps in the marketeers' separate procession outside of town, in the elite women's trend toward performing cross-dressed in male roles, or in the arrival on the scene of the rural people called Indians to protest their representation and to demand their inclusion in national life, there is room in the pageant (or in discourse about it) for productive contestation, although it is yet difficult to imagine how such pageantry might be inverted to posit the ideal citizen-subject as an Indian. This postcolonial predicament is truly historically deep and convoluted; still, it is also a particularly American, and Bolivian, one.

NOTES

I attended and/or researched carnival pageants both in Oruro and elsewhere in Bolivia repeatedly and for varying lengths of time between 1980 and 1999, with fellowship support and in the margins of other projects. Fulbright-IIE supported my work on carnival in Oruro during 1987–1988; return visits to Oruro and work on Potosí's San Bartolomé and Cochabamba's Urqupiña festivals were possible in 1989, 1991, 1992, 1995, 1996, 1998, and 1999 in part with the support of faculty travel grants from the University of Miami and New York University. Analyses of this material have been presented in many face-to-face and a few published contexts, including "La fiesta del carnaval postcolonial en Oruro: Clase, etnicidad y nacionalismo en la danza folklórica," *Revista Andina* 20.2 (1992): 279–352. My personal and intellectual debts incurred in the process of research and writing are legion, and many are acknowledged in prior publications. Particularly formative for my work were challenging commentaries by Xavier Albó, Rossana Barragán, Carlos Echevarría, Marta Irurozqui, Zoila Mendoza, Deborah Poole, and Ben Orlove, appended to my essay in the *Revista Andina* publication. Since then commentaries by William Christian, Beth Penry, Silvia Rivera Cusicanqui, and James Scott have been helpful. Comments by many graduate students at the University of Miami and New York University have also been important. My work on recent indigenous "invasions" of carnival was sparked by the 1995 conference Las Figuras Nacionales del Indio (organized in Mexico City by Jacques Galinier and Anath Ariel de Vidas) and has been published in part in my commentary on essays in a special issue of the *Journal of Latin American Anthropology* (December 1998), edited by Mark Rogers. Comments by the organizers and participants of the After Spanish Rule workshop have also been instrumental. Note that all translations are mine unless indicated otherwise.

1 Claudio Lomnitz, "Nationalism as a Practical System: Benedict Anderson's Theory of Nationalism from the Vantage Point of Spanish America," in *The Other Mirror: Grand Theory through the Lens of Latin America*, ed. Miguel Angel Centeno and Fernando López-Alves (Princeton: Princeton University Press, 2001), 329.

2 Ann Laura Stoler, *Race and the Education of Desire: Foucault's History of Sexuality and the Colonial Order of Things* (Durham: Duke University Press, 1995).

3 Ann Laura Stoler, "Making Empire Respectable: The Politics of Race and Sexual Morality in Twentieth-Century Colonial Cultures," *American Ethnologist* 16 (1989): 634–60.

4 Doris Sommer, *Foundational Fictions: The National Romances of Latin America* (Berkeley: University of California Press, 1991).

5 William A. Wilson, "Herder, Folklore, and Romantic Nationalism," *Journal of Popular Culture* 6.4 (1972): 819–35; Raymond Williams, *The Country and the City* (New York: Oxford University Press, 1973).

6 Authoritative sources on the Creole predicament include David Brading, *The First America: Spanish Monarchy, Creole Patriots, and the Liberal State, 1492–1867* (New York: Cambridge University Press, 1991); Bernard Lavallé, *Las promesas ambiguas: Ensayos sobre criollismo colonial en los andes* (Lima: Pontificia Universidad Católica del Perú, 1993).

7 Marisol de la Cadena, "Silent Racism and Intellectual Superiority in Peru," *Bulletin of Latin American Research* 17.2 (1998): 143–64.

8 On Oruro's carnival, see Abercrombie, "La fiesta del carnaval postcolonial en Oruro: Clase, etnicidad y nacionalismo en la danza folklórica," *Revista Andina* 20.2 (1992): 279–352, and references there.

9 On the procession of Gran Poder in La Paz, see Xavier Albó and Mathias Preiswerk, *Los Señores del Gran Poder* (La Paz: Centro de Teología Popular, 1986). The pilgrimage-pageant of Quillacollo is described in Robert Albro, "Neoliberal Ritualists of Urkupiña: Bedeviling Patrimonial Identity in a Bolivian Patronal Fiesta," *Ethnology* 37.2 (1998): 133–64; and María Luisa Lagos, "'We Have to Learn to Ask': Hegemony, Diverse Experiences, and Antagonistic Meanings in Bolivia," *American Ethnologist* 20.1 (1993): 52–71.

10 In Bolivia, the category "Indian" is a construct largely of elites and anthropologists. I use the term (with or without quotes) in reference to these categorical constructs. Since the 1952 revolution *Indio* was displaced for a time by the euphemism *campesino* ("peasant"), but the latter term has also become stigmatized. "Indian" has recently been reappropriated by the mostly-urban *indianista* (as opposed to *indigenista*) movement led by Aymara- and Quechua-speaking intellectuals (see Xavier Albó, "El retorno del indio," *Revista Andina* 9.2 [1991]: 290–366), but it remains for most rural people an insult. On the problem of ethnic, racial, and language labeling in the Andes, see my "To Be Indian, to Be Bolivian: 'Ethnic' and 'National' Discourses of Identity," in *Nation-States and Indians in Latin America*, eds. Greg Urban and Joel Sherzer (Austin: University of Texas Press, 1991), 95–130. See also Marisol de la Cadena, *Indigenous Mestizos: The Politics of Race and Culture in Cuzco, Peru, 1919–1991* (Durham: Duke University Press, 2000); Cecilia Méndez, "República sin indios: La comunidad imaginada del Perú," in *Tradicion y Modernidad en los Andes*, ed. Henrique Urbano (Cuzco: Centro Bartolomé de las Casas), 15–41; Mary Weismantel and Stephen F. Eisenman, "Race in the Andes: Global Movements and Popular Ontologies," *Bulletin of Latin American Research* 17.2 (1998): 121–42.

11 This insight is further elaborated in Joanne Rappaport, "Fictive Foundations: National Romances and Subaltern Ethnicity in Latin America," *History Workshop Journal* 34 (1991): 119–31; Julie Skurski, "The Ambiguities of Authenticity in Latin America: Doña Bárbara and the Construction of National Identity," *Poetics Today* 15.4 (1994): 605–42.

12 Sommer, *Foundational Fictions*, 109–10.

13 Although there is no space to develop the issue in this essay one might also extend Sommer's thesis to encompass nonheteronormative challenges to such heterosexual erotics, some of which are suggested here.

14 Rereadings of the dreams on which Freud based his oedipal theory point to the centrality in his sexual fantasies of his family's servant, who he analytically took to be a substitution for the forbidden mother.

See Peter Stallybrass and Allon White, *The Politics and Poetics of Transgression* (Ithaca: Cornell University Press, 1986); and Stoler, *Race and the Education of Desire.*

15 On the embodiment of social memory, see Paul Connerton, *How Societies Remember* (New York: Cambridge University Press, 1989); on forms of festively enacted social memory in rural towns not far from Oruro, see my *Pathways of Memory and Power: Ethnography and History among an Andean People* (Madison: University of Wisconsin Press, 1998).

16 On the process of surrogation in the (anglophone) carnival of the Atlantic world, see Joseph Roach, *Cities of the Dead: Circum-Atlantic Performance* (New York: Columbia University Press, 1996).

17 Stallybrass and White, *Politics and Poetics of Transgression*, 5, quoted in Roach, *Cities of the Dead*, 39.

18 On the performance history of Inca plays in the area, see Margot Beyersdorff, *Historia y drama ritual en los Andes Bolivianos, siglos XVI-XX* (La Paz: Plural, 1991). One such playscript is analyzed in Nathan Wachtel, *Vision of the Vanquished* (New York: Barnes and Noble Imports, 1977).

19 This dance has been studied in detail by Julia Elena Fortún in *La danza de los diablos* (La Paz: Ministerio de Educación y Bellas Artes, 1961).

20 Accounts are offered in Augusto Beltrán Heredia, *Carnaval de Oruro* (Oruro: Editorial Universitaria, 1956); and Niver Montes Camacho, *Proceso íntimo del carnaval de Oruro* (Oruro: Editorial Universitaria, 1986).

21 The outfit is fully depicted in M. Lissette Canavesi de Sahonero, *El traje de la chola paceña* (La Paz: Amigos del Libro, 1987).

22 For example, see Peter Burke, *Popular Culture in Early Modern Europe* (New York: Harper and Row, 1978).

23 The pin-up "virgin" of one group in 1988's anticarnival (a hazing ceremony for engineering students) identified them as "conchalitas devotas a la virgencita de la cocainita" (little chola devotees of the little virgin of cocaine), a rhyming-slang burlesque linking the cholitas' allure to illicit sexual fantasy (*concha*, "shell," is also a slang term for vulva).

24 See Miri Rubin, *Corpus Christi: The Eucharist in Late Medieval Culture* (Cambridge: Cambridge University Press, 1991); Frances George Very, *The Spanish Corpus Christi Procession: A Literary and Folkloric Study* (Valencia: Tipografía Moderna, 1962); Antoinette Molinié, "Dos celebraciones de Corpus Christi, en los Andes y en La Mancha," *Antropología* (Madrid), no. 10 (1995): 41–72; Antoinette Molinié, ed, *Celebrando el Cuerpo de Dios* (Lima: Universidad Católica del Peru, 1999); and Carolyn Dean, *Inca Bodies and the Body of Christ: Corpus Christi in Cuzco* (Durham: Duke University Press, 1999).

25 On censuses, see Armando Guevara-Gil and Frank Salomon, "A Personal Visit: Colonial Political Ritual and the Making of Indians in the

Andes," *Colonial Latin American Review* 3.1–2 (1994): 3–36. On *relaciones geográficas*, maps, and plans, see Richard L. Kagan, *Urban Images of the Hispanic World, 1493–1793* (New Haven: Yale University Press, 2000); on imperial bureaucracy, see Richard L. Kagan, *Lawsuits and Litigants in Castile, 1500–1700* (Chapel Hill: University of North Carolina Press, 1981).

26 See María Justina Sarabia Viejo, *Francisco de Toledo: Disposiciones gubernativas para el virreinato del Perú, 1569–1574; Vol. 2: Ordenanzas generales para la vida común en los pueblos de indios*, (Seville: Escuela de Estudios Hispano-Americanos, 1989).

27 For more on reducción, see my *Pathways of Memory and Power*. On confession and other missionary techniques, see Regina Harrison, "The Theology of Concupiscence: Spanish-Quechua Confessional Manuals in the Andes," in *Coded Encounters: Writing, Gender, and Ethnicity in Colonial Latin America*, ed. Francisco Javier Cevallos-Candau, Jeffrey A. Cole, Nina M. Scott, and Nocomedes Suárez-Araúz (Amherst: University of Massachusetts Press, 1994), 135–50.

28 On the "crisis of the aristocracy" and resulting efforts to discipline *el vulgo*, see José Antonio Maravall, *Culture of the Baroque* (Minneapolis: University of Minnesota Press, 1987).

29 See Thomas A. Abercrombie, "Q'aqchas and the Plebe in Rebellion," *Journal of Latin American Anthropology* 2 (1996): 62–111.

30 On the transfer of such spectacles to the Indies, see José Juan Arrom, *Historia del teatro hispanoamericano (época colonial)* (Mexico City: Eds. de Andrea, 1967); Othón Arroniz, *Teatro de evangelización en Nueva España*, (Mexico City: Universidad Autónoma de México, 1979); Max Harris, *Aztecs, Moors, and Christians: Festivals of Reconquest in Mexico and New Spain* (Austin: University of Texas Press, 2000); and Margot Beyersdorff, *Historia y Drama Ritual en los Andes bolivianos* (La Paz: Plural, 1997).

31 Fray Alonso Ramos Gavilán, *Historia de Nuestra Señora de Copacabana* (1621; La Paz: Empresa Editora Universo, 1976), 221.

32 Bartolomé Arzáns de Orsúa y Vela, *Historia de la Villa Imperial de Potosí*, 3 vols. (1702–1735; Providence: Brown University Press, 1965) 1:95–99.

33 Arzáns's description of the fiestas of 1608 is analyzed by Lewis Hanke in "The 1608 Fiestas in Potosí," *Boletín del Instituto Riva-Agüero* (Lima) 3 (1956–57): 107–28. On the foundation and layout of Oruro and its single large ranchería, see José de Mesa and Theresa Gisbert, "Oruro: Origen de una villa minera," in *La minería hispana e iberoamericana: Contribución a su investigación histórica; Vol. 1: Ponencias del I coloquio internacional sobre historia de la minería* (León: Cátedra San Isidoro, 1970), 559–90. On the laboring indio forastero population there, see Ann Zulawski, *They Eat from Their Labor: Work and Social Change in Colonial Bolivia* (Pittsburgh: University of Pittsburgh Press, 1995).

34 Compare the analysis of like sites in Michael Taussig, "History as Sorcery," in his *Shamanism, Colonialism, and the Wildman* (Chicago: University of Chicago Press, 1987).

35 Karen Spalding, *Huarochiri* (Stanford: Stanford University Press, 1984), 273–74.

36 Enrique Tandeter, *Coercion and Market: Silver Mining in Colonial Potosí, 1692–1826* (Albuquerque: University of New Mexico Press, 1993); Abercrombie, "Q'aqchas and the Plebe in Rebellion."

37 Archivo General de Indias (hereafter AGI), Lima 807, "Potosí 1751: Testimonio de la causa contra varios yndios por querer seguir la costumbre del robo de metales."

38 AGI, Charcas 481, no. 19, 2°, "Gremio de Azogueros al Superintendente," 1762.

39 These well-documented events are analyzed in Fernando Cajías de la Vega, "Los objetivos de la revolución indígena de 1781: El caso de Oruro," *Revista Andina* 1.2 (1983): 407–28. A partial review of these events is presented in Oscar Cornblitt, *Power and Violence in the Colonial City* (New York: Cambridge University Press, 1995).

40 Sarah C. Chambers, *From Subjects to Citizens: Honor, Gender, and Politics in Arequipa, Peru (1780–1854)* (University Park: Pennsylvania State University Press, 2000); Juan Pedro Viqueira Albán, *Propriety and Permissiveness in Bourbon Mexico*, trans. Sonya Lipsett-Rivera and Sergio Rivera Ayala (Wilmington: SR Books, 1999).

41 On the sixteenth- to eighteenth-century European creation of a "high public culture" as distinguished from plebian practice, see Burke, *Popular Culture in Early Modern Europe*. Charles III officially forbade the public performance of autos sacramentales during Corpus Christi in 1780 (242).

42 On such strictures, see, for example, Susan Socolow, "Acceptable Partners," in *Sexuality and Marriage in Colonial Latin America*, ed. Asuncion Lavrin (Lincoln: University of Nebraska Press, 1989).

43 Helen Nader, *Liberty in Absolutist Spain* (Baltimore: Johns Hopkins University Press, 1990); Jordana Dym, " 'A Sovereign State of Every Village': City, State, and Nation in Independence-Era Central America, ca. 1760–1850" (Ph.D. diss., New York University, 2000); S. Elizabeth Penry, "The *rey común*: Indigenous Political Discourse in Eighteenth-Century Alto Perú," in *The Collective and the Public in Latin America: Cultural Identities and Political Order*, ed. Luis Roniger and Tamar Herzog (Brighton: Sussex Academic Press, 2000); François-Xavier Guerra, "De la política antigua a la política moderna, la revolución de la soberanía," in *Los espacios públicos en Iberoamerica: Ambigüedades y problemas, siglos XVIII-XIX*, ed. F. X. Guerra and Annick Lampérière (Mexico City:

El Colegio de Mexico, 1992); and the review in Lomnitz, "Nationalism as a Practical System."

44 Abercrombie, "Q'aqchas and the Plebe in Rebellion."

45 On the simultaneous existence of these two forms of sovereignty, see Tristan Platt, "The Janus State," paper presented at the workshop After Spanish Rule, Gainesville, Florida, October 1999.

46 Cf. Stoler, *Race and the Education of Desire.*

47 See Stuart B. Schwartz and Frank Salomon, "New People and New Kinds of People: Adaptation, Readjustment and Ethnogenesis in South American Indigenous Societies (Colonial Era)," in *The Cambridge History of Native American Peoples; Vol. 3: South America,* (part 2), ed. Frank Salomon and Stuart B. Schwartz (New York: Cambridge University Press, 1999), 443–501.

48 Alberto Flores Galindo, *Buscando un Inca: Identidad y utopía en los Andes* (Lima: Instituto de Apoyo Agrario, 1987).

49 See Tristan Platt, "Liberalism and Ethnocide in the Southern Andes," *History Workshop Journal* 17 (1984): 3–18.

50 Manuel J. Rodriguez, in *La Palestra,* February 28, 1924.

51 On the emergence of indigenismo in Bolivia, see Michelle Bigenho, "Imaginando lo imaginado: Las narrativas de las naciones bolivianas," *Revista Andina* 14.2 (1996): 471–507.

52 See, for example, Laura Gotkowitz, "Indigenous Resistance, Mestizo Revolution," (Ph.D. diss., University of Chicago, 1998).

53 See Rossana Barragán, "Entre polleras, ñañacas y llicllas: Los mestizos y cholas en la conformación de la "Tercera República," in *Tradición y Modernidad* ed. Urbano, 43–73.

54 The novel is also analyzed in Robert Albro, "The Populist Chola: Cultural Mediation and the Political Imagination in Quillacollo, Bolivia," *Journal of Latin American Anthropology* 5.2 (200): 30–88. See also consideration of Bolivia's earlier indigenista work, *Juan de la Rosa,* in Marcia Stephenson, *Gender and Modernity in Andean Bolivia* (Austin: University of Texas Press, 1999); and Gotkowitz, "Indigenous Resistance, Mestizo Revolution."

55 Carlos Medinaceli, *La Chaskañawi: Novela de costumbres bolivianas* (La Paz: Amigos del Libro, 1947), 250–51.

56 The butchers' union maintains its integrity by limiting its dance membership to butchers and their families and taking a tax on cattle entering the slaughterhouse.

57 See Niver Montes Camacho, *Proceso intimo del carnaval de Oruro* (Oruro: Editorial Universitaria, 1986), for a pocket history of carnival groups.

58 Ayllu Sartañani, *Perspectivas de descentralización en Karankas: La vision comunaria* (La Paz: PROADE/ILDIS, 1995).

59 For discussion of a Peruvian case of the distinct performance styles of dances held to be Indian as opposed to mestizo, see Zoila Mendoza, *Shaping Society through Dance* (Chicago: University of Chicago Press, 2000).

60 Albro, "The Populist Chola."

61 This asymmetry has been noted by Linda Seligmann in "To Be In-Between: The Cholas as Marketwomen," *Comparative Studies in Society and History* 31.4 (1989): 694–721, 705.

62 See ibid.

63 See Mark Burkholder, "Honor and Honors in Colonial Spanish America," in *Faces of Honor*, ed. Lyman Johnson and Sonia Lipsett-Rivera (Albuquerque: University of New Mexico Press, 1998), 18–44.

64 See Mary Weismantel, *Cholas and Pishtacos: Stories of Race and Sex in the Andes* (Chicago: University of Chicago Press, 2001), for a bold study of the place of the chola in the Andean imaginary. See also Silvia Rivera Cusicanqui et al., "Trabajo de mujerres: Explotación capitalista y opresión colonial entre las migrantes aymaras de La Paz y El Alto, Bolivia," in *Ser mujer indígena, chola o birlocha en la bolivia postcolonial de los años 90*, ed. Silvia Rivera Cusicanqui (La Paz: Ministerio de Desarrollo Humana, 1996), 163–300.

65 For accounts of provincial folklore pageants in which such performances are rehearsed, see Stuart Alexander Rockefeller, "There Is a Culture Here: Spectacle and the Inculcation of Folklore in Highland Bolivia," *Journal of Latin American Anthropology* 3.2 (1999); and Thomas James Solomon, "Mountains of Song: Musical Construction of Ecology, Place, and Identity in the Bolivian Andes" (Ph.D. diss., University of Texas at Austin, 1997).

66 I refer to the story of the "rise of the West" as institutionalized in anglophone and francophone academies, which thoroughly marginalizes Iberian empires and colonies. On Spanish studies in the United States, see Richard Kagan, "Prescott's Paradigm: American Historical Scholarship and the Decline of Spain" *American Historical Review* (April 1996). See also Enrique Dussel, "Eurocentrism and Modernity," in *The Postmodernism Debate in Latin America*, ed. John Beverley, Michael Aronna, and José Oviedo (Durham: Duke University Press, 1995), 65–76.

67 See, for example, Walter D. Mignolo, *Local Histories/Global Designs: Coloniality, Subaltern Knowledges, and Border Thinking* (Princeton: Princeton University Press, 2000).

68 On the modernism inculcated in the shift from festival to spectacle in the countryside, see Rockefeller, "There Is a Culture Here."

69 See de la Cadena, *Indigenous Mestizos* and "Silent Racism and Intellectual Superiority in Peru."

3. POLITICA

Governmentalities, States, Subjects

MARIXA LASSO

Revisiting Independence Day

Afro-Colombian Politics and Creole Patriot

Narratives, Cartagena, 1809–1815

On November 11, 1811, an angry mob of black and mulatto patriots armed with lances, daggers, and guns stormed Cartagena's government palace. After insulting and beating the members of the Creole-led revolutionary junta, the mob forced them to sign the Declaration of Independence against their will. What is the meaning of this independence scene? It certainly does not fit with the exalted nationalist narratives of the early republican period, that glorified independence, the birth of the nation, and the historical role of founding Creole fathers. Yet it also does not sit well with more recent social historical narratives of Spanish America, which would have a difficult time explaining an Independence Day in which Afro-Colombians called the shots.

Although the scene described above faithfully follows most contemporary witness accounts of Cartagena's Independence Day, today it seems incredible, almost absurd. Its shocking effect derives from its resemblance to a popular revolutionary scene. We have been taught that the wars of independence in Spanish America were anything but popular revolutions. An entrenched historical tradition has argued not only that the lower classes had little if any political influence in the independence war; it has also questioned the revolutionary nature of the war itself.[1] Like the revisionist readings of the French Revolution, social historical narratives of the independence wars have made the revolution into a political and intellectual "illusion" of change. In the French case, the revisionist argument goes, revolutionaries deluded themselves in thinking that they were actually destroying a feudal system, of inaugurating a modernity that, in reality, had already been destroyed by underlying social forces. In the words of Jacques Rancière, "The Revolution is the illusion of making the Revolution, born from ignorance of the Revolution already being made."[2]

In contrast, the "enlightened illusion" of the Spanish American revolutions consisted in proclaiming a political modernity that failed to arrive.[3] Like the French Revolution, at one level it was a problem of timing, of disjunction between speech and event.[4] In Spanish America the revolution anteceded modernity, which would not arrive until the second half of the nineteenth century with the consolidation of national states and the "delayed" integration into the world economy.[5] At another and more profound level, the revolution is declared a nonevent because it was geographically misplaced.[6] Enlightened revolutionary ideology had little relevance to Spanish American "reality." The revolution was out of place because it had no place in Spanish American society. Unlike in France, modernity in Spanish America was and is constantly in question.[7]

The misplacement of the Spanish American revolutions of independence is intrinsically related to the notion that the political ideas of the age of revolution had no relevance for the lower classes. Whether the lower classes are considered the essence of Spanish American society or mere demographic majorities, it is their assumed disconnection that made revolutionary politics a mere illusion of the Creole elite.[8] The lower classes neither participated in revolutionary politics nor were they affected by political changes. Their primitive state prevented them from understanding the trappings of revolutionary politics, which were the exclusive domain of enlightened elites enamored of foreign ideas.[9] When the lower classes do appear in independence narratives it is mainly in the role of the shadowy reflection of Creole fears. Their only political influence was to strengthen the conservative and royalist inclinations of the Creole elite in places where that elite feared Indian or slave insurrections.[10] In its more radical interpretation, this narrative of fear also contributed to the nonevent status of the wars of independence. The wars had secured independence from Spain but nothing else: "Same mule, new rider." The revolution was a mirage, a matter of mere rhetoric.

In this essay I trace the historiographical construction of elite illusion and lower-class naivete back to the earliest Creole narratives of independence. My examination of this discourse addresses the ways in which Afro-Colombian politics were inscribed in the first Creole patriotic historical narratives of the Colombian city of Cartagena, an autonomous republic from 1811 to 1815.

The first master narratives of the wars of independence presented a drama in which Creole patriots struggled against numerous obstacles to create an independent, free, and modern nation.[11] In these narratives the lower classes were counted among those obstacles that Creole patriots had to overcome.[12] José Manuel Restrepo—a protagonist in the struggles for independence, the minister of the interior under Simón Bolívar, and a historian and founder of the master narrative of the Colombian wars of independence—was clear in his appraisal of the lower classes: they were primitive, in need of education, and prone to follow demagogues; if uncontrolled, they would drag the nation down the road to anarchy.[13] In Restrepo's foundational history, lower-class participation in the wars of independence is not erased but deauthorized.[14] In treating Cartagena's revolution, Restrepo acknowledges Afro-Colombian (pardo) participation and its decisive influence in the movement for independence, but he immediately depoliticizes Afro-Colombian actions. Booze and cash rather than patriotism explains their participation in the independence movement.[15] Afro-Colombian participation was not positive proof of popular patriotism; instead it demonstrated the "insolence and preponderance of people of color, which became fatal for public peace."[16] In short, Restrepo's history inscribes the acts of Afro-Colombian patriots in a discourse of danger and irrationality that sets them in sharp contrast to the noble and political conduct of the Creole elite.

In such nineteenth-century Creole narratives modernity is the commendable aspiration of Creole patriots, and one of the principles that would justify independence from Spain. It is no accident that one of Restrepo's opening scenes in his founding narrative of the Colombian wars of independence presents Nariño's's translation and printing of the Rights of Man, followed by his subsequent trial and imprisonment by the Spanish authorities.[17] Yet early narratives of the independence wars also offer some of the first admonitions about the perils of adopting modern politics in Latin America. These texts do not condemn modern politics per se but rather its excesses. Simón Bolívar's attacks on lawyers, demagogues, and incendiary theoreticians for their failure to understand that modern politics could not be transferred to Spanish America without sufficient attention to local reality are well known.[18] According to Bolívar, the new Spanish American nations needed strong government, without which they would inevitably fall into chaos and anarchy.[19] The legacy of the conservative Bolivarian narrative was to drive an epistemic wedge between the struggles and debates over forms of popular and regional representation and the societies that expressed them by transforming them into the political pipedreams of a handful of enlightened lawyers.[20]

With the emergence and institutional establishment of social history the discourse of illusion reached new levels. As social historians compared the nature and degree of social and economic changes from colonial times through the nineteenth century, they concluded that the lower classes gained nothing with independence, and if anything they lost.[21] Although many social historians acknowledged the social conflicts and economic changes that permeated the wars and their aftermath, most found little of interest in a period during which the hierarchical social order remained unaltered.[22] Changes in political culture were quickly dismissed as "mirages" that shrouded a cruel social reality. It is no accident that the apogee of social history during the 1970s coincided with a low point in research and publication on the independence period. In spite of their opposition to the nineteenth-century master narratives, social historians remained trapped by elitist understandings of the political, in particular by the characterization of the lower classes as primitive rebels. Social historians shifted the blame for the democratic failures of the independence period from the lower classes to the elite. The lower classes ceased being a barrier to the nation's modernity only to become the helpless victims of a project that they had no relation to and that did not care to include them. They were betrayed by an elite illusion of modernity that proclaimed the equality of all citizens and provided for ample suffrage rights, but was characterized in reality by *caciquismo* (bossism) and electoral fraud, which proclaimed racial equality but continued colonial practices of racial discrimination.[23]

More recent historical work is challenging the dominant narrative of the wars of independence as a nonevent and an illusion of modernity, during which the Creole elite copied foreign models with little relevance to Spanish American societies. These new works have illustrated the complexities and political richness of this period, and they have also begun to situate the wars of independence within the larger historical context of the age of revolution. These studies have recovered the sentiments of historical novelty characteristic of the period—sentiments that provided an opportunity to depose a colonial ancien régime and to construct modern, free, and just societies. They have examined how different actors across the empire read and debated contemporary theories of "good government" in terms of the "realities" of the metropole and its overseas territories.[24]

These new works tend, albeit incompletely, to go beyond the check-list model of revolution, in which the Spanish American revolutions are compared to the French and United States models to see where they failed as modern bourgeois revolutions. Antonio Annino, for example, has pointed out that the more recent Black Legend of Spanish American political history, which denounces nineteenth-century suffrage as a practice dominated by *caudillos* (chieftains), corruption, and ignorance, merely mimics the views of contemporary elites. Instead, he argues that it is more useful to situate the contemporary views of elites within a general nineteenth-century debate on the problem of how to conciliate social order and hierarchy with the new politics of citizenship and representation. In this early republican debate Latin America occupies a special place, not only for its early ample suffrage participation but, more important, because it does not fit within Europe's evolutionary model of the rise of political consciousness, which predicts a gradual increase in participation. On the contrary, in Spanish America early ample suffrage rights were later replaced by more restrictive codes.[25]

Nevertheless, sophisticated political analyses like Annino's often fail to register the participation of people of African descent. Significantly, this blind spot is not because the new political historians are unaware of lower-class participation in the wars of independence; these historians also do not deny the receptiveness of the lower orders to certain revolutionary ideas. One of the more sophisticated political historians of the period, François-Xavier Guerra, acknowledges the participation of people of African descent in the wars, as well as the influence of French, and particularly Haitian, revolutionary ideas in slave revolts.[26] Yet he quickly dismisses such events as exceptional and inconsequential, events that at most tended to make the Creole elite more conservative. Thus, Guerra delivers his grand generalization that what sets the Spanish American revolutions apart from other contemporary revolutions is the lack of participation of the lower classes in modern politics.[27]

But in Venezuela and Caribbean Colombia, both of which were crucial war theaters and important exporters of revolutionary armies (later marching on Ecuador, Peru, and Bolivia), people of African descent were a demographic majority and thus constituted the corps of the patriot army. Why do historians still insist on their insignificance? This insistence in denying Afro-Colombians' interest, participation, and contribution to republican politics speaks to the weight that historians generally give to nineteenth-century political narratives, which continue to be read as documentary evidence of lower-class attitudes. Anthony Pagden's analysis of the relationship between Bolívar's political thought and the blacks and mulattoes at Angostura provides a clear example of the limits of this historical narrative. Angostura, a small city on the banks of the Orinoco River, played a crucial role in the independence period as the seat of the first Constitutional Congress of Gran Colombia (present-day Venezuela, Colombia, and Ecuador). While most of the region, including the principal cities, remained occupied by Spanish forces, the Bolivarian army gathered at Angostura to set the constitutional basis of the imagined new nation. Dominique De Pradt described the event in the following terms:

> Sybarites of the civilization of Europe, preachers of liberty, I would wish to see your tribunals set by the banks of the Orinoco, your benches of senators mingled with a horrible mixture of Blacks, Mulattos, Cowboys, Creoles, of men suddenly dragged out of the depths of slavery and barbarity to be transformed into legislators and heads of state! The same blood, the same language, the same customs, a common heritage of grandeur and of talent, an advanced civilization, all these hold together all the several parts of the societies of Europe. In America all is diversity, the principles of division, and absence of civilization. In Europe one plays, in America one must create.[28]

One of the most striking features of De Pradt's observation is its endurance. Anthony Pagden uses him to point out Bolívar's failure to understand that his lofty republican ideals would do poorly within such a social environment. Oddly, he accuses Bolívar of not following his own precepts: the need to adapt laws to the regional specificities, and the fact of not being able to see the chimerical nature of his own program. According to Pagden, local people needed a nationalist ideology based on emotional, historical, or religious nationalism instead of abstract republican precepts with which they had no connection.[29]

In Pagden's analysis what passes unnoticed is one of the salient characteristics of De Pradt's description: The presence of black and mulatto legislators in Angostura. One could ask who these senators were; what they thought about their legislative duties; who the black and mulatto soldiers at Angostura were; how they experienced, participated, and followed the congressional debates; and did they have any influence on their outcome? Did Bolívar or any of the legislators feel their presence as an important public in preparing their addresses? In addressing such questions a different picture of the origins of modernity in Spanish America may emerge. This questioning requires, however, going beyond the conservative narrative of the wars of independence, of which Bolívar, Restrepo, and De Pradt are but some of the best-known examples. These narratives reiterate the unfitness of republican ideals to Spanish American societies, the proclivity of the lower classes to follow demagogues, and the need for strong governments in societies rifted by racial and social differences. They should be seen not as necessarily insightful descriptions of lower-class political characteristics but rather as only one variation among several political programs and commentaries that emerged during the wars.[30] These conservative readings need to be confronted with other readings that emerged during the revolution and are understood as part of a larger debate over the nature of political change and the role of color and the lower classes in the new republics.

Recent works that situate the Spanish American wars of independence within the general context of the age of revolution can prove to be extremely useful for this type of analysis because they help to situate the debates about race and politics in Spanish America within the larger debates on freedom and citizenship in the Atlantic world. One of the fascinating characteristics of the political culture of this period is the fluidity and openness that accompanied the emergence of multiple questions and debates about the nature of political representation, sovereignty, and citizenship. In places where people of African descent were in the majority, the crucial question of the racial and social limits of modern political participation was acute.[31] Similar to other peoples of African descent in the French and English Caribbean, many Afro-Colombians partake of the republican enthusiasm and rhetoric that characterized this period. They appropriate liberal rhetoric that decried Spanish obscurantism and declared a new era of republican freedom, not only to defend and further older aspirations for freedom and justice but also to fight for new notions of racial equality.[32]

Let us return to the opening scene of Cartagena's independence and ask who were these patriot Afro-Colombians? Why were they so eager to force Cartagena's Creole junta to sign the Declaration of Independence? Why did they feel entitled to do so? And why did the junta not wish to sign? By the time the day of independence had arrived, the Afro-Colombians who stormed into the chambers of the City Council had two full years of political experience as patriot conspirators under their belt. When the City Council or *cabildo* decided to depose the Spanish governor and create a junta that would rule in the name of the king, they needed to secure the support of the local blacks and mulattoes. According to a local witness, the City Council sought the support of persons close to the common people before overthrowing the Spanish governor. Thanks to this alliance they secured the participation of the black and artisan quarter of Getzemaní.[33] On the appointed day, the City Council deposed the governor with help from men armed with machetes and from a crowd from Getzemaní.[34] In this Cartagena was not unique. In the nearby city of Mompox, the *zambo* (half Indian, half black) José Luis Muñoz was part of the 1810 City Council conspiracy against the Spanish authorities. According to the Spanish military commander, it was necessary to win back the support of Muñoz because of his influence with mulattoes and zambos.[35] This pattern of securing alliances for urban patriot conspiracies continued until the very end of the independence struggle. In 1819, for example, the Spanish authorities discovered yet another patriot conspiracy in Mompox in which Creoles colluded with zambo artisans.[36]

The participation of Afro-Colombians as fellow patriots confronted the Creole elite with the predicament of how to deal with lower-class political participation under the new regime. On the one hand, the Creole elite had to call on people of African descent to support their political actions against the Spanish. These actions were glorified in Creole patriotic rhetoric as the righteous attempt of "the people" to recover its freedom and sovereignty. It was this crowd, as the people, that helped to legitimate the Creoles's seizure of power. On the other hand, the Creole elite feared that blacks and mulattoes might escape from their political control.[37] The legal and electoral system upheld the notion that sovereignty had returned to "the people," which included both blacks and whites without racial distinction. The electoral instructions for the Suprema Junta of the province of Cartagena of December 1810 included all races: "All parishioners, whites, Indians, mestizos, mulattoes, zambos and blacks, as long as they were household heads and lived from their own work, were to be summoned for elections." Only "vagrants, criminals, those who were in servile salaried status, and slaves are excluded."[38] This law not only helped secure the essential support of Afro-Colombian artisans for the patriot cause and led to the participation of a few influential Afro-Colombians in the government, but also conformed to the liberal notion that many Creole patriots then adhered to, namely that political power should be in the hands of men of merit regardless of their origin.

It was quite a different matter, however, to allow an uncontrolled crowd of black and mulatto artisans to determine the political future of the city. The novelty of the electoral process and of the notion of the people's sovereignty led to ambivalences over the legitimacy and extent of street actions. For example, during the election of the newly expanded junta on August 11, 1810, a crowd led by an Afro-Colombian militia officer gathered in the front of the government palace to request the election of José María García Toledo, a prominent Creole patriot, as president of the junta. García Toledo vehemently rejected their expression of support and explained to the crowd that this election "did not belong to the people but to their representatives."[39] Moveover, García Toledo made sure to have a personal conversation with their leader, during which he reproached him for his audacious initiative and obtained his word that he would not do it again when the representatives gathered to elect the president of the junta. To García Toledo's satisfaction, "not a soul was in the plaza" when the junta elected him as their president.[40]

The event reveals something of the fluidity that the notion of election had at the time. In this instance, the issue was not who would be elected but how and by whom. It was agreed that the junta president would be elected by the people, but in what manner? Would he be elected by the crowd, by the representatives with the support of the crowd, or exclusively by the representatives? The people in the crowd had acted under the assumption that they were entitled to directly express their choice.[41]

Although in this particular case Creole leaders resolved their conflicts with Afro-Colombian patriots to their satisfaction, the opposite was more often the case. Afro-Colombians tended to take the anti-Spanish rhetoric to extremes that the junta would not countenance. For example, after the discovery of a Spanish conspiracy against the junta, crowds of blacks and mulattoes filled the streets of Cartagena for two days, attacking and looting the houses of wealthy Spaniards whom they considered accomplices. The junta, which had not yet declared independence from Spain, and which also held property rights in high esteem, strongly disapproved of these attacks. Yet it could do nothing to stop them. Not only was it hard to control the hundreds of armed men who filled the streets, but, more important, it was difficult to justify the repression of a crowd that was acting not as a riotous mob but as a patriotic defender of the junta.[42]

Such conflicts over the nature and extent of lower-class political participation began to divide Cartagena's patriots into two distinct camps: the Piñeristas, or "demagogues," and the Toledistas, or "aristocrats." Although the Creole revolutionary junta had initially solicited the cooperation of Afro-Colombians to depose the Spanish governor, in the process granting equal legal rights to all races, it grew increasingly wary of Afro-Colombians' political participation. Gathered around its president, García Toledo, the junta tried to control the political activities of local Afro-Colombians by confining political actions to institutional channels. They opposed the mob's attacks on Spanish property and saw the humiliation of prominent Spaniards at the hands of Afro-Colombians as an attack on social order. The Piñeres brothers, who belonged to wealthy and prestigious Creole families, led the other camp. They based their political power on the support of the Afro-Colombian artisans, an alliance that quickly earned them the label of demagogues. They were compared to Danton and Marat, and one of them signed as "the fervent."[43] Not only were they not afraid to call black and mulatto artisans into the streets, but their revolutionary rhetoric emphasized the end of aristocracy and the equality of all men, and they were not afraid to denounce unpatriotic aristocratic manners and behavior among the local elite. The Piñeres and their followers took the anti-aristocratic rhetoric of racial equality to extremes that most members of the local Creole elite would not accept. They linked anti-Spanish sentiment with a revolutionary antiaristocratic rhetoric that not only promoted racial equality but also favored the active participation of lower-class Afro-Colombians in city politics.

The refusal of junta president García Toledo to sign the Declaration of Independence was directly linked to the divisions between the (Piñeristas) "demagogues" and the (Toledista) "aristocrats." Although García Toledo supported independence, he was very concerned about when, and especially how, it would be achieved. He feared a tumultuous independence movement during which a riotous crowd would call the day. He strongly believed that independence should not be declared until the election of the national convention in January 1812. In his mind only the convention, as the representatives of the people, had the legal right to take such a momentous step.[44] Independence should only be declared by "the Convention in tranquility without demagogy, which was the legal, political, and convenient procedure."[45] If the convention declared independence, the Toledista Creole elite who dominated the junta would maintain its traditional control. It would be quite a different matter if it were declared in advance with the support or under the pressure of the new patriot militia, then controlled by the Piñeristas.

Yet it was not to be the convention that declared independence but rather a helpless Creole junta threatened by armed crowds of blacks and mulatto patriots. With the backing of these pardo patriot militias (los Lanceros de Getzemaní), the Piñeristas conspired to petition the junta to declare independence on November 11, 1811, and establish a republican government. Because local blacks and mulattoes had not left records of their reasons for forcing the junta to declare independence, we can only infer their motives. One possible explanation derives from the development of social and racial politics in Cartagena and the larger Spanish Empire. As Alfonso Múnera has pointed out, it was probably not a coincidence that Cartagena's independence followed the Spanish refusal to grant citizenship rights to people of African descent in the new 1812 constitution.[46] This refusal came after a passionate debate widely followed across the empire, during which American and Spanish deputies took opposite sides on this crucial issue. Patriots used Spanish opposition to African American citizenship to rally the support of Afro-Colombians.[47] Patriot rhetoric incorporated racial conflicts within a larger republican discourse that sharply distinguished between an archaic, despotic, and oppressive Spanish past and a new republican future of freedom, equality, and justice. Patriots also weaved a rhetoric of harmony that considered racial conflicts and divisions yet another legacy of Spanish rule. It was aristocratic Spain that instituted racial discrimination and slavery; as such it would disappear in the era of republican virtue.

It is telling that the conspiracy centered around the pardo artisan quarter of Getzemaní. The main leaders of the republican conspiracy were all persons of influence among the artisans of Getzemaní, and the rebellion was headquartered in the house of the artisan Pedro Romero, a pardo officer in the Lanceros. After agreeing to stop work on that day the artisans of Cartagena followed the junta's deliberations from Romero's house, and when their agents reported that the junta was going to end the session without considering their petition for independence, they decided to march into the city. The patriot pardo militia took control of the city bastions and a large crowd of people from Getzemaní went to the city armory and forced the door. Armed with lances, daggers, and guns, they continued on to the government palace. There they requested through their spokespersons that the junta approve their petition for independence. In spite of the crowd's belligerency and the junta's lack of military support, García Toledo refused to comply. Irritated by this opposition the crowd, led by Gabriel Piñeres, invaded the sessions hall. Treating García Toledo with disrespect and violence, the crowd imprisoned him, and under duress, the junta, including García Toledo, signed the Declaration of Independence.[48] That day and the next the defeated junta had to endure a city controlled by the crowd from Getzemaní. It is not surprising that García Toledo would later describe Independence Day as a "nefarious and dangerous day" and the next as "a day of tears and scandal, not only for this city and its province but for the entire country."[49]

Following independence the Creole elite confronted the vital issue of whether or not they would recover political control of the city. Cartagena was sharply divided between the two patriot camps, and it was unclear which group would control the city. Both sides were represented in government. Although in the minority, the Piñeristas were represented in Congress and the Piñeres brothers often occupied some of the most important offices. The military was also divided, with the patriot militia supporting the Piñeristas, the standing army or fijo supporting the Toledistas, and the rest oscillating between both camps. Although the Toledista or "aristocratic" party counted on the support of most of the Creole elites, contemporary accounts constantly emphasize the political strength, influence, and belligerence of the "demagogues" during the following four years. Even if the governing junta remained under the control of a Toledista majority, it was the Piñeres brothers who "imposed their opinions, by hook or by crook, supported by the militias and the people of color."[50]

Descriptions of the events of these years abound in which the elite were forced to endure acts in which pardo patriots showed little inclination to give up the power and sovereignty that they as "the people" had achieved. However, the greatest challenge to the "aristocratic" faction came in December 1814 during the gubernatorial elections. On December 17 the republic's electoral college gathered to vote for the new governor. García Toledo won with fifteen votes while Germán Gutierres de Piñeres came in second with ten votes.[51] In spite of his victory Toledo did not become governor. The people in the galleries interrupted the electoral process by shouting their rejection of García Toledo and demanding the election of citizen Gabriel Piñeres. It was "the will of the people." This crowd, which denominated itself as "the people," was described by the Toledistas not as "the household heads, the honest neighbors, or the virtuous patriots of Cartagena, but the scum, a throng of obscure men with nothing to lose."[52] Some Piñerista members of the electoral college joined forces with the crowd. Muñoz accused García Toledo of pro-Spanish sentiments, while Germán Gutierres de Piñeres defended his brother's candidacy by stressing his contribution and sacrifices for independence and pointing out his popularity as "the idol of the people."

Piñerista deputies also denounced an electoral system in which the electors were all friends and clients of García Toledo. They argued that the tumult in the galleries was the natural result of this clique's ignoring the will of the people. The Toledista deputies responded that the electoral college had lost its freedom and was muzzled by fear, and that any decision taken that day would be invalid. They proposed to end the session and wait for things to calm down, but the people in the galleries would have none of it. Armed with machetes and cutlasses, they closed the doors and forced the electors to continue the debate and to come to a final decision that day. After a long debate Gabriel Piñeres proposed a compromise, moving that he and García Toledo both be nominated as consuls with equal power. This was not enough for the people in the galleries, however, who shouted that they wanted "Gabriel without crutches." After some

Piñerista deputies explained the reasons and convenience of this agreement, the riotous galleries acquiesced.

The tumult at the electoral college received much attention from contemporaries, and for good reason. The event had exposed the weakness of the Creoles's political control and, perhaps more important, the lack of an authoritative, established political discourse that could provide automatic answers to such crucial issues as who were the people and who had the right to represent the people. In spite of the lack of established political rules about proper procedures, there was a conventional republican rhetoric that set limits if not on political actions at least on the ways in which these actions could be framed and understood. All political actors were obliged to avoid accusations of demagoguery, aristocracy, anarchy, and tyranny, and to frame their actions in terms of virtue, freedom, and equality. But in Cartagena the meaning of these political keywords was not always shared. It was this tension between a shared and newly established republican rhetorical framework of political virtue on the one hand and a fluid and conflictive political reality on the other that characterized the independence period.

For the anti-Piñeristas the tumult in the electoral college was the culmination of the anarchy, violence, and turmoil that had afflicted Cartagena under the rule of the Piñeres. In their version the crowd had attempted to replace a constitutional representative government with a despotic and dictatorial one.[53] If the electoral college did not recover the freedom lost to these seditious men, disorder and anarchy would triumph over the legal and constitutional order.[54] However, it was insufficient to argue that the crowd had no right to impose its will on the elected representatives. The Toledistas had to demonstrate that the riotous galleries and the Piñeristas as a whole were not *the people*. For this, they appealed to those elements of the republican imaginary that would help them delegitimize crowd actions. Piñeres was not the idol of *the* people but instead a demagogue who based his popularity on his ability to corrupt zambos with money and liquor.[55] According to the Toledistas, the men in the crowd were only men *who claimed to be the people*. The men in the galleries had no right to representation, were merely "scum; men without house and family and with nothing to lose." Nor were they "real patriots" but rather opportunists who had taken advantage of the situation to subject respectable Cartageneros to three years of insults and vexations.[56]

The Piñerista narrative of these events presents a completely different reading. Their version was expressed in a published pamphlet defending their actions in the electoral college.[57] Although this pamphlet shared in the early republican discursive framework, it differs in its interpretation of what constitutes demagoguery, aristocracy, factions, and anarchy. Piñeristas claimed to follow the laws of the republic, and they accused the Toledistas of destroying all that independence and republicanism stood for. The election of Toledo went against the constitution, which guaranteed a government for the common good of the people and not for the benefit of any one man, family, or particular class of men. Toledo wanted to impose his aristocratic ideas on the people, without regard for the suffering of humanity or the perdition of the fatherland.[58] Piñerista rhetoric emphasized the antiaristocratic nature of the independence movement, linking the struggle for independence to the struggle against the social divisions of the old colonial regime. In the words of the pamphlet: "Independence destroyed the basis of aristocratic pride, opening the door to merit and virtue alone, and its liberal system sanctioned legal equality. That is what displeases these so-called nobles."[59] Moreover, Toledo had betrayed his pro-Spanish sentiments by publicly declaring that November 11, Independence Day, had been sad and nefarious. He also had placed the government in the hands of clients. Such actions were further proof of his aristocratic inclinations, and it followed that Toledo's rule would annihilate the people. Citing Cicero and the Bible, the pamphlet defended the legitimacy of rebellion in order to save the fatherland. It rejected the notion that the tumult at the electoral college was an attempt by the rabble to hinder the freedom of the electoral system; instead, it had been a patriotic act through which the people had saved the liberty of the republic.

After a period of conflict and negotiations the Toledistas managed to gain control of the city. Soon a public health committee, headed by Toledo himself, decreed the expulsion of "dangerous" Piñerista elements,[60] and the Creole elite prepared to celebrate its victory. Commemorative acts whose goal was to portray the role of prominent Creoles in saving the city from "chaos" and "anarchy" were orchestrated. Creole heroism would be painted on the senate chamber, narrated in the books of meritorious citizens, and the heroes' names would be inscribed in golden letters to immortalize their glory.[61] These commemorative acts were among the first attempts to invent an official narrative of independence in which the participation of the colored lower classes was erased altogether. But events were too recent to be so easily forgotten, and so the still-vivid actions of lower-class elements were depoliticized and rewritten in local accounts as attacks on law and order. Afro-Colombian patriotism and support for independence would be presented as a sordid pretext that concealed their seditious and factious intentions. They became a "faction who had taken hold of government under the shield of independence." The uproar at the electoral college revealed their true intentions to continue "their horrible projects of plunder, murder, and desolation."[62] Virtuous and law-abiding citizens had endured these insults of factious and seditious men long enough. Thus Creole patriotic history made raucous bandits of Afro-Colombian patriots.

The difficulties of the elites in controlling the lower-class politics of the Piñeristas were inscribed in a complementary discourse of elite illusion. In the midst of the Piñerista-Toledista conflict, Cartagena resident Miguel Diaz Granados wrote to his brother-in-law that he was extremely displeased "at having to stay in this Babylon . . . a better acquaintance with the purposes and lack of order and morality in the prevailing system, made me soon desire to separate myself from an illusion which, like Plato's Republic, only existed on paper."[63] For this Cartagenero the alleged virtues of republicanism were only good on paper. In Cartagena, the republic had only brought disorder and immorality. Significantly, what made republicanism an illusion was not the indifference of the lower classes toward modern politics but their excessive participation. Yet by inscribing their participation in a discourse of disorder, this Cartagenero divorced the lower class from republican politics, transforming the republic into an elite illusion ill-suited to local reality.

Contemporary attempts to inscribe the antiaristocratic republican activities of Afro-Colombians in a discourse of chaos and demagoguery had a lasting impact on independence narratives. Depicted as victims of or obstacles to modernity, the lower classes were expunged from the political sphere. They now became the perennial subjects of pedagogical projects that sought to educate the lower classes in modern forms of political participation. Then as now these master narratives of Spanish American independence concealed the multiple readings of and conflicts over republicanism and democracy. Terms such as the now official and emblematic *patria boba* (foolish fatherland), enshrined in the historiography to denominate the initial years of republican experience in Colombia, effortlessly operationalize a broad historical language of chaos and illusion.[64]

Analyses of the emergence of the myth of racial democracy during this period tend to be inscribed within these narratives of chaos and illusion.[65] Promises of legal equality itself are quickly dismissed by social historians as empty promises that hid the cruel reality of slavery and a pervasive racial discrimination. In this version, such discourses were merely hegemonic tools for securing control of the lower classes. Contemporary realities and discourses were more complex, however. In Colombia slavery did remain legal for another thirty years. However, in regions such as the province of Cartagena not only did the number of slaves diminish by 50 percent during the course of the independence wars, but it became increasingly difficult for the slave-owning elite to reestablish social control over slaves who had become accustomed to the new opportunities opened by the revolution.[66] Nor could slave owners justify their claims within a political discourse that openly declared slavery to be at odds with a liberal and enlightened nation.[67] Similarly, although racial discrimination continued after independence legal equality was not merely empty rhetoric. People of African descent achieved an unprecedented degree of social mobility as some became generals, senators, and governors; more important, at the time it was not at all clear how much further these changes would reach.[68]

I am not arguing that the wars of independence shattered previous social structures; rather, I contend that the "failure" of the liberal project to fulfill its promises of equality was not predetermined by its lack of connection to Spanish American reality. Although few scholars at present would use the weight of the Spanish cultural legacy to explain contemporary political cultures, such a rationalization continues to enjoy great popularity in nonacademic circles. Its enduring appeal probably derives from the lack of a new paradigm or better general explanations for the continuity of certain colonial characteristics.

Fernando Coronil's proposal that nineteenth-century social struggles in Latin America be understood not as a confrontation between tradition and modernity but as a dispute among different notions of modernity suggests such an avenue.[69] The myth of racial democracy is a case in point. The republican wars of independence invited a myriad of political interpretations. Many Afro-Colombians embraced republicanism in the hope of freeing themselves from oppression and discrimination. Throughout the wars and their aftermath Afro-Colombians pressured the Creole elite for inclusive notions of equality and citizenship. It is now necessary to understand the pervasive racism and social inequality of the nineteenth and twentieth centuries not as a historical continuation of colonial patterns but as novel and modern constructions of inequality.[70] Let us not forget that today's myth of racial democracy is a nationalist, modern, republican construction. Its main trait, a nationalist discourse that declares racial language and identifications to be unnational, emerged during the wars. Its conflictive legacy of inclusion, silence, and discrimination is the product of the particular ways in which Spanish American nations "resolved" the tensions raised by a new universal language of citizenship in societies characterized both by racial inequality and alternative forms of political practice.

NOTES

I gratefully acknowledge the financial support of the Wenner-Gren Foundation for Anthropological Research, Inc., the Social Science Research Council, and the Tinker Foundation to conduct research in Colombia. I especially wish to thank Mark Thurner for his ideas and suggestions. This essay, and the dissertation on which it is based, would not have been possible without his encouragement. Note that all translations are mine unless indicated otherwise.

1 For a recent assessment of the revolutionary nature of the Spanish American wars of independence, see Eric Van Young, "Conclusion— Was There an Age of Revolution in Spanish America?" in *State and Society in Spanish America during the Age of Revolution*, ed. Victor M. Uribe-Uran (Wilmington: Scholarly Resources, 2001), 219–46.

2 Jacques Rancière, *The Names of History: On the Poetics of Knowledge*, trans. Hassan Melehy (Minneapolis: University of Minnesota Press, 1994), 22.

3 I borrow the term "enlightened illusion" from Luis Castro-Leiva, *La Gran Colombia, una ilusión ilustrada* (Caracas: Monte Avila, 1985).

4 Rancière, *The Names of History*, 31–39.

5 For a summary of mid-nineteenth-century social, political, and economic changes, see Tulio Halperín Donghi, *The Contemporary History of Latin America*, ed. and trans. John Charles Chasteen (Durham: Duke University Press, 1993), 116–57.

6 I borrow this term from Roberto Schwarz, *Misplaced Ideas: Essays on Brazilian Culture* (London: Verso, 1992).

7 For an insightful criticism of this perspective, see Fernando Coronil, "Beyond Occidentalism," *Cultural Anthropology* 11.1 (1996): 51–88.

8 Building on the methodological developments of the recent literature on peasant studies, recent works on the independence wars have begun to provide a more nuanced conception of the appropriation of elite political discourse by plebeians and their participation in the processes of state formation in the new republics. For the literature on peasants and politics, see Florencia Mallon, *Peasant and Nation: The Making of Postcolonial Mexico and Peru* (Berkeley: University of California Press, 1995); Mark Thurner, *From Two Republics to One Divided: Contradications of Postcolonial Nationmaking in Andean Peru* (Durham: Duke University Press, 1997); and Peter Guardino, *Peasants, Politics, and the Formation of Mexico's National State: Guerrero, 1800–1857* (Stanford: Stanford University Press, 1996). On the plebe and politics, see Sarah C. Chambers, *From Subjects to Citizens: Honor, Gender, and Politics in Arequipa, Peru, 1780–1854* (University Park: Pennsylvania State University Press, 1999); Margarita Garrido, *Reclamos y representaciones: Variaciones sobre la política en el nuevo reino de Granada, 1770–1815* (Bogotá: Banco de la República, 1993); Virginia Guedea, "De la infidelidad a la infidencia," in *Patterns of Contention in Mexican History*, ed. Jaime E. Rodríguez (Wilmington: Scholarly Resources, 1992); Alfonso Múnera, *El fracaso de la nación: Región, clase y raza en el Caribe colombiano (1717–1821)* (Bogotá: Ancora Editores, 1998); and Hilda Sabato, *The Many and the Few: Political Participation in Republican Buenos Aires* (Stanford: Stanford University Press, 2001). Although some of these works openly challenge the assumption of a strong ideological divide between the elite and the lower classes, the revolutionary nature of the wars continues to be hotly contested. Even Eric Van Young's sophisticated analysis of the Mexican wars of independence continues to question the relevance of modern politics for the Mexican lower classes; see his *The Other Rebellion: Popular Violence, Ideology, and the Mexican Struggle for Independence, 1810–1821* (Stanford: Stanford University Press, 2001). A similar approach is taken by Charles Walker in *Smoldering Ashes: Cuzco and the Creation of Republican Peru, 1780–1840* (Durham: Duke University Press, 1999). It is not yet clear how the master narratives of the independence period will incorporate these new works.

9 For one of the more well-known academic representatives of this view, see E. Bradford Burns, *The Poverty of Progress: Latin America in the Nineteenth Century* (Berkeley: University of California Press, 1980).

10 John Lynch, *The Spanish American Revolutions, 1808–1826* (New York: Norton, 1973); Benedict Anderson, *Imagined Communities: Reflections on the Origin and Spread of Nationalism*, 2nd ed. (London, 1991), 48; and

François-Xavier Guerra, *Modernidad e independencias: Ensayos sobre las revoluciones hispánicas* (Madrid: MAPFRE, 1992), 41.

11 Germán Colmenares, *Las convenciones contra la cultura* (Bogotá: Tercer Mundo 1987), 94–95.

12 Ibid., 78–89.

13 José Manuel Restrepo, *Historia de la revolución de la República de Colombia*, vol. 1 (1858; Medellín: Bedout, 1974), 37.

14 Pierre Bourdieu, *Language and Symbolic Power* (Cambridge: Cambridge University Press, 1991), 43–89; Bruce Lincoln, *Authority: Construction and Corrosion* (Chicago: University of Chicago Press, 1994), 9–11, 47–54; and Eric Wolf, *Envisioning Power: Ideologies of Dominance and Crisis* (Berkeley: University of California Press, 1999), 56, 129.

15 Restrepo, *Historia de la revolución*, 190.

16 Ibid., 189.

17 Ibid., 89–94.

18 For recent analyses of Bolívar's intellectual legacy, see David Brading, *The First America: The Spanish Monarchy, Creole Patriots, and the Liberal State, 1492–1867* (Cambridge: Cambridge University Press, 1990), 603–20; Castro Leiva, *La Gran Colombia*; and Anthony Pagden, *Spanish Imperialism and the Political Imagination: Studies in European and Spanish American Social and Political Theory, 1513–1830* (New Haven: Yale University Press, 1990), 133–53.

19 See, for example, Bolívar to Santander, Magdalena, July 8, 1826; Bolívar to Mariano Montilla, Sátiva, March 24, 1828; and Carta a Mariano Montilla, Fusca, January 7, 1828, in *Obras Completas de Bolívar* (Havana: n.p., 1950); "Mensaje a la Convención de Ocaña," May 1, 1828, in *Proclamas y Discursos del Libertador* (Carácas: Lit. y tip. del comercio, 1939), 367; and Castro Leiva, *La Gran Colombia*, 119.

20 This line of argument is strikingly similar to that of the French revisionists who blame the intellectuals for the excesses of the French Revolution. For a critique, see Rancière, *The Names of History*, 40.

21 Lynch, *The Spanish American Revolutions*.

22 Victor M. Uribe, in "The Enigma of Latin American Independence," *Latin American Research Review* 32.1 (1997): 236–55, notes the "limited impact" of social history in the historiography of the wars of independence. For a broader assessment of the difficulties that social history has had in providing a comprehensive analysis of political culture in Latin America, see William Taylor, "Between Global Process and Local Knowledge: An Inquiry into Early Latin American Social History, 1500–1900," in *Reliving the Past: The Worlds of Social History*, ed. Oliver Zunz (Chapel Hill: University of North Carolina Press, 1985), 115–90.

23 Lynch, *The Spanish American Revolutions*, 347; Burns, *The Poverty of Progress*.

24 Anderson, *Imagined Communities*, 47–65; Antonio Annino, ed., *Historia de las elecciones en Iberoamérica, siglo XIX* (Mexico: Fondo de Cultura Económica, 1995); Brading, *The First America*; Guerra, *Modernidad e independencias*; Pagden, *Spanish Imperialism*, 133–53; Jaime Rodríguez, *The Independence of Spanish America* (Cambridge: Cambridge University Press, 1998); Eduardo Posada-Carbó, ed., *Elections before Democracy: The History of Elections in Europe and Latin America* (New York: St. Martin's Press, 1996); Victor M. Uribe-Uran, *Honorable Lives: Lawyers, Family, and Politics in Colombia, 1780–1850* (Pittsburgh: University of Pittsburgh Press, 2000); Marie Laure Rieu-Millan, *Los diputados americanos en las cortes de Cádiz* (Madrid: Conselo Superior de Investigaciones Científicas, 1990); and Manuel Chust, *La cuestión nacional americana en las cortes de Cádiz, 1810–1814* (Valencia: UNED, 1999).

25 Annino, *Historia de las elecciones*, 1–13. For a recent review of works on the early history of citizenship in Spanish America, see Hilda Sabato, "On Political Citizenship in Nineteenth-Century Latin America," *American Historical Review* 106.4 (October 2001): 1290–315. See also Hilda Sabato, *La política en las calles: Entre el voto y la movilización, Buenos Aires, 1862–1880* (Buenos Aires: Sudamericana, 1998).

26 François-Xavier Guerra, *Modernidad e independencias*, 41. For an analysis of the influence of the Haitian revolution on Venezuela's slave population, see Pedro M. Arcaya, *Insurrección de los negros de la Serranía de Coro* (Caracas: Panamanian Institute of Geography and History, 1949), Federico Brito Figueroa, *Las insurrecciones de los esclavos negros en la sociedad colonial venezolana* (Caracas: Cantaclaro, 1961), 41–88; and Julius S. Scott, "The Common Wind: Currents of Afro-American Communication in the Era of the Haitian Revolution" (Ph.D. diss., Duke University, 1986). For Afro-Venezuelans' interest in the constitutional debates at Cadiz, see James King, "The Colored Castes and American Representation in the Cortes of Cadiz," *Hispanic American Historical Review* 33.1 (1953); and King, "A Royalist View of the Colored Castes in the Venezuelan Wars of Independence," *Hispanic American Historical Review* 33.4 (1953): 526–37.

27 Guerra, *Modernidad e independencias*, 36.

28 I am taking De Pradt's quote from Pagden, *Spanish Imperialism*, 148.

29 Pagden, *Spanish Imperialism*, 152–53.

30 I am inspired here by Ranajit Guha, "The Prose of Counter-Insurgency," in *Selected Subaltern Studies*, ed. Ranajit Guha and Gayatri Chakravorty Spivak (New York: Oxford University Press, 1988); and Michel-Rolph Trouillot, *Silencing the Past: Power and the Production of History* (Boston: Beacon, 1995), 70–107.

31 The degree to which the historiography on the wars of independence

has ignored the rich and sophisticated historical literature on the French Caribbean is surprising. This literature has examined the multiple ways in which slave and free people of African descent appropriated French revolutionary discourse. In addition, it has shown the importance of colonial revolutionary events in the development of European notions of race and citizenship. See Laurent Dubois, "A Colony of Citizens: Slave Emancipation during the French Revolution" (Ph.D. diss., University of Michigan); C. L. R. James, *The Black Jacobins* (New York: Dial, 1938); D. B. Gaspar and David Geggus, eds., *A Turbulent Time: The French Revolution and the Greater Caribbean* (Bloomington: Indiana University Press, 1997); David Geggus, ed., *The Impact of the Haitian Revolution in the Atlantic World* (Columbia: University of South Carolina Press, 2001); and Mimi Sheller, *Democracy after Slavery: Black Publics and Peasant Radicalism in Haiti and Jamaica* (Gainesville: University of Florida Press, 2000).

32 I treat this topic in some detail in my "Race and Republicanism in the Age of Revolution: Cartagena, 1745–1831" (Ph.D. diss., University of Florida, 2002).

33 Manuel Ezequiel Corráles, comp., *Documentos para la historia de la Provincia de Cartagena de Indias, hoy Estado Soberano de Bolívar, en la Unión Colombiana*, vol. 1 (Bogotá, 1883), 127–28.

34 Corráles, *Documentos*, 127–28.

35 "Informe del Comandante de Ingenieros, Don Vicente Talledo, al Virrey Amar, sobre conatos de revolución en Cartagena y Mompox," in Corráles, *Documentos*, 53–54.

36 "Testimonio de lo que resulta de la Causa Principal contra Don José Manuel de la Paz, Administrador General de Tabacos de la Villa de Mompox: Indiciado de haber entrado en la conspiración tramada en Mompox contra las armas del Rey," Archivo General de Indias (hereafter AGI), Cuba, 719 A. Similarly, the list of patriot conspirators in 1819 Ocaña includes men and women, whites and blacks, free and slaves. See "Relación de las persona que resultaron cómplices en la sorpresa y asesinato verificados en esta ciudad de Ocaña el 10 de Noviembre de 1819," AGI, Cuba, 719 A.

37 Garrido, *Reclamos y representaciones*, 277–97. This, of course, was not unique to Colombia or Spanish America. Back in 1959 George Rudé, in *The Crowd in the French Revolution* (London: Oxford University Press, 1959), described how the French bourgeoisie confronted a similar predicament.

38 "Instrucciones que deberá observarse en las elecciones parroquiales, en las de partido y en las capitulares, para el nombramiento de diputados en la Suprema Junta de la provincia de Cartagena," December 11,

1810, in Manuel Ezequiel Corrales, *Efemérides y anales del Estado de Bolívar*, vol. 2 (Bogotá, 1889), 48.

39 José María García de Toledo, "Defensa hecha por el señor José María García de Toledo de su conducta pública y privada, contra las calumnias de los autores de la conmoción del 11 y 12 del presente mes," in Corrales, *Documentos*, 373.

40 Ibid.

41 My analysis of Cartagena's crowd builds on the theoretical insights of Colin Lucas in "The Crowd and Politics between 'Ancien Régime' and Revolution in France," *Journal of Modern History*, 60.3 (1988): 421–57; Natalie Zemon Davis, *Society and Culture in Early Modern France* (Stanford: Stanford University Press, 1975); Rudé, *The Crowd*; and Edward P. Thompson, *Customs in Common* (New York: New Press, 1991).

42 "Manuel Trinidad Noriega to Don Francisco Bustamante," Cartagena, February 10, 1811, in Corrales, *Efemérides y anales*, 64–70.

43 Gabriel Jiménez Molinares, *Los Mártires de Cartagena de 1816 ante el consejo de guerra y ante la historia*, vol. 1 (Cartagena: Impr. Departmental de Bolívar, 1950), 302.

44 Ibid., 242–44.

45 Ibid., 246.

46 Alfonso Múnera, "Failing to Construct the Colombian Nation: Race and Class in the Andean-Caribbean Conflict, 1717–1816" (Ph.D. diss., University of Connecticut, 1995), 237.

47 King, "A Royalist View of the Colored Castes," 533; Lasso, "Race and Republicanism."

48 "Exposición de los acontecimientos memorables relacionados con mi vida política, que tuvieron lugar en este país desde 1810 en adelante," Manuel Marcelino Nuñez, Cartagena, February 22, 1864; and "Diligencias actuadas que tienen relación con la transformación política de Cartagena de Indias, que se toman de una documentación del Coronel Bonifacio Rodríguez," in Corrales, *Documentos*, 412–13.

49 García Toledo, "Defensa hecha," 380, 390. For a description of the events of November 12, see Jiménez Molinares, *Los Mártires*, 258.

50 "Imponían sus puntos de vista, a las buenas o a las malas, apoyados en las milicias y en el paisanaje de color" (Jiménez Molinares, *Los Mártires*, 260). See also "Ley del estado de Cartagena de Indias, de honores a los ciudadanos Pedro Gual, Manuel del Castillo, y José María García de Toledo," February 13, 1815, in Corrales, *Efemérides y Anales*, 180.

51 The description of the electoral college session is taken from "Primer oficio del gobernador de la provincia de al secretario del Estado y Relaciones Exteriores del Gobierno de la Unión," Pedro Gual, Car-

tagena, January 30, 1815, AGN, Restrepo, rollo 5, folio 113–17; and "Extracto de las sesiones del Colegio Electoral y Revisor de la Constitución del Estado de Cartagena de Indias," in Corrales, *Efemérides y Anales,* 162–65.

52 "Primer oficio del gobernador," folio 114.

53 Major General José Salvador de Narvaéz, "Operaciones del Ejército de Cartagena situado en la línea occidental del río Magdalena, desde el 22 de diciembre de 1814 hasta el 18 de enero de 1815, con motivo de lo ocurrido en el Colegio electoral y Revisor el 17 de Diciembre citado," January 30, 1815, in Corrales, *Efemérides y Anales,* 172–73.

54 Salvador de Narvaéz, "Operaciones del Ejército," folio 177; and "Primer oficio del gobernador de la provincia de al secretario del Estado," folio 115.

55 Salvador de Narvaéz, "Operaciones del Ejército," folio 175, 178–79.

56 "Primer oficio del gobernador," folio 114.

57 "El honor vindicado y brevisima exposición de los motivos que han obligado al pueblo de Cartagena a rechazar el nombramiento de Gobernador en el señor García de Toledo," AGN, Restrepo, rollo 5, folio 281–83.

58 Ibid., folio 281.

59 Ibid.

60 Salvador de Narvaéz, "Operaciones del Ejército," folio 175–77; and "Primer oficio del gobernador," folio 115–16. For a list of the expatriated men, see Jiménez Molinares, *Los Mártires,* 196–97.

61 "Ley del Estado de Cartagena de Indias de honores a los ciudadanos Pedro Gual, Manuel del Castillo y José María García de Toledo," February 13, 1815, in Corrales, *Efemérides y Anales,* 181–83.

62 Ibid.

63 Quoted in Jiménez Molinares, *Los Mártires,* 287.

64 For recent criticisms of the language of chaos that has traditionally characterized nineteenth-century politics in Spanish America, see Donald Fithian Stevens, *Origins of Instability in Early Republican Mexico* (Durham: Duke University Press, 1991); and Rebecca Earle, ed., *Rumors of War: Civil Conflict in Nineteenth-Century Latin America* (London: n.p., 2000).

65 For elite use of a republican rhetoric of equality to attract the black population to their side during the wars of independence, see Lynch, *The Spanish American Revolutions;* and Winthrop R. Wright, *Café con Leche: Race, Class, and National Image in Venezuela* (Austin: University of Texas Press, 1990).

66 See the 1780 and the 1825 censuses for the province of Cartagena in Hermes Tovar Pinzón, *Convocatoria al poder del número: Censos y estadísticas*

de la Nueva Granada 1750–1830 (Bogotá: AGN, 1994); and Gustavo Bell Lemus, "Deserciones, fugas, cimarronajes, rochelas y uniones libres: El problema del control social en la provincia de Cartagena al final del dominio español 1816–1820," in *Cartagena de Indias de la Colonia a la República* (Bogota: Fundación Simón y Lola Guberek, 1991).

67 Jaime Jaramillo Uribe, "La controversia jurídica y filosófica librada en la Nueva Granada en torno a la liberación de los esclavos y la importancia económica y social de la esclavitud en el siglo XIX," *Anuario de Historia Social y de la Cultura* (Bogotá), no. 4 (1969): 63–86. *Observaciones de G.T. sobre la ley de Manumisión del Soberano Congreso de Colombia* (Bogota, 1822). "Los Hacendados y Vecinos de la Provincia de Cartagena de Colombia al Congreso," November 30, 1822, Archivo Legislativo del Congreso de Colombia, Camara, Peticiones, 33, folio 24–31.

68 See, for example, the lives of the black generals José Padilla, Manuel Piar, Laurencio Silva, and José Domingo Espinar described in the following works: Enrique Otero D'Costa, *Vida del Almirante José Padilla, 1778–1828* (Bogota: Imprenta de las Fuerzas Militares, 1973); José Carrillo Moreno, *José Laurencio Silva, paradigma de lealtad* (Caracas: Presidencia de la República, 1973); Asarubal González, *Manuel Piar* (Valencia: Vadell, 1979); and Ernesto J. Castillero Reyes, *General José Domingo Espinar (1791–1865): Médico, ingeniero y militar; Fundador de la independencia del Perú* (Panama: Portobelo, 1997).

69 Coronil, "Beyond Occidentalism." For a reexamination of the notion of colonial legacies, see Jeremy Adelman, ed., *Colonial Legacies: The Problem of Persistence in Latin American History* (New York: Routledge, 1999).

70 Gilberto Freyre, *The Masters and the Slaves: A Study in the Development of Brazilian Civilization* (New York: Knopf, 1956); Frank Tannenbaum, *Slave and Citizen: the Negro in the Americas* (New York: Vintage, 1946); Marvin Harris, *Patterns of Race in the Americas* (New York: Walker, 1964); Carl Degler, *Neither Black nor White: Slavery and Race Relations in Brazil and the United States* (New York: Macmillan, 1971); Florestan Fernandes, *A integração do negro na sociedade de classes* (São Paulo: Universidade de São Paulo, 1965); Emilia Viotti da Costa, *The Brazilian Empire: Myths and Histories* (Chicago: University of Chicago Press, 1985); George Reid Andrews, *Blacks and Whites in São Paulo, Brazil, 1888–1988* (Madison: University of Wisconsin Press, 1991); Peter Wade, *Blackness and Race Mixture: the Dynamics of Racial Identity in Colombia* (Baltimore: Johns Hopkins University Press, 1993); and Ada Ferrer, *Insurgent Cuba: Race, Nation, and Revolution, 1868–1898* (Chapel Hill: University of North Carolina Press, 1999).

PETER GUARDINO

Postcolonialism as Self-Fulfilled Prophecy?

Electoral Politics in Oaxaca, 1814–1828

✷ In recent years Latin Americanists have engaged in often-heated discussions about the wisdom of importing theoretical perspectives and language from other disciplines or the historiography of other parts of the world.[1] To me, it seems important to distinguish between recognizing the utility of terms or concepts and agreeing with every position of the authors that employ them. For example, my frequent use of the term subaltern certainly results from my readings of South Asian historiography, but it does not imply agreement with the theoretical positions of everyone who has ever used the word. Indeed, that would be impossible because subaltern studies groups hold some quite contradictory theoretical positions.[2] Sometimes I use "subaltern" as a useful shorthand when I am making a point that I believe applies to subordinated peoples in a variety of social categories, thereby saving me from constantly repeating phrases like "indigenous peasants and the mixed-race urban poor." Other times I employ "subaltern" because it is a more political term than peasant or worker, which are in the end more rooted in economic relationships than in political ones. The political character of "subaltern" makes it more like the terms the people I write about use in eighteenth- and nineteenth-century documents. They most often use terms that express political connections to the whole, terms such as subjects, citizens, or sons of the village.

I believe we can accept the term postcolonial in the same way. As Mark Thurner points out, the term stresses politics, a politics after colonialism but of the same cloth.[3] But we do not need (or in my case, want) to appropriate much of what "postcolonial" brings with it in literary criticism. The element I like least about some versions of postcolonial theory is the effort to discard metanarratives. The criticism of metanarratives is certainly important: our knowledge is shaped by them, and knowledge can as a result conceal and oppress as much as it enlightens or liberates.[4]

Yet the effort to do away with metanarratives brings two problems. First, as several critics of postcolonial theory have pointed out, metanarratives have a way of sneaking in the back door, and arguably a hidden metanarrative is much more insidious than an explicit or even an implicit one.[5] The second problem is that without metanarratives there might be no narrative at all, and it is almost impossible to write about causes without constructing a narrative. Without causative understandings, political action is probably not possible. In consequence, as grateful as I am to postcolonial and other postmodern theorists for focusing serious attention on how dangerous our teleologies are, I believe that abandoning them altogether is both impossible and useless. What we need instead is an increased awareness and sense of responsibility about how we think and write about change and causation.

The feature that makes "postcolonial" particularly useful as a term for the period after independence is the emphasis it places on politics. More precisely, as Patricia Seed points out, using the term postcolonial highlights "the relation of the political processes of nation formation to colonialism."[6] This emphasis brings with it another feature I'm quite willing to borrow from South Asian and other postcolonial historiography; namely a sense of how much is obscured by triumphalist, totalizing nationalist narratives.[7] Yet we should keep in mind the specificity of the narratives produced in nineteenth-century Latin America. In most countries, initial triumphalist interpretations of the political present and future were quite rapidly replaced by expressions of despair over the failure of the new nations to achieve political stability and economic growth. Interpretations that stressed victory over decadent Spanish colonialism could not explain postcolonial failures. Newer, more pessimistic views soon replaced them. In Mexico these bifurcated between liberal pundits who stressed the pernicious persistence of features of Spanish colonialism and conservatives who argued the inadequacy of political and cultural systems that were not grounded in the successful work of Spanish colonialism.[8] In both of these versions the colonial system remained a dominant topic of political conversation through the 1860s.

I would argue that both of these pessimistic visions of Mexico's project were postcolonial in the sense put forward by some practitioners of postcolonial studies in South Asia, particularly Partha Chatterjee.[9] The political projects of the new elite were shot through with the assumptions about subalterns that had underpinned the vision of late-colonial elites of their own political position. The new elite saw itself as surrounded by a sea of ragged, alien people incapable of understanding the finer points of political philosophy and, even worse, of civil property law. Liberals argued that these alien subalterns should be transformed; conservatives doubted that subalterns had the basic virtues that would make such a transformation possible. They instead believed that subalterns could only be controlled with more familiar forms of government. Yet these liberal and conservative voices of pessimism were preceded and later accompanied by others who argued that subalterns could and did react in a conscious and measured way to the political innovations of the 1810s and 1820s. In Mexico, the optimists even predominated in the early 1820s as the institutional frameworks of the national and regional states were set up.

The optimism of some political pundits was paralleled by an important phenomenon among subalterns. The leaders and intellectuals of different subaltern groups almost always sought to engage the new, postindependent, republican state. They took notice of the new political symbols and terms being trumpeted by elites and state institutions, and they struggled to make sense of them for their own purposes. In doing so these leaders and intellectuals made possible a series of encounters between lawmakers and former colonial subjects that verged on transcending the continuities of colonial domination. This transcendence was rarely realized, and even where it was realized it was contingent and momentary. Nevertheless, these encounters had important consequences for the politics of postcolonial states, and their study can tell us much about the limits of both domination and resistance.

The existence of this history of postcolonial engagements should not surprise us—it follows a history of colonial engagements that were very similar. These colonial engagements familiarized subalterns with the conceptual language of the colonizers and the ways that language could be redeployed. Moreover, engagements were virtually mandatory, both before and after independence. Subalterns could not ignore politics, as they often appealed to state power in conflicts over resources, even with other subalterns.

These engagements must be approached with caution. They were always mediated by the institutions and actors that shaped the discursive strategies that individuals could deploy. Moreover, the discourses themselves were fashioned to influence particular audiences. Only rarely do we find documents directed from one subaltern individual or group to another, where more equal relations of power might allow us to suppose more direct access to subaltern thought. Even then, the texts themselves are fraught with the forms, arguments, and metaphors learned in dialogues with the colonial and postcolonial state, and, moreover, the texts usually represent the only available evidence about the often-anonymous individuals who built them. We are forced to contextualize the documents by surrounding them with information about plebes, artisans, or Indian peasants. At best we might map the bare outlines of a particular Indian peasant village that we know contained divisions of gender, class, age, and kinship—divisions that simply didn't leave enough documentary evidence to allow us to do justice to their complexity.

Despite all these reasons for caution, I believe it is imperative that we seriously research the encounters between postcolonial states and subaltern subjects. The alternatives are unappealing. One could assume that the discourses, laws, and ideologies constructed by postcolonial elites had no effect on the lives of subalterns, or that these hegemonic projects were so effective in penetrating and constraining those lives that researching them is irrelevant.[10] I do not think that the evidence can be reasonably interpreted as supporting either of these alternatives. Instead it mostly suggests engagement and mutual influence.[11] The engagements and influences were unequal, and power certainly was unevenly distributed in these encounters. Yet to deny their existence is to turn our backs on a key arena of postcolonial state formation. Moreover, this denial would, ironically, confirm both the most pessimistic visions of postcolonial elites and the most radical claims of some postcolonial theorists. In the former, subaltern populations were seen as so alien that they could not engage the new political paradigms of national identity and individual freedom at all.[12] In the latter, those new political paradigms so successfully marginalized and controlled subalterns that they became virtually voiceless.[13] In both cases postcolonialism, or postcoloniality, becomes a kind of self-fulfilled prophecy.

One of Latin America's most bitter postcolonial disappointments was the failure of the new political rules adopted after independence to assure peaceful and orderly politics. By the middle of the nine-teenth century electoral politics were rarely the dominant mecha-nism for choosing political leaders or even the most important means for legitimating them. Surprisingly, until recently historians have made little effort to understand this particular failure. Generally they have simply dismissed the problem by asserting without evi-dence that electoral rules excluded the majority of people from the polls or that elections were always a sham. Only in the past decade have historians begun serious research on electoral history and prac-tices in the first half of the nineteenth century. In the remainder of this essay I combine an analysis of the bloody breakdown of electoral politics in the southern Mexican city of Oaxaca along with some further reflection on the utility of postcolonial theory.

Elections provide a particularly interesting window on the relation-ship between subaltern groups and politics in postcolonial Latin America. The most important difference between the legitimating discourse of colonial politics and those of postcolonial politics was the transfer of sovereignty from metropolitan monarchs to Latin American peoples. The specifics of this differed from country to country, and for several the various stages of change began even before nominal independence in response to events in Iberia. Yet everywhere elections became the key symbolic link between newly sovereign "people" and governments. Elections were the principal arena where the new ruling fiction of sovereignty was acted out. Sometimes the connection was purely symbolic, but particularly in the early years these political acts were often important in choosing officeholders and determining policies. Although engagements be-tween subalterns and the efforts of postcolonial elites to form and dominate new polities also took place in rebellions and in the judicial system, elections were the one arena where elites openly encouraged such engagement. In many ways this made the eventual abandon-ment of elections as the principal mechanism for choosing of-ficeholders particularly disappointing.

On August 15, 1828, large numbers of voters gathered in Oaxaca's central square to cast ballots in a key legislative election. Tensions were high, and they overflowed when voters realized that one of the city's two electoral parties had gained complete control of the valida-tion and counting of ballots. Angry arguments escalated, and soon the state militia opened fire and charged the crowds. Within a few minutes several men were dead and many more were wounded.

In constructing the extremely brief account above I restricted myself to information about which both parties were in agreement. Yet even this very flat account points to some key features of electoral politics in Oaxaca in the period: elections were well attended; there were two political parties; and those parties disagreed passionately. Eventually electoral politics lost relevance in Oaxaca, but it was not because elections were not competitive or because people were indifferent to them. Again, what we see here is not disengagement from postcolonial politics but rather engagement.

In the period in question the city of Oaxaca had around twenty thousand inhabitants. It was nestled in a pleasant location where three of Mexico's most fertile valleys joined. These valleys were shared between indigenous farming villages and small estates owned by mestizos and whites. Oaxaca's location also gave it access to several different mountainous zones, where hundreds of indigenous villages occupied distinct ecological and economic niches.

Oaxaca was at the time the capital and market center for a large area where the majority of people made most of their living in agriculture. Even so, the cost of transportation meant that agricultural commodities could not be profitably exported to Atlantic markets or to the cities of central Mexico. The region instead exported two other products that owed their more concentrated value to laborious and difficult-to-supervise handwork. The more famous of these was cochineal, a dye made from the dried bodies of an insect that indigenous peasant men collected from maguey plants. The second product was cotton cloth, which was produced both by male mestizo weavers in the city and by indigenous peasant women in mountain villages.

The city's wealthiest families owed their riches to commerce. Merchant families funneled the dye and textile production from indigenous villages and urban artisans into Mexico's larger economy and, in the case of dye, into the world economy. These merchant families sought to maximize the social distance between themselves and the majority of the region's population. In the late colonial period they stressed their identity as Spaniards in a sea of more darkly colored people. They also emphasized their monopoly of offices in the city's municipal government. These offices were purchased with payments to the Crown, but the members of the municipal council often arbitrated among pretenders for a given vacancy. The offices brought great prestige manifested in positions of honor at civic and religious celebrations.

The vast majority of the city's population was neither so economically well off nor so obsessed with ethnicity. There were around eight hundred weavers in 1800, but much of the population provided services for either the city's elite or the villages and haciendas of its hinterland.[14] The city was ethnically diverse, and for most of the population ethnicity was gaining force as a marker of identity. It was increasingly self-reported on official occasions such as baptism, marriage, or census taking.[15]

Both ethnic and occupational differences proved to be important in the passionate party politics that eventually led to the electoral violence of 1828. Several developments drove this process of polarization. Economic opportunity for all urban residents collapsed. Political and philosophical trends in other parts of the Atlantic world led to the designation of political officials through elections and the end of official ethnic distinctions. Individuals and groups had to cope simultaneously with the end of older official social categories and the institution of new political practices. Their search for new ways of making politics led them to adopt political identities that stressed the old absolute of religion and the new one of national allegiance.

Economic opportunities for both merchants and artisans began to decline before independence due to Mexico's problematic connection to world markets. The major market for dye was European, and when Spain's intermittent wars with Great Britain closed the seas to Mexican exports the dye trade faltered.[16] In contrast, the major markets for Oaxacan textiles were in central and northern Mexico. These textiles could not compete in price and quality with the products of English factories, so when Spain was at peace with England the Oaxacan textile trade languished. After independence matters only worsened. The dye trade suffered from Guatemalan competition, and competition from English factories increased with Mexico's formal adoption of free trade policies. The declining demand for both products in wider markets reduced profits for Oaxaca's merchants. Moreover, the lower demand for cloth wiped out the livelihoods of urban weavers. Oaxaca had eight hundred working looms in 1800 but only thirty in 1827.[17]

In the midst of this economic decline Oaxaca's official political and social order also underwent dramatic changes. Although local forces and groups engaged and modified these innovations the impetus came largely from forces outside their control. Events and trends in Spain and other areas of Mexico brought pressure toward ethnic and political leveling and introduced electoral politics.

Pressure toward ethnic and political leveling began with the Hispanic world's effort to reorganize itself to resist Napoleon after 1808. In Spain this defense was first undertaken by multiclass movements under the leadership of local notables and then restructured by liberal politicians based in Cadiz. Rumors of French invasion fleets and attempts to subvert allegiance to the king and Catholicism surged back and forth through Mexico, gaining force when bishops and colonial officials repeated them in calls for donations.[18] In Oaxaca they took on even more force when news of the Hidalgo rebellion reached the city in October 1810. Different social groups competed to organize militia forces. The merchants set up two well-equipped and decorously dressed companies. The city's artisans also organized two companies, and they insisted that their finances allowed, and their honor required, that they dress in the same uniforms as the merchant companies. As the artisans put it, "Since the cause we all defend and the monarch we serve are the same, we should not be made unequal."[19]

The reworking of social categories in Oaxaca took on more force when the Spanish Cortes abolished caste privileges in 1812, a decree that reached Oaxaca right before insurgent leader José María Morelos captured the city that November. Morelos also abolished caste distinctions.[20] The insurgent leader also added another element that would prove crucial in the evolution of political identities after the war—namely, he disseminated insurgent arguments about the peculiar perfidy of European Spaniards. Insurgents argued that European Spaniards were in league with Napoleon against the king and true religion, conspiring for New Spain's ruin. Insurgents also claimed that the European Spaniard's monopolistic and usurious business practices bled New Spain's poor.[21] These arguments set up the Spanish both as scapegoats for the declining fortunes of the urban poor and as likely conspirators against Mexican independence.

The royalists recaptured Oaxaca in 1814, yet royalist troops brought little comfort to the city's elite. The royalists did not revive caste distinctions because at that point the liberal Spanish constitution of 1812 was in force in royalist Mexico. Moreover, the constitution brought political change along another, related dimension—it set in place virtually universal suffrage and indirect elections, the two basic electoral procedures that would govern Mexican elections until the middle of the 1830s. Lawmakers desired widespread participation in elections but they also wanted buffers to prevent capricious voters from choosing officeholders. In other words, they felt the need to engage subalterns in legitimating the state but sought to prevent any subaltern influence on policy making. With wide suffrage and indirect elections, voters were supposed to simply choose prominent, intelligent, and honorable men who would in turn make the important decisions. Officeholders would be chosen in elections but subalterns would not do the choosing. Lawmakers did not believe that the vast majority of voters in the Hispanic world should debate alternative policies and then seek to shape government policies through elections.

The effort of Hispanic writers of the constitution to avoid party politics was frustrated from the beginning. Richard Warren, Antonio Annino, and Virginia Guedea have shown how elections held under the 1812 constitution in Mexico City became occasions of intense political organizing and conflict.[22] Political groups quickly realized they could circumvent the indirect nature of elections. They prepared lists of candidates to serve as electors and then distributed the lists before parochial elections. Rather than being forced to choose electors known to them personally and then allow these electors to vote their consciences, parochial voters could avail themselves of strangers pledged to support a particular candidate or slate of candidates for office. This technique suddenly made the partisan mobilization of even relatively poor voters the key to electoral success.

This innnovation did not immediately spread to Oaxaca, but the delay did not prevent electoral controversy. Oaxaca's first constitutional elections were held in 1814. Although there was apparently little political organizing in this election, the elite families who had previously dominated municipal offices received a rude surprise. An Indian and a mestizo artisan were elected to the town council, and hence municipal office was no longer a marker of exclusive status. Fortunately for the mercantile elite, barely six months later Fernando VII repudiated the constitution and overturned all elections held under it. Nevertheless, when the constitution was put in force again in 1820 the city's first families again felt threatened when no less than four councilmen from humble origins were elected. The elite families proceeded to denigrate these councilmen, calling them *vinagres*, or vinegars. The intention to belittle backfired, however, and within a few years those who opposed the pretensions of the city's elite proudly called themselves vinagres and their opponents *aceites*, or oils.[23]

The egalitarian principles of the Spanish constitution were confirmed in the Plan de Iguala that made Mexico an independent empire in 1821. In Oaxaca, party conflict continued. Records of the disputed 1822 election suggest the stakes and arguments of this early party politics. The aceites succeeded in choosing the majority of secondary electors, and these electors selected only aceites to join the council. The aceites argued that carrying out the laborious, uncompensated duties of councilmen and buying the required uniform were too burdensome for relatively poor men. The vinagres feared that the better-organized aceite party would permanently exclude from office lower-class men from mestizo or indigenous backgrounds, despite official egalitarianism.[24]

The vinagres immediately organized a protest. A large group presented a petition asking the governor to nullify the election. The document's nominal authors were the leaders of the city's barrios, but they also claimed to have the backing of the officers of the city's military garrison. They argued that, according to law, elected officials had to demonstrate "good reputation, allegiance to Independence, and services to the cause," and they claimed that many of those elected had not even shown "even a simulated addiction to the liberty of the Empire, have fled from the public ceremonies that have been held, and only accepted their posts due to a Spirit of ostentation."[25] The writers went on to say that some of those elected "splutter in explaining themselves to produce a Peninsular [Spanish] style as if this were a virtue" and others pointed with pride to their roots in the few families that had dominated municipal offices.[26] The writers also criticized the manner in which the secondary election was held, saying that it was a result of a "plot" because fifteen of the secondary electors met beforehand to decide whom they would elect to each office.[27] The petition was signed by over one hundred individuals and listed a similar number of supporters who could not sign their names. This impressive organizational effort was accompanied by surreptitious threats against European Spaniards, questioning the legitimacy of European Spaniards holding political office in an independent Mexico.[28]

In 1823 the vinagres and the city's military garrison lobbied municipal and state officials to proclaim the state's support for a new, republican federalist constitution. The organizational effort on this occasion was very similar to that of 1822. Large crowds accompanied delegations to authorities and military officers coordinated their efforts with leaders of the city's poor. Their statements exalted equality and liberty.[29] Mexico became an independent republic, but this did not eliminate the new party conflict or even give the vinagres an appreciable advantage in it.

The vinagres and aceites contested every subsequent election of the 1820s. Each election brought ever more sophisticated electoral organizing and ever more virulent electoral propaganda. After the completion of parish elections the two groups would joust for position in secondary elections by challenging the credentials and aptitudes of secondary electors. Moreover, after each election the parties debated their fairness and the legitimacy of the particular forms of organizing used.[30] Yet even as they pursued practical strategies for winning office the two parties also struggled to define their own political identities. These discursive battles were tied to the organizational ones, but ultimately they had more ominous implications.

Under the threat of losing elections each party adopted discourses that stressed how alien their opponents were to local society and culture. The aceites came to argue that the vinagres were heretics whose excesses would lead to the wrath of God. The vinagres in turn identified the aceites with Spanish colonialism and efforts to return Mexico to Spanish rule. In a sense these were both conspiracy theories wherein one's political opponents were imagined as the internal allies of powerful outside forces.[31] The outside forces supposedly aided by heretical vinagres were the rationalism and skepticism let loose by the Enlightenment and the French Revolution. In theory they operated through societies of Masons, which met periodically in secret with special quasi-religious rites.[32] The outside forces supposedly abetted by aceites, though oft-rumored, in the end were very concrete. In 1829 Spanish exiles invaded Mexico hoping to return it to the realm of Fernando VII. Again, though, the rhetoric that accompanied the belief that aceites were secret allies of the Spanish king was one of conspiracy, as vinagres constantly denounced clandestine meetings.

The vinagres increasingly identified the aceites with both the European Spaniards who remained in Mexico and with conspiracies to restore Mexico to Spanish rule. The identification of the aceites with the European Spaniards and threats to Mexican independence was part of a national phenomenon, the growth of radical popular alternatives to the status quo.[33] One driving force behind this othering of a group that the polity officially tolerated was the scapegoating of Spanish merchants for the way cotton growers and weavers foundered under a tide of cheap foreign textiles. Anti-Spanish sentiment was tightly linked with calls for protectionism.[34] The political attitudes of the aceites prepared them for identification with the Spaniards: in the years before independence they had flaunted their Spanish roots. Now the aceites defended resident Spaniards from pressures for expulsion and did nothing to alleviate the plight of the city's artisans because they subscribed to the economic orthodoxy that interference in markets benefited no one.[35]

Arguably, though, even urban economic miseries were not enough to give the anti-Spanish movement the political momentum it developed. Its force was magnified and multiplied by the Spaniards' association with rumored and real conspiracies to end Mexico's new political independence. The substrate of these ideas was laid in the years after 1808, when the Spaniards were rumored to be in league with Napoleon to turn Mexico over to the godless French. After independence, suspicion of disloyalty to the king was replaced with that of disloyalty to the new nation. Even relatively conservative political figures played this particular tune.[36]

As the 1820s went on these allegations took on greater and greater force because there was credible evidence behind them, both at the national level and in Oaxaca. In early 1827 Spanish friar Joaquín Arenas approached military officers in Mexico City seeking their cooperation in returning Mexico to Spanish rule. He was arrested, tried, and executed. Authorities also discovered a conspiracy much closer to home, on the coast of Oaxaca. Again those responsible were imprisoned, but one escaped and tried to subvert Oaxaca's garrison before he was subdued.[37] These real plots were magnified in pamphlets that accused tyrannical Spaniards of seeking to plunge Mexico into civil war.[38]

The vinagres initially had the best of the electoral competition.

They made the most of their opponents' undemocratic statements and positions of 1822–1823, when the aceites had arranged the secondary elections for the municipal council to deny the artisans' positions. In 1824 the vinagres gained a substantial number of places in the state legislature, which wrote the state constitution. In 1826, though, the aceites recouped much of the ground they had lost, apparently by organizing through a number of confraternities based in the city's cathedral parish. In this electoral campaign the aceites accused the vinagres of impiety.[39] The aceites chose one of their own, José Ignacio de Morales, for state governor.

After 1826 the aceite legislature shielded Oaxaca's Spanish population from pressures for expulsion. Their protection was severely damaged in 1827. On November 21, Santiago García, the commander of the state's military garrison, issued a printed statement that the state's Spaniards should be expelled because of their efforts to return Oaxaca to Spanish rule. In response, the state legislature passed a much milder expulsion decree. Customarily, laws were published in a ceremony in which an official read them aloud in prominent places accompanied by a military escort, drummer, and trumpeter. García, however, refused to provide an escort for the publication of the mild expulsion decree, and instead republished his own proclamation with troops in dress uniform accompanied by "the din of church bells, fireworks, and a large part of the People."[40] He insisted that the state legislature and governor had prevented "the Oaxacan People" from expressing their desire for protection from Spanish plots; something he said was shown by their vocal support for his efforts. Vinagre José Mariano Torres led large groups of civilian citizens to lobby the town council and state legislature for a severe expulsion law. The town council acquiesced, but the legislature instead moved its deliberations to a village away from the city's crowds. Eventually the national government sent new troops to control the unrest, and García capitulated, content because the national government had recently passed an expulsion law more severe than the one he had proposed.[41]

The anti-Spanish agitation of 1827 was crucial for several reasons. García articulated both the fear of Spanish subversion and the frustration with the aceite-dominated legislature's apparent insensitivity to shifting political opinion. He also expressed the vinagres' growing belief that the state and municipal governments were preventing vinagres from expressing their political beliefs. On November 24, he told the governor that "many citizens have come to complain to me that the police sergeant Pedro Calderón walks around armed, preventing citizens from coming to my headquarters to manifest their desires."[42] García's opponents shared this fear of curbs on political expression. García allowed scheduled municipal elections to take place while he controlled the city. After he stood down, the state legislature annulled these elections due to the "lack of liberty which prevented the vast majority of citizens from voting" and rescheduled them for January 1828.[43] Here again is the fear that an opponents' legal or extralegal control of the streets was used to prevent political expression.

The vinagres won the new municipal elections after a period of intense political organizing, as both parties held nocturnal meetings to elaborate lists of candidates for distribution to voters.[44] In August 1828 another crucial election would determine the composition of the state legislature for the next two years. Ominously, each party accused its adversary of using government institutions to harass opponents. Prominent vinagre Ignacio María Ordoño accused Governor Morales of arbitrarily imprisoning him and placing aceites in the state militia.[45] As the August elections neared, Morales prohibited nocturnal meetings in the street of more than four men and prevented the publication of a vinagre pamphlet.[46] Yet even though the aceites controlled the state government they also complained about vinagre violence and harassment. Morales claimed that groups of vinagres assaulted a state congressman and threatened electoral meetings of aceites.[47] In June 1828 the aceite paper *Cartas al Pueblo* charged that the vinagre municipal judge Manuel Varela had illegally imprisoned Antonio Valdés y Moya, director of the state's government press, for beating his wife.[48] This imprisonment prevented an issue of the aceite newspaper from appearing.

Political temperatures were driven to the boiling point in 1828 by the local conflict between aceites and vinagres. Yet they were raised even further by Mexico's first contested presidential election. Radicals championed Vicente Guerrero, who they argued would maintain a firm anti-Spanish stance and act to preserve the interests of artisans besieged by foreign competition. Their opponents favored Secretary of War Manuel Gómez Pedraza, a former royalist officer who seemed to promise more peace and security to Mexico's elite.[49] Not surprisingly in Oaxaca the aceites favored Gómez Pedraza, while the vinagres idolized Guerrero.

In March 1828 a group of vinagres founded Oaxaca's first Masonic lodge, and other York rite lodges soon followed it. The vinagres also founded several "Guadalupan" societies. In club meetings vinagres praised vinagre periodicals and criticized the aceite press. They also mocked effigies of their opponents. In Guadalupan meetings they met under the image of the Virgin of Guadalupe and promised to uphold Mexican independence against conspiracies. It seems that the York rite lodges were mostly for vinagre political and military leaders while the Guadalupan societies were designed to attract the urban public,[50] apparently in an effort to compete with the aceite's use of established confraternities in electoral organizing.

In summer 1828 the vinagres were caught in an institutional bind. Although they hoped to win the August legislative elections, the new legislature would not take office until after two crucial votes. In July the outgoing legislature would choose the governor for the next term. In September it would cast Oaxaca's sole vote in the presidential election. These asynchronisms had been built into the political system to damp down the potentially dangerous waves of public opinion. Now from the vinagres' point of view they would thwart the popular will. Yet the vinagres did everything in their power to derail the apparently predetermined course of events, and one of their tactics added dramatically to political tensions in the city.

The state's governor was chosen in a two-step process. The lower house of the state legislature selected a list of six preferred candidates and forwarded it to the state senate, which would then choose the winner. In July 1828 the aceites had a clear majority in the lower house, and they forwarded a list of aceite candidates to the senate. The senate was also dominated by the aceites, but there were still two vinagre senators who had been elected in 1824. The vinagre senators could not win the gubernatorial election for the vinagres, but they halted the election by leaving so that the senate would not have a quorum. A crowd of cheering vinagres met them at the door. As in November 1827, the aceites controlled the institutions but their aims were frustrated by the vinagres' control of the streets. Two weeks of tense standoff ensued, ending only when the government compelled one of the vinagre senators to attend the session in which aceite Joaquín Guerrero was elected governor.[51]

By the time the August 1828 elections arrived the city was primed for political disaster. Two political parties, each capable of mobilizing large numbers of voters, eyed each other warily. The aceites and vinagres could both plausibly expect political repression if they failed to win the election. Each had made emotionally charged appeals that stressed the consequences of losing. The vinagres argued that an aceite victory was a step toward the subversion of Mexican independence by Spain. The aceites countered with the accusation that the vinagres would weaken Oaxaca's devotion to Catholicism. Both parties had also impugned the legitimacy of their opponents' political tactics. Each argued that the other had committed fraud and lied to its supporters, duping them into cooperation. Both aceites and vinagres hoped for the best, a clear electoral victory; yet each feared the worst, a violent usurpation by their opponents.[52] In hindsight, it is a wonder the violence was not more severe.

The first voters present named the polling officials. These officials were crucial, as they would count the vote and determine whether voters were qualified. In past elections naming the table's officials had been a tumultuous affair, and most recently the vinagres had won this preliminary battle for the January 1828 municipal elections.[53] Both vinagre and aceite accounts agree that the officials named for the August election were aceites. The aceites claimed that this victory was gained according to legal, established procedure. According to the vinagres, Manuel María Fagoaga, the aceite official in charge of the election, arranged for the table's officials to be named before the bulk of voters arrived.[54] When the vinagres discovered this they began to object, and Fagoaga immediately ordered the imprisonment of several vinagre leaders. A delegation led by José María Pando and Ignacio Fagoaga (ironically, Manuel's brother) went to the governor's residence to protest. Many vinagre voters followed them a few minutes later.

After the delegation departed the situation at the voting table became confused. The officials began receiving votes, apparently over the shouted protests of a throng of vinagres. Expecting problems, Manuel Fagoaga had asked for a detachment of militia to guard the voting table. According to the aceites one or two men in the crowd fired pistols toward the table.[55] The vinagres denied this, but in any event the militia opened fire on the crowd, and the bloodletting began.

Meanwhile at the governor's house Ignacio Fagoaga and Pando had tried unsuccessfully to convince Governor Joaquín Guerrero to restrain Manuel Fagoaga's partiality. Guerrero argued that he had no legal authority to give orders to Manuel Fagoaga. As they conversed, a crowd of vinagre voters arrived at the governor's door, where they were prevented from entering by a small militia. When Pando and Ignacio Fagoaga left they heard the firing begin a few blocks away in the plaza. According to Pando a militia patrol arrived immediately at the governor's house and attacked the crowd with firearms, bayonets, and swords. In contrast the aceite militia claimed that Ignacio Fagoaga fired two pistols at the patrol, which responded in self-defense. In either case several men were killed and wounded right in front of the governor's house.[56]

Between the two separate outbreaks of violence five vinagres were killed or mortally wounded and several more were injured. Yet in the long term the most important casualty was the electoral system. Guerrero suspended the parish or primary elections and canceled the second scheduled day. Secondary elections proceeded on schedule because Guerrero claimed that elections elsewhere in the state returned such a preponderance of aceite electors that the city's election was a moot point.[57] The secondary electors chose a legislature dominated by the aceites. Authorities imprisoned twenty-seven vinagres and exiled two others from the state. As predicted, the outgoing state legislature cast its ballot in the presidential election for Manuel Gómez Pedraza.

Soon thereafter Antonio López de Santa Anna led his army into Oaxaca, which he occupied in support of the successful rebellion that sent Gómez Pedraza into exile and placed Vicente Guerrero in the presidential palace. Embittered vinagres supported Santa Anna during his occupation of Oaxaca, especially when he was besieged for weeks by government forces. Afterward the vinagres successfully forced the annulment of the August 1828 legislative election. This spiral continued through the rest of the decade as well as the first half of the 1830s. Although vinagres and aceites continued to compete in elections, the actual holding of office was increasingly determined by which group had military control of the state, and this in turn was increasingly a question of trends in national politics. Competition in elections was no longer the principal road to power in state politics.

Was the demise of electoral politics in nineteenth-century Mexico a case of postcolonialism as self-fulfilled prophesy? Did the barriers of class and ethnic identity that colonial elites carefully built and tenaciously defended to legitimate their privileged position prevent them from fulfilling their later dream of constructing a Mexican nation-state able to compete on par with its European and North American contemporaries? If we look at the founding moment of party politics in Oaxaca, when the city's leading families expressed their fear of social leveling by denigrating less-privileged members of the town council as "vinagres," this certainly appears to be the case. Yet there are limits to this line of analysis. Despite their fears, these wealthy and powerful families did not seek income qualifications for voting until the 1830s, and they never contemplated continuing the official recognition of ethnic hierarchies and categories. They also did not construct elections as fictions. For a time elites were willing to choose political leaders through elections with broad suffrage.

The demise of electoral politics was also not a case of postcolonialism as self-fulfilled prophecy in other senses found both in some nineteenth-century analyses of politics and in some varieties of postcolonial theory. These perspectives suggest that gaps between elite projects and subaltern mentalities were so large that the two never met. The evidence against this is clear. Subalterns in Oaxaca very definitely engaged the new practices and discourses of politics. The numbers of voters alone indicate that the poor of the city turned out in large numbers for elections. Clearly they believed that the new practices and policy alternatives of government had some relevance to their lives. Moreover, this engagement was not one in which the ideologies and discourses of elites were so successful in ordering or reordering the social world that subaltern agency became impossible or meaningless. Richard Graham has made a fairly plausible case for this kind of elite success in his analysis of nineteenth-century Brazilian elections, which he interprets as rituals emphasizing social hierarchy.[58] Elites were not so successful in Oaxaca. The vinagre program against foreign merchants and for protectionism was for its day a very radical alternative, and it seems to have had a great deal of resonance for parts of Oaxaca's urban population.

François-Xavier Guerra has produced the most systematic body of work analyzing the difficulties of introducing electoral politics in Spanish America. Recently, together with Marie Demélas-Bohy, he has attributed the failure of Spanish America to successfully adopt what he calls modern forms of politics to the persistence of family cliques, clientage networks, and municipal bodies, the "collective participants of the old society."[59] Patron-clientage is difficult to document under the best of circumstances, and there is little evidence of its operation in urban Oaxaca. In 1832 a vinagre newspaper did accuse the aceites of assigning government posts on the basis of family cliques, yet the posts involved were strictly for people of means and education.[60] The collapse of urban textile production makes it particularly difficult to imagine what patronage vinagres or aceites could offer the urban poor. The apparent importance of confraternities in electoral organizing would seem to lend some support to the thesis of Guerra and Demélas-Bohy. Nevertheless, in Oaxaca the activities of these confraternities stressed ideological argument rather than blind loyalty to corporate bodies. Moreover, neither party deployed corporatist rhetoric: both stressed the deciding role of the individual will of citizens in elections.

I would argue that the demise of electoral politics was more complicated than any of these analyses suggest. The postcolonial failure I have tried to explain here was more a breakdown of pluralism than it was of democracy. Elections were not sustained as a method for distributing political power because in the 1820s political parties built discourses and worldviews that stressed the apocalyptic consequences of losing elections. They constructed their opponents as perverse and subversive enemies of the values both sides agreed were foundational. Ironically this both increased each party's fear that losing elections would result in repression and increased their incentive to persecute their enemies if they won.

Pluralism notably proved to be almost as much of a problem in Spain before the 1980s as it was in Latin America. There are two aspects of the Hispanic historical experience that worked against political pluralism. The first was that religious tolerance was not worked out in the early modern period. Circumstances in the colonial United States and Great Britain prevented religious unity or the preponderance of single religious groups in different politics, and this eventually led to practical religious tolerance, laying some ideological precedent for political pluralism. The second aspect of the Hispanic historical experience that worked against political pluralism was the fear of factionalism. Calls against organized political division within polities or communities were omnipresent in the Spanish world.[61] The belief that one's political opponents represented a faction tended to preclude tolerating them. The absence of pluralism, in other words, may be related to the Hispanic legacy of Spanish America without being a result of colonialism.

Yet I would not say the question is one of a Hispanic authoritarian tradition that can be counterpoised to Anglo-Saxon legacies of plu-ralism and democracy. The early leaders of the nascent United States also abhorred factionalism, and they instituted systems of indirect representation to moderate the impact of wide suffrage. The nascent United States experienced more than one major controversy over the repression of political opponents. In fact, suffrage was wider in Mex-ico in the 1820s than it was in the United States or Great Britain. Yet the United States immediately following independence was in a much better position to strengthen pluralism and eventually democ-ratize politics. Its economic situation was much better and it did not face significant efforts on the part of Great Britain to return it to colonial rule.

Electoral politics and popular sovereignty were introduced in Oa-xaca under extremely unfavorable circumstances. The economy was in decline and social hierarchies based on ethnicity and class were suddenly deemed incompatible with the ideals of the new state. Par-ties were a practical inevitability, but Hispanic political traditions abhorred them. Moreover, the political arguments bequeathed by the years of civil and international war after 1808 were mostly about the danger of pernicious plots against church and state. The circum-stances made for a political culture of conspiracy theory that under-mined trust between groups and encouraged those who controlled the state to wield repression against their enemies. Seen this way, the demise of elections as a practical method of choosing officeholders seems more an inevitable tragedy than a self-fulfilled prophecy.

NOTES

Note that all translations are mine unless indicated otherwise.

1 See, for example, Florencia Mallon, "The Promise and Dilemma of Subaltern Studies," *American Historical Review* 99.5 (December 1994): 1501; Richard Slatta, "Bandits and Social History: A Comment on Joseph," *Latin American Research Review* 26 (1991): 145–51; J. Jorge Klor de Alva, "The Postcolonialization of the (Latin) American Experi-ence," in *After Colonialism: Imperial Histories and Postcolonial Displacements*, ed. Gyan Prakash (Princeton: Princeton University Press, 1995), 247, 263–69; and Stephen Haber, "The Worst of Both Worlds: The New Cultural History of Mexico," *Mexican Studies/Estudios Mexicanos* 13.2 (summer 1997): 363–83.

2 Among others Florencia Mallon, in "Promise and Dilemma," 1497–

99, has identified these, although she believes they are tensions rather than contradictions.

3 Mark Thurner, "Historicizing 'the Postcolonial' from Nineteenth-Century Peru," *Journal of Historical Sociology* 9.1 (March 1996): 3.

4 Gyan Prakash, "Introduction: After Colonialism," in Prakash, ed., *After Colonialism*, 4–6.

5 Anne McClintock, "The Angel of Progress: Pitfalls of the Term 'Post-Colonialism,'" *Social Text* 31/32 (1992): 85–86; Fernando Coronil, "Can Postcoloniality Be Decolonized? Imperial Banality and Postcolonial Power," *Public Culture* 5.1 (fall 1992): 99–100.

6 Patricia Seed, "Subaltern Studies in the Post-Colonial Americas," *Dispositio/n* 19.46 (1994): 219.

7 Prakash, "Introduction" 9–10; Subaltern Studies Group, "Founding Statement," *Dispositio/n* 19.46 (1994): 8.

8 The best work on this intense ideological split remains Charles Hale's *Mexican Liberalism in the Age of Mora* (New Haven: Yale University Press, 1968).

9 Partha Chatterjee, *The Nation and Its Fragments: Colonial and Postcolonial Histories* (Princeton: Princeton University Press, 1993), 159.

10 Piers Larson has recently criticized some proponents of postcolonial theory for taking this latter position; see his "Capacities and Modes of Thinking: Intellectual Engagements and Subaltern Hegemony in the Early History of Malagasy Christianity," *American Historical Review* 102.4 (October 1997): 996–99.

11 One leading postcolonial theorist who also stresses engagement is Partha Chatterjee; see, for example, *The Nation and Its Fragments*, 159–60.

12 The examples are myriad. For the Mexican case, see José María Luís Mora, *Méjico y sus revoluciones*, vol. 1 (1836; Mexico City: Porrua, 1950), 63–73. The most famous Latin American contemporary to espouse this view was, of course, Domingo Sarmiento; see his *Life in the Argentine Republic in the Days of the Tyrants; or, Civilization and Barbarism* (New York: Hurd and Houghton, 1868), esp. 59–60.

13 The most prominent statement to this effect was of course Gayatri Spivak's "Can the Subaltern Speak?" in *Marxism and the Interpretation of Culture*, ed. Cary Nelson and Lawrence Grossberg (Urbana: University of Illinois Press, 1988), 271–313.

14 Brian Hamnett, *Politics and Trade in Southern Mexico, 1750–1821* (Cambridge: Cambridge University Press, 1971), 187; John Chance, *Race and Class in Colonial Oaxaca* (Stanford: Stanford University Press, 1978), 160.

15 Chance, *Race and Class*, 155–85.

16 Hamnett, *Politics and Trade*, 114–15.

17 Carlos Sánchez Silva, *Indios, comerciantes, y burocracia en la Oaxaca post-colonial, 1786–1860* (Oaxaca: Instituto Oaxaqueño de las Culturas, Fondo Estatal para la Cultura y las Artes, Universidad Autónoma Benito Juárez de Oaxaca, 1998), 91–110.

18 For Oaxaca, see various pastoral letters from the bishop in the Biblioteca Pública del Estado de Oaxaca, Fondo Martinez Gracida, vol. 68.

19 Archivo General de la Nación (hereafter AGN), Operaciones de Guerra, 103, fol. 6–69 (quote from 61v). The artisans' argument here is an early example of the kind of assertion of honor based on virtue that Sarah Chambers found in early republican Arequipa; see her *From Subjects to Citizens: Honor, Gender, and Politics in Arequipa, Peru, 1780–1854* (University Park: Pennsylvania State University Press, 1999), 160–87.

20 Ernesto Lemoine, *Morelos: Su vida revolucionaria a través de sus escritos y otros testimonios de la época* (Mexico City: Universidad Nacional Autónoma de México, 1965), 264.

21 Peter Guardino, *Peasants, Politics, and the Formation of Mexico's National State* (Stanford: Stanford University Press, 1996), 61–65.

22 Richard Warren, "Elections and Popular Political Participation in Mexico, 1808–1836," in *Liberals, Politics, and Power: State Formation in Nineteenth-Century Latin America*, ed. Vincent Peloso and Barbara Tenenbaum (Athens: University of Georgia Press, 1996), 34–36; Antonio Annino, "The Ballot, Land, and Sovereignty: Cádiz and the Origins of Mexican Local Government, 1812–1820," in *Elections before Democracy: The History of Elections in Europe and Latin America*, ed. Eduardo Posada-Carbó (New York: St. Martin's Press, 1996), 67–73; and Virginia Guedea, "Las primeras elecciones populares en la ciudad de México, 1812–1813," *Mexican Studies/Estudios Mexicanos* 7.1 (winter 1991): 9–13.

23 I have not located any sources that discuss the connection between the everyday use of these terms and their political and social connotations. One possibility is that it has to do with the way oil rises to the top in combinations of oil and vinegar. Another is that vinagre began as a pejorative reference to spoiled wine, and aceite was a pejorative reference to something slippery and slimy that does not mix well with vinegar.

24 AGN, Gobernación Legajo 1936 caja 2 exp. 6, fol. 5.

25 Ibid., fol. 12v.

26 Ibid., fol. 13.

27 Ibid., fol. 13–14v.

28 Ibid., fol. 31–34v.

29 AGN, Gobernación s/s caja 48 exp. 12; Fondo Manuel Martinez Gracida, vol. 38.

30 Un Espectador Imparcial, *Elecciones parroquiales de Oajaca en los dias 15 y*

16 del corriente (Oaxaca, 1826); *Cartas al Pueblo*, April 12, 1828; *Dos clérigos y un coyote pueden más que un batalón, ó sea Diálogo entre un Sensato y un Mayordomo Oajaqueño* (Mexico: Imprenta de Mariano Galván, 1826); *Los Americanos por Naturaleza, Contestación al comunicado del Oajaqueño por adopción del número del Sol que abajo se expresa* (Oaxaca: Imprenta Liberal, dirigida por Nicolás Idiaquez, 1826); and Pablo Villavicencio (El Payo del Rosario), *Ya tenemos en Oaxca parte de la Santa Liga* (1826), reproduced in James C. McKegney, *The Political Pamphlets of Pablo Villavicencio "El Payo del Rosario,"* vol. 2 (Amsterdam: Rodopi N.V., 1975), 598–607.

31 This brings to mind François Furet's argument about the genesis and particular power of the specter of the "aristocratic plot"; see his *Interpreting the French Revolution* (New York: Cambridge University Press, 1981), 55–56.

32 *Cartas al Pueblo*, April 23, 1828; *Cartas al Pueblo*, August 16, 1828.

33 I have discussed this process extensively in *Peasants, Politics*, 113–27.

34 Peter Guardino, "Identity and Nationalism in Mexico: Guerrero, 1780–1840," *Journal of Historical Sociology* 7.3 (September 1994): 314–42.

35 *Memoria que el Gobernador del Estado de Oaxaca presentó en la apertura de las sesiones ordinarias del Segundo Congreso Constitucional del mismo, verificado el 2 de julio de 1827* (Oaxaca: Imprenta del Gobierno, 1827), 8.

36 Carlos María de Bustamante, *A los habitantes de la Provincia de Oaxaca* (Mexico City: Imprenta Americana de Alejandro Valdés, 1822); *La Revolución de Oajaca, o sean los efectos de la revolución que intentaron hacer en aquella provincia los desconocidos españoles, el día 9 del presente, en que se hizo la Jura de nuestro digno emperador. Carta particular. Oajaca diciembre 8 de 1822* (Puebla: La Liberal de Moreno Hermanos, 1822).

37 Archivo Histórico de la Ciudad de Oaxaca (herafter A H C O), Delitos Contra la Seguridad del Estado, 1826; Jorge Fernando Iturribarría, *Historia de Oaxaca 1821–1854* (Oaxaca: Ediciones E R B, 1935), 82–83.

38 *Manifiesto que los oaxaqueños dirigen a sus compatriotas de los Estados, por los acontecimientos de Matamoros* (Puebla: Reimpreso en la Oficina del Patriota, 1827).

39 *Un Ciudadano, A mis conciudadanos de Oajaca y todo el Estado* (Oaxaca: n.p., 1826); Villavicencio, *Ya tenemos en Oaxaca*; Ignacio María Ordoño, *Manifesto al público imparcial* (Oaxaca: Imprenta Liberal a Cargo de Nicolás Idiáquez, 1826); *Dos clérigos y un coyote pueden más que un batalón, ó sea Diálogo entre un Sensato y un Mayordomo Oajaqueño* (Mexico City: Imprenta de Mariano Galván, 1826); *El Enemigo Irreconciliable de los Pícaros, ¿Si tendremos monarquía a prestesto de heregía?* (Mexico City: Imprenta del Aguila, Dirigida por José Ximeno, 1826).

40 A G N, Gobernación, Legajo 66 exp. 1.

41 Iturribarría, *Historia de Oaxaca*, 83.

42 AGN, Gobernación Legajo 66 exp. 1.

43 Archivo General del Estado de Oaxaca (hereafter AGEO), Fondo Impresos, 28/01/1828.

44 Libro de Actas Secretas del Senado, January 1828, AGEO, Fondo Legajos Encuadernados, Sección Decretos, vol. 70, 1825; Ignacio María Ordoño, *Acusación al público contra el Supremo Gobierno* (Mexico: Imprenta del Correo por C. C. Sebring, 1828), 21.

45 Ordoño, *Acusación al público*, 21.

46 AHCO, Tesorería Municipal, 1764–1829; AGN, Gobernación Legajo 76 exp. 1.

47 AGN, Gobernación Legajo 76 exp. 1.

48 *Cartas al Pueblo*, June 21, 1828. Later it claimed that another vinagre municipal judge assaulted an aceite and his wife. *Cartas al Pueblo*, July 16, 1828.

49 Guardino, *Peasants, Politics*, 125.

50 AGN, Gobernación Legajo 76 exp. 1; *Cartas al Pueblo*, July 9, 1828, August 20, 1828, and August 30, 1828.

51 AGN, Gobernación Legajo 76 exp. 1; *Cartas al Pueblo*, July 19, 1828.

52 For an explicit expression of this fear see Ordoño, *Acusación al público*, 28.

53 *Cartas al Pueblo*, September 10, 1828.

54 AGEO, Fondo Gobernación, vol. 2, s/e.

55 *Cartas al Pueblo*, August 16, 1828; AGN, Gobernación Legajo 76 exp. 1.

56 AGN, Gobernación Legajo 76 exp. 1; AGEO, Fondo Gobernación, vol. 2, s/e.

57 AGN, Gobernación Legajo 76 exp. 1.

58 Richard Graham, *Patronage and Politics in Nineteenth-Century Brazil* (Stanford: Stanford University Press, 1990), 101–21.

59 François-Xavier Guerra and Marie Demélas-Bohy, "The Hispanic Revolutions: The Adoption of Modern Forms of Representation in Spain and America, 1808–1810," in *Elections before Democracy: The History of Elections in Europe and Latin America*, ed. Eduardo Posada-Carbó (New York: St. Martin's Press, 1996), 56.

60 *El Zapoteco*, September 7, 1832.

61 François-Xavier Guerra, *Modernidad e independencias: Ensayos sobre las revoluciones hispánicas* (Mexico: Fondo de Cultura Económica, 1993), 361.

ANDRÉS GUERRERO

The Administration of Dominated Populations

under a Regime of Customary Citizenship

The Case of Postcolonial Ecuador

Translated by Mark Thurner

✴ This essay is, more than anything else, an exploration of regions poorly illuminated in the construction of a regime of citizenship and political representation of the republican kind that simultaneously and organically incorporates forms of domination. I am most concerned with those modalities that I call the "administration of populations": the management, under republican regimes, of demographic groups (particularly in the nineteenth century) that are not considered apt for the quotidian forms of exchange inherent to the relationship of equality among citizens (that is, for the most part, populations classified as uncivilized).

This problematic takes part in a wider discussion about the various forms that citizenship may assume in different historical contexts. Working at the intersection of various perspectives (of class, ethnicity, race, gender) some authors have raised the problem of citizenship conceived not merely as a modality of inclusion and egalitarianism (a notion inherent in its own universalizing discourse), but as a historical construction tinted by the semantics of domination and contingent on social conflicts and relations of power.[1] This problem, in my view, is particularly pertinent for those postcolonial states (like the republic of Ecuador) that harbor significant indigenous populations under conditions of social, political, and economic subordination.

Today in the Andes and in Mesoamerica the so-called Indians have attained protagonist roles in social movements. They now erupt in public space and on the national political scene, provoking political conjunctures, albeit under a sign doubly paradoxical. First, these movements emerge precisely at a moment when the architecture of citizenship and of republican representation—some two hundred years old—is totally consolidated. Second, they occur at a moment when the public opinion of "citizens in the common sense" (a notion I will define below, but by which here I mean the Creole or white-mestizo² population) was convinced (a sort of consensus among the dominant) that Indians were essentially obliterated populations or, in the best of cases (what some authors strove to catalog as) "witnesses" to a past long gone, "fossil" cultures, or perhaps peasant communities cornered in remote "refuge regions."³ Thus, under the shadow of citizenship, indigenous peoples were rendered as invisible populations stripped of social protaganism; their economic and cultural contribution to the nation was reduced; and, of course, they were denied any political relevance. Indians constituted a kind of historical residue, peoples and cultures that silently faded away before the open gates of national integration, globalization, migratory movements, and above all the process of mestizaje, or miscegenation, which implied the bodily incorporation of natives into the ideal image of the white-mestizo national citizen.

As a means of bringing this problematic into focus, I have adopted a modality of narration that does not intend to unravel a historical intrigue, but that does seek to draw taut associations between three levels of analysis.⁴ I begin by narrating two historical conjunctures, each of which left an enduring mark on the formation of citizenship in Ecuador. Cutting the thread of this historical narration, I then intercalate two types of "detour" that connect with other themes. The object is to spin a significant web of linkages that associate both conjunctures with two kinds of problems. The first problem, which is theoretical, derives from the necessity to think through the paradoxical variation of a form of citizenship that is constructed as a system for the administration of populations. The second problem is a methodological one that arises from the process of writing, and of reading in the archives, the history of citizenship as a quotidian relation of domination in a postcolonial republican context. These problems, imposed on the historian by both past and present social realities, arise when she or he attempts to decode and analyze the documents that lay before her or his eyes.

The two narrated conjunctures are located in 1843 and 1857. They concern the constitution of citizenship by initiative of the state. The

Administration of Dominated Populations   273

first removes the dust from a failure buried among the many amnesias of the national cause. In effect, the recently founded national state attempted in 1843 to amplify the juridical equality of citizenship and extend it to all the populations of the republic, including the indigenous. However, the state had to reverse itself in the face of a social rebellion ignited by the white-mestizo population, and particularly by the popular classes that formed part of this group of de facto citizens.

In contrast, the second conjuncture (1857) achieved an enduring success: without dissent the parliament voted for the legal equality of the indigenous population with the rest of the country's citizens. Nevertheless, the juridical leveling did not erradicate the administration of dominated populations; on the contrary, it brought it up to date. A shift occured in the system of domination, from an explicit modality of management—concentrated in the state and in the legacy of the colony—to a republican form that decentered domination toward the diffuse and variegated periphery of what Pierre Bourdieu calls "fields of power" located in the private sphere.[5] A system of domination over the indigenous population that was compatible with republican principles and laws and inscribed in citizenship was implanted. Thus, in 1857 the management of the indigenous population (the de facto noncitizens) was delegated to the patriarchal and patrimonial institutions of citizens.

I have selected these two conjunctures because in my view they accentuate crucial aspects, both theoretical and historical, of the architecture of citizenship. I am referring to the fact that the effective content of this relationship, in the sphere of everyday life, is the geometric result of a historical process. It depends politically, socially, and culturally on the fields, conjunctures, and relations of power on which it is laid. In other words, under certain circumstances citizenship may integrate modalities of domination over those populations classified and discriminated against as noncitizens, by virtue of a constitutive habitus of practice, an inborn structure of mentality of the politically, culturally, and racially "legitimate" population. This form of domination utilizes a system of classification with colonial origins that is proper to the "legitimate" population as defined by racial criteria and political and cultural attributes. Thus, in practice, the formation of citizenship is a component of the *world of common sense*. This world is articulated with forms of thought and the system of habitus, both historically constituted and incorporated by the dominant population during the colonial period and reinvented in the republican period. This view of citizenship as historically constituted modalities in the world of common sense leads me to formulate theoretical considerations that, in my "detours" into the usages of the notion of citizenship, I attempt to link back to the historical narrative.

Over the course of my ongoing research on the relation between the indigenous populations in the nineteenth century and the formation of the republican state it has become increasingly clear to me that— in the Ecuadorian context and also for those countries of the region with large indigenous populations—to adhere to the conventional, merely juridical definition of citizenship, or to define it exclusively in terms of relations between populations and the state, is to render the notion reductivist. The problem of a form of domination decentered from the state and delegated to private powers remained unelucidated within the context of a political system that implanted, relatively early on, juridical equality among all (adult male) inhabitants of the country. This is what occured in Ecuador after 1857 and has come down to the present. The problem, at most, might be interpreted as one of intersubjective relations between individuals, of intolerance as a consequence of ethnic emotivities. In any case, it was not a pertinent subject for the history of the political construction of the republic.

The question for us now concerns choosing the conceptual tools that can be manipulated to achieve some theoretical understanding of the problem. The possibility that I explore in this essay consists of orienting the analysis toward a notion of citizenship conceived of as a field of power for social agents in the political public sphere as conceived by Jürgen Habermas.[6] This notion required removing citizenship from its significant site focused on the state and resituating it in the context of immediate and quotidian strategies of power between populations. At the same time, I make use of Michel Foucault's warnings about the insufficiency of any juridical explanation of power (which fits so well with the notion of citizenship conceived only in terms of rights), and of his project to reveal certain phenomena of domination in terms of the "administration of populations."[7] In these pages I also make use of two theoretical propositions drawn from the feminist critique of the political. In order to analyze the constitution of the dominated subject and those who dominate, I draw upon, on the one hand, Carole Pateman's proposal to interrogate the forms of domination nested in the myth of the social contract, the notion of citizenship, and the separation of public from private, and, on the other, Judith Butler's suggestion that forms of domination, the domain of politics, create a "determining exterior" that is "pre-" or "non-" political where the "Other" is situated.[8]

The final theme of the "detours" that interrupt the narrative thread of the historical conjunctures to tie some loose ends in related themes has to do with the political representation of the indigenous population under a regime of citizenship. This problem leads me to the linked phenomena of, with the construction of citizenship, the process of making certain populations invisible in the public-state sphere, which is directly linked to the presence and legitimate discourse of social agents in the political. Given that indigenous peoples as a group of populations are shoved into the distant recesses of the public sphere of citizens; subordinated to the sphere of private powers; and situated in a "constitutive outside," two questions arise. First, under such conditions how is the political representation of this type of population (which is, ultimately, one of subjects) executed under a regime of citizenship? Second, what significance may the historian assign to those archival documents called "representations" (*representaciones*) that are addressed to state functionaries and in which invisible populations emerge? How should we interpret documents written by citizen intermediaries, the social agents who put the words in the mouths of Indians and down on paper? Who speaks and what is said? This essay closes, then, by proposing a form of representation that I call ventriloquy, which, along with the problem of transcription, implicates the writing of history.

CITIZENS AGAINST UNIVERSAL EQUALITY

In 1843, thirteen years after the founding of the republic of Ecuador, the country's first president drew a grim picture of the nation's fiscal situation before the parliament.[9] The newly founded national state was bankrupt. The brand-new bureaucracy had not been paid for months and the authorities were without funds for planned public works projects. Funds had to be collected. The president asked senators and deputies—the country's first generation of "representatives"—to vote for a new law designed to resolve the financial crisis. He made two proposals aimed, he explained, not only at the fiscal crisis but also at a "painful and flagrant" political contradiction that created an injustice nested in the very principles of the republic.[10] In effect, his two proposals for revenue collection eliminated a long-standing political distinction—rooted in the colonial period, and which the new republic had not suppressed—that had been drawn between two types of populations.[11] On the one hand, Spanish-speaking Creoles or "whites" and mestizos, those whom the state recognized as active or passive citizens, composed what one might call the "natural" members of the republic, endowed with obvious contextual and implicit historical rights assumed and nested in the *sentido común* or commonsense world that informed the founding fathers of the nation-state.[12] However, and despite being citizens, they paid no personal or poll tax and, as the president announced, they "contributed almost nothing toward the maintenance of the state."[13] On the other hand, "indigenous taxpayers"—that is, adult males of dominated populations—paid a "tribute or contribution" (head tax) in cash, if for no other reason than the tautology of having been classified by the republic as indigenous persons.

The president gave the parliament two options. The first was a straightforward abolition of the tribute now paid by indigenous persons, to be replaced, in accordance with sound republican principles, "by other taxes imposed on every citizen in proportion to his assets." The second option was to extend or generalize tribute to all citizens: "To extend the contribution to that *part of the people* [la parte del pueblo; my emphasis] otherwise exempt from its payment [the white-mestizo population], so that, extended or generalized in this manner, two great goals may be reconciled: that of justice, by abolishing a bad principle, and that of [the state's fiscal] necessity, which forces us to close the deficit."[14]

Both proposals would produce the necessary revenues to continue the project of republican state making, while at the same time establish the principle of civil equality (fraternal and patriarchal) among the various populations of the republic.[15] The proposals were also innovative. By suppressing Indian tribute they broke the vertebral column of colonial domination inherited from Spain. The bond of tribute was extended in the first century of colonial rule (1570) between the Spanish Crown and the colonized peoples; it lent coherence to a complex architecture of material and symbolic ties of domination prior to the foundation of the republic.

On the other hand, the president's proposal sprung from those ideals that had guided the independence movement from Spain: the utopia born of the Enlightenment and the Anglo-American and French revolutions. It was about constructing a new and rational political order, making a clean sweep of history, and erecting the sovereign people's state; in short, building a republic of free and equal individuals based on universal principles of citizenship.

Once the collection of the universal levy was decreed in 1847, an event took place that presents a historical paradox when regarded from today's perspective; that is, from those categories already constituted in current national systems. A violent rebellion swept the most densely populated area of the country from north to south (inhabited by whites-mestizos and Indians). Except for Quito—capital of the republic and site of the domestic life and political activities of "notables" (especially landowners) and the ruling white-mestizo urban classes, where there were no confrontations—revolutionary fervor spread through the villages and towns of the sierra. The president ordered the army to stamp out the insurrection, and battles, death, and destruction ensued for nearly three months. Spirits were calmed by a further decree, and finally the rebellion ceased as the government backed off. The president revoked the act that had extended the levy imposed on Indians to the adult male "white" population—that is, to the population defined as citizens both de facto and by law, in the commonsense world and by the state.

Meanwhile, the levy was maintained for the indigenous population, who had always, over the last three centuries, paid tribute to the state in their capacity as colonial subjects. In effect up to the midnineteenth century the republican state financed itself, to a level fluctuating around 15 percent and 30 percent of its total income—by means of the levy.[16] In the words of the minister of the interior and finance, the state kept itself afloat thanks to a levy based on "an outrageous inequality, *so very contrary to* the (republican) form of government we have adopted" (my emphasis).[17] For its connotations, it is worth pointing out that this minister of the interior, Ecuador's first to advocate universal republican equality, was a credentialed member of the landlord class, and the owner of an *obraje* (textile mill) and several haciendas. Of course, on his properties and in his house he administered several generations of indigenous families.

When talking about citizenship in the early nineteenth century one must keep in mind that it was still a notion in formation, not only in Ecuador but around the world. In its "broad definition" it was part of quotidian discourse, signifying adherence to a political system both vast and scarcely codified.[18] In the early years of the republic one may distinguish a spectrum of meanings that range, first, from tacit and quotidian rights, derived from the commonsense world of the population sensitive to independence; and, second, to those rights that were progressively defined in a restrictive way by republican laws, particularly political rights. The general usage, derived from habitus, granted, as many documents demonstrate, a de facto right of citizenship to the local, white-mestizo elite.[19] Such usage included white-mestizo females, albeit in a situation of paternal and conjugal subordination. Simultaneously, the usage rooted in the commonsense world obviously, and without discussion, excluded indigenous persons. However, in law the extension of citizenship to include the exercise of representation rights (electors and elected) was limited by propriety, plus other restrictions.[20] Obviously, those laws that granted full rights to (active) citizens referred only to adult males, and they ratified the double legal exclusion—applied unequally—of women and Indians (men and women). Furthermore, the term citizen is in many official papers interchangeable with the word Ecuadorian—a usage that was widespread in state and political discourse, indeed nearly quotidian, ruled above all by the commonsense world rather than by any juridical codification. As the nineteenth century unfolds, the state's definition annuls and prevails over usages anchored in the commonsense world. Citizenship was converted into an almost purely juridical notion defined in terms of a state that "recognizes" a certain population and excludes the rest.

The Paradoxes of Equality

To understand this rebellion of the citizens, we must take pause at the manner in which the "popular" sectors of the white-mestizo population perceived the government's attempt to generalize the "contribution" paid by the indigenous population and thereby implement the principle of equality. Official accounts and the sporadic writings of the rebels (handwritten by themselves, being Spanish speakers) coincide in that they rebelled because they understood that the government intended, in an underhanded way and via the pretext of a "universal tax" (*contribución general*), to impose on them a levy that—by analogy with the colonial *tributo de indios*, or Indian tribute—they qualified in their pamphlets as a *tributo de blancos*, or white tribute. The republican fiscal equalization was not entirely new; it had colonial antecedents. In the 1780s the Bourbon state attempted to expand the tax base of the colonial system, precisely by extending the Indian tribute to include *cholos* (urban Indians) and mestizos. Moreover, in the first decade of the seventeenth century the liberal Cortes of Cadiz momentarily suppressed the fiscal and civil distinctions between Indian and non-Indian populations in the Americas. In 1788 in the region of Riobamba (south of Quito), for example, a significant uprising took place that was led by the so-called mestizos of the towns and cities, bilinguals who strove to situate themselves in a non-Indian condition. The rebellion was a response to the Bourbon reforms that attempted to extend the caste categories. The fiscal equalization enacted by the state could have been experienced as the symbolic equivalent of a return to the condition of Indian tributary. It is conceivable that the rebellion of 1788 against downward equality could still reverberate sixty years later, as seen in the acts and words of the poor white-mestizos.[21]

The use of the word "tribute" contained meanings that resonated in the mental perceptions and emotional sensibilities of the citizen rebels. The word was imbued with precise material and symbolic content; it signaled the government's transgression of a "moral" threshold of political legitimacy.[22] In effect, "poor whites" in the Andes constituted a social group that in the postcolonial context both fits and clashes with the Gramscian notion of "subalterns." White-mestizo peasants with scarce lands, wage workers, artisans, itinerant merchants, shopkeepers, muledrivers, day laborers, domestic servants—all were dominated, albeit in the bosom of the dominant colonial group. They shared the common colonial class situation of seeing themselves as white-mestizos; and on their farms and in their homes, and in those of their masters as well, they dealt with the dominated indigenous persons (both men and women) who worked for them in a permanent or sporadic capacity.

In everyday life and in public spaces the poor white-mestizos adopted strategies of distinction that reproduced an ethnic frontier in the dense web of exchanges with, and in certain proximity to, the life of indigenous villagers. They interacted on a daily basis and forged links (in a social and emotive sphere plagued by ambiguity and ambivalence) with those indigenous peasants under their power (*bajo su férula*), be they inferiors or fictive kin. At certain moments they appealed to unity so as to weave alliances against landlords or the state.

The equalization of rights decreed by the state had repercussions in these poor and middle sectors; especially, one suspects, in the new social groups emerging in the small towns. I allude here to that fringe of families located in an indiscernible proximity to the condition of the Indian, and who took advantage of the transformation of the colonial system, opting for a silent strategy of ethnic declassification. Due to their very cultural and generational proximity (being bilingual, the offspring of mixed unions, or having indigenous ancestors) these social strata renewed their symbolic and material strategies of distinction and distancing from the situation of the Indian both in the small towns and in the countryside.

It is significant, for example, that in the first decade of the republic, and still under the rigor of the tributary regime, legislatures attempted to define criteria that would reclassify populations because, they argued, indigence "is spreading to the towns."[23] To this end the Arancél de Derechos Parroquiales (Tariff on Parish Fees) was created. The manifest purpose of the tariff was to impede abuses and control the fees collected by the Catholic Church for the celebration of marriages and burials. In the text of the tariff four classes of population are defined—"those who were formerly known with the name of Spaniards"; "those who used to call themselves highlanders" (*montañeses*); "indigenes"; and "slaves and freed slaves"[24]— each of which was to pay variable amounts in accordance with status and rank.

The intermediate category between the first class of "those formerly known with the name of Spaniards" and the third class of "indigenes" presents a stumbling block for the process of identification. Effectively, how are "highlanders" to be identified? In addition, the tariff law omits an important group that is perceptible without conjecture under the matrix of classification that operates in the world of common sense: the "mestizos." The issue here is to find an answer to a concrete and quotidian problem: the parish priests and sextons needed to distinguish the ethnic and racial identities of their clients so as to determine the amount to charge for performing the two usual ceremonies. The law allows for confusion when it comes to the middle sectors. One diocesan priest wrote to the minister asking that he specify who should be considered "mestizos." The Cabinet or Council of Ministers (Consejo de Ministros) offered the circular response "that those who have indigenous grandparents be taken for mestizos."[25] The clarification only mires itself in a new swamp, which in any case is foreseeable: another prelate of the church begged for yet another clarification of the difference (juridical) between the "highlanders" mentioned in the tariff law and the "mestizos" of the circular issued by the Council of Ministers. Another meeting of the Cabinet produced a second round of definitions that, as one might expect, were even more confusing: the Council of Ministers declared "that there is no difference" between highlanders and mestizos but that "as a general rule all mestizos who are subject to the payment of the indigenous head tax (*contribución personal de indígenas*) correspond to the third class."[26] That is, with the force of law and strict bureacratic incoherence, a paradoxical identity is verified: mestizos who pay the personal contribution cease being so and become members of the class of indigenes. This is precisely the reading that the poor whites of the towns made one year later when the government attempted to generalize the principle of equality under the law. They considered that if they paid the personal contribution, as the indigenous populations had been doing, they would likewise become indigenes for the republic. Consequently, they rebelled against a paradoxical equalization of a colonial stamp that would change their identity and degrade them from citizens to the status of Indian.

The absurdity manifested in the attempt to determine with precision the classes of populations enumerated in the tariff, coming from high functionaries who tended to reduce things to juridical logic, uncovers a breach through which a social fact may filter. It is not about incapacity or bureaucratic error; rather, a divergence becomes evident, a certain marginal aberration in sensibility or perhaps a contradiction between, on the one hand, the state's ordering of the classes and statuses of populations and, on the other, the strategies of catalogization contrived in the commonsense world of quotidian exchanges. These are two different functioning principles of citizenship. The one is guided by juridical definitions that require minuscule precisions and authenticating affirmations of identities to govern relations among citizens and with the state. The second citizenly principle employs schemes of mental perception that are matrices of ordering strategies evident in quotidian power relations. The state principle establishes (and requires) rigid scales and reiterative techniques of identification for the purpose of recognizing identities conceived as immutable. Common sense, on the other hand, plays with the relativity of identities that vary according to situations of power: the validity of practical identification remains delimited to quotidian contexts of social exchange, the here and now of the everyday.

In the end, the uprising of poor whites in 1843 appears to have occurred when the state attempted to implant its vision of the universal equality of citizens under the law (i.e., the parliament and the executive). The initiative violated the reigning consensus tied together by a shared mentality and sensibility. In effect, citizenship was not perceived from the perspective of the world of postcolonial common sense to be constitutive of universal equality; rather, it was the privilege of social and racial hierarchy, an *inter paris* among the dominant.

The early-nineteenth-century postcolonial transition to the republican system, the change of laws, the organization of a new state apparatus with the replacement of functionaries, and the creation of new jurisdictions, as well as certain changes in the agrarian structure, particularly the sale of commons, all permit the suspicion that the power relations among populations were profoundly altered. A process ocurred in which ethnic gradations were amplified and re-signified (both in the mental and structural senses). In the towns, groups of different status intermix; in the rural indigenous communities whites take up residence among the Indians; and, even in the strict domain of the hacienda, mestizos are "Indianized" and Indians "mestizize" themselves. Diffuse intuitions sprout from the early republican documentation: the problems of identification that functionaries attempt to resolve give the impression that in these decades modifications in the strategies of symbolic distinction are at work. In short, conditions appear propitious for the distension of categories and the emergence of new social groups.[27] In the commonsense world of citizens these new social groups appear to be "seen" (the metaphor implies visual classification and social reconfirmation of identity) as nonindigenous. The payment of a "general contribution" placed these groups, by force of circumstance, on the same plane as the indigenes. The state had stumped the ethnic frontier that traversed the world of common sense, imposing a downward leveling of society. As such, citizenly equalization was resented by "the people" as a detestable imposition, an illegitimate act of the state at the very moment in which rising social sectors were exerting considerable effort to distinguish themselves from indigenous tributaries. As they did this, the old binary matrix that ordered relations between whites and Indians was becoming more ambiguous and less polarized. As one rebel denounced, for this "part of the people" (recall that the president employed the same phrase in his discourse) the levy implies that sooner or later they would succumb to the necessity of having to "sell oneself into bondage on the haciendas."[28] To pay the tax, the "poor whites" would have to work as "concerted" peons. They would be "enslaved" and "attached" (adscritos) to the landlords for generations to come, with their spouse and children included. Being legitimate citizens in the world of common sense, the state would reconvert them, by force of tax law, into Indians.

In effect, the tributary circuit that linked the state to the haciendas and its indigenous populations was by 1847 a consolidated and ancestral colonial habitus. This circuit benefitted from the difficulties peasants faced in obtaining cash in an agrarian economy with restricted money circulation and a broad subsistence sector where barter prevailed. Obviously, landlords (big, medium, and small) had access to cash. They sold their harvests in urban centers for cash. Since the colony, the state knew about and took advantage of this circuit. Consequently, when a peon was contracted to a hacienda the state required the landlord to assume payment of his tribute on a semester basis.[29]

The "Attached Condition" of the Indian

The financial obligation imposed on landowners by tribute law was not unilateral: the landowner was politically compensated with an acknowledgment of rights. In return for paying the tribute of their indigenous workers, the republican state adjudicated to landowners a modality of rule over a space and its inhabitants. A circular (quasi-law) issued by the minister of the interior defined the so-called attached condition of indigenous laborers on the haciendas.[30] In essence, it consisted of a sort of delegation of republican sovereignty to a "master citizen" (patrón ciudadano) for the administration of indigenous persons who, grouped in communities, inhabited his private property.[31]

In this "attachment" the republican state acknowledged a formation of power of colonial origin. It is a realm of domination inscribed in quotidian modalities of asymmetrical reciprocity (material and symbolic) between landlord and indigenous families. For instance, peons could hardly abandon their masters, and their children (sons) were dependent on the proprietor's tutelary power.[32] In turn, the master citizen "took charge" of "his" indigenous workers, securing the reproduction of generations and providing protection; he administered a species of justice (at the hacienda courtyard, or *patio de hacienda*) and his powers stretched over individual and domestic life cycles, as well as the generational cycle of the population. Finally, the master citizen presided over the ritual calendar, and his acts of power were endowed with sacral meanings.[33]

With rare exceptions, the circuit I have just described was aimed at conquered populations. It concerned the king of Spain's colonial "subjects," not the "Creoles" and *castas*, or mestizos, which were excluded as the privileged colonial group. Thus, in the early republic the rebellion of the poor "whites" against "tribute" meant that "popular" citizens (it is known that "notables," mainly landowners, were not involved in the revolt) violently rejected a generalization or extension of the colonial situation intrinsic to "Indian" populations.[34]

In summary, universalizing the principle of equality elicited a paradox: the republic demotes "common" citizens from their colonial status. It annuls the social hierarchies that impregnate the concrete signifiers of citizenship and equates them with a colonial preeminence. It converts "poor white" citizens into state subjects, since they are obliged, like the indigenous population, to enter the sphere of power of the landowners.

THE REPUBLIC'S INVISIBLE POPULATIONS

The Weight of Demographics

In quantitative terms, which populations fit or did not fit the commonsense notion of citizenship during the first decades of the republic? The importance of this question for the construction of postcolonial citizenship is accentuated when we consider the future historical implications of certain demographic disproportions among the inhabitants of a territory. It is a problem that has to be situated in terms of the social conflicts that emerge between (dominant and dominated) colonial populations in the process of nation-state formation. With independence, certain groups become citizens and others become "subjects." Whatever political form that these conflicts over citizenship adopt, and regardless of the alliances that are tied and the result obtained by the process, such postcolonial relations among populations are an unavoidable problematic for national history,[35] particularly if what we want to comprehend is the system of citizenship as a form of domination not so much from the perspective of the state but from the commonsense world of practice.

In 1846 some seven hundred thousand inhabitants were living in the former Royal Audiencia of Quito, the administrative unit of the Spanish empire over which the republic of Ecuador, like other Latin American countries, was remapped and illustrated with territory, inhabitants, and state. The national census of that year classified the population (male and female) by ethnic and juridical categories: "whites," 41 percent; "Indians," 52 percent; "free mulattoes," 4 percent, "mulatto slaves," 1 percent; "free blacks," 1 percent; "black slaves," 1 percent.[36] Plagued by errors and absences rather than by a reflection of demographic realities, the census figures should be read as a quantitative image that the state, enlisting the positivist halo that surrounds numbers, attempts to disseminate among the instructed social sectors—that is, the small cenacle of readers of the Diario Oficial (Official Bulletin). Perhaps the implicit function, if it had one, was not so much bureacratic as political: it promoted citizenly reading and communication. The publication of the census figures and their revision stimulated commentary in both the public and domestic spheres; its evidence nurtured the mental perceptions of the citizenly public and as such contributed to its consolidation. To a certain extent the construction of the republic was legitimated in the world of common sense. The state provided the proof of an objective reality. It produced in numbers the existence of Ecuadorians; it ratified ethnic and racial differences and in doing so delineated the objective of the construction: the civilizing process. The state created an imaginary fact that the citizens could confront and judge because it confirmed those certainties ostensibly engendered by the wisdom of everyday experience.

The activity of recounting (in the sense of both numerating and narrating) in order to assemble the nation in statistical tables grants an immediate and sensible existence to the social group that counts and recounts the Others. It constructs citizens in the common sense and it draws a line of difference between citizens and "subjects." The state and its citizens verify an imagined reality. The "demographic people" (pueblo demográfico) is molded in the objectification of columns of numbers deployed within ideal national borders by places— towns and cities, provinces, counties, and parishes. Particularly in the nineteenth century the census appears more than anything to be a ritual act whose principal (implicit) function may be to sketch a symbolic representation of the nation in the social imagination. In the act of reading such acts the (white-mestizo) citizens confirm their reality in much the same way as it is constructed by the *Official Bulletin*—the repository of the legitimate public word of the state—in the statistical tables it prints. The collectivity of citizens reads and comments on itself. In recognizing itself, synchronic time and narration is created, and the census thus assists the public and citizenly narration of the nation, which is to be lived collectively.

Be that as it may, the census numbers are converted into a kind of demographic imaginary of the state's ordering of populations which, given its fictional character, serves as a qualitative "index" of the collective construction of certain mental classificatory schemes that contribute to the citizenly formation of common sense, the deus ex machina that operates in the private and everyday administration of populations.

That 41 percent of the population baptizes itself "white" constitutes the demographic group par excellence of the ideal of citizenship in the first half of the nineteenth century. In accordance with the census classification form developed by state functionaries, itself guided by criteria of distinction that emanate from the "shared significance of the world,"[37] it was this population that granted onto itself, simultaneously, its preeminence as citizens with an equality that was, before the rest, hierarchical inter paris. In the classifications of the census, the catalogings of the "shared significance of the world" coincided with the norms of the state. The "whites," represented by the census interviewers, instituted themselves as the historical group that legitimately counted itself; consequently, they exercised the right to identify, quantify, and arrange hierarchically the other populations. Despite its unconstitutionality, the procedure inaugurated during this period was still observed a century later. In 1947, the *Special Instructions for Enumerators* of the general census of Otavalo still defined the procedure and criteria for counting the identification: "Race: [The enumerator] will record 'White' when [the person interviewed] is dressed in the way that *we are accustomed* [*acostumbramos*] to, and has pink or white skin; 'Mestizo' when it is observed that there has been mixing with the indigenous [race]; and 'Indigene' when [the person interviewed] is dressed like an Indian and his mother tongue is Quechua" (my emphasis).[38]

I emphasize that the *Special Instructions* were thought out and designed for the enumerators of the municipality who were included in this obvious "we," in the equality of those who "[dress] in the way that we are accustomed to" and look like us (visual metaphor of the strategies of classification), the pink or white skinned. The self-identity of oneself as "white" (constructed in the very process we are describing) establishes the necessary parameter of reference (although always implicit) and the production of the forms for taking the census. It also marks the procedure of identification of the enumerators and the possibility of classifying and quantifying the other inhabitants on an ethnic and racial gradation.

In the nineteenth century the statistical tables published in the *Official Bulletin* always place the "whites" in the first column. One of these published documents shows an official who let run his imagination. Capitalizing on the statistical columns, he sketched the front of a Greek or Roman temple over the table, thus improvising on the metaphor and configuring the censused republic (*republica censada*). From left to right the order of the columns that sustains the architecture acquires significance because it opens a hierarchical succession that is always led by the "white" numbers.

When the census was drawn up in 1846 the "white" category was a motley minority of Spanish speakers, although no doubt many of these "whites" could also express themselves fluently in Quechua. This group enjoyed a privileged colonial status despite the fact that within its bosom it propagated abysmal economic and cultural inequalities, as well as unequal access to the exercise of power. This was the population that was disposed to a revolutionary sensibility (worldview and emotivity) of independence.[39] On the other hand, there were cases when "Indian" communities in the Andes, when they did not actually oppose independence, pursued their own strategies: they supported, alternately, the "Creole pioneers" and the Spanish colonial troops.[40] Those 52 percent of "Indians," although included as "Ecuadorians" by the state, unquestionably fell, in the mental maps and social strategies of ("white") citizens, on the other side of the froniter of the "rational being" (an expression from common speech) and of civilization—which is to say, finally, citizenship. This majority of "Ecuadorians" (the "Indians") thus became republican subjects that the citizens were to administer.

In 1830 the delegates of the "whites"—that is, the "notables" (big landlords, miners, merchants, and intellectuals)—met in "constitutive assemblies of the republic" and founded the parliament of Ecuador. They were the unquestionable "representatives of the people" or of the "republic"[41]; they wrote the political constitution of the state. Ideally, the sovereign power of citizens resides in the juridical body of persons that invents an identity: the nation of Ecuadorians within its borders.

Nevertheless, the same act of instituting republican reality excludes "Indians." The myth invents, implicitly and by consensus, those populations "outside" of the rational and civilized. The foundational myth excludes, hides, and covers over the demographic majority throughout the nineteenth century and nearly to the end of the twentieth. It creates the internal stranger, a hidden referent of the citizen, a tacit and undefinable category: the Indian subject of the republic. Conceptually, it is a "blank space" that is constitutive of the sovereignty of republican law. It is a domain external to the principles of "the people" that grants legitimacy to a political system via deliberation and common accord. It is an undefined space that, as it traces a border (social, political, historical, and ethnic) structured by a matrix of colonial classifications that distinguishes the "white" population from the rest, in turn permits the definition of the legitimate citizen and establishes a historical goal: the civilizing process for the rest of the nonwhite populations.[42]

This constitutional blank indicates that the formation of the republic and the construction of citizenship depends on the play of power. The republic has to emboss the indigenous populations as "rational" Ecuadorians whose faces carry the effigy of the white-mestizo individual. An obvious continuity unfolds between the colonial process and the postcolonial construction of the civilizing nation-state as the administrator of populations.

Extending Citizenship

Keeping in mind the demographic proportions of republican state formation raises a more complicated, undoubtedly less obvious, question: Does the form of domination change when rights of citizenship are extended to all adult males? That is, more precisely, exactly how are Indian subjects administered under a generalized system of citizenship?

In 1847 the Ecuadorian parliament approved a law that suppressed the status of "indigenous tributary" by establishing that "in the republic the tax known by the name of *contribución personal de indígenas* (tribute) is abolished, and *individuals of this class are now equal to the rest of the Ecuadorians* in terms of the obligations and rights imposed and granted by the fundamental charter (the Constitution of the republic)" (my emphasis).[43]

To illustrate this problem I will focus on an important sector of the dominated population: the social web of peasant heads of households (*huasipungueros*) living within the haciendas. In the Andes, the hacienda was firmly institutionalized as a formation of power both by the state (as private property) and by the nearly autonomous structure of social relations of domination (reciprocity among unequals). Moreover, in over three centuries of colonialism the Ecuadorian hacienda had achieved an unrivaled dominance over land and people. For this reason the hacienda offers a lucid example of the shift in domination induced by the mid-century extension of citizenship into the periphery of the republican order.

With the suppression of indigenous status and the amplification of equality, it is necessary to keep in mind two situations that together define a strategy of domination: first, the very organizational logic of the republican state; and second, the economic (or class) interests of landlords or hacendados.

According to the logic of the nation-state, to maintain a tax (tribute) destined exclusively for certain populations (the natives) while exempting others (white citizens) was a "barbaric" violation of principles. All (adult males) Ecuadorians should enjoy the same rights and obligations; all should "contribute to the state each according to his fortune."[44] No reason could possibly justify that one "part of the people" be made to pay a form of tribute derived from a classificatory scheme elaborated under a colonial political rationality, which is to say by an exogenous logic contrary to the self-referentiality of the principles of citizenship and of the popular sovereignty. This irrationality is accentuated above all in the judicial system. Under the postcolonial tribute system, natives were in a threefold status both Ecuadorians and tributary populations, as well as "miserable persons." Contradictory and ambiguous, this last category served to place Indian subjects in a situation of state tutelage and to integrate them into the code of citizenship; that is, the state's judicial system recognized the dominated populations as Ecuadorians unfit to exercise the rights of citizenship. Thus, a series of judicial procedures were prescribed and a corps of "Indian protectors" was organized so that they should be "represented" in the courts and before the state.[45] In synthesis, the condition of tributary populations imposed on the state and the indigenous peoples a relationship that implied the presence of a strata of intermediary functionaries: a bureaucracy for the administration of populations. The situation contradicted the logic of the republic, including one of its cornerstones: the republican regime of representation.[46]

The extension of citizen's rights to natives also coincided with the economic interests of hacendados. Indeed, in the vote for the abolition of tribute there was no opposition but instead wide consensus in a parliamentary body where landlords were preponderant.[47] How is this to be understood? In my view we must revisit the economic circuit of state/tribute/haciendas. In effect, the state treasury collected from hacendados the tribute which, in principle, it assumed on behalf of those indigenous workers (huasipungueros) who inhabited his estate. With the abolition of the state/tribute/haciendas circuit the landlords were freed of the obligation to pay the tax. Moreover, by mid-century (if not before) the hacienda had consolidated its own forms of recruitment, maintenance, and reproduction of the indigenous labor force. The tributary circuit was no longer indispensable; the haciendas had achieved autonomy from the state.

For its part, the republic continued to recognize the "attachment" of workers to the haciendas until the late nineteenth century. This meant that, part de facto and part de jure, the practice of administering populations found within the circumscription of power of the landed estates was legalized. Even the legislative activity of the formulation and approbation of a few flaccid guidelines for "labor contracts" between landlords and (indigenous) peons was delegated to the diminutive municipal councils of the rural counties. Obviously, in these local bodies the interests of landlords were heard with few inhibitions. Thus, the central state delegated to the private sphere, at the confines of the public-state sphere, the codification of labor relations between citizens and natives.[48]

We now arrive at the question of the historical forms (processes and structures) that the administration of populations may adopt under a regime of citizenship of the postcolonial type; that is, the problem of domination when equality under the law is generalized. As a historical variant, this is Foucault's "state of domination" noted earlier, which we could almost say is the opposite of an "apartheid" type system, and in which no attempts are made to impede access, either by juridical or political means, to the equality of citizenship.

In an "apartheid" type system the administration of subjects (the de facto noncitizens) concerns the public-state sphere. As in the colonial tributary situation (before the mid-nineteenth century), it requires a legal corpus, administrative apparatus, and even assigned territorial circumscriptions for populations. Its government embodies the citizenly concern for the "common good": it is a "public affair." Indeed, when a republican system erects an impenetrable juridical "wall" between citizens and subjects, it is worth researching the question of whether domination requires that the state directly assume at least six inescapable functions: the identification, registration, locating, tracking, protection, and repression of the segregated "part of the people." Consequently, the "state of domination" that is configured locates the management of these "technologies of rule" over populations in the nucleus of the public and state sphere: such a government becomes a weapon in the political field of citizens.[49]

Domination and the Private Sphere

The derogation of republican tribute and the legal extention to all populations of the equality of citizenship unleashes, in my view, a curious "strategy of power." Decentered with respect to the public-state axis, a citizenly field for the exercise of power over indigenous peoples is configured. In short, in the second half of the nineteenth century the administration of populations is no longer a "public affair," and it remained so until the indigenous uprisings of 1990 and 1994 that paralysed the country (I return to this point below). What is more, at first glance this "strategy of power" feigns the dismantling of the functions realized by the state's "administrative technologies": domination appears to disappear. Nevertheless, seen from up close what happens is that the extension of citizenship, particularly in the case of the haciendas, consists of the following: the state abandons the administration of indigenous tributaries. With the abolition of tribute the statutes, classificatory (juridical) code, and the bureaucratic apparatus of intermediaries that permitted the state to recognize its "indigenous contributors" are suppressed: natives thus become invisible in the public-state sphere. The new strategy displaces the administration of populations toward the private sphere, and particularly toward the territorial power of propertied citizens who own haciendas.

Detour 3

After 1857 the astonished and frustrated historian verifies an archival amnesia: oversight has attacked the official memory of the state. In the national archives (of the executive, the parliament, and the courts) housed in the capital of the republic, the word "indigenous" or "Indian" vanishes. A gap is left on the archive's shelves; a blank space appears in the documents (for the understood but unwritten context). In the "instruments" of rule (official reports and correspondence, laws, decrees, and regulations) the equality of citizenship erases the words that had once made it clear that certain measures pertained only to a "part of the people"—that is, to the "Indians" or "indigenous." The information therefore becomes indiscernible in relation to dominant and dominated populations, and in the censuses the columns that had ordered and hierarchically arranged the (symbolic and demographic) body of "Ecuadorians" under three grand rubrics—"whites," "Indians," and "blacks"—disappear.

With the abolition of the tribute and the erasure of the classification "Indian" the statistics bear witness to a fact deemed natural because biological: they delineate a body contour organized in three components prior to history: "men," "women," and "minors." The image of the nation as a human biological group crystallizes as unitary and ultimately without differences. Once again, the universalization of the rights of citizens renders Indian peoples invisible in the official registers.

But when the historian leaves the capital of the republic and abandons its national archives, between surprise and intrigue she or he discovers that its forgetfulness does not affect texts produced in the periphery. The specifications "Indians" and "indigenous" reappear in those papers piled up in places that don't quite qualify as "archives" and rather less as depositories of official memory. The omitted appellations appear in the correspondence of petty functionaries, in the proceedings of the municipal council, in the case files of the lower courts, and in the account books of the haciendas. These are texts that sweep up in the written word the dregs of the oral and the marks of practice. The fiction of the naturalized, unitary, and homogenous body-nation grows dim.

Indeed, the historian verifies that these provincial functionaries reinsert the omitted words. It happens in the process of applying the measures dictated by the central government. It is an obvious situation: the law will be executed in the context of the exercise of quotidian strategies of power between white and indigenous, in the confines of the public, and in the private sphere of a periphery mottled by local bosses. The colonial logic of practice serves to reveal that, rather than being forgotten, those words are actually avoided by the republican state; nevertheless in the process of writing the "instruments of rule" they are consciously thought.[50]

Under the new republican form by which populations are administered, the state utilizes a technology of communication inherent to the usual procedures of commonsense formation. Officials communicate between the different levels of the state; they decipher and codify texts. The deciphering applies to communications that travel from center to periphery, especially when executing measures prescribed by law or quasi law. The deciphering is a pragmatic act of interpretation, and it passes unnoticed because it is taken for granted. On the edge of the public-state sphere, the same law will be deciphered (understood) in one way or another in relation to citizens and indigenes, in accordance with the situation of the moment. Officials reinsert the elided categories and words; procedures hardly require an attentive will or a rigorous conscience. The same goes for lawyers, landowners, and townspeople. Measures are applied by the case in face-to-face relations in a periphery dominated by a motley entanglement of local and private powers. The categories easily reinserted by the common-sense reading of high official language have a performative effect that reclassifies: subject populations are identified, talked about, and worked on without much effort and with little vacillation.

Codification occurs in the communication that flows in the other direction, from the periphery to the center of the state. Petty functionaries like the *tenientes políticos* (district officers) for example, relate events to their immediate superiors, the *jefes políticos* [district governors], in their reports and correspondence. The obligatory channel follows the steplike path that connects each of the various levels of the state. At the end of the chain, when one compares the relation of a teniente político with the report that arrives on the desk of the minister of the interior, the categories used to specify populations barely protrude the surface of the text. The written language and explicit references of the teniente político, which are closer to the tonalities of speech that resonate in quotidian exchanges, are stumped as the communication moves up the ladder of instancies of the state. By the end of the circuit the color is washed out: the state imposes a language of communication written in the vocabulary of the law and under the logic of universal principles.

In short, each level or instancy of the state bureacracy is, according to the proximity or distance of the periphery from the center, a place of textual processing where the logic of law and common sense intervene. In the conflicts of everyday life between citizens and subjects the swarming classifications of common sense reign; in the plexus of the state (the juridical code) the unifying logic of the code of citizenship rules. Both are inscribed on various levels of the archive.

From a heuristic point of view, for the historian the hacienda presents an even greater advantage: it offers a dense mass of documentation untypical of other formations that, because they are inserted into a misty and evanescent quotidian orality, devise furtive plays of power. Such is the case, for example, of Bourdieu's notion of the strategies of symbolic domination obtaining among a certain kind of (white-mestizo) village intermediary who assumes a ritual role: the so-called founders of Christian cults, or the fictive godparents of an unequal kinship between white and indigenous families, the *compadrazgo*. For such formations of power the historian may only intuit—by means of a retrospective gaze activated by an ethnographic present—the many intrigues and machinations of the field of intimate and immediate domination.

The delegation of power to the haciendas offers an example of the most evident and institutionalized modality in the private administration of populations. Besides constituting a geographical space, the hacienda is, in effect, a consolidated power formation endowed with symbolic codes, rituals, and mechanisms of repression and consensus making. Moreover, it unambiguously belongs to the private and patriarchal sphere: landlords conserve a jealous autonomy in the management of their properties, which is a "private affair." Although the hacienda is the most obvious case, it was not the only peripheral power formation that assumed administrative functions. In reality, everything having to do with Indian people was decentered toward the limits of the state, ending up in the realm of a nebula of powers located either in the plexus of the private sphere (that is, the hacienda) or in the blurred threshold of the public (that is, in the hands of the petty functionaries who confused the public with the private, the personal, and the domestic).

Let me summarize the shift in domination that occured in 1857 as a result of the abolition of tribute and the extension of citizen's rights to include the indigenous populations:

First, the generalization of republican rights carries with it a well-known trick of concealment and exclusion.[51] It displaces the administration of populations from the dense nucleus of the public-state sphere toward the dispersed plexus of the private. Among citizens it opens a polygon of forces in relation to indigenous populations: it becomes an *enjeu* (stake) in the private sphere.[52] Finally, it delegates domination to a periphery of quotidian and heterogenous patriarchal powers. It is a "state of domination" ruled by the furtive and velvet strategies of practice and symbolic violence. With one trick the republic achieves several objectives: first, it preserves the purity of the principle of citizenship as established in the constitution; and second, it delivers to citizens direct access (personal and private) to indigenous populations. This access was a prerequisite for the (material and symbolic) reproduction of the dominant social group insofar as it became a citizen group in the nineteenth century.

Second, once more I rely on the suggestive work of Carole Pateman, which includes civil society and the state in the public sphere while the private is seen as a domain of conjugal and patriarchal power. The division derives from the imaginary (liberal) institution of political society (the social contract among *frater* [brothers]). In effect, in Andean Ecuador the private sphere is neither constructed nor defined merely by a process of differentiation with respect to the public-state sphere. It is not a sphere of familial sensibility self-centered on the "intimacy" of the home; rather, it outlines a terrain of strategies between citizens and subjects, between the private (domestic and patriarchal) and indigenous (domestic and communal) domains.[53] The state converts this polygon of strategies between populations and citizens into a legal vacuum. It lies beyond the public-state and the private: it falls outside the principles that organize the constitutive dichotomy of a republic of citizens.[54] Thus, for example, indigenous communities (land, members, authorities) cease to exist in the law after the abolition of tribute. They were legally recognized only in 1937, a century after the foundation of the republic. During this entire period they existed as the taken-for-granted context for citizens and as a legal vacuum for the state, a kind of "indifference zone or a non-localizable place."[55]

The problem of the hacienda analyzed above exemplifies clearly the existence of these domains of social relations that are extrinsic to the republican dichotomy. For a citizen it is private property and the place of familial "intimacy," but what rules is a sociability of domination that does not fit the logic or horizon of meaning inherent in the categories of public and private. These are colonial relations that have nothing to do with the dialectic between the individual and the state, the particular and the universal, corporate interests and the common good, and so forth. Nevertheless, they construct the historical significance of the republican private and public-state spheres.

Third, as the state sheds its administrative functions, a new and less costly economy of domination is implanted. Specifically, it no longer utilizes "technologies of rule" over indigenous peoples, which require legal codes, a bureaucracy, and written procedures of identification, surveillance, and registration. The multiplicity of private powers employs diffuse knowledges of domination that appear as innate skills, tacit and personal, that are not formulated nor formulable and that do not leave written traces. They are "colonial knowledges" erected in systems of habitus, "made bodily" in the transgenerational socialization of a centuries-long experience of domination. It is Bourdieu's *sens du jeu* (logic of interests) in a field of domination and everyday resistance.

Fourth, what happens to the conflicts between whites-mestizos and Indians under a regime where the administration of populations is decentered from the state sphere? I will mention here only two aspects. First, as it passes to the private sphere domination is converted into personal skirmishes between individuals—that is, between white-mestizo and indigenous (men).[56] Domination is diluted and disaggregated in strategies that vary according to the fields of power. Conflicts are euphemized, converted into "symbolic domination" and, consequently, into "everyday resistance" to oppression.

Violence becomes an attribute of subjectivity. The second aspect (related to the first) is that the new form of domination excludes the "thematicization" (as noted by Habermas) of conflicts between citizens and Indians in the public, state, and political spheres: they do not become the subject of political debate. At most, they present themselves, insofar as they are problems, as "interethnic relations" or "cultural" differences, or as the age-old intolerance between "human groups"; that is, they belong to the naturalized domain of hate and affection between persons of "human groups." They are not subjects that structure the political field.

Finally, "with the assimilation of politics to public life" under the republic, relations between citizens and Indians (and among the latter) become a sphere of "essential exclusion."[57] They form a space of social relations and conflicts that borders the public-state sphere at its "contingent" limits: depending on the historical conjuncture, this space may temporarily erupt in the public sphere and later disappear. Its presence is neither inherent nor constitutive of the political field, as in the case of conflicts among citizens and with the state, which by definition are part of the public. Citizenship (as a polygon of forces) constitutes itself via this exclusion; it intuits an "indigenous outside" consisting of those populations lacking rationality, those uncivilized subjects of the republic. These are social groups that require a civilizing pedagogy (a disciplinary process) to become citizens modeled on the mold of the white-mestizo Spanish-speaking individual.

I am drawing on the "insistence" of Judith Butler "that a political field is of necessity constructed through the production of a determining exterior. In other words the very domain of politics consitutes itself through the production and naturalization of the 'pre-' or 'non-' political. In Derridean terms, this is the production of a 'constitutive outside.' "[58] Butler refers above all to women but she extends her argument to other dominated groups. One may say that the domain of indigenous populations (their territories, forms of government, symbolic codes), which for the republican state are neither public nor private, becomes a "constitutive outside" for the political field of citizens.

To amplify these themes goes beyond the intent of these pages. Nevertheless, they all devolve to a final problem that is inscribed in the formation of citizenship, and can be illuminated by examining the following questions: What form does the representation of subjects adopt under a regime of citizenship? What is the status of the discourse of Indian subjects? What do the documents—in which they "speak" for the historian—actually say?

CITIZEN VENTRILOQUISTS FOR THE DOMINATED

In effect, under an exclusionary regime of (republican) citizenship, where the dominated are relegated to a contingent space neither public nor private, a question presents itself. By what channel is communication established between state and populations? That is, in what manner are they represented in the public-state sphere? Further, what role do citizens play in the process of representing subjects otherwise excluded from the political field?

In all cases it must be remembered that the republican state cannot completely deny the existence of Indian people even though it does not recognize them and dilutes their presence under the regime of equality by citizenship. Among citizens, the plays of power centered on the administration of populations are vectors that structure the political. This is also the case of the state apparatus in the periphery: in the parishes and county seats these plays of power constitute the political. In a "semi-public affair" local functionaries need natives to carry out the very functions of the state and the municipalities: Indian peasants maintain and supply the urban centers, execute public works, and provide transportation and communications services. Moreover, part of the judicial function of the state is to exercise tutelage over what goes on in the private sphere, that is, to oversee the family and the conjugal bonds of citizens. As a consequence, a linkage of communication and representation is in some way made between the public-state sphere and what goes on in the borders of the private sphere and even in the heart of Indian life. Because subjects are "invisible" in the public sphere, conflicts engendered by the strategies of domination find ways to emerge by virtue of the circuit of mediations. They appear in the courts or are "recognized" by the chain of "political" functionaries (district chiefs, provincial governors, ministers, the president). In other words, certain conflicts between citizens and Indians and among the dominated that are not resolved by the strategies of domination, surge (contingently) into the public sphere and become a "public-state problem."

To approach this "problem" it is worth jumping forward from the past to the present, from the nineteenth century to the late twentieth. In effect, in 1990 and 1994—a century and a half after the foundation of the republic of Ecuador—two big "indigenous uprisings" paralyzed the country, in each case for nearly a month. The indigenous population, hundreds of thousands of people, left the cover of their rural communities and erupted in public spaces: they blocked the highways, shut down the markets, protested in city streets, and occupied the mass media (radio and television stations).

I use the singular "indigenous population" because the dominated "populations" (plural) of the nineteenth century today conform to one unified social group in terms of Benedict Anderson's notion of an "imagined community" that defines itself as "indigenous."[59] Without provoking confusion, one may assert today the unitary profile of "the Ecuadorian native" (*el indígena ecuatoriano*) in the social imaginary of both the indigenous and white-mestizo populations with only scarce regional variations. Moreover, the indigenous 52 percent of the 1847 census is now a minority between 15 percent and, at most, 20 percent of the country's total population. Still, in some rural zones in the Andean provinces the indigenous population is the majority.[60]

Their leaders address the (white-mestizo) citizenry and the government. With these two mass actions—located in an indiscernible threshold between the political and the ritual—they institute themselves as social agents in the public sphere. The movement of Ecuadorian Indians emerges, its eruption recasts the political field. The movement elaborates its own discourse; it debates the political forces (parties, pressure groups, intellectuals, labor unions, the church). The Indian people delegate their representation to leader-intellectuals (men and women) who in the conjuncture speak of "the indigenous people of Ecuador." Their rejection of domination includes aspects of the "common interest of the people." They denounce oppression in general (of Indians, peasants, and the white-mestizo urban poor); outline political economic measures; elaborate legislative proposals for official recognition (in the constitution of the republic) of their languages and cultures; demand cultivatable lands; protest against the decline in living standards; and solicit social services. Finally, they declare themselves to be an autonomous "people" that includes various "nationalities" whose authorities should be recognized by the republic.

During the two uprisings in the early 1990s the president and his ministers had to receive the indigenous leaders, grouped together in a "national" organization, in the old colonial palace of Carondelet, which is the present seat of government.[61] They initiated a long series of negotiations that was broadcast on radio and television, day by day. This act—the mass diffusion of the scene of negotiation—disrupted the national imaginary. For the first time in republican history natives were seen taking their own positions in the political field and negotiating directly and publicly with the big powers (government, landlords, industrialists, the church, the military). In public opinion, for the state and the political parties, and among the military, natives are now an essential and modern social agent located in the plexus of the public sphere. Their organizations are among the principal forces of the country, with representatives (intellectuals) who have emerged from the fold, and with their own discourse. The subjects break the barriers of the private: from everyday forms of resistance to public action they become political agents.[62]

I return now to the nineteenth century to clarify the significance of the eruption of indigenous peoples in today's public sphere. The problem has to do with the representation of the invisible populations (of subjects) under a regime of citizenship. In effect, with the two "indigenous uprisings" of 1990 and 1994 a breaking point is reached with the colonial and republican past. A nodal aspect of the republican "state of domination" was that with the construction of citizenship in the mid-nineteenth century the indigenous populations came to form a "constitutive outside" for the public and private spheres. The process of exclusion situated indigenous peoples in a species of third sphere, a space of domination of colonial origin in the republic. To raise the question of self-representation, or of the legitimacy of their discourse, was simply impertinent. The words of traditional leaders were unintelligible to the state and the political forces; in the public sphere, they were populations not yet civilized.[63]

What these populations (their discourses) "say" through the mouths of their authorities—presence, representation, discourse—only acquires sense in the limits of the private sphere. For practice it is a translucent discourse; it arises in the personalized gambits that are hatched by peripheral power formations (haciendas, domestic units, municipalities, local functionaries). It is the constitutive discourse (ritualized utterance and gesture) of the fields of quotidian power.

Again, in what ways may Indian populations be represented in the political sphere of citizens, being subjects? The historian sifts through the local documents, he or she dusts off the mid-nineteenth-century correspondence between provincial functionaries of the republic and the minister of the interior and reads proceedings preserved in a file labeled "representations." In bureaucratic jargon these are solicitations, complaints, and problems expressed by Indians before a state authority. One such document begins with the following phrase: "I, José M. de la Cruz, governor of natives . . . before your excellency, for his part and in the name of the rest [of the natives], respectfully say" (José M. de la Cruz gobernador de indígenas . . . ante Usted respetuosamente por si y por los demás digo).[64] The phrase exhibits an obvious grammatical error that I wish to emphasize. In correct Spanish it should read "I . . . for my part . . . say" (por mi . . . digo); that is, it should correspond to the first-person form, which would indicate that the same person carries out two actions: he speaks and writes. But here one reads for his part (por si) in the third person, followed by say (digo), the first-person conjugation. The (grammatical) "person" of the pronoun does not agree with the verb form. In grammatically correct writing there are two alternatives: "I . . . for my part . . . say" (por mi . . . digo) when the same person speaks and writes, or "He . . . for his part . . . says" (por si . . . dice) when there are two persons, one who speaks and another who writes.

The error, the discordance in the (grammatical) "person," opens an ambiguity about the (historical) person who realizes the act of speaking and writing. Who speaks in this document? He who speaks or he who writes? It is obvious that the governor of Indians does not write the representation in his own hand. To address the functionary to state his problem he resorts to an intermediary who does the writing for him. Roaming around in the text is a social agent (a scribe) who, although indispensable to the act of speaking via writing, nevertheless remains incognito and, at the same time, present in the words. In effect, and as it must be, the indigenous authority, not the writer, signs the petition. What functions are fulfilled by this intermediary who, in the end, makes it possible for the governor of the natives to be rendered comprehensible to the state functionary and who, in the public sphere, represents for his part and in the name of the rest?

It may be worthwhile to uncover an answer. The function of the scribe who produces the document is not entirely derived from his control over the writing. It is also not reduced to the problem of translating, from the tongue (oral Quechua) of the populations that the governor of natives represents, to the language (written Spanish) of the republic and its citizens. The unknown intermediary carries out at least two additional functions. On the one hand, he becomes a ventriloquist because he makes a voiceless indigenous authority speak in the public-state sphere. He presents the problem in the state's code; he assembles a legitimate and legal discourse. On the other hand, as he writes the "representation" he is the author of a strategy. He carries out both functions insofar as he is an individual who possesses a recognized presence in the public sphere, knows the "rules of the game" in the political field, and above all knows the functionaries personally. In short, he's a white-mestizo—a citizen.

As the historian reads the text he or she notes that the document does not reproduce the words spoken aloud to the scribe by the indigenous authority. This is what the syntactic slippage in the phrase explains: for his part (*por si*) the scribe speaks, practiced in law; "I . . . say" (*digo*) the ventriloquist makes the indigenous governor speak to the state functionary. Thus, the intermediary agent neither transcribes nor translates: he elaborates a complex practice that may be defined as "trans-writing" (*trans-escritura*). His writing seeks a performative effect that prolongs the text beyond the words.[65]

In the "representation" the historian does not discover the words spoken by the native governor. Still, the document offers something more: a kind of geometric semblance. In drawing up the document the scribe delineates on a reduced scale the local political polygon, and he centers its axis on the conflict related by the indigenous authority. On the margins of his outline, but in the outer confines of the political, he arranges, first, the shadow of the governor who he tries to represent "for his part and . . . the rest" of the natives (*por si y los demás*); he then tries to provoke state intervention in that no-man's land between the private-citizen sphere and the dominated, or among the latter. But to do this he must possess a guide's knowledge of the topography of the political terrain. Second, the scribe makes a calculation of the local vectors present (interests and forces) that impinge on the subject. Finally, he orients the text toward a key social agent, addressing it to a state authority. In order to play the part of strategist, the ventriloquist must be a seasoned player who occupies a position in the local play of material and symbolic interests. He has firsthand knowledge of how to plot gambits of attack and defense, and he is capable of analyzing the positions of social agents and thus propose alliances. In a word, he possesses a political skill embodied in the habitus.

I leave open an analysis of the complex plays of power, the webs of clientage and asymmetrical reciprocity (symbolic domination), implied by this system of representation by ventriloquy. I will also not dwell here on the consequences that political ventriloquy carries with it: the undeniable transformation (in discourse and l'njeu, in the issues at stake) that a conflict raised in the indigenous domain undergoes when it is made to emerge in the public sphere. That is, the prismatic divergence that mediates between the play of the indigenous governor and the play of the scribe constitutes the strategies of representation in the domain of the voiceless and dominated and also in its audibility in the public-state sphere.

NOTES

I thank Mark Thurner for translating this essay and for his numerous critical suggestions.

1 M. Mann, "Ruling-Class Strategies and Citizenship," *Sociology* 21 (1987): 339–54; Carole Pateman, "The Fraternal Social Contract," in *Civil Society and the State: New European Perspectives*, ed. John Keane (London: Verso, 1988); B. Turner, "Outline of a Theory of Citizenship," *Sociology* 24 (1990): 189–217; and Mark Thurner, *From Two Republics to One Divided: Contradictions of Postcolonial Nationmaking in Andean Peru* (Durham: Duke University Press, 1997), 27.

2 By "mestizo" or "white" I mean the social group that under the colony was classified into different juridically defined "castes." Under the republic, this group identified itself as "white." I am using "white" as a qualifier and as a classification parallel to "indigenous," which was used by the state and citizens and today is still in use in everyday life. In addition, nowadays former populations qualify themselves as "Ecuadorian indigenes" in their organizations and discourse.

3 Alfonso Caso, *La comunidad indígena* (Mexico City, 1971); Darcy Ribeiro, *Las Américas y la Civilización; Vol. 1: Los pueblos testimonio* (Buenos Aires: Centro Editor de América Latina, 1969); and Gonzalo Aguirre Beltrán, *Regiones de refugio* (Mexico City: Instituto Indigenista Interamericano, 1989).

4 On the notion of intrigue as an organizing thread of the historical

account, see Paul Ricoeur, *Temps et récit*, vol. 2 (Paris: Seuil, 1983); and Jacques Ranciére, *Les noms de l'histoire: Essai de poétique du savoir* (Paris: Seuil, 1992).

5 Pierre Bourdieu, *Le sens pratique* (Paris: Minuit, 1980).

6 Jürgen Habermas, *The Structural Transformation of the Public Sphere: An Inquiry into a Category of Bourgeois Society*, trans. Thomas Burger (Cambridge: MIT Press, 1989).

7 Michel Foucault, *Il fant defender la société: Cours au Collège de France, 1976* (Paris: Gallimard, 1997).

8 Carole Pateman, "The Fraternal Social Contract," in *Civil Society and the State: New European Perspectives*, ed. John Keane (London: Verso, 1988), 101–27; Judith Butler, "Contingent Foundations: Feminism and the Question of 'Postmodernism,'" in *Feminist Contentions: A Philosophical Exchange*, ed. Seyla Benhabib, et al. (New York: Routledge, 1995).

9 Territories and populations belonging to the Royal Audiencia of Quito (a colonial district) were organized into an independent national state in 1830, when the republic of Gran Colombia (founded in 1822) was divided up into three nation-states: Colombia, Ecuador, and Venezuela.

10 "Report from Gral. J. J. Flores, President of the Republic, to the Senate," *Gaceta del Ecuador*, January 24, 1841.

11 The status of "Indian tributary" was suppressed in 1821 during the war of independence and citizenship was extended to all populations; however, in 1828 Simón Bolívar reestablished the tribute, now known as "contribution."

12 Bourdieu, *Le sens pratique*, chap. 3. This notion has been translated into English as "practical mastery" as well as "the logic of practice," but for the sake of style is translated here as "customary." See Craig Calhoun, ed., *Bourdieu: Critical Perspectives* (Chicago: University of Chicago Press, 1993), 225.

13 "Report from Gral. J. J. Flores, President of the Republic, to the Senate," *Gaceta del Ecuador*, January 24, 1841.

14 Ibid.

15 Pateman, "The Fraternal Social Contract."

16 Mark Van Akken, "La lenta expiración del tributo indígena en el Ecuador," *Cultura* (Quito) 16, (1983): 49–80.

17 *Exposición del Ministro Secretario de Estado presentada al Congreso 1° Constitucional del Ecuador, 1831* (Quito: Imp. del Gobierno, 1831). *Ligera Exposición que el Ministro de Estado en los Departamentos del Interior, Relaciones Exteriores y Hacienda, presenta a la Convención Nacional en 1835* (Quito: Imp. del Gobierno, 1835).

18 "The inevitable consequence (of the extended use) was that the term 'citoyen' was packed with multiple, ambiguous and contradictory

meanings, and that it became a focus of passionate political struggles [between 1789 and 1800]" (W. H. Sewell Jr., "Le citoyen/la citoyenne: Activity, Passivity, and the Revolutionary Concept of Citizenship," in *The French Revolution and the Creation of Modern Political Culture*, ed. Colin Lucas (New York: Pergamon, 1987), 106, 114. See also Ferdinand Brunot, *Histoire de la langue française des origines à nos jours; Vol. 9: La révolution et l'empire*, part 2: "Les événements, les institutions et la langue" (Paris: A. Colin, 1967), 678–98.

19   For the uses of the word "citizen" (*ciudadano*) in Peru, see Thurner, *From Two Republics*, where he states: "Literally, *peruano* was used to mean common *indio* . . . It seems that the local elites had not yet included themselves in this new 'national' category (they preferred the highbrow *ciudadano* or *vecino*)" (27).

20   *Leyes de Colombia, 1821–1827* (Caracas, 1840).

21   On colonial fiscal reforms in Peru, see Thurner, *From Two Republics*, 20–25. On the 1788 rebellion , see S. Moreno Yañez, *Sublevaciones indígenas en la audiencia de Quito* (Quito: Abaya Yala, 1985), 208, 224.

22   E. P. Thompson, "The Moral Economy of the English Crowd in the Eighteenth Century," *Past and Present* 50 (1971).

23   *Gaceta del Ecuador*, April 18, 1839.

24   Ibid.

25   *Gaceta del Ecuador*, September 26, 1842.

26   *Gaceta del Ecuador*, October 10, 1842. The *informaciones* and "*comunicaciones*" or *instrucciones* of the ministers had the status of quasi-laws.

27   An example: the *corregidor* (republican tax collector) of Otavalo requested instructions in order to execute a ministerial resolution that insisted that in spite of laws to the contrary the corregidor collect the indigenous head tax "from the legitimate offspring of Indian men wed to White women, and from the 'natural or spurious' offspring of Indian women, even if their fathers are Whites." The corregidor confirms in his reply that "that class of persons" does indeed exist in his county. Archivo Nacional Histórico, Quito (hereafter A N H/Q), Series of Correspondence from the Governor of Imbabura to the Minister of the Interior, September 29, 1838.

28   A N H/Q, Series of Correspondence from the Governor of Imbabura to the Minister of the Interior, August 16, 1843 and October 22, 1843.

29   *Gaceta del Ecuador*, November 3, 1842.

30   Circular issued by the Minister of the Interior on November 18, 1831, ABFL/Q.

31   Compare this postcolonial situation with the features highlighted by Eric Hobsbawm in the constitution of the nation-state, which eliminates intermediary bodies of power and establishes a direct link be-

tween individuals and the state: "In short, the state ruled over a territory, its agents increasingly reaching down to the humblest inhabitant
of the least villages" (E. J. Hobsbawm, *Nations and Nationalism since
1780: Programme, Myth, Reality* [Cambridge: Cambridge University
Press, 1992], 80).

32 *El Protector de indígenas a nombre de los menores hijos de Alejo Gualca, pidiéndo
se los declare libres del concertaje celebrado con el Sr. A. Mora,* Archivo Histórico, Instituto Otavaleño de Antropología (hereafter AH/IOA); EP/J,
box 1 (1843–46; 720). *Manuela Toacaza vda. de Martín Sisa contra el Sr.
Francisco Carcelé,* AN H/Q, Serie Indígenas, Notaría 6, 1832.

33 See my *La semántica de la dominación, el concertaje de indios* (Quito: Libri
Mundi 1991), 119–213.

34 Report from a civil servant, Series of Correspondence from the Governor of Imbabura to the Minister of the Interior, August 16, 1843,
AN H/Q.

35 The national bibliographies on republican citizenship in Latin America are considerable, but the problem of *the administration of populations
subject to the state* is at best mentioned as a problem of "exclusion" or,
following the modernization telos of T. H. Marshall in his *Citizenship
and Social Class and Other Essays* (Cambridge: Cambridge University
Press, 1950) as an "unfinished process" or perhaps an "impediment"
that "distorts" the historical formation of the citizenry and the national "political culture." See, for instance, J. Murilo de Carvalho,
"Dimensôes da Cidadania no Brasil do seculo XIX," paper presented
at the seminar on citizenship, Bogota, 1994. See also Anthony Marx,
*Making Race and Nation: A Comparison of South Africa, the United States, and
Brazil* (Cambridge: Cambridge University Press, 1998), 267–77.

36 Report from the Minister of Interior to the Senate in 1846, Censo
General de la Poblacion, 1846, Serie Empadronamientos, AN H/Q. On
the unreliability of census data, see M. Lucena Samoral, "La población
del Reino de Quito en la época del reformismo borbónico, circa 1784,"
Revista de Indias, 54.200.

37 The automatic incorporation of a shared principle of vision and division, of similar cognitive structures of evaluation among a social
group "is the fundament of immediate, prereflexive consensus of a
sense of the world; consensus is the origin of experience of the world
as 'the world of common sense' " (Bourdieu, *Méditations pascaliennes*
[Paris: Seuil, 1997], 206).

38 Censo General de Otavalo, *Instrucciones especiales para los enumeradores,*
AH/IOA, Serie Municipalidad, box 1, October 5, 1947.

39 A "new awareness," the idea that they were creating a new society, a
new type of man; François-Xavier Guerra, *Modernidad e independencias:*

Ensayos sobre las revoluciones hispánicas (Mexico: Fondo de Cultura Económica, 1993), 13.

40 John Lynch, *The Spanish American Revolutions, 1808–1826* (New York, 1986).

Cecilia Méndez, "Rebellion without Resistance: Huanta's Monarchist Peasants in the Making of the Peruvian State, Ayacucho 1825–1850" (Ph.D. diss., State University of New York, Stony Brook, 1996).

41 Both terms appear interchangeably in the constitutions of the republic of Ecuador from 1830 to the present.

42 Norbert Elias emphasizes the unambiguous relation between the "civilizing process," colonial expansion, and the formation of nation-states, see his *El proceso civilizatorio: Investigacions sociogenéticas y psicogenéticas* (Mexico City: n.p., 1987), 95–96.

43 Congressional Law of October 21, 1857, ABFL/Q.

44 Proceedings of floor debate and commissions, 1856–1857, ABFL/Q.

45 Laws relevant to tribute include the Law of October 15, 1828 in *Indice del Registro Oficial de la República de Colombia* (1828–1829), *Registro Oficial*, no. 20 y 21, 156–63; the Law of June 3, 1851, in *El Nacional*, no. 370, 29/7/1851; the Law of November 23, 1854 in *El Seis de Marzo*, no. 132, vol. 1851–1858; all located in ABFL/Q.

46 A history of republican political representation in Latin America may be found in François-Xavier Guerra, "The Spanish American Tradition of Representation and Its European Roots," *Journal of Latin American Studies* 26 (February 1994): 1–35. This study deals with the premodern impediments that "distort" republican representation, but it barely mentions the exclusion of indigenous populations.

47 Proceedings of floor debate and commissions, 1856–1857, ABFL/Q.

48 "Leyes de Regimen Municipal," in *El Nacional* no. 54, June 20, 1861, ABFL/Q.

49 The reference here to Foucault is mandatory, particularly regarding the terms "administration," "technologies of rule," "population," "state of domination," and "strategies of power." See Foucault's "Cours du 14 janvier 1976," in *Il faut défendre la société* (Paris: Gallimard-Seuil, 1997), 21–36, and his "L'Ethique du souci de soi comme pratique de la liberté," in *Dits et Ecrits* vol. 4 (Paris: Gallimard, 1994), 728.

50 See my "La coutume et l'etat: Curagas et lieutenants politiques à Otavalo au XIX siècle," *Annales E.S.C.* (Paris) (March-April 1992): 331–54.

51 See Carole Pateman, "Feminist Critique of the Public/Private Dichotomy," in *Public and Private in Social Life*, ed. S. I. Benn and Gerald F. Gauss (London: Croom Helm, 1973), 281–82.

52 Ibid., 102–3.

53 For Jürgen Habermas the "petty patriarchal family" is, in Europe, the

formative nucleus of the private; see his "Prefacio a la nueva edición alemana," in *Historia y Crítica de la Opinión Pública* (Barcelona: n.p., 1994), 8–9. About intimacy and the private, see Phillipe Ariès, "Para una historia de la vida privada," in *Historia de la vida privada*, vol. 3, ed. Georges Duby (Madrid, 1989).

54 Guerrero, "La coutume et l'etat."

55 G. Agamben, *Homo Sacer: Le pouvoir souverain et la vie nue* (Paris, 1997), 27.

56 The theme of the exclusion of women, daughters, and spouses is of singular importance for the strategies of postcolonial domination decentered from the state, but exploring this issue goes beyond the scope of this essay.

57 Butler, "Contingent Foundations," 55 n.1. See also my "La coutume et l'etat." Otaualo (Équateur) 2 (1992): 331–54.

58 The notion of a "constitutive exteriority" is borrowed from Jacques Derrida, *De la Grammatologie* (Paris: n.p., 1992), 441–43.

59 See Gregory Knapp, *Geografía Quichua de la Sierra del Ecuador* (Quito: Abya Yala, 1991); and Leon Zamosc, *Estadísticas de predominio étnico del a Sierra ecuatoriana: Población rural, indicadores cantonals y organizaciones de base* (San Diego: University of California, 1994).

60 The Confederation of Indigenous Nationalities of Ecuador (CONAIE), founded in 1986, coordinates at least seventeen provincial organizations in the Ecuadorian sierra.

61 A similar process has ocurred in Mexico: the indigenous organizations in Chiapas erupt in the political public sphere, forcing the state to negotiate, and thereby constitute themselves, as social agents. On the uprisings of 1990 and 1994 in Ecuador, see Jorge Leon, *El levantamiento indígena: De campesinos a ciudadanos diferentes* (Quito: Cedime, 1994); and my "Le soulevement indigène national de 1994: Discours et représentation politique," *Problèmes d'Amérique Latine* (Paris) 19 (October-December 1995): 51–75.

62 Benedict Anderson, *Imagined Communities: Reflections on the Origins and Spread of Nationalism* (London: Verso, 1991).

63 See my "The Construction of a Ventriloquist's Image: Liberal Discourse and the 'Miserable Indian Race' in Late-Nineteenth-Century Ecuador," *Journal of Latin American Studies* 29.3 (October 1997): 1–36.

64 Correspondence of the Governor of Imbabura Province to the Ministry of Interior, (Solicitudes, 1856); ANH/Q.

65 On this notion, see my "De protectores a tinterillos: La privatización de la administración de poblaciones indígenas (dominadas)," in *Las sociedades campesinas del siglo XIX en los Andes*, ed. Heraclio Bonilla (Santander, Colombia: Universidad de Santander, 1996).

JOANNE RAPPAPORT

Redrawing the Nation

Indigenous Intellectuals and Ethnic Pluralism

in Contemporary Colombia

✴ In June 1999, the Panamerican Highway between the Colombian cities of Cali and Popayán was blocked for eleven days by twelve thousand representatives of indigenous communities of the southwestern department of Cauca, bringing transportation to a halt on this major north-south artery in the country. Led by a steering committee comprised of representatives of the Regional Indigenous Council of Cauca (CRIC) and other indigenous organizations, and joined by the governors of reservation councils belonging to the Guambiano, Nasa (Páez), and Yanacona ethnic groups, Cauca's indigenous peoples demonstrated in response to government noncompliance of a number of agreements concerning the provision of crucial services (health, education, and land reform, among others) to indigenous communities, which rank among Colombia's poorest people.[1] These accords were reached as a result of similar mobilizations in previous years.[2]

The mass mobilization also called for a recognition of CRIC, a modern regional indigenous organization, as a "traditional authority," analogous to the reservation councils that have existed since the colonial period. The demonstrators also demanded that indigenous authorities participate in an expanded version of the peace negotiations that Colombian president Andrés Pastrana has conducted with the major guerrilla organization FARC (Revolutionary Armed Forces of Colombia), a dialogue in which civil society has been conspicuously absent. This extraordinary event established a microcosm of Caucan indigenous society at a site called La María, complete with a regional council made up of the governors of the various participating reservations, a civic guard, a corps of shamans, and numerous "neighborhoods" in which different communities pitched their tents. Alongside negotiations with government officials that took place at the tent serving as the mobilization headquarters, almost one hundred shamans performed rituals and shared knowledge among themselves and with interested spectators. Musicians played while participants danced away the sleepless nights to fight against the cold and the uncomfortable conditions.

The negotiators and other participants in the council confronted the state in a variety of ways. When government representatives challenged the native occupation of a major artery, they responded that La María was already constituted as indigenous territory before the Spanish invasion of the sixteenth century and that it was not their fault that the Panamerican Highway had been built there. The first ministerial delegation's visit was greeted by a thunderstorm that the shamans were said to have created. The director of the Division of Indigenous Affairs—himself an Ingano whose government position was achieved as a result of pressure from the indigenous movement—was censured for his choice of identifying as a member of the government and not as a native person. As the days wore on, the mobilization's leadership rejected a number of drafts of agreement, forcing the government to accept its principal demands and to open extended negotiations with indigenous representatives.[3]

This massive affirmation of indigenous identity is not new in Cauca, where in the past three decades, regional organizations such as CRIC and national movements such as AICO (Indigenous Authorities of Colombia) and ONIC (National Indigenous Organization of Colombia) have played a key role in strengthening local-level indigenous authority, repossessing lands usurped from reservations in previous centuries by nonnative landlords, and impelling the Constitutional Assembly to recognize Colombia as a pluriethnic nation in its 1991 constitution.[4] Since the constitutional mandate was adopted, indigenous communities have won the right to supervise their own educational systems, to administer tax funds, to organize their own public health systems, and to devise a culturally sensitive system of justice. Thus, it is no longer possible (although it really never was) for anthropologists to study indigenous cultures in Colombia without paying heed to the multiple articulations between local communities and regional, national, and international institutions, whether the latter be representatives of the Colombian state, the indigenous movement and its supporters, or the guerrilla organizations whose confrontation with the state in recent years has transformed the Colombian countryside into a battlefield.[5]

At the interface between the indigenous movement and representatives of the broader Colombian society stand indigenous intellectuals, leaders of native communities who are conversant with the discourses of both the state and of their own constituencies. Unlike the native leaders of the past, this new sector is increasingly cosmopolitan: many have university degrees, even postgraduate degrees; they are world travelers; they are as comfortable speaking before the United Nations or with representatives of the World Bank as they are speaking to their own constituencies; and they have become national celebrities. These intellectuals fill multiple roles, from serving as negotiators at La María and framers of the 1991 constitution to being the authors of local development projects and the coordinators of bilingual education programs that prepare members of native communities for participation on the national stage.[6]

In this essay I explore the quandaries facing indigenous public intellectuals in millennial Cauca. The indigenous movement has effectively achieved political participation on the regional and national stages, as well as a place in the constitutional framework through the creation of the fiction of a multiethnic nation; they have also won numerous municipal mayoralities in Cauca and in nearby Nariño, thereby permitting them to assume public administration in localities with an indigenous majority. They have been successful in introducing culturally sensitive projects in native communities, designed in accordance with innovative ethnographic and linguistic research produced by native scholars. Now, however, that they have become important public interlocutors with the state, effectively exerting the pressure necessary so that indigenous authorities can assume state functions on the local level, the movement's leaders are finding it increasingly difficult to translate their elegant cultural theories into political practice. The cultural discourse that has always accompanied the movement and has nourished its multiple projects has proven antithetical to the exercise of administrative duties, producing ambivalences and contradictions in which the multiple constituencies and interlocutors of the indigenous movement are at odds.[7] As was expressed to me by an aide to the Nasa mayor of Toribío, indigenous government functionaries are discovering that once they become part of the *alcaldía*, or municipal mayor's office—which we can read as the most immediate and local instance of "state"—they are no longer treated as members of the community, those governed by a *cabildo* (town council), because they identify and become identified with state interests, as did the Ingano director of the Division of Indigenous Affairs, who was rebuffed by the forces mobilized at La María.[8]

In addition to the ambivalence that indigenous leaders experience when they are forced to choose between divergent sets of interests in their quest to capture political autonomy, their objective of reconfiguring the state from a pluralist vantage point is contradicted by the very terms of their culturalist discourse. On an intellectual level, the indigenous leadership of Cauca had striven to "provincialize Europe" and to focus on categories and practices that place their own (oppositional) culture in the foreground; as we shall see in an exploration of Guambiano historical research, this has been achieved on the level of academic analysis through the elaboration of new organizing models that permit indigenous intellectuals to narrate history in culturally specific ways.[9]

But the next step, the reconceptualizing of the nation-state in practice, with the goal of achieving effective and culturally rooted public administration, has been highly elusive. In effect, indigenous activists have discovered that the adoption of a multiculturalist discourse by the Colombian state is part of a political strategy that effectively co-opts or disarms the indigenous leadership, framing their novel attempts at decentering Colombian political narratives with those very same political discourses and practices they have been confronting. As a result, indigenous political projects ultimately serve to strengthen the Colombian state instead of producing the radical pluralist democracy that the movement seeks.[10] I will explore this issue in the concluding section of this essay through an analysis of the problems surrounding the codification of customary law in Nasa communities.

THE NATURE OF
INDIGENOUS IDENTITY IN LATIN AMERICA

Indigenous identity in Latin America can only be understood in relation to the dominant society, a point that is underscored by Diane Nelson in her analysis of the pan-Mayan movement in Guatemala:

What I am naming Quincentennial Guatemala might also be termed "postcolonial" in the sense that after five hundred years we have no access to a moment before the articulations among Europe, the Americas, Africa, capitalist modes of production, milpa (corn) agriculture, Christian god, Mayan gods, Spanish and the array of indigenous languages, and so on: in another word, all of the relations joined into Columbus' mistaken coining of Indian. There are no identifications in Guatemala that are not formed in relation.[11]

It has become a truism to make this assertion in anthropological writing. Nevertheless, it bears restatement from a variety of vantage points. First, the historical depth of this relationship is frequently passed over by ethnographers who have not carefully traced the paths by which cultural forms evolve in relation to the dominant society. Second, it is precisely by articulating their cultural, intellectual, and political agendas within a practice that locates indigenous demands and projects in relations of equivalence with that of other social movements in opposition to the overwhelming power of the state that indigenous public intellectuals are forging a pluralist politics in relation to their allies.[12] Since the colonial period of the sixteenth to eighteenth centuries when the population of indigenous communities in what is today Colombia was decimated by disease and war, and then was regrouped into urban units and isolated from colonial society in order to ensure the population's availability as a source of labor and its undivided attention directed at resident Catholic missionaries, indigenous identity has existed in relation to the dominant society.

During the colonial period, Colombian indigenous communities were organized into resguardos (an English gloss of which might be "reservation"), communal landholding corporations administered by cabildos or councils. Both the institutions of resguardo and cabildo were preserved in somewhat altered form as even less autonomous entities under postindependence legislation, their existence reaffirmed by the 1991 constitution.[13] These institutions, colonial in nature, did not provide for the administrative autonomy of indigenous authorities, but constituted the cabildo as a mediator between the community and the state, the latter serving as recipient of tribute or taxes, labor levies, and military conscripts, as well as administering justice. The meaning of the terms "indigenous," "authority," and "community" have thus for centuries involved specific administrative and legal statuses within Colombia. Over time, membership in a resguardo and the authority of the cabildo came to stand for what it means to be indigenous, lending a highly charged political nature to ethnic identity. The politicization of identity was further intensified with the appearance of the indigenous movement in the 1970s, whose program of land claims obliged self-identification as indigenous to be greeted as a subversive act by the repressive apparatus of the state and of organized landlords.[14] Since the 1991 constitution, the state, in its move toward decentralization, recognized cabildos as entities entitled to receive and administer *transferencias*, or tax funds, for public works, leading to a curious melding of ethnic identity within the framework of the nation: it is difficult today to draw a diametric opposition between indigenous community and state, given that the cabildo has increasingly taken on state functions.[15]

In the last decade of the twentieth century, the Colombian state has been forced to face up to its own deterioration: its failure to maintain effective military control over its territory and economic control over its markets, as well as its inability to administer needed services to its population. Operating within a neoliberal paradigm, as are other Latin American governments, the state's solution has tended toward decentralization. The power of the indigenous movement since its inception and its key alliances with other sectors (at the writing of the constitution, their most significant ally was the M-19, a guerrilla group turned legal political party that enjoyed a powerful plurality in the Constitutional Assembly) permitted native leaders an opportunity to pressure the state to recognize the plural nature of the Colombian nation and to insert its demands for ethnic autonomy into the decentralization program. The significance of this victory is particularly momentus given that only 1.5 percent of the Colombian population identifies itself as indigenous.[16]

Mark Thurner has suggested that the "postcolonial" is an apt gloss for referring to such unaccustomed relationships to the nation as we find in late-twentieth-century Cauca: "When microhistorical, textually sensitive research in the field and the local archive reveals the silences of the available rubrics under which it labors, *particularly where the problematics of colonial and national state and subject formation are concerned*, then the 'postcolonial' may be usefully deployed to name predicaments and subjectivities otherwise unrecognized or unimagined in the master teleologies of, say 'the nation,' or 'the modern,' or 'capital.' "[17] In the Colombian case—and in a broader sense across

Latin America, as several other contributions to this volume suggest—what is unimagined in the teleology of "the nation" is the notion that indigenous identity could intimately transform national identity, that indigenous institutions could double for state institutions, and that the state in its constitutional discourse would recognize this ambiguous situation[18]—ambiguous because neither indigenous organizations nor the national legislature and executive are completely comfortable with this amalgamation. Hence, we see an ethnic organization seeking to be recognized as a "traditional authority," a contradictory term given that underlying its appeal to tradition lie the specifically modern connotations of citizenship and political participation, articulated within the contemporary constitutional space. Further, we see a troubled state that formally recognizes indigenous authority but backtracks when twelve thousand ethnic citizens block the Panamerican Highway because it cannot meet those demands that it has already affirmed in its constitution and in numerous prior accords.

INDIGENOUS PUBLIC INTELLECTUALS AND MULTICULTURAL POLITICAL SPACE

The indigenous public intellectuals who are key participants in the reformulation of the Colombian state are urban-based activists, most of whom are well-schooled and working as educational policymakers, community development specialists, legislators, and politicians under the aegis of the numerous indigenous organizations that operate on the Caucan stage. Most of them were born in rural communities and have moved to town centers and cities as professionals, unlike the vast majority of indigenous migrants to urban areas, who arrive in the city as unskilled laborers and work largely in the informal sector. The intellectuals, in contrast, are highly articulate and literate in Spanish, although many of them also speak indigenous languages.[19] Gayatri Chakravorty Spivak would argue in this light that indigenous public intellectuals are not appropriately termed "subalterns" given their facility with manipulating and subverting hegemonic discourses; instead, they function as organic intellectuals within an emergent multicultural popular social sector.[20] I am not sure, either, that these intellectuals would refer to themselves as subalterns, except as a political tactic: the position they occupy in the national and regional political arenas is not so much defined by their subordination, as by the cultural difference that is emblematic of their political platform. In a continent in which the occupier/occupied distinction was blurred in the colonial period by mestizaje, it is precisely by underscoring ethnic difference that the indigenous movement can forge a political space distinct from that of other social sectors.[21]

A common set of conditions underlies the development of a sector of indigenous intellectuals in the Andes. The return of liberal democracy in many countries and the growth of ethnic movements has created scenarios in which native intellectuals can find their voice, identify their publics, and participate in open political action. The growth of nongovernmental organizations and grassroots social movements with external funding has facilitated the funds necessary to launch their research initiatives, writing, and publications. The expansion of secondary and higher education to rural and native peoples has permitted the training of these scholars, while the growth of adult education and of native-controlled channels of electronic communication have created the conditions for a dialogue to take place, as much within the native intellectual sector as between native intellectuals and metropolitan intellectuals, on the one hand, and native intellectuals and their communities, on the other. Finally, the 1992 quincentenary of the invasion of the Americas provided a catalyst and a space for reflection by native writers and thinkers.

These new political and intellectual actors have developed alongside a significant shift in the nature of indigenous political authority. Since the Colombian state began to formally recognize indigenous communities as distinct cultural entities by incorporating their functionaries into the public administration, a new layer of local leaders, particularly cabildo governors, has arisen: high school educated men and women with well-developed linguistic and literacy skills in Spanish, who are nominally comfortable with drawing up development plans and devising municipal budgets, and who move with ease between rural communities and regional or national administrative centers. Thus, when CRIC demanded it be recognized as a "traditional authority," it was not referring to the cabildos of old whose dominion was marginal and who were extremely timid when it came to engaging state discourse (although they were effective at mobilizing their communities in contestatory politics). Instead, the organization saw itself as representing a new breed of political leader, one able to move across cultural contexts.[22]

Postcolonial indigenous political activists can be aptly designated as "inappropriate Others," whose simultaneous exercise of insiderness and outsiderness defies the attribution of neat, discrete, and polarized identity. In the words of Trinh T. Minh-ha:

> The moment the insider steps out from the inside, she is no longer a mere insider (and vice versa). She necessarily looks in from the outside while also looking out from the inside. Like the outsider, she steps back and records what never occurs to her the insider as being worth or in need of recording. But unlike the outsider, she also resorts to non-explicative, non-totalizing strategies that suspend meaning and resist closure. (This is often viewed by the outsiders as strategies of partial concealment and disclosure aimed at preserving secrets that should only be imparted to natives.) She refuses to reduce herself to an Other, and her reflections to a mere outsider's objective reasoning or insider's subjective feeling . . . Undercutting the inside/outside opposition, her intervention is necessarily that of both a deceptive insider and a deceptive outsider. She is this Inappropriate Other/Same who moves about with always at least two/four gestures: that of affirming "I am like you" while persisting in her difference; and that of reminding "I am different" while unsettling every definition of otherness arrived at.[23]

Exemplifying the "inappropriate Other" is the indigenous intellectual who works in the offices of the indigenous organization, traveling to New York, Paris, or Mexico City to attend international conferences and returning to observe community assemblies in Toribío or Guambía; who is fluent in Nasa Yuwe (the Nasa language) or Guambiano, but writes in Spanish; and who is responsible for directing a process of cultural revitalization by creating educational policy for rural groups, but lives in the city. While all Others are in a sense inappropriate, ethnic activists consciously deploy their inappropriateness in the political arena. The Caucan "inappropriate Other" juxtaposes indigenous and metropolitan discourses and identities in an effort to produce discomfort, to demand that listeners reflect on the fact that the speaker is an indio but is highly sophisticated and that she or he is culturally different but not subordinated: the Caucan "inappropriate Other" forces other Colombians to rethink what "indigenous" means, insisting that they engage the cultural pluralism to which they have paid lipservice over the past decade.

The Nasa definition of *cosmovisión*, or worldview, presents a good example of how indigenous intellectuals reinscribe Western ethnographic methodology with specifically Nasa conceptual agendas, thus engaging in pluralist forms of cultural expression and political practice. The English term "worldview" brings to mind a secularized vision of the cultural filters through which groups understand and act on their surroundings, suggesting a bounded and static concept of culture. In contrast, Nasa intellectuals interpret their notion of cosmovisión as a more holistic (integral, in Spanish) vision of the universe that takes into account both the fit between the natural and supernatural worlds and the articulation of indigenous cultural visions within a broader pluralist reality. In the Nasa translation of the constitution, for example, "culture" is defined as wët üskiwe'n'i. Wët signifies "harmony"; üs translates as "permanence"; kiwe is "territory"; and the suffix n'i links these terms into a cause-effect relationship. Thus, an English translation of the Spanish back-translation in the glossary reads: "The form of behavior resulting from a permanent harmonic relationship with Nature."[24] Harmony is understood here as the interpenetration of past, present, and future. Nasa leader Jesús Enrique Piñacué speaks of it as a distinct system of causation, within which events do not "cause" other events to occur but rather coexist within a constellation of experiences that cannot be ordered chronologically because they are distributed in space, not in time; only the shaman, or te'wala, can determine their logic.[25]

Nasa notions of cosmovisión draw on anthropological discourse, inasmuch as they describe Nasa culture as a coherent and discrete whole. Nevertheless, this vision is by no means static nor bounded, as are essentialist definitions of culture. For example, Nasa intellectuals' explanations of the idea of harmony draw on linguistic models of space and time as described in the publications of indigenous linguists trained in postgraduate university programs, who argue that in Nasa Yuwe the past is located in front of the speaker.[26] Nasa linguists have appropriated their experience of translating the constitution into Nasa Yuwe in their task of creating a Nasa research methodology. In countless meetings as well as in publications, concepts from the dominant society ranging from development and educational systems to science and history are analyzed through their translation into Nasa Yuwe, thus creating a Nasa hierarchy of knowledge.[27]

For example, at a meeting held in the CRIC offices, in which Nasa and Western intellectuals contrasted Colombian and Nasa notions of what would constitute an educational system, the word "education" was translated into Nasa Yuwe by Abelardo Ramos, one of CRIC's linguists and the principal translator of the constitution into Nasa Yuwe. Ramos—who earlier told me that from a Nasa point of view a system is like a web or net with multiple critical nodes, constituted by the cultural planners or intellectuals—translated "education" as *nasa neesn'i*, a heritage of abstract qualities (*neesn'i*), including identity, history, and tradition, that serve as a basis for determining policy and for negotiating with the state. Abelardo also linked this notion to the Nasa concept of culture (*wët üskiwe'n'i*), generating a telling commentary from Inocencio Ramos, his brother and another CRIC intellectual: "Allí estarían las formas de transmitir e investigar" (This is where we would find the forms of transmission and research).

Western science is thus appropriated within Nasa notions of harmony, necessarily shifting the terms of reference of cosmovisión but accomplishing this on Nasa terms. This process of reinterpretation of the West and the consequent reconfiguration of a hybrid Nasa thought is, moreover, described as a *political* exercise: that is, it takes place in a pluralist context in which culture and cosmovisión are necessarily understood by indigenous intellectuals as oppositional (*contestatario*) categories employed in negotiation with the state.[28] As we shall see, this politicization of ethnic categories, which releases indigenous identity from the taxonomic binary of "Indian/white" that has characterized anthropological descriptions of interethnic relations over the years, is mobilized in forms of cultural revitalization aimed at carving out an autonomous space for Colombian indigenous communities. This strategy, moreover, internalizes the notion of "pluralism" so that it not only refers to the multiculturalism espoused by the constitution but also focuses indigenous conceptions of culture so that they are also pluralistic, fostering a recognition at the local level, particularly in educational venues and in the creation of multiethnic cabildos, that Nasa or Guambiano cultural forms interact and intermingle with those of their mestizo or Afro-Colombian neighbors.

The goal of indigenous research is to deepen the impact of pluralist politics within the indigenous movement and between native organizations and other representatives of popular sectors; it eschews the primordial roots of Nasa culture to concentrate on how the Nasa have developed their identity *within* Colombian society, thus establishing an indigenous identity *in relation to* political allies. Pluralism thus means more than simple political representation by multiple interests, which is the way it has been conceived by the Colombian elite who adopted multiculturalism along with administrative decentralization as a neoliberal strategy for shoring up a deteriorating state.[29] Instead, it is at once a collaborative research strategy and a political project in which native peoples have come to engage the fact that they are simultaneously Nasa or Guambiano *and* Colombian and that they cannot be one without being the other—"inappropriate Otherness" refocused on entire populations operating as political actors within new social movements that have not only entered the political stage but have attempted to restructure it.[30]

Euro-American anthropological narratives have, however, played a key role in defining Colombian indigenous identity at various points during the past century. Law 89 of 1890, the central piece of legislation legitimizing the resguardo before the adoption of the 1991 constitution, classified indigenous communities through an evolutionary taxonomy that distinguished between levels of economic and sociopolitical integration, thus defining the extent of state tutelage they were to receive. When indigenous groups of the first half of the twentieth century were found to have "moved up" the evolutionary ladder, their resguardo status was liquidated. Anthropological narratives of acculturation and culture loss played a crucial role in the creation of policies for resettling the Nasa in isolated localities after a 1994 earthquake destroyed their territory.[31]

It is with the appearance on the political stage of indigenous public intellectuals that ethnography has been turned to other purposes, its narratives serving as a framework for cultural revitalization through the production of ethnographies written from an indigenous perspective. Rey Chow suggests that indigenous ethnographers can only examine themselves from the vantage point of those who have been already looked at by others.[32] It is precisely this consciousness of previous academic and administrative surveillance, which impinges on indigenous intellectual production to produce an ethnographic subject *in relation to*, that exemplifies the definition of culture within the contemporary indigenous movement. Sometimes this is as simple as the production of historical studies that refute previous research by nonnative scholars.[33] At other times, as I will demonstrate in my analysis of Guambiano historical writing, it involves the reworking of academic genres so that they reflect native cosmovisión. Even those intellectual contributions by "inappropriate Others" that focus exclusively on native worldviews and cultural traditions are necessarily framed by the reformulation of the Colombian nation as ethnically pluralist; their very construction is lodged within the intimate relationship that ethnography has enjoyed with the state in the construction of Indianness.

In effect, indigenous intellectuals are not essentialist at all but rather articulate seemingly essentialist arguments within highly constructionist frameworks. In a perceptive analysis of the cultural discourses of Native American activists in California, Les Field has pointed out that these intellectuals are simultaneously essentialist and constructionist: essentialist insofar as they focus on those aspects of culture that demonstrate their difference from the dominant society, constructionist in their emphasis on cultural reconstruction (as opposed to maintenance) and in their fight to gain recognition as sovereign political actors by claiming social and cultural continuity through nonessentialist means.[34] In this sense, indigenous public intellectuals (and their metropolitan academic collaborators) deploy essentialism and constructionism in ways different from those of scholars in the academy. Native Americans embrace essentialism strategically, unlike their academic counterparts, but simultaneously they recognize that it is through essentialist discourses that the U.S. government has controlled processes of tribal recognition; however, they criticize the constructionism of metropolitan academics insofar as it shies away from producing needed cultural descriptions of contemporary indigenous groups.

Over the past decade, I have noticed a move away from essentializing discourses and toward a more constructionist approach on the part of Nasa public intellectuals, particularly in their treatment of the notion of cosmovisión and its applications within educational planning. Where once they embraced cosmovisión as an unchanging and universal cultural trait, many indigenous educators are now turning their attention toward the diversity that characterizes Nasa territorial space, both in terms of the linguistic and cultural differences among the two hundred thousand Nasa who live in radically differing rural and urban environments and in terms of the need for the Nasa to interact on a cultural level with their mestizo and Afro-Colombian neighbors.

The move from essentialism to constructionism can be traced along various paths. First, the educational formation of many indigenous public intellectuals has historically been in linguistics, given the priorities that the movement has traditionally placed on bilingual education, resulting in an emphasis on cultural models that are linguistically derived (something that I will touch on below in my interpretation of Guambiano historical writing). One of the earliest university programs to seek out indigenous students and provide them with scholarships was the ethnolinguistics program at the Universidad de los Andes in Bogotá, a project meant in part to contribute to the training of indigenous educators (as well as to produce Colombian-born linguists in order to supplant the U.S.-born missionary/linguists of the Summer Institute of Linguistics). The curriculum was focused on structural linguistics and, as founder Jon Landaburu told me, led to an initial euphoria on the part of native students, who embraced structuralism as a vehicle for "finding themselves." But as these students have found themselves confronted by the more complex sociocultural realities in which their bilingual schools are situated and as they have branched out to read constructionist anthropological and historical works, they have moved toward a different position in which they reject as impossible and simplistic the possibility of arriving at a "universal grammar of Nasa culture," a point driven home to me by Abelardo Ramos in a discussion about the curriculum of CRIC's university program for bilingual teachers.[35]

There are also tangible political realities that have fostered this transformation. Traditionally, CRIC has located the "center" of Nasa culture in an isolated region called Tierradentro, a place from which the Nasa have migrated over the past four centuries, first fanning out in the sixteenth and seventeenth centuries along the mountains immediately to the east of Popayán, and since the 1960s colonizing the Pacific coastal plain to the west of the Caucan capital, establishing homesteads in the eastern tropical lowland departments of the Caquetá and Putumayo, and moving to the urban centers of Cali, Popayán, and Santander de Quilichao.

While Tierradentro remains emblematic of Nasa culture, its inhabitants have been among the least politically active of the Nasa, preferring to maintain their allegiances to the establishment Liberal Party and the traditionalist Catholic Church that has ruled over the territory for the better part of the twentieth century, thanks to the Colombian government's Concordat with Rome. The people of Tierradentro have associated themselves with CRIC as clients receiving a variety of needed services, but hardly as leaders. On the other hand, CRIC was founded in 1971 in Toribío, a municipality in northern Cauca where the organization remains strong to this day.

The north is characterized by less culturally isolated indigenous communities, who have interacted on a daily basis with nonnative popular sectors that have honed their political militancy on a protracted struggle against sharecropping and the hacienda system and that are intimately linked to the regional market economy, both licit and illicit.[36] In Toribío, only a third of the population speaks Nasa Yuwe, a proportion much higher than the significant Nasa populations inhabiting the southern margins of the Cauca Valley, communities that play an important role in CRIC politics—in Corinto, for instance, only 10 percent are Nasa Yuwe speakers. Given these political realities and the fact that most of the organization's pilot schools—whose curricular planning and supervision is in the hands of Nasa public intellectuals—are located in the north, it has become increasingly difficult to sustain an essentialist agenda.

Let us now turn to an example of the intellectual production that characterizes indigenous Cauca, moving from the Nasa to their Guambiano neighbors, whose research exhibits a similar juxtaposition of essentialist cultural description within pluralist agendas and methods.

RECONCEPTUALIZING AND PLURALIZING HISTORY

Members of the Caucan intellectual elite have always identified the Guambianos as originating in Peru, interlopers in the mountainous territory they inhabit adjacent to Popayán. Since 1981, when the cabildo of Guambía embarked on a project of repossessing usurped lands within the resguardo boundaries, the indigenous leadership has felt it imperative that they debunk such theories once and for all. Beginning in 1983, the Guambiano History Committee, composed of young schooled intellectuals as well as elder traditional historians, initiated collaborative research with cultural anthropologist Luis Guillermo Vasco of the National University of Colombia and Bogotá archaeologist Martha Urdaneta to ground in history the territorial claims that the community was making through land occupations, by proving their primordial connections to the land.

The publications of the Guambiano History Committee attempt to engage in dialogue with metropolitan readers and researchers, as well as with the Guambiano community, through the adoption of a new language for interpreting the past. On the part of the Colombian anthropologists concerned, this has meant privileging Guambiano debates and theories over those of their own academic community. Unlike many of their North American counterparts, many Colombian anthropologists view collaboration with indigenous organizations as an integral part of their work since the inception of the movement in the 1970s.[37] For the Guambianos, this endeavor has also involved the embracing of a new language (Spanish) for engaging in historical interpretation as well as a new medium for encoding this discourse with its own distinct literary conventions. What emerges is a hybrid type of writing, not strictly metropolitan academic discourse but certainly not "typical" Guambiano orality, either.[38]

The juxtaposition of plural senses of the past is conveyed in both archaeological and historical publications of the Guambiano History Committee, especially in a long article, "En el segundo día, la Gente Grande (Numisak) sembró la autoridad y las plantas y, con su jugo, bebió el sentido" (On the second day the Great People (Numisak) sewed authority and the plants and, with its juice, drank their meaning), published in an anthology edited by the Instituto Colombiano de Antropología, in which the theoretical underpinnings of a dialogue between Guambiano historians and metropolitan anthropologists are depicted in the very act of narration.[39]

The article contains stories of the origin of Guambiano settlement, of colonial chiefs, of the loss and reclaiming of lands, and of the forces that have operated against Guambiano autonomy (the Catholic Church, the introduction of commercial fertilizers, opium poppy cultivation, etc.), interspersed with interpretive segments on the nature of Guambiano culture, some of which evince the hand of Luis Guillermo Vasco Uribe, the anthropologist; some the pen of young Guambiano analysts; and others the voice of Abelino Dagua Hurtado, the elder who was the driving force behind the committee. Although almost none of these fragments is identified by author, it is not difficult to distinguish the voices of the different committee members. The narrative moves from one voice to another in a spiral that rolls and unrolls, a metaphor that, we shall see, provides the central organizing model of the article. The very dialogic structure of the article, which constructs a narrative to accompany Guambiano models of cosmovisión, suggests that this novel form of historical writing has arisen not from an exclusively Guambiano subject position but from a pluralist environment in which Guambiano intellectuals engage and reinterpret the theories and methodologies of metropolitan social scientists, an intercultural dialogue in which Nasa intellectuals have also engaged.[40]

One of the most elegant segments of this history interprets the past as a spiral structure embodied in various examples of material culture:

Time is like a wheel which turns; it is like a pøtø, a ring, which returns to the original time; this is the path of the sun above the earth, this is the form in which the køsrømpøtø, the rainbow, walks, when it makes a circle upon turning around. But it is also like the snail or like the rainbow, which has a tøm, an articulation through which everything is related, marking the epoch or the period. Time goes and returns, passes and returns, passes and returns.

To speak of history implies a progression that is not linear but not circular either. It is like a spiral in three dimensions, whose center is on high: the Guambianos say that it is a srurrapu, a snail. Many rocks in various localities of the reservation are engraved with petroglyphs; among them there is a dominant motif: the spiral. Simple, double, inscribed in concentric circles, its presence is obvious and repetitive. The traditional hat of men and women, the kuarimpøtø, composed of a long woven band with various threads sewn into a spiral around a center, repeats the motif of the snail shell. The elders can read history in it, just as [they see] their vision of society as a whole and the ways in which things are interconnected. In it, the origins of time and space are marked. At its center everything begins and returns.[41]

This notion of spiral space was first developed by Guambiano linguists who, through an analysis of linguistic categories and temporal terminologies, describe time as something that rolls and unrolls in multiple temporal bands. Guambiana linguist Bárbara Muelas argues that this movement of time occurs in the relationships that Guambiano families establish with their geographic surroundings: "When one or more people who live in a house are invited to leave for other sites, they are invited with the expression pichip mentøkun, which literally means 'let us unroll.' The opposite situation, when they are invited to return home, is kitrøp mentøkun, which means 'let us roll up' or 'let us collect ourselves.' "[42]

Similarly, this action of rolling and unrolling defines the Guambiano relationship with time:

As the years unfold, in lived time, in the voyage of life and through the world, the ancestors have marked a path, they have opened a trail on which those who come behind, their descendants from today, must advance to make history. The past goes in front and the future comes behind. It is as though our ancestors had returned to look for their descendants or as though those who have already left (died) had returned to "judge" what their descendants have accomplished in their absence. It is as though a turn were made in the vast circular space, a new meeting with the ancestor, [of] past and future, an illusion, a hope, in Guambiano thought. The space before us and lived time (conserved in tradition) orient human life. They go ahead [of us] in life, and [continue] after life. The space that is left behind and time not yet lived are a space and a time that must still unroll.[43]

The entire publication of the Guambiano History Committee, comprised of semiindependent fragments with distinct authors, can itself be seen as a spiral, a pøtø, that continuously returns to or "sights upon" recurrent themes such as the pishimisak, the people of the cold, who are the ancestors of the Guambiano, or the nature of time in the Guambiano worldview. Similarly, the history committee's text rolls and unrolls, moving back and forth from the present into the distant past of the ancestors, the more recent past of the abuses of the hacienda, the decisive moment of the recovery of cabildo authority and the repossession of usurped lands. This is not a linear chronological narrative but a constant resighting on key moments in Guambiano history, which come up, again and again, as significant teachings.

The early history of Guambía focuses on the appearance of Mama Manuela Caramaya, the foundational chief (or cacica) of Guambía, who was born in the river and defended Guambiano lands from indigenous and European invaders. Mama Manuela's story is followed by an earlier event, the creation of the world and of the earliest people, the pishimisak, who simultaneously possessed masculine and feminine qualities and whose lives were intimately connected with the circulation of water from the high peaks of the Andes (the páramo) that they inhabited to the lower reaches, where the Guambiano now live.

The narrative then turns to the chiefdoms of the time of the Spanish invasion, looking back again at the pishimisak, who are called the fathers and mothers of the cabildo. The narrative moves then to the 1980s, when the Guambianos clashed with the leadership of CRIC. It paints the Guambiano as a peaceful people, like their pishimisak ancestors. This peacefulness was reoriented toward the occupation of the hacienda Las Mercedes and its reincorporation into the resguardo, leading to a politicization of the cabildo and, ultimately, to the founding of AICO. The narrators then turn to a discussion of the problems that have arisen as increasingly the Guambiano cultivate opium poppies. This is abruptly followed by a shift to the distant past, with a story of how the Guambiano settled the cordillera, moving from the hot Cauca valley to the highlands. Then follows a history of how Guambiano lands were lost to large landowners in the nineteenth century. Suddenly, however, full circle is made, with a return to the pishimisak and the founding cacica: the need to reclaim Las Mercedes is explained in terms of the sacred importance of place, since the hacienda is located at the confluence of the two major rivers, male and female, located at the place where the cacica was born.

A series of other stories follow: a description of the 1980 occupation of Las Mercedes; the collusion of earlier Guambiano governors with the landlords (undated); visions of the Virgin Mary (undated); the entrance of the missionary sisters of Mother Laura into Guambía and how they taught the Guambianos to wear shoes (first half of the twentieth century); how municipal authorities forced the Guambianos to assign individual plots to resguardo members (1920s); and the entrance of the Summer Institute of Linguistics into Guambía (1955). These historical events are then framed, through the exegesis of key Guambiano terms, by a discussion of what community and reciprocity mean and through an analysis of the need to revitalize Guambiano culture. Clearly, this is not a chronological narrative but a history consciously made to roll and unroll, as a spiral, with the territory itself and the topographic features in which foundational beings live on, providing an axis for recounting the past. The spiral organizing model is explicitly stated in those segments that engage in cultural exegesis; it was reaffirmed for me in discussions with Guambiano intellectuals.

A second format simultaneously structures the narrative. At the end of the article there is a lengthy discourse by Abelino Dagua Hurtado, the elder who was the motor behind the history project. Taita Abelino, as he is respectfully called by Guambianos, reiterates the history of the Guambiano and the need for cultural and territorial revitalization by framing the entire narrative as a political speech, much as he might do in a public assembly. This is reminiscent of the strategies of Bolivian filmmakers working in collaboration with local indigenous activists, who found that their work was more clearly comprehended by native communities when sandwiched between oral recountings by respected storytellers of the events depicted in the film.[44] Taita Abelino's overwhelming influence on the project can be appreciated when we consider that most of the early history being recounted was unknown to most Guambianos before the history committee was founded. His voice provides an organizing thread, teaching and advising Guambiano readers and listeners, much as he accompanies the cabildo.

Here we have an attempt to rewrite history, not only in its contents but in its very form, so that it reflects what the authors maintain is a Guambiano worldview (*cosmovisión*) and political practice. While it appears to succeed in conceptually "decentering Europe," however, Guambiano history is not entirely successful. Its very hybridity, which makes this history a powerful tool within pluralist politics, also inhibits its reception by the Guambiano community. First, it is coauthored by a Colombian anthropologist who does not speak Guambiano, thus forcing the history committee to write in Spanish—a cumbersome and possibly counterproductive exercise given that their publications must be retranslated into Guambiano for use in the schools. Second, the exercise was written in response to the earlier theories of Guambiano origins of the Caucan elite, thus reflecting Guambiano recognition of their previous status as an object of ethnography and, consequently, forcing them to take up an external agenda. Finally, the project is framed by the educational institutions in which it is employed: the Guambiano school system, run by Guambiano intellectuals and recognized by the Education Ministry of Bogotá. I will briefly consider here the implications of these issues.

History as written by the Guambianos is based almost exclusively on oral narrative, despite the history committee's extensive—and unanalyzed—archival research. While this may have something to do with the fact that the members of the committee (including Vasco) are not trained in paleography or in the interpretation of archival materials, it probably has a great deal more to do with Guambiano characterizations of their own culture. Anthropology has traditionally painted native Andean cultures as oral in nature, neglecting the very significant ways in which they have participated in literate society since the Spanish invasion. In particular, the drafting of legal documents was ubiquitous after the sixteenth century, incorporating native peoples into a Spanish "lettered city" in which power was exercised through specific generic and political forms of the written word.[45] Following the anthropological model, Guambiano intellectuals have also characterized themselves as oral but with a twist: orality stands here in opposition to the literacy of the dominant society. For this reason, written history, which marks a presumed departure from (or reconstruction of) Guambiano culture, is primarily oral in nature. Thus, the history committee perpetuates traditional anthropological typologies that treat them as primitive Others. Significantly, young Guambiano historians who have joined the committee more recently have begun to incorporate locally held written documents into their corpus of data, although they have not published their findings.

The othering of Guambiano history by the Guambianos themselves is a source of other dilemmas. While "En el segundo día" is indeed innovative, it does not depart substantially enough from academic genres of writing, however experimental its form. It is published in Spanish, typeset in a recognizable visual form, contains footnotes and bibliographies, and was incorporated into an academic anthology—all of which invite a metropolitan intellectual audience and not a Guambiano readership. Thus, it remains inextricably connected to the notion of the "lettered city," locked in a "contact zone" in which Guambiano writers communicate with the outside and not with their own people.[46] In effect, "En el segundo día" and other writings of the Guambiano History Committee are not widely read in Guambía itself, where their contents are transmitted orally in the schools and in public meetings, following the traditional educational practices of memorization and repetition. Although they provide new narratives for a future cabildo leadership, they do not project the very intellectual terms on which the history project is constituted.

CUSTOMARY LAW

Indigenous public intellectuals clearly demonstrate success in their efforts to reconceptualize historical and ethnographic research within alternative frameworks arising out of a dialogue between an exegesis of their own cultures and an appreciation of the broader context within which indigenous identity formation has taken place.

The results of their research are elegant and innovative. But to what extent are they able to carry them into practice? Extended discussions with Nasa cultural planners working in CRIC's bilingual education program suggest that many intellectuals see their work as addressing culture in the "past tense"—as not successfully interacting with the concerns or forms of understanding local communities, and as operating in a hybrid "contact zone" that the intellectuals perceive as "inauthentic."[47] These activists' very preoccupation with such matters indicates that they are continually framing and reframing their activities and their own identities in relation to both the dominant society and their own constituencies. By exploring the problems that have arisen in the introduction of customary law among the Nasa I will attempt here to address the impasse in which they find themselves.[48]

The 1991 constitution, which reconstructs Colombia as a decentralized and multiethnic nation, recognizes through the creation of a system called indigenous special jurisdiction the capacity of native communities to construct their own modern legal systems based on customary law. Within this system, all offenses, ranging from petty crimes to murder, are to be tried within the indigenous community, based upon the usos y costumbres (uses and customs) of the native group.[49]

The identification of usos y costumbres is complicated, however, by the fact that indigenous legal forms have been subordinate to European forms for over four centuries; thus, any local indigenous practices that survived within the colonial system were framed and impoverished by the dominant system. Nonindigenous anthropologists have attempted to codify customary law through the positivist identification of the penalties paid for particular crimes across a small sample of cases, presupposing that a coherent corpus of rules constituting usos y costumbres exists in native communities. In contrast, indigenous leaders, whose assertions are founded in processes of investigation and judgment in the communities, have suggested that it is impossible to codify usos y costumbres, because they operate according to a different cultural logic.[50] Here, once again, the cultural constructions of indigenous intellectuals come into play, particularly in their understandings of the concept of cosmovisión (worldview).

It is from within the notion of cosmovisión that the Nasa leadership has developed a strategy for generating customary law. Working on the basis of recently abandoned practices, such as the use of public whippings and of the stocks, the cabildos that comprise C R I C have reintroduced what they see as Nasa forms of punishment.[51] The condemned are whipped on their legs after guilt has been determined in an investigation conducted by the cabildo in collaboration with shamans. The stocks are a roughly hewn apparatus some six feet high, with multiple holes from which the accused are hanged by their feet for periods of two or three minutes to a half hour. Most sets of stocks were destroyed, buried, or abandoned by communities in the 1950s and 1960s, but were reerected in the 1990s in the wake of constitutional reform.

While many human rights activists condemn as barbaric the stocks and public whippings, the movement defends these practices as humane alternatives to incarceration in Colombian prisons because they do not separate offenders from their communities for lengthy periods of time and expose them to hardened criminals. Moreover, these procedures are seen as forms of promoting reconciliation, not as punishment, because they are associated with lengthy periods during which cabildo members and shamans accompany the guilty party, providing him or her with advice and empathy with the aim of reincorporation into the community; indeed, in some cases, those punished go on to hold positions in the cabildo.

Such forms of punishment, moreover, are seen as essential to restoring harmony to the community. Their significance is explained by Nasa intellectuals in terms of their relevance to Nasa cosmovisión. The whip is viewed as a representation of lightning (*rayo*), a major figure in Nasa oral tradition and cosmology that restores order to the community by mediating between light and darkness. Punishment in the stocks is seen as a renewal of harmony, insofar as its use is determined by shamanic séance and the object and the prisoner are "refreshed" by shamans before its use. Carlos Gaviria Díaz, the judge whose landmark decision regarding corporal punishment in indigenous communities opened the floodgates for the use of the stocks, summarizes the relationship between cosmovisión and customary law in the following way: "In the first case [the Colombian justice system], punishment occurs because an offense has been committed, in the second [the Nasa justice system] punishment occurs in order to re-establish the order of Nature . . . The first rejects corporal punishment as an attempt against human dignity, the second considers it a purifying element, necessary so that the accused subject feels liberated."[52]

What is significant here is the fact that the state, operating according to pluralist doctrines, has felt it necessary to legitimize corporal punishment in indigenous communities by recourse to the contemporary construct of cosmovisión, and that these autochthonous practices, now legal thanks to the court, will be forever framed by the Colombian legal system. Significantly, the judge bases his decision on cultural traits, thus sidestepping the more thorny issue of investigation and determination of guilt by shamans, which constitutes the centerpiece of indigenous analyses at public forums. The incipient Nasa system of justice—incipient because for the past four centuries the colonial Spanish state or the Colombian state have administered European forms of justice in these communities, thereby supplanting indigenous forms—is thus defined in relation to the Colombian system, using positivist ethnographic forms of explanation.

Despite such court decisions, however, the use of such forms of corporal punishment, particularly the stocks, has become a bone of contention in Nasa communities, spurring a series of constitutional lawsuits (tutelas) brought by community members against their cabildos, arguing that their human rights as Colombian citizens are violated by these practices; the state, through the Constitutional Court has nevertheless repeatedly upheld their use as an appropriate example of usos y costumbres.[53] In the most publicized of these tutelas, the question was considered of whether or not such forms of corporal punishment were, in fact, traditional, and it was decided that despite their origins in Spanish colonial practice—a criticism currently being made by youth in some communities—their traditional nature is ensured by their place within a coherent cosmovisión.[54] In effect, the question of what is tradition is under dispute, both within and outside the community. Both inside the movement and beyond its borders tradition is perceived as malleable, forged ideologically within a political process.

Notwithstanding this very contemporary understanding of tradition, the use of the stocks is highly problematic across Nasa communities. In a recent incident in Tóez, a twelve-year-old girl was hanged in the stocks in retribution for having run away from her adoptive parents and taken up with "mafiosos." Given that her adoptive father was governor of the community some saw her punishment as a case of family problems being aired in a communal setting, while others were disturbed by the fact that such a young person would be subject to this drastic punishment. On multiple occasions I was told that the stocks had been discontinued in the past when a pregnant woman was hanged by her feet and died as a result. While the formulaic nature of these accounts suggests that they might be better understood as a contemporary analysis of the reasons for abandoning the practice rather than an account of what "really" happened, this gendered condemnation of the stocks, like the criticism surrounding the punishment of the young girl in Tóez, establishes some of the limits beyond which indigenous forms of punishment cannot encroach. Such limits, however, have been exploded by constitutional reform. Nowadays, Nasa communities face the prospect of judging and punishing all lawbreakers within their populations, thus forcing them to rethink the role of the stocks, which until now was held to be a method of last resort and used only a handful of times a year by each cabildo. More commonly, the accused was transferred to the Colombian justice system in an attempt to avoid having the cabildo come to a decision.

It is precisely in this decision-making process that Nasa intellectuals and leaders have come up against a major barrier. In summer 1996, Marden Betancourt, the indigenous mayor of Jambaló, was murdered by the Ejército de Liberación Nacional guerrillas, who accused him of having set up paramilitary groups in the region. A number of local leaders who were at odds with Betancourt were charged by the community with having incited this political assassination. The accusations and the cabildo's decision to punish the offenders by public whipping led to a flurry of local, national, and even international criticisms of contemporary Nasa constructions of usos y costumbres. A public assembly was called to review the findings against the defendants before the eyes of the cabildos of Cauca and the press. The transcript of the trial suggests that cabildo authorities, who were unable to arrive at a judicial procedure that departed sufficiently from that of the Colombian state and instead adhered almost religiously to it, felt inadequate to the task given their lack of legal literacy and the investigator's and witnesses' confusion about how to present and review evidence.

At the center of their difficulties lay also the problem of heterogeneity in Nasa communities—an ethnic group with more than two hundred thousand members with differing commands of Spanish and Nasa Yuwe; living in radically diverse economic and social conditions; practicing various religions; and sharing their territories with members of different ethnic groups, such as the Guambiano defendants in the Jambaló trial, men who had until then been considered community members, even serving on the cabildo. Various participants in the assembly voiced their concern over the application of usos y costumbres in such a fragmented community, where the punishments deemed to be "traditional" by one cabildo are bluntly rejected as European by another.

Clearly, the interpenetration of Nasa cosmovisión with the legal and constitutional worldview of the dominant Colombian society is highly problematic when it is put into practice on the ground. Processes of cultural construction, which work so well in opening interethnic dialogue, in expanding the space of intercultural collaboration, and in galvanizing cabildos to extend their autonomy, must be framed in practical procedural models that have not yet been clearly formulated, a point driven home in the recent writings of Nasa political theorists.[55]

CONCLUSION

In closing I would like to open a new area of discussion as opposed to revisiting the analyses I have already shared: I would like to explore how my ethnography itself becomes part of the reality I have been studying. As the product of a collaborative fieldwork enterprise with Nasa intellectuals and of ongoing participation in discussions and projects with the Bilingual Education Program of CRIC, my research would not have been possible had I chosen to use traditional modes of participant observation, which would not only have confined me to a more limited sphere of operation "outside" the processes I have chosen to study but also would have denied me the opportunity to engage in such full exegesis with the very intellectual actors about whom I write.[56] It was only through constant movement from one political site to another (meetings, workshops, and assemblies throughout Andean Cauca), as well as through a commitment to intellectual exchange based on the terms set by indigenous intellectuals who chose the kinds of activities in which they felt my participation would be most fruitful for them, that I came to perceive the contradictions and complexities of the indigenous movement's relationship to the Colombian state and to a sense of Colombian nationhood, embodied in the problematic notion of ethnic pluralism.

This is not to say that I became a CRIC activist, which is certainly not the case, but that I became an interlocutor within the pluralist dialogue that nourishes indigenous intellectual and political projects. As such, I became privy to their novel research methodologies, motivations for investigation, and preoccupations with the course of their intellectual projects. But at the same time, as Universidad de los Andes linguist Tulio Rojas once told us in a meeting at CRIC, this also meant that I had to begin to assume the consequences of my research; that is, my interpretations would not only be subjected to critique by my indigenous interlocutors, with whom I would work to construct a fruitful research agenda, but would ultimately be presented publically in various Nasa venues. As a result, the kinds of issues and interpretations I have chosen diverge, to some degree, from those that have characterized an anthropology influenced by postcolonial theory and cultural studies, particularly in my treatment of the meaning in Cauca of essentialist and constructionist ethnographic strategies; in my insistence on a continued focus on indigenous communities, as opposed to turning my ethnographer's eye toward issues of mestizaje; and in my reticence to view these complex political actors as subalterns.[57] While these theoretical approaches have, clearly, influenced the sorts of analysis in which I engage in this article, they also establish a playing field that inhibits a politically committed ethnography. In short, the intention of my text ultimately is to be reinscribed, perhaps under very distinct terms, in Nasa constructionist intellectual process rather than in our own.

NOTES

The research on which this essay is based was conducted during the summers of 1995 through 1999. From 1996 to 1997 my research was supported by a grant given by Colciencias, the Colombian national research institute, to the Instituto Colombiano de Antropología, for a team project in which I participated. I thank María Victoria Uribe, director of ICAN, Claudia Steiner, then-director of social anthropology in ICAN, and María Lucía Sotomayor, coordinator of the research team, for the opportunity to participate in the project. In 1998 and 1999 I received summer research support from the graduate school of Georgetown University. In 1999, in conjunction with Myriam Amparo Espinosa, David Gow, Adonías Perdomo, and Susana Piñacué, I received an international collaborative grant from the Wenner-Gren Foundation for Anthropological Research, which provided a critical arena for discussion of the issues brought up here. Others also provided critical insights into identity formation, law, and the rise of intellectuals, for which I am deeply thankful: Antonio Bonanomi, Herinaldy Gómez, Rosalba Ipia, Jean Jackson, Jon Landaburu, Manuel Molina, Bárbara Muelas, Jessica Mulligan, Abelardo and Inocencio Ramos, Tulio Rojas, Mark Thurner, Vicente Tunubalá, Arquimedes Vitonás, Kay Warren, and the students of CRIC's Licenciatura en Pedagogía Comunitaria. George Baca, Daín Borges, Les Field, Charlie Hale, Naomi Moniz, Bettina Ng'weno, and Gyan Pandey provided welcome and useful commentaries on written drafts of this essay; however, I alone am responsible for what I have written here. Note that all translations are mine unless indicated otherwise.

1 Edmundo Carvajal, *Censo de población* CRIC-Nasa Kiwe en el area del desastre de Tierradentro, Cauca, CRIC-Nasa Kiwe: Análisis descriptivo de la producción y usos del suelo e impacto del desastre del 6 de junio de 1994 en la región de Tierradentro (Popayán: Consejo Regional Indígena del Cauca/Corporación Nasa Kiwe, 1995); Carlos Alfredo López Garcés, *Censo de población* CRIC-Nasa Kiwe en la zona de desastre del 6 de junio de 1994: Análisis descriptivo del medio ambiente en Tierradentro (Popayán: Consejo Regional Indígena del Cauca/Corporación Nasa Kiwe, 1995).

2 CRIC (Consejo Regional Indígena del Cauca), *Congreso Extraordinario Indígena Regional del Cauca: Declaratoria de emergencia social, cultural y económica de los pueblos indígenas del Cauca; reconfirmación autoridad tradicional indígena al Consejo Regional Indígena del Cauca—CRIC declaratoria territorio de convivencia, diálogo y negociación* (Territorio Indígena Guambiano La María Piendamó, mimeographed, 1999).

3 On October 12, 1999, La María was constituted by the movement as a "Territory of Coexistence, Dialogue, and Negotiation," in which multiple popular sectors would meet to press for participation as civil society in national dialogues for peace and in which regular training sessions would take place for leaders of new social movements, traditional indigenous authorities, and for indigenous municipal mayors.

4 República de Colombia, *Nueva Constitución política de Colombia* (Pasto: Minilibrería Jurídica Moral, 1991).

5 In addition to FARC, other armed actors include the ELN (Army of National Liberation), a smaller guerrilla group, and various paramilitary organizations. The latter were originally created by the Colombian army and continue to receive its unofficial (but hardly disguised) support. All of these armed actors operate on the Caucan stage.

6 Three native leaders, Lorenzo Muelas of Guambía, Alfonso Peña Chepe of the Nasa community of La Laguna, and Embera representative Francisco Rojas Birry, participated in the Constitutional Assembly that drafted the 1991 constitution. Since then, indigenous candidates for the national Senate have competed in a special jurisdiction whereby

the electorate at large choose two indigenous senators. In addition to Muelas and Rojas Birry, various Guambiano, Nasa, and Kamsá leaders have served as senators, while others have been elected to the national House of Representatives. Interestingly, these indigenous candidates were elected largely by nonindigenous, urban, intellectual voters.

7 For example, the national state carefully monitors municipal mayors, requiring them to disburse funds according to national administrative guidelines. In municipalities in which the mayor is indigenous, contradictions with cabildos have arisen because the latter are more free to govern according to "uses and customs," causing the mayors to appear to side with the state as opposed to their indigenous constituencies.

8 Here, I will simplify what I mean by the term the state, ignoring the complexities of its multiple instances (local government, national government, ministries and institutes, military) that impinge on the indigenous movement. In addition, owing to space limitations I will refrain from touching on the issue of the multiple states that coexist in Colombia—the Colombian government, the FARC and other guerrilla organizations, and the paramilitary. For an ethnographic appreciation of how the state is perceived on the local level, see Akhil Gupta, "Blurred Boundaries: The Discourse of Corruption, the Culture of Politics, and the Imagined State," *American Ethnologist* 22.2 (1995): 375–402.

9 Dipesh Chakrabarty, "Postcoloniality and the Artifice of History: Who Speaks for 'Indian' Pasts?" *Representations* 37 (1992): 1–26. See also Vicente Rafael, *Contracting Colonialism: Translation and Christian Conversion in Tagalog Society under Early Spanish Rule* (Durham: Duke University Press, 1993).

10 Ernesto Laclau and Chantal Mouffe, *Hegemony and Socialist Strategy: Towards a Radical Democratic Politics* (London: Verso, 1985).

11 Diane M. Nelson, *A Finger in the Wound: Body Politics in Quincentennial Guatemala* (Berkeley: University of California Press, 1999), 3.

12 "It must be stressed that such a relation of *equivalence* does not eliminate *difference*—that would be simple identity. It is only insofar as democratic differences are opposed to forces or discourses which negate all of them that these differences are substitutable for each other. That is, the 'we' of the radical democratic forces is created by the delimitation of a frontier, the designation of the 'them'; it is not a homogeneous 'we,' predicated on the identity of its components. Through the principle of equivalence a type of commonality is created that does not erase plurality and differences and that allows diverse forms of individuality" (Chantal Mouffe, "Democratic Politics and the Question of Identity," in *The Identity in Question*, ed. John Rajchman [London and

New York: Routledge, 1995], 38.) See also Laclau and Mouffe, *Hegemony and Socialist Strategy*.

13 Joanne Rappaport, *The Politics of Memory: Native Historical Interpretation in the Colombian Andes* (Durham: Duke University Press, 1998).

14 On the history of CRIC, see Jesús Avirama and Rayda Márquez, "The Indigenous Movement in Colombia," in *Indigenous Peoples and Democracy in Latin America*, ed. Donna Lee Van Cott (New York: St. Martin's Press/Inter-American Dialogue, 1995), 83–105; Christian Gros, *Colombia indígena: Identidad cultural y cambio social* (Bogotá: CEREC, 1991); Trino Morales, "El movimiento indígena en Colombia," in *Indianidad y descolonización en América Latina: Documentos de la Segunda Reunión de Barbados*, ed. Grupo de Barbados (México City: Nueva Imagen, 1979), 41–54. On the history of AICO, see María Teresa Findji, "From Resistance to Social Movement: The Indigenous Authorities Movement in Colombia," in *The Making of Social Movements in Latin America: Identity, Strategy, and Democracy*, ed. Arturo Escobar and Sonia Alvarez (Boulder: Westview, 1992), 112–33.

15 Under the 1991 constitution, the decentralization of the Colombian administrative apparatus is to include the creation of Indigenous Territorial Entities (ETIs), which will function in the place of municipalities and departments (or provinces) in indigenous territories, further confounding the community-state opposition; ETIs have not yet been created, due to opposition in the Colombian legislature. See Joanne Rappaport, ed., "Ethnicity Reconfigured: Indigenous Legislators and the Colombian Constitution of 1991," special issue of the *Journal of Latin American Anthropology* 1.2 (1996).

16 In Cauca, where some 40 percent of the population is indigenous, the pressure is even more intense, as was revealed in fall 1999 when month-long blockages of the Panamerican Highway by a multiethnic alliance forced the governor of the department, a member of the Popayán elite, to identify with indigenous and peasant interests. Since then, a joke has been circulating within the indigenous movement, which identifies the departmental government as another cabildo—the cabildo of Popayán.

17 Mark Thurner, "Introduction: After Spanish Rule," position paper presented at the Wenner-Gren workshop After Spanish Rule, Gainesville, Florida, October 1999, p. 21.

18 Of course, contemporary Latin American national imaginings have traditionally appropriated a glorious precolumbian past; what is different here is that indigenous political demands have forced Colombia to reimagine itself as multiethnic, leading to a fusing of indigenous and Colombian structures of governance. On the politics of the inclu-

sion of indigenous issues in the Colombian constitution as compared to a similar process in Bolivia, see Donna Lee Van Cott, *The Friendly Liquidation of the Past: The Politics of Diversity in Latin America* (Pittsburgh: University of Pittsburgh Press, 2000). On the impact of indigenous movements in other Andean countries, see Jorge León Trujillo, *De campesinos a ciudadanos diferentes* (Quito: CEDIME/Abya-Yala, 1994); Galo Ramón Valarezo, *El regreso de los runas: La potencialidad del proyecto indio en el Ecuador contemporáneo* (Quito: Comunidec/Fundación Interamericana, 1993); Estéban Ticona, Gonzalo Rojas, and Xavier Albó, *Votos y wiphalas: Campesinos y pueblos originarios en democracia* (La Paz: Fundación Milenio/CIPCA, 1995).

19 It is not uncommon among the Nasa for entire communities to be composed of monolingual Spanish-speakers.

20 Gayatri Chakravorty Spivak, "Can the Subaltern Speak?" in *Marxism and the Interpretation of Culture*, ed. Cary Nelson and Lawrence Grossberg (Urbana: University of Illinois Press, 1988), 271–313. On organic intellectuals, see Antonio Gramsci, "The Intellectuals," in *Selections from the Prison Notebooks* (1947; New York: International Publishers, 1971). In this sense, the intellectuals of whom I speak are not comparable with the local intellectuals studied by scholars such as Claudio Lomnitz in his *Exits from the Labyrinth: Culture and Ideology in the Mexican National Space* (Berkeley: University of California Press, 1992) or Florencia Mallon in her *Peasant and Nation: The Making of Postcolonial Mexico and Peru* (Berkeley: University of California Press, 1995). In their analyses, local intellectuals are seen as articulating hegemonic discourses within local spaces, and might more appropriately be termed "traditional intellectuals"; in contrast, the public intellectuals of whom I speak are attempting to articulate counterhegemonic discourses. Further, it is not correct to term these Colombian activists "peasant intellectuals," after the work of Steven Feierman (*Peasant Intellectuals* [Madison: University of Wisconsin Press, 1990]), given that they are cosmopolitan urban actors living in a postpeasant era in which rural people are distinctly linked to urban areas through migration and through proletarianization (See Michael Kearney, *Reconceptualizing the Peasantry* [Boulder: Westview, 1997]).

21 On the differences between Latin America and other parts of the postcolonial world, see Paulo Emílio Salles Gomez, *Cinema: Trajetória no subdesenvolimento* (São Paulo: Editora Paz e Terra, 1980), 77. This emphasis on difference as opposed to subalternity creates great discomfort among nonindigenous activists: they, too, can identify as subalterns but they cannot distinguish themselves as culturally different.

22 In addition to such transformations in local political leadership, CRIC

has seen its authority shrink with the rise of regional cabildo associations, a development detailed in David D. Gow and Joanne Rappaport, "The Indigenous Public Voice: The Multiple Idioms of Modernity in Native Cauca," in *Indigenous Movements, Self-Representation, and the State in Latin America*, ed. Jean Jackson and Kay B. Warren (Austin: University of Texas Press, 2000).

23 Trinh T. Minh-ha, *When the Moon Waxes Red: Representation, Gender, and Cultural Politics* (New York: Routledge, 1991), 74. Nelson, who uses the term "inappropriate Other" in *A Finger in the Wound*, also calls Maya intellectuals "hackers" in order to describe a social layer that successfully appropriates technology but resists being appropriated by the society from whence the technology came.

24 "[La] forma de comportamiento que resulta de la permanencia en relación armónia con la naturaleza." The constitutional articles relevant to native communities have been translated into a variety of major indigenous languages by indigenous translators with formal linguistic training. The translation by Abelardo Ramos into Nasa Yuwe is titled, *Ec ne'hwe's': Constitución política de Colombia en Nasa Yuwe* (Bogotá: CCELA–UNIANDES, 1994), 116.

25 Jesús Enrique Piñacué, "Aplicación autonómica de la justicia en comunidades paeces (una aproximación)," in República de Colombia, *Del olvido surgimos para traer nuevas esperanzas—la jurisdicción especial indígena* (Bogotá: Ministerio de Justicia y del Derecho/Ministerio del Interior, Dirección General de Asuntos Indígenas, 1997), 32–33.

26 Marcos Yule, "Avances en la investigación del Nasa Yuwe (lengua páez)," *Proyecciones Lingüísticas* (Popayán) 1.1 (1995): 23–30.

27 Adonías Perdomo, *Escuela del pensamiento Nasa, resguardo indígena de Pitayó: Memorias del primer y segundo encuentro* (Pitayó, manuscript, 1996).

28 Piñacué, "Aplicación autonómica," 32–33.

29 See Christian Gros, "Los indios en el marco de las recientes transformaciones constitucionales colombianas," paper presented at Coloquio Las Figuras Nacionales del Indio, organized by CERMACA, México, D.F., September 1995; and Gros, "Derechos indígenas y nueva Constitución en Colombia," *Análisis Político* (Bogotá) 19 (1993): 8–24.

30 See Paul Gilroy, *"There Ain't no Black in the Union Jack": The Cultural Politics of Race and Nation* (Chicago: University of Chicago Press, 1987); and Stuart Hall, "New Ethnicities," in *Stuart Hall: Critical Dialogues in Cultural Studies*, ed. David Morley and Kuan-Hsing Chen (1989; London: Routledge, 1996), 441–49.

31 The Nasa, who in the late nineteenth century were perceived as more "primitive" than the Guambiano, were assigned to the category of

territorios de misiones, regions in which Catholic missionary orders (the Vicentian Community, in this case) would supervise education. See Correa Rubio, François, "Estado, desarrollo y grupos étnicos: La ilusión del proyecto de homogenización nacional," in *Identidad*, ed. M. Jimeno, G. I. Ocampo, and M. Roldán (Bogatá: ICFES, 1989). On the liquidation of resguardos, see Joanne Rappaport, *Cumbe Reborn: An Andean Ethnography of History* (Chicago: University of Chicago Press, 1994). On the use of evolutionary anthropological frameworks in the late twentieth century, see Joanne Rappaport and David D. Gow, "Cambio dirigido, movimiento indígena y estereotipos del indio: El Estado colombiano y la reubicación de los nasa," in *Antropología en la modernidad*, ed. María Victoria Uribe and Eduardo Restrepo (Bogotá: Instituto Colombiano de Antropología, 1997), 361–99.

32 Rey Chow, *Primitive Passions: Visuality, Sexuality, Ethnography, and Contemporary Chinese Cinema* (New York: Columbia University Press, 1995), 180.

33 Abelino Dagua, Misael Aranda, and Luis Guillermo Vasco, *Somos raíz y retoño: historia y tradición guambianas* (Cali: Ediciones Colombia Nuestra, 1989).

34 Les Field, "Complicities and Collaborations: Anthropologists and the 'Unacknowledged Tribes' of California," *Current Anthropology* 40.2 (1999): 199–200.

35 CRIC, Programa de Educación Bilingüe and Consultores en Educación y Desarrollo S.C., *Propuesta de formación superior: Licenciatura en pedagogía comunitaria* (Popayán, manuscript, 1997).

36 See Myriam Amparo Espinosa, *Surgimiento y andar territorial del Quintín Lame* (Quito: Editorial Abya-Yala, 1996); and María Teresa Findji and José María Rojas, *Territorio, economía y sociedad páez* (Cali: Editorial Universidad del Valle, 1985).

37 For a similar discussion on Brazil, see Alcida Rita Ramos, "Ethnology Brazilian Style," *Cultural Anthropology* 5.4 (1990): 452–72.

38 Martha Urdaneta Franco, "Investigación arqueológica en el resguardo indígena de Guambía," *Boletín del Museo del Oro* 22 (1988): 56.

39 Luis Guillermo Vasco Uribe, Abelino Dagua Hurtado, and Misael Aranda, "En el segundo día, la Gente Grande (Numisak) sembró la autoridad y las plantas y, con su jugo, bebió el sentido," in *Encrucijadas de Colombia amerindia*, ed. François Correa (Bogotá: Instituto Colombiano de Antropología, 1993), 9–48.

40 A similar example of the espousing of pluralism through joint authorship is Luis Angel, Gustavo Mejía, Benjamín Dindicué, *Quintín Lame: La caida del coloso colombiano* (Popayán, manuscript, 1989), I, a reorganization of Manuel Quintín Lame's *Thoughts of the Indian Who was Educated in*

the Colombian Jungles. Lame's book is an enigmatic text, written in the late 1930s by a Nasa sharecropper who led the native peoples of southern Colombia to organize themselves against the sharecropping system and in favor of strengthening cabildos. See Lame, *En defensa de mi raza* (1939; Bogotá: Comité de Defensa del Indio, 1971); an English translation of *Los pensamientos* is provided, in addition to a detailed analysis of the text, by Gonzalo Castillo-Cárdenas in *Liberation Theology from Below: The Life and Thought of Manuel Quintín Lame* (Maryknoll, N.Y.: Orbis, 1987). The treatise has become a foundational text for the indigenous movement. *Quintín Lame: La caída del coloso colombiano* was prepared by members of the Quintín Lame Armed Movement, a multiethnic guerrilla group that operated in defense of the indigenous communities of Cauca during the 1970s and 1980s. The text is particularly interesting insofar as its author, Luis Angel Mejía Dindicué, is actually a pseudonym constructed from a composite of the names of three fallen leaders: one Afro-Colombian (Luis Angel Monroy—the first comandante of the movement); another, mestizo (Gustavo Mejía—instrumental in the founding of CRIC); and another, Nasa (Benjamín Dindicué—an important CRIC leader in the 1970s). Thus, the pen name exemplifies and stands for the pluralistic nature of both the movement and its intellectual project. For a more sustained analysis of this text, see Joanne Rappaport, "Hacia la descolonización de la producción intelectual indígna en Colombia," in *Modernidad, identidad y desarrollo: Construcción de sociedad y re-creación cultural en contextos de modernización,* ed. María Lucía Sotomayor (Bogotá: Instituto Colombiano de Antropología, 1988), 17–45.

41 "El segundo día," in Abelino Dagua, M. Aranda, and L. G. Vasco, *Somos raíz,* 10–11.

42 Muelas, "Relación espacio-tiempo," in *Somos raíz,* 32.

43 Ibid., 35–36.

44 Jorge Sanjinés and Grupo Ukamau, *Teoría y práctica de un cine junto al pueblo* (Mexico City: Siglo XXI, 1979).

45 This point has been theorized by Angel Rama in *The Lettered City* (Durham: Duke University Press, 1996) and examined empirically for native peoples by Rolena Adorno, *Guaman Poma: Writing and Resistance in Colonial Peru* (Austin: University of Texas Press, 1986); Roberto González Echevarría, *Myth and Archive: A Theory of Latin American Narrative* (Cambridge: Cambridge University Press, 1990); Regina Harrison, *Signs, Songs, and Memory in the Andes: Translating Quechua Language and Culture* (Austin: University of Texas Press, 1989); Rappaport, *The Politics of Memory;* Silvia Rivera Cusicanqui, *"Oprimidos pero no vencidos": Luchas del campesinado aymara y qhechwa, 1900–1980* (La Paz: HISBOL, 1980).

46 On the problems inherent in academic genres of writing, see John Beverley, *Subalternity and Representation: Arguments in Cultural Theory* (Durham: Duke University Press, 1999). On the notion of the contact zone and the culturally hybrid genres that operate there, see Mary Louise Pratt, *Imperial Eyes: Travel Writing and Transculturation* (New York: Routledge, 1992). In contrast, more grass-roots publications, handwritten in comic book form and composed in native languages and in Andean Spanish, with all of the grammatical errors that the vernacular exhibits from the point of view of the "lettered city," depart more radically from the generic model. This point was brought home to me by Nasa university students who embraced an Aymara history written in this form (Alejandro Mamani Quispe, *Historia y cultura de Cohana* [La Paz: Hisbol/Radio San Gabriel, 1988]) as more "authentic" and potentially liberatory to them.

47 I address these issues in my "Los nasa de frontera y la política de la identitidad en el Cauca indígena," paper presented at the ninth Congreso de Antropología en Colombia, Popayán, July 2000.

48 I concentrate here on criminal procedures, which are at the heart of political battles in contemporary Cauca. The application of customary law within the civil realm is not as bitterly contested, making its development less visible.

49 Article 246 of the 1991 Constitución política. See also República de Colombia *Del olvido surgimos;* Herinaldy Gómez, "El derecho étnico ante el derecho estatal," *Convergencia* (Mexico) 3.8–9 (1995): 295–316; Herinaldy Gómez, "Crisis de la justicia y la jurisdicción indígena en Colombia," *Convergencia* (Mexico) 6.18 (1999): 285–308; and Esther Sánchez Botero, *Justicia y pueblos indígenas de Colombia* (Bogotá: Universidad Nacional de Colombia, Facultad de Derecho, Ciencias Políticas y Sociales, 1998). See also Robert V. H. Dover, "Fetichismo, derechos e identidad en el pensamiento político indígena," in *Modernidad, identidad y desarrollo: Construcción de sociedad y re-creación cultural en contextos de modernización,* ed. María Lucía Sotomayor (Bogotá: Instituto Colombiano de Antropología, 1998), 41–50.

50 Carlos César Perafán Simmonds, in *Sistemas jurídicos paez, kogi wayúu y tule* (Bogotá: Colcultura/Instituto Colombiano de Antropología, 1995), presents a codification of customary law in various indigenous communities. For indigenous arguments against codification, see República de Colombia, *Del olvido surgimos.*

51 I was told that the stocks have been adopted recently in Guambía as well.

52 Carlos Gaviria Díaz, "Diversidad étnica y cultural—reconocimiento constitucional," Sentencia no. T-523/97, Sala Cuarta de Revisión de

Tutelas de la Corte Constitucional, Santafé de Bogotá, 1997, n.p. Note the difference between explanations of Nasa corporal punishment and Michel Foucault's interpretation of the function of public execution in Europe before the nineteenth century: "It is a ceremonial by which a momentarily injured sovereignty is reconstituted. It restores that sovereignty by manifesting it at its most spectacular . . . Its aim is not so much to re-establish a balance as to bring into play, at its most extreme point, the dissymetry between the subject who has dared to violate the law and the all-powerful sovereign who displays his strength" (Foucault, *Discipline and Punish: The Birth of the Prison* [New York: Vintage, 1979], 48–49).

53 Gow and Rappaport, "The Indigenous Public Voice"; Gloria Isabel Ocampo, "Diversidad étnica y jurisdicción indígena en Colombia," *Boletín de Antropología* (Medellín) 11.27 (1997): 9–33; Sánchez Botero, *Justicia y pueblos indígenas*.

54 Leoxmar Benjamín Muñóz Alvear, "Acción de tutela impetrada por el señor Francisco Gembuel Pechené, en contra de los señores Luis Alberto Passú, Gobernador del Cabildo Indígena de Jambaló y Luis Alberto Fiscué, Presidente de la Asociación de Cabildos de la Zona Norte del Departamento del Cauca," Juzgado Primero Penal Municipal, Santander de Quilichao (Cauca), January 8, 1997.

55 Adonías Perdomo, "Autonomía, autoridad y justicia interna en los resguardos de Pitayó Silvia, Pioyá Caldono y Pat Yu' Cajibío" (Pitayó, manuscript, 1999).

56 I was most able to develop this relationship with CRIC and, to a lesser degree, with the subregional organization working in northern Cauca and the representatives of some politically independent communities, based on my longstanding research commitment to the Nasa and the circulation in translation of many of my publications, which provided a tangible basis for dialogue. I was not as successful with the Guambiano, whose intellectual activities I have been forced to observe only at a distance (perhaps in part because I am in dialogue with CRIC, their rival; because I write about the Nasa; and because the Guambiano reject collaboration with most external anthropologists, with a few exceptions, like Vasco). Thus my interpretations of the process in Guambía have been filtered through the analytical approaches derived from my contact with CRIC.

57 This particular essay arose from numerous discussions with Nasa intellectuals and will be further subjected to discussion in translated form, something that is already occurring with other written results of my research; ultimately, we hope to write joint-authored studies. The issue of accountability to the indigenous activists we study is dis-

cussed in detail in Les Field, "Academic and 'Real World' Analyses of Mestizaje: A Ramble about Privilege, Positioning, and Politics," paper delivered at the annual meeting of the Latin American Studies Association, Miami, March 2000; and in Jean Jackson, "The Politics of Ethnographic Practice in the Colombian Vaupés," *Identities* 6:2–3 (1999): 281–317.

Contributors

THOMAS A. ABERCROMBIE is Associate Professor of Anthropology at New York University. He is the author of *Pathways of Memory and Power: Ethnography and History among an Andean People* (1998).

SHAHID AMIN is Professor of History at Delhi University and a founding editor of *Subaltern Studies*. He is the author of *Event, Metaphor, Memory: Chauri Chaura, 1922–1992* (1995) and *Sugarcane and Sugar in Gorakhpur* (1984).

JORGE CAÑIZARES-ESGUERRA is Associate Professor of History at the University at Buffalo. He is the author of *How to Write the History of the New World: Histories, Epistemologies, and Identities in the Eighteenth-Century Atlantic World* (2002).

PETER GUARDINO is Associate Professor of History at Indiana University. He is the author of *Peasants, Politics, and the Formation of Mexico's National State: Guerrero, 1800–1857* (1996).

ANDRÉS GUERRERO is an independent scholar affiliated with the Facultad Latinoamericana de Ciencias Socialas (FLACSO) in Quito, Ecuador. He is the author of *De la economía a las mentalidades* (1991), *La semántica de la dominación: El concertaje de indios* (1991), and *Curagas y tenientes políticos: La ley de la costumbre y la ley del estado, Otavalo 1830–1875* (1990).

MARIXA LASSO is Assistant Professor of History at California State University, Los Angeles. She is the author of "Race and Republicanism in the Age of Revolution: Cartagena, 1795–1831" (Ph.D., diss., University of Florida, 2002).

JAVIER MORILLO-ALICEA is Visiting Professor of History at Carlton College. He is currently writing his doctoral dissertation in Anthropology and History at the University of Michigan.

JOANNE RAPPAPORT is Professor of Anthropology with an appointment in the Department of Spanish and Portuguese at Georgetown University. She is the author of *Cumbe Reborn: An Andean Ethnography of History*

(1994), and The Politics of Memory: Native Historical Interpretation in the Colombian Andes (1990).

MAURICIO TENORIO-TRILLO is Associate Professor of History at the University of Texas at Austin. He is the author of Argucias de la historia: Siglo XIX, cultura y "América Latina" (1999), and Mexico at the World's Fairs: Crafting a Modern Nation (1996).

MARK THURNER is Associate Professor of History and Anthropology at the University of Florida. He is the author of From Two Republics to One Divided: Contradictions of Postcolonial Nationmaking in Andean Peru (Duke University Press, 1997).

Index

Library of Congress Cataloging-in-Publication Data

After Spanish rule : postcolonial predicaments of the Americas /
edited by Mark Thurner and Andrés Guerrero; foreword by Shahid
Amin.
p. cm. — (Latin America otherwise)
Includes bibliographical references and index.
ISBN 0-8223-3157-8 (cloth : alk. paper) — ISBN 0-8223-3194-2
(pbk. : alk. paper)
1. Latin America—History—1830–1898. 2. Latin America—
Historiography. 3. Postcolonialism—Latin America. 4. Literature
and history—Latin America. 5. Latin America—Relations—Spain.
6. Spain—Relations—Latin America. 7. Latin America—Relations—
Foreign countries. 8. Nationalism—Latin America. I. Thurner,
Mark. II. Guerrero, Andrés. III. Series.
F1413.A43 2003
980'.03—dc21   2003009339

DATE DUE

NOV 2 0 2004			
REC 03 REC'D			
OhioLINK			
JUN 3 0 REC'D			
OhioLINK			
NOV 2 9 REC'D			
OhioLINK			
JUN 1 4 REC'D			
DEC 2 1 2007 OCT 0 7 REC'D			
	WITHDRAWN		
GAYLORD			PRINTED IN U.S.A.

F 1413 .A43 2003

After Spanish rule